The Goldendoodle Handbook

LINDA WHITWAM

ISBN- 13: 978-1535247290

Copyright

Approved by GANA (Goldendoodle Association of North America)

Contributing Authors

Amy Lane

Christy Stevens

Debbie Dixon

Janece Schommer

Lynne Whitmire

Acknowledgements

My sincere thanks go to GANA, the Goldendoodle Association of North America, and the Goldendoodle breeders as well as owners and canine experts who have generously contributed their time and expertise to this book. Their knowledge and love of their dogs shines through and without them, The Goldendoodle Handbook would not have been possible.

Special thanks to: Amy Lane, Candice Farrell, Christy Stevens, Debbie Dixon, Donna Shaw and Kelly Milne, Dyvonia Bussey, Janece Schommer, Kelsey Huffer, Laura Chaffin, Lynne Whitmire, Melissa Farmer, Michael and Lisa Ross, Renee Sigman, Sandra Beck, Steve and Neelie Smith, Wendi Loustau, IDOG International, Doodle Trust and Dr Sara Skiwski.

Contributors' details are listed at the back of the book.

TABLE OF CONTENTS

1. Meet the Goldendoodle

Goldendoodles first began to appear in the United States in the 1990s. The originals were all large dogs, as they were the offspring of Standard Poodles. While Standards are still very popular, the more recent introduction of Miniature and Toy Poodles into breeding programs has resulted in the appearance of Petite, Miniature and Medium Goldendoodles, which has widened their appeal.

Australian Wally Conron bred the first Labradoodle in the 1980s to act as a guide dog for a visually impaired American woman whose husband suffered from pet allergies. Word spread and the cat was soon out of the bag — or in this case, the Doodle.

People all across the world began pairing many different breeds with a Poodle (with varying degrees of success) in search of the Holy Grail of hybrids; the low shedding coat. There was a big rush to cash in on the craze for these new 'designer dogs' with unscrupulous breeders churning out hybrid (crossbreed) puppies with scant attention to health and temperament, resulting in these so-called 'designer dogs' getting a bad Press.

Some of those mixes did not result in a good match with the Poodle, but people who breed or own Goldendoodles believe that they have hit the jackpot. They say that their hybrid is the perfect combination of the best qualities of both parent breeds; Poodle and Golden Retriever. Indeed, it is hard to find anyone who has a bad word to say about Goldendoodles. When properly socialized and given sufficient exercise, and mental stimulation, there is no doubt they make superb family pets and are suitable even for first time dog owners. :)

(Photo of her F1B Standard Goldendoodle, Stella, by Debbie Dixon, Zippity Doodles, Colorado.)

And when it comes to buying a puppy, the Goldendoodle has two major advantages over many other crossbreeds. Firstly, it has an excellent parent breed club in the USA which promotes and protects the Goldendoodle: GANA, the Goldendoodle Association of North America. This is an excellent first port of call for any potential owner, who would be well advised to look for either a GANA registered breeder, or one who adheres to their Code of Ethics — whatever country they live in.

Secondly, there has been a recent breakthrough in genetics. A gene has been discovered which produces the flat type of coat which is most likely to shed — and the type many potential owners wish to avoid. Many forward thinking Goldendoodle breeders are now testing for this gene and increasing the chances of breeding puppies with low shedding coats.

What Exactly is a Goldendoodle?

The Goldendoodle is not a purebred or pedigree, but a crossbreed or hybrid. That means you cannot get AKC or Kennel Club registration papers with your dog - although you can register him or her with the Continental Kennel Club at https://ckcusa.com. And if you live in Canada or the USA, you can apply for your dog to be included in the only Goldendoodle registry currently available, run by GANA at www.goldendoodleassociation.com/Owner_registry_search.aspx

A Goldendoodle is the result of breeding a Golden Retriever with a Poodle, which is the dog of choice when it comes to hybrids, due to the unique, low shedding fleecy coat. The Poodle originated in Germany (not France), where the name means something akin to 'puddle dog,' and was bred as a gundog to retrieve ducks and other fowl. The Poodle is highly intelligent – the second smartest of all the breeds after the Border Collie – and is very quick to learn new things, so needs mental as well as physical exercise to prevent boredom. Poodles are also regarded as

intuitive, picking up on owners' moods, and some do not respond well to stress, tension and loud noises.

The Golden Retriever (pictured) is known for his stellar temperament, admired by breeders and dog lovers worldwide. He is well-balance, cheerful, steadfast, loyal, easy to please, eager to please you, and great with children. He's also very intelligent and easy to train, making the breed a popular choice on both sides of the Atlantic.

Well-bred Goldendoodles exhibit the best qualities of the two parent breeds. They are intelligent, social, biddable, non-aggressive with other animals and excellent with children. They enjoy life to the full and can bowl you over with their enthusiasm – sometimes literally, if not properly trained! They will play all day long if you will, and are friendly with everybody (so don't make good guard dogs) and, like their ancestors on both sides, love water. Many also have low shedding coats. For much more information on coats and colors, see **Chapter 11**, and if pets make you sneeze, read **Chapter 4. Goldendoodles for Allergy Sufferers.**

Goldendoodles are sometimes described as 'Velcro dogs', as they are people-oriented and very attached to their owners. They do not do well when left alone for long periods, resulting in a tendency to suffer from separation anxiety. Their coats and love of people mean that they are not suitable to be kept outdoors. They are bred as companion dogs, not guard dogs, and thrive on being with others.

As a relatively new type of dog, the Goldendoodle is to some extent still a 'work in progress,' which is why – particularly with the new genetic developments in health testing and coat types – it pays to choose a breeder with a proven track record of producing healthy pups with good temperaments and low shedding coats. Prices range from a few hundred dollars, or pounds, up to $3,000, or more than £1,000 in the UK. Well bred, fully health tested dogs are at the top end of this scale. Most good breeders will not sell their dogs for less than $1,200 or around £900 in the UK (in 2016.) If a puppy is cheap, you have to ask why; corners have been cut somewhere - and it's often health testing and proper socialization. Although the Goldendoodle is generally healthy, any dog bred from unhealthy parents can inherit problems.

You might come across 'teddy bear Goldendoodles,' a phrase which some breeders use and others dislike. This refers to North American Goldendoodles bred from English Creme (or Cream, sometimes also called European) Golden Retrievers. English and American Golden Retrievers are variations of the same breed. However, some US breeders have imported English Cremes for a couple of reasons.

The first is health; the (UK) Kennel Club says: "There are certain health differences between the American Goldens and the English Creme. American Goldens have a significantly higher chance of getting cancer as compared to English Cremes. This is based on research and statistics. The median age of American Goldens is 10 years and eight months, while the median age for English Cremes is 12 years and three months." American Goldens are also statistically more likely to have hip or elbow dysplasia. That's not to say that all American Goldens are unhealthy; this is far from the case. You should always ask to see the parents' health certificates, whatever type of puppy you buy.

The other main reason is the look and color of the English, which are bigger-boned and have a lighter, denser coat. They also have a larger, squarer head; hence the 'teddy bear' look.

All original Goldendoodles were all known as Standards as they were bred from Standard Poodles; today there are four different sizes. This is how GANA describes them:

➢ **Petite range:** Height: below 14 inches, typically 25lb or less

➢ **Miniature range**: Height: over 14 but under 17 inches (35cm to 42cm) at wither (shoulder), typically 26-35lb

➢ **Medium range:** Height: over 17 but under 21 inches (43cm to 52cm) at wither, typically 36-50lb

➢ **Standard range:** Height: over 21 inches (53cm to 63cm) at wither, typically 51lb or more

As the Goldendoodle is a hybrid, there are more variables than with purebreds, so sizes and weights are not written in stone. GANA adds: "Final size category of a dog will be determined at adulthood and is measured at the withers (shoulders.) Please be aware that the estimated size of a puppy by a breeder is an educated guess. Therefore, a puppy's final size may vary somewhat from a breeder's initial calculation." (Photo of F1B Cameo by breeder Lynne Whitmire, Fountain Falls Goldendoodles, South Carolina.)

The size of the adult dog depends upon the parents. Today, all three types of Poodle - Standard, Miniature and Toy - are used to breed Goldendoodles, and each has its own different set of typical character traits. When considering a Goldendoodle, think about temperament as well as size; a Miniature Goldendoodle will not behave exactly like a Standard Goldendoodle.

As a hybrid, the Goldendoodle has no Breed Standard like purebred dogs. There may be one in the future, but for now this crossbreed is still developing and improving. In the meantime, GANA members have voted on what they believe to be important:

❦ A balanced mix of physical characteristics of the Golden Retriever and the Poodle

❦ A consistently friendly, social temperament similar to that of the Golden Retriever

🐾 Consists of Poodle and Golden Retriever only - no other breed infusion is accepted

🐾 No tail docking or body altering other than the removal of dew claws - dew claw removal is optional

F Numbers Explained

In the canine world, F numbers have nothing to do with photography or Formula One motor racing, instead they describe the generation of a crossbreed dog. The F comes from the Latin *filius* (son) and means "relating to a son or daughter." Many - but by no means all - Goldendoodle breeders are working towards a **multigen** (or multigenerational) dog which shows a consistency of size, temperament and low shedding coat. A multigen is the result of successive Goldendoodle to Goldendoodle breedings, rather than breeding a Golden Retriever to a Poodle.

An **F1** Goldendoodle is a **first generation** cross between a Golden Retriever and a Poodle. Some breeders and canine experts believe that an F1 may benefit from 'hybrid vigor.' The next generations are worked out by always adding one number up from the lowest number parent. An **F2** could be the offspring of two first generation Goldendoodles, F1 x F1, or it could be the product of an F1 x F2, or higher, cross. An **F3** is the offspring of one F2 parent where the other parent was F2 or higher.

Then there are the **B** numbers - **F1B, F2B**, etc. The **B** stands for Backcross. This occurs when a litter has been produced as a result of a backcross to one of the parent breeds – usually a Poodle, e.g. when a Goldendoodle is bred with a Poodle, usually to increase the chance of a low shedding coat.

....

'Hybrid Vigor'

This is the theory that the first cross between two unrelated purebred lines is healthier and grows better than either parent line. And Goldendoodles and other so-called 'designer dogs' are causing a big debate in the canine world. Does hybrid vigor - or heterosis, to give it its scientific name - exist or not?

Creating a dog by crossing two existing breeds increases the gene pool and some people believe that this reduces the risk of inherited problems in puppies. When done responsibly, breeding is **by design**. In other words, it is breeding between a deliberately chosen healthy sire and dam, and this parentage can give the crossbreed puppy the advantage of hybrid vigor – or robustness. (Pictured is F1 English 'teddy bear' Mini Goldendoodle, Sage, bred by Dyvonia Bussey, of Grace Goldens, Alabama.)

The theory is that the puppy may be stronger and healthier as he is less likely to inherit the inbred genetic faults of both purebred (pedigree) parents. Many dog breeds have health problems which have been bred in over the years; some Dalmatians are deaf, some Labradors have hip problems, Dachshunds may suffer from back problems, and so on. This is because as well as breeding the good points into a purebred, the genes with the faults have also been inadvertently passed on.

How wonderful it would be if you could take any two purebred dogs, cross breed them and automatically ensure a 100% healthy dog. Unfortunately, it is not as simple as that. Although the gene pool is larger with crossbreeds, health checks still have to be made on the parents. If your Goldendoodle pup has a Golden Retriever with a hip problem or a Poodle with an eye issue as a parent or ancestor, there is still a chance that he or she will inherit that fault.

Due to the mixed gene pool, there are also more variables with hybrids; size, color and coat are just some of the inconsistencies with Goldendoodles – even within the same litter - although leading breeders are working towards a consistent Breed Standard. Similarly, many Goldendoodles are sold as non-shedding and hypoallergenic. Many families with allergies live perfectly happily with Goldendoodles, but no breeder can categorically say that you will NOT be allergic to their dogs. All allergies are different. Despite most Goldendoodles being low shedding, there are no cast iron guarantees - odds are that even the other littermates didn't turn out exactly the same as your dog.

There are also studies, such as the one published in the Journal of the American Veterinary Medical Association http://news.vin.com/VINNews.aspx?articleId=29634, which call into question the whole notion of hybrid vigor! If you do decide to get a Goldendoodle, the best thing you can do is select a good breeder who health tests her breeding stock.

Labradoodle V Goldendoodle

The Goldendoodle followed in the footsteps of the Labradoodle about a decade later. In some ways, the two hybrids are similar. They both have a Poodle parent or ancestors but, as the names suggest, the Labradoodle has Labrador Retriever heritage, while the Goldendoodle has Golden Retriever heritage. (Photo: Janece Schommer.)

We asked a number of Goldendoodle breeders what, if any, differences exist. Amy Lane, Fox Creek Farm, West Virginia and Founder of GANA: "In the early generations (F1, F1B), the Goldendoodle's coat is more reliable, in that it will be a full, fluffy coat with a good chance of being non-shedding. The early generations of Labradoodles almost always shed and many have a sparse, wiry coat that is not typical of the multigen Labradoodle.

"I personally have found the Labradoodle to be a higher energy dog than the Goldendoodle. I think this goes back to the differences between the Golden Retriever and the Labrador Retriever, as I have always found the Golden Retriever to be easier to train and have a moderate energy level."

GANA Vice President Janece Schommer, Goldendoodle Acres, Wisconsin, who is one of the breeders at the forefront of genetic testing: "In regard to the coat types, there can be a huge difference in first generations. An F1 Labradoodle has at least one short coat gene from its Labrador parent and one long coat gene from the Poodle. This can make for some interesting coats, to say the least. F1 Goldendoodles don't have to deal with this as both Goldens and Poodles have long hair coat genes. By the time you get to F1b, it's hard to tell a Labradoodle from a Goldendoodle pup."

Donna Shaw, Donakell Goldendoodles, Aberdeenshire, Scotland: "Well for me that is easy to answer as I originally bred Labradoodles but they didn't have the look I was looking for. There is such a difference in them, especially when it comes to their natures; Labradoodles are far more boisterous and not so easy to train and tend to be like this for a good few years, not just puppyhood, compared to the Goldendoodles. From a breeding point of view, Goldendoodle coat types are so predictable when having a litter, especially in the early generations." (Pictured is Donna's red Standard Goldendoodle, Nikita, aged six months.)

Laura Chaffin, Cimarron Frontier Doodles, Oklahoma, breeds both: "First generation Labradoodles can have a scruffy look to them, and perhaps a wiry texture, but this does not compromise their wonderful temperaments. I think sometimes Labradoodles can be a little more active than the Goldendoodles, but this really depends on the temperaments of the parents."

Renee Sigman, Yesteryear Acres, Ohio, also breeds both hybrids: "Labradoodles tend to be a little more driven; they like having a job to do. They aren't as content to lie around all day long and really need to have some sort of exercise routine to be happy. Our Goldendoodles are very laid back and would be just as happy hiking all day as just hanging out watching TV. They are mellow love bugs!"

Wendy Loustau, Mustard Seed Ranch Goldendoodles, Georgia: "In the first generation the coat is a huge difference. You get few, if any, really good coats in an F1 Labradoodle, whereas all F1 Goldendoodles have a good coat. By the F1B generation, though, it evens out."

The Appeal of the Goldendoodle

Ask anyone who has spent any time with a Goldendoodle and they will all say the same: there is something really special about this dog. Many of the breeders involved in this book were originally breeding other dogs...until they came across Goldendoodles and found them irresistible.

Lynne Whitmire, Fountain Falls Goldendoodles, South Carolina, tells her story: "The first time I saw a Goldendoodle was at Grant Park in Atlanta. My daughter Paralee, who had been talking about this cool "new kind of dog", asked me to meet her friend who had a six-month-old Goldendoodle. When I saw this dog come bounding at me across the park, I was smitten. I just sat down and said: "You are incredible; I want one of these. Goldendoodles are like no other dog. Over my lifetime I've been involved and have bred Dalmatians, Dobermans, Poodles and Great Danes. The health problems, short lifespan and other issues in the breeds had left me discouraged. As I began to learn more about Goldendoodles I couldn't find anything not to love. They come in all sizes, they are beautiful and they don't shed! What I like most about Doodles is their personality. They have the sharp intelligence of a Poodle and the people-loving quality and loyalty of the Golden Retriever. They are the perfect blend of the two breeds. I've also discovered through my therapy dog work and personal experiences that they have incredible empathy. They are perfect for therapy work and as Service dogs.

"Our Doodles come in all colors; some of our litters are all cream to white, some are all buff colors. The litters that I like best are what we call 'rainbow litters.' I had one litter with six different colors: black, cream, black phantom, chocolate phantom, chocolate and white parti and black and white parti! That litter was my largest litter at 14, the mom was an F1 English cream and the dad was a chocolate and white parti Poodle."

Others breeders tell of how they got The Doodle Bug, starting with Sandra Beck, Beck Kennel, Iowa: "The first Goldendoodle I met was a therapy dog at my daughter's high school. He won the hearts of all the students and would seek out those that seemed stressed, helping to put them at ease. Goldendoodles have eyes that almost seem human to me and have such happy-go-lucky personalities.

"I always loved the Poodle and Golden Retriever breeds and the Goldendoodle is the perfect combination of both breeds...with much less shedding compared to a Golden Retriever. Goldendoodles are your biggest fans and follow you everywhere. They love attention and thrive in an active home where they can be included. Early training is important to help you communicate with your Goldendoodle. They really have a high desire to please their owners."

Kelsey Huffer, Alki Goldendoodles, Washington State: "I was first attracted to the non-shedding coat, but was quickly won over by their charming and goofy personalities. They love to have fun, and love for you to be included. They have the ideal temperament; easy going and eager to please." (Pictured is Kelsey's F2 female Alki's She's My Ginnie, who weighs 45lb at three years old. Photographer: Jamie Pitts of Simple Life Created.)

Michael and Lisa Ross, Chai Kennels, Elgin Canada, have been breeding Standard and Medium Goldendoodles and Standard Poodles since 2007. They said: "Originally we did not plan to cross them. But with the incidence of Golden Retriever lovers with allergies we decided to go ahead and try a few litters....We fell in love with Goldendoodles and have never looked back! They are fun loving and adaptable."

Scotland's Donna Shaw: "I have been breeding Goldendoodles since 2002. I was a Poodle breeder and saw Goldendoodles online in America, where I fell in love with them. I Googled them in the UK and none showed up, so started with my own Standard Poodle and Golden Retrievers to get my first ones and took it from there. My Doodles are the standard size and have whites, creams, chocolate, apricot, red and two new phantom girls of eight months. Mine range from F1 to F2 and F1b and F2b, I have personally found that the middle generations have a lot of throwbacks to the Retriever side of the breed."

Renee Sigman, Yesteryear Acres, Ohio: "We raised Labrador Retrievers for many years prior to raising Doodle puppies. The most appealing thing is the temperament combined with the low shedding coat. We breed cream, apricot and red Goldendoodles in Medium and Standard size. They are great family dogs with very little dog hair. We get requests for all sizes, but we do not breed Minis, as I like the temperaments of the bigger dogs better."

Neelie Smith, River Falls Goldendoodles, South Carolina, also breeds Standards and Mediums and adds: "Temperament is the most appealing quality of a Goldendoodle; they are unlike any other breed. They seem to almost be on the same level as you are."

Wendy Loustau, Mustard Seed Ranch Goldendoodles, Georgia: "I bred Great Pyrenees years ago. Originally it was the look and, of course, the lower shedding that attracted me to the Goldendoodle. The cross just works. It combines the intelligence of the Poodle and the loyalty, affection and dedication of the Golden, with the added benefit of low to non-shedding. And there aren't many larger non shedding dogs that are as family friendly either."

Melissa Farmer, FarmerDoodles, Ohio, has been breeding all generations, Mediums and smaller, since 2006: "I love the Goldendoodle's unique personality that is almost human. I feel like one day my Doodles may actually talk back to me as I am conversing with them! They have the most fun and comical behavior when playing and I LOVE the fact that keeping my home clean is easier with less hair. Goldendoodles love children and other animals and do exceptionally well with them. I enjoy working with families with special needs children or adults and have placed many puppies in these environments, including an adult who now lives in an assisted living facility."

Finally, we asked breeders to sum up their Goldendoodles in a few words

- 🐾 Best furry love bug companion ever!

- 🐾 Smart, fun, loving

- 🐾 Lapdog, best friend; social, family-oriented

- 🐾 Loveable, affectionate, loyal

- 🐾 Adorable fur bundles of love

- 🐾 Safe for families! (from a mother-of-five)

- 🐾 Fun, loving, goofy

- 🐾 Cheerful, obedient, sociable and affectionate

- 🐾 Paws down, The Best!

(Photo of Stella fully grown by Debbie Dixon.)

2. Choosing a Goldendoodle Puppy

Once you have decided that the Goldendoodle is the dog for you, the best way to select a puppy is with your head - and not with your heart. With their big appealing eyes, silky soft fur and endearing personalities, there are few more appealing things on this Earth than a litter of Goldendoodle puppies. If you go to view a litter, the pups are sure to melt your heart and it is extremely difficult – if not downright impossible - to walk away without choosing one.

So, it's essential to do your research before you visit any litters to make sure you select **a responsible breeder with health-tested parents** (of the puppy, not the breeder!) and who knows Goldendoodles inside out. After all, apart from getting married or having a baby, getting a puppy is one of the most important, demanding, expensive and life-enriching decisions you will ever make. Just like babies, puppies will love you unconditionally - but there is a price to pay. In return for their loyalty and devotion, you have to fulfill your part of the bargain.

In the beginning you have to be prepared to devote several hours a day to your new puppy. You have to feed him several times a day and housetrain him virtually every hour, you have to give him your attention and start to gently introduce the rules of the house as well as take care of his general health and welfare. You also have to be prepared to part with hard cash for regular healthcare and pet insurance. (Pictured is Eva, a multigen Mini Goldendoodle aged 11 weeks bred by Christy Stevens, of Winding Creek Ranch, Indiana.)

If you are not prepared, or unable, to devote the time and money to a new arrival – or if you are out at work all day – then now might not be the right time to consider getting a puppy. Goldendoodles like to be with their humans. Separation anxiety is not uncommon and if left alone too long, their natural sunny temperaments can change when they become unhappy. If you are out at work all day then these may not be the dogs for you; to leave a Goldendoodle alone for long periods is just not fair on this lovable crossbreed that is happiest when he's involved in family life. Pick a healthy pup and he or she will probably live to 11, 12 or even into the teens, so it is definitely a long-term commitment. Before taking the plunge, ask yourself some questions:

Have I Got Enough Time?

In the first days after leaving his - or her - mother and littermates, your puppy will feel very lonely and probably even a little afraid. You and your family have to spend time with your new arrival to make him feel safe and sound. Later in this chapter breeder Christy Stevens has written an excellent article which gives an insight into the minds of young Goldendoodle puppies.

Ideally, for the first few days you will be around all of the time to help him settle and to start bonding with him. If you work, book a couple of weeks off, but don't just get a puppy and leave him alone in the house a few days later.

As well as housetraining (potty training), after the first few days, once he's feeling more settled, start to introduce short sessions of a couple of minutes of behavior training to teach your new pup the rules of the house. Goldendoodle puppies can be very boisterous and early teaching to stop puppy biting and jumping up are recommended. Even before his vaccinations have finished, start the socialization process by taking him out of the home to see buses, trains, noisy traffic, kids, etc. - but make sure you CARRY HIM if he's not clear after his vaccinations. Puppies can be very sensitive to all sorts of things and it's important to start the socialization process as soon as possible. The more he is introduced to at this early stage, the better. A good breeder will already have started the socialization process.

Once he has had the all-clear following his vaccinations, get into the habit of taking him out of the house and garden or yard for a short walk every day — more as he gets older. New surroundings stimulate his interest and help to stop him from becoming bored and developing unwanted character traits. He also needs to get used to different noises. Spend some time gently brushing your Goldendoodle and checking his ears are clean to get him used to being handled and groomed right from the beginning. Many breeders will recommend that you have your pup checked out by a vet within a few days of taking him home. You'll also need to factor in time to visit the vet for regular healthcare visits and annual vaccinations.

How Long Can I Leave Him?

This is a question we get asked all of the time and one which causes a lot of debate among owners and prospective owners. All dogs are pack animals; their natural state is to be with others. So being alone is not normal for them, although many have to get used to it. The Goldendoodle has been bred to be a family pet, not a guard dog; he or she wants to be around you.

Another issue is the toilet; all Goldendoodles have smaller bladders than humans. Forget the emotional side of it, how would you like to be left for eight hours without being able to visit the bathroom? So how many hours can you leave a dog alone? Well, a useful guide comes from the canine rescue organizations. In the UK, they will not allow anybody to adopt if they are intending to leave the dog alone for more than four or five hours a day.

Dogs left at home alone all day become bored and, in the case of Goldendoodles and other breeds which are highly dependent on human company, they may well become depressed. Of course, it depends on the character and temperament of your dog, but a lonely Goldendoodle may display signs of unhappiness by being destructive, digging, chewing, barking or urinating.

A puppy or fully-grown dog must NEVER be left shut in a crate all day. It is OK to leave a puppy or adult dog in a crate if he or she is happy there, but all our breeders said the same, the door should never be closed for more than a few hours during the day. A crate is a place where a puppy or adult should feel safe, not a prison. Ask yourself why you want a dog – is it for selfish reasons or can you really offer a good home to a young puppy – and then adult dog – for a decade or longer? Would it be more sensible to wait until you are at home more?

Is My Home Suitable?

Goldendoodles are adaptable; they can live on a farm or in an apartment. However, they all have exercise requirements and so need regular access to the outdoors. Part of this time should ideally be spent off the lead. Don't forget that your puppy's ancestors - the Poodle and the Golden Retriever were originally bred as sporting dogs and to work all day on a shoot. One of the reasons why some Goldendoodles – particularly larger ones - end up in rescue centers is that the owner did not realize how much exercise and stimulation the dog needed

Goldendoodles are highly intelligent and sensitive, and breeders find them one of the easiest (cross)breeds to housetrain – provided you are diligent in the beginning. See **Chapter 5** for more information on how to housetrain your puppy. If you are one of the Goldendoodle owners who lives in an apartment, it is very important to take him outside to perform his duty many times a day to start with if you don't want your pup to eliminate indoors. If you can continue to do this three or four times daily then there is no need to indoor housetrain him. And if you live in a house with a yard or garden, don't leave your puppy unattended; dognapping is becoming increasingly common, particularly with the high price of pups. Make sure there are no poisonous plants or chemicals out there which he could eat or drink. Common plants toxic to dogs include crocus, daffodil, azalea, wisteria, cyclamen, sweat pea, lily of the valley, tulips, hyacinth and lily.

Goldendoodle puppies are little chewing machines and GD-proofing your home should involve moving anything sharp, breakable or chewable - including your shoes - out of reach of sharp little teeth. Make sure he can't chew electrical cords – lift them off the floor if necessary, and block off any off-limits areas of the house, such as upstairs or your bedroom, with a child gate or barrier, especially as he will probably be following you around the house in the first few days. There's more specific advice from breeders on preparing your home later in this chapter.

Family and Children

One of the reasons you have decided on a Goldendoodle may be because you have children and GDs have a reputation for being excellent family pets. Your children will, of course, be delighted about your new arrival; one of the wonderful things about Goldendoodles is how naturally good they are with youngsters. But what about the other members of your family – your husband/wife, or parents, do they all want the puppy as well? A puppy will grow into a dog which will become a part of your family for many years to come and it's important to make sure that everybody in the household is on board with the decision to get a dog. (Photo courtesy of Lisa Ross, Chai Kennels, Elgin, Canada.)

But remember that puppies are small and delicate, as are babies, so you should never

leave babies or very small children and dogs alone together – no matter how well they get along. Small kids lack co-ordination and a young Goldendoodle may inadvertently get poked in the eye or trodden on if you don't keep an eye on him or her. Often puppies regard children as playmates (just like a small child regards a puppy as a playmate) and so the young dog might chase, jump and nip with sharp teeth. This is not aggression; this is normal play for puppies. Train yours to be gentle with your children and your children to be gentle with your dog. See **Chapter 8. Exercise and Training** on how to deal with puppy biting. Discourage the kids from constantly picking up your gorgeous new puppy. They should learn respect for the dog, which is a living creature with his or her own needs, not a toy.

Make sure your puppy gets enough time to sleep – **which is most of the time in the beginning** - so don't let your children constantly pester him. Sleep is very important to puppies, just as it is for babies. Also, allow your Goldendoodle to eat at his or her own pace uninterrupted; letting youngsters play with the dog while eating is a no-no as it may promote gulping of food or food aggression. Another reason some dogs end up in rescue centers is that owners are unable to cope with the demands of small children AND a dog. On the other hand, it is also a fantastic opportunity for you to educate your little darlings (both human and canine) on how to get along with each other and set the pattern for wonderful life-long friendships.

Single People

Many single adults own dogs, but if you live alone, getting a puppy will require a lot of dedication on your part. There will be nobody to share the responsibility, so taking on a dog requires a huge commitment and a lot of your time if the dog is to have a decent life. If you are out of the house all day as well, it is not really fair to get a puppy, or even an adult dog. Left alone all day, they will feel isolated, bored and sad. However, if you work from home or are at home all day and you can spend considerable time with the pup every day, then great; a Goldendoodle will become your best friend.

Older People

If you are older or have elderly relatives living with you, the good news is that Goldendoodles are great company. Provided their needs are met, they are affectionate, easy going and love to be with people. If you are older, make sure you have the energy and patience to deal with a young puppy - consider getting a smaller Goldendoodle, a Standard may be a step too far. All dogs of whatever size benefit from daily walks away from the home. In fact, dogs can be great for older people. My father is in his mid-80s, but takes his dog out walking for an hour to 90 minutes every day - a morning and an afternoon walk – even in the rain or snow. It's good for him and it's good for the dog, helping to keep both of them fit and socialized! They get fresh air, exercise and the chance to communicate with other dogs and their humans.

Goldendoodles are also great company indoors – you're never alone when you've got a dog. Many older people get a dog after losing a loved one (a husband, wife or previous much-loved dog.) A pet gives them something to care for and love, as well as a constant companion. However owning a dog is not cheap, so it's important to be able to afford annual pet insurance, veterinary fees, a quality pet food, etc. The RSPCA in the UK has estimated that owning a dog costs an average of around £1,300 ($2,000) a year.

Other Pets

However friendly your Goldendoodle puppy is, if you already have other pets in your household, they may not be too happy at the new arrival. Goldendoodles generally get on well with other animals, but it might not be a good idea to leave your hamster or pet rabbit running loose with your pup; most dogs have some prey instinct. In the beginning, spend time to introduce them to each other gradually and supervise the sessions. Goldendoodle puppies are naturally curious, lively and playful and they will sniff and investigate other pets. You may have to separate them to start off with, or put your boisterous and playful Goldendoodle puppy into a pen or crate initially to allow a cat to investigate without being mauled by the hyperactive pup, which thinks the cat is a great playmate.

This will also prevent your pup from being injured. If the two animals are free and the cat lashes out, he or she could scratch your pup's eyes. Just type 'Goldendoodle and cat' into YouTube to see how the two might interact. A timid cat might need protection from a bold, playful Goldendoodle - or vice versa. A bold cat and a timid young Goldendoodle will probably settle down together quickest! Pictured is a scene of domestic bliss at the home of Amy Lane.

If things seem to be going well with no aggression after one or two supervised sessions, then let them loose together. Take the process slowly, if your cat is stressed and frightened he may decide to leave. Our feline friends are notorious for abandoning home because the food and facilities are better down the road. Until you know that they can get on, don't leave them alone together.

Goldendoodles generally get on well with other dogs. If you already have other dogs, supervised sessions from an early age will help them to get along and for the other dogs to accept your friendly new Goldendoodle. If you are thinking about getting more than one pup, you might consider waiting until your first Goldendoodle is an adolescent or adult before getting a second, so your older dog is calmer and can help train the younger one. Coping with, training and housetraining one puppy is hard enough, without having to do it with two. On the other hand, some owners prefer to get the messy part over and done with in one go and get two together – but this will require a lot of your time for the first few weeks and months.

As with all dogs, how well they get on also depends on the temperament of the individuals. If you have another dog, it is important to initially introduce the two on neutral territory (rather than in areas one pet deems his own) as you don't want one dog to feel he has to protect his territory. If you think there may be issues, walking the dogs parallel to each other before heading home for the first time is one way of getting them used to each other.

Gender and Color

You have to decide whether you want a male or a female puppy. In terms of gender, much depends on the temperament of the individual dog - the differences WITHIN the sexes is greater than the differences BETWEEN the sexes. Unless you are planning to breed your dog, size and temperament should be your major considerations – with males generally being larger than females.

If you already have dogs or are thinking of getting more than one, you do, however, have to consider gender. You cannot expect an un-neutered male to live with an unspayed female without problems. Similarly, two uncastrated males may not get along; there may simply be too much testosterone and competition. If an existing dog is neutered (male) or spayed (female) and you plan to have your puppy neutered or spayed, then the gender should not be an issue. Often Goldendoodle breeders – including all GANA members - will specify that your pup has to be spayed or neutered within a certain timeframe. This is not because they want to make more money from breeding Goldendoodles, it is to protect the (cross)breed by preventing indiscriminate breeding.

Despite the name, not all Goldendoodles are golden and some people make a decision based on color. As well as various shades of gold, other colors include black, white, cream, red, chocolate, apricot, silver, and parti (white and one other color.) However, we would suggest that color is not as important as size and temperament. Color can also change between puppyhood and adulthood, and may get lighter as the dog ages. Chat with the breeder, she knows her puppies well, and discuss which one would best fit in with your household and lifestyle. That beautiful red puppy with the slightly timid disposition may not be the best choice if you have a busy house full of lively kids and other pets.

More than One Dog

Owning two dogs can be twice as nice - or double the trouble, and vet's bills. There are a number of factors to consider. Here is some advice from UK rescue organization The Doodle Trust:

"Think about why you are considering another dog. If, for example, you have a dog that suffers from separation anxiety, then rather than solving the problem, your second dog may learn from your first and you then have two dogs with the problem instead of one. The same applies if you have an unruly adolescent; cure the problem first and only introduce a second dog when your first is balanced." (Pictured is a two-week-old litter of black and chocolate Medium Goldendoodles bred by Sandra Beck, of Beck Kennel, Iowa.)

"A second dog will mean double vet's fees, groomer's fees, insurance and food. You may also need a larger car, and holidays will be more problematic. Sit down with a calculator and work out the expected expense – you may be surprised. Two dogs will need training, both separately and together. If the dogs do not receive enough individual attention, they may form a strong bond with each other at the expense of their bond with you.

"If you are tempted to buy two puppies from the same litter - DON'T! Your chances of creating a good bond with the puppies are very low and behavior problems with siblings are very common.

"Your dog may be sociable with other dogs but will not necessarily accept another dog into the household. You may find it useful to borrow a friend's dog which is familiar with your own and have a "dummy run" of life in a two-dog household. Research your considered breed well, it may be best to buy a completely different breed to add balance. If you have a very active dog, would a quieter one be best to balance his high energy or would you enjoy the challenge of keeping two high energy dogs?

"You will also need to think of any problems that may occur from keeping dogs of different sizes and ages. If you own an elderly Chihuahua, then an adolescent Labradoodle or Goldendoodle may not be a good choice! If you decide to purchase a puppy, you will need to think very carefully about the amount of time and energy that will be involved in caring for two dogs with very different needs. (Photo courtesy of Dyvonia Bussey, of Grace Goldens, Alabama.)

"A young puppy will need to have his exercise restricted until he has finished growing and will also need individual time for training. Dogs of the same sex can and do live amicably in the same household, although harmony is more likely with a dog and bitch combination. If you decide to keep a dog and bitch together, then you will obviously need to address the neutering issue."

Top 10 Tips For Working Goldendoodle Owners

We would certainly not recommend getting a Goldendoodle if you are out at work all day, But if you're determined to get one when you're out for several hours at a time, here are some useful points:

1. Either come home during your lunch break to let your dog out or employ a dog walker (or neighbor) to take him out for a walk in the middle of the day. If you can afford it, leave him at doggie day care where he can socialize with other dogs.

2. If not, do you know anybody you could leave your dog with during the day? Consider leaving your dog with a reliable friend, relative or elderly neighbor who would welcome the companionship of a Goldendoodle without the full responsibility of ownership.

3   Take him for a walk before you go to work – even if this means getting up at the crack of dawn – and spend time with him as soon as you get home. Exercise generates serotonin in the brain and has a calming effect. A dog that has been exercised will be less anxious and more ready for a good nap.

4. Leave him in a place of his own where he feels comfortable. If you use a crate, leave the door open, otherwise his favorite dog bed or chair. You may need to restrict access to other

areas of the house to prevent him coming to harm or chewing things you don't want chewed. If possible, leave him in a room with a view of the outside world; this will be more interesting than staring at four blank walls.

5. Make sure that it does not get too hot during the day and there are no cold drafts in the place where you leave him.

6. Food and drink: Although most Goldendoodles love their food, it is still generally a good idea to put food down at specific meal times and remove it after 15 or 20 minutes if uneaten to prevent your dog becoming fussy or 'punishing' you for leaving him alone by refusing to eat.

    Make sure he has access to water at all times. Dogs cannot cool down by sweating; they do not have many sweat glands (which is why they pant, but this is much less efficient than perspiring) and can die without sufficient water.

7. Leave toys available to play with to prevent destructive chewing (a popular occupation of bored Goldendoodles or one suffering from separation anxiety.) Stuff a Kong toy – pictured - with treats to keep him occupied for a while. Choose the right size of Kong, you can even smear the inside with peanut butter or another favorite to keep him occupied for longer.

8. Consider getting a companion for your Goldendoodle. This will involve even more of your time and twice the expense, and if you have not got time for one dog, you have hardly time for two. A better idea is to find someone you can leave the dog with during the day; there are also dog sitters and doggie day care for those who can afford them

9. Consider leaving a radio or TV on very softly in the background. The 'white noise' can have a soothing effect on some pets. If you do this, select your channel carefully – try and avoid one with lots of bangs and crashes or heavy metal music!

10. Stick to the same routine before you leave your dog home alone. This will help him to feel secure. Before you go to work, get into a daily habit of getting yourself ready, then feeding and exercising your Goldendoodle. Dogs love routine. But don't make a huge fuss of him when you leave as this can also stress the dog; just leave the house calmly

Similarly when you come home, your Goldendoodle will feel starved of attention and be pleased to see you. Greet him normally, but try not to go overboard by making too much of a fuss as soon as you walk through the door. Give him a pat and a stroke then take off your coat and do a few other things before turning your attention back to him. Lavishing your Goldendoodle with too much attention the second you walk through the door may encourage needy behavior or separation anxiety.

....

Puppy Stages

It is important to understand how a puppy develops into a fully grown dog. This knowledge will help you to be a good owner. **The first few months and weeks of a puppy's life will have an effect on his behavior and character for the rest of his life.** This Puppy Schedule will help you to understand the early stages:

Birth to seven weeks	A puppy needs sleep, food and warmth. He needs his mother for security and discipline and littermates for learning and socialization. The puppy learns to function within a pack and learns the pack order of dominance. He begins to become aware of his environment. During this period, puppies should be left with their mother.
Eight to 12 weeks	At the age of eight weeks, the brain is fully developed and **he now needs socializing with the outside world**. He needs to change from being part of a canine pack to being part of a human pack. This period is a fear period for the puppy, avoid causing him fright and pain.
13 to 16 weeks	Training and formal obedience should begin. **This is a critical period for socializing with other humans, places and situations.** This period will pass easily if you remember that this is a puppy's change to adolescence. Be firm and fair. His flight instinct may be prominent. Avoid being too strict or too soft with him during this time and praise his good behavior.
Four to eight months	Another fear period for a puppy is between seven to eight months of age. It passes quickly, but be cautious of fright or pain which may leave the puppy traumatized. The puppy reaches sexual maturity and dominant traits are established. Your Goldendoodle should now understand the following commands: 'sit', 'down', 'come' and 'stay'.

Plan Ahead

Most puppies leave the breeder for their new homes when they are seven or eight weeks old – Toy breeds may be a little older. It is important that they have time to develop and learn the rules of the pack from their mothers and litter mates. Some puppies take a little longer to develop physically and mentally, and a puppy which leaves too early may suffer with issues, for example a lack of confidence throughout life. Breeders who sell their pups at six weeks or younger are probably more interested in a quick buck than a long-term puppy placement. In the USA, many states specify that a puppy may not be sold before eight   or seven - weeks of age.

And if you want a well-bred Goldendoodle puppy, it certainly pays to plan ahead as most good Goldendoodle breeders have waiting lists. (Pictured is a litter bred by Steve and Neelie Smith, of River Falls Goldendoodles, South Carolina.)

Choosing the right breeder is one of the most important decisions you will make. Like humans, your puppy will be a product of his or her parents and will inherit many of their characteristics. His temperament and how healthy your puppy will be now and throughout his life will largely depend on the genes of his parents. Responsible breeders DNA test their dogs, they check the health records and temperament of the parents and only breed from suitable stock - and good breeding comes at a price.

Expect to pay upwards of $2,000 in the USA, C$1,200 in Canada and £900 in the UK for a puppy from fully health-tested parents. If a Goldendoodle pup is being sold for less, you have to ask why.

Because of these high prices, unscrupulous breeders with little knowledge of the breed have sprung up, tempted by the prospect of making easy cash. A healthy Goldendoodle will be your irreplaceable companion for the next decade or more, so why buy an unseen puppy, or one from a pet shop or general advertisement? Would you buy an old wreck of a car or a house with structural problems just because it was cheap? The answer is probably no, because you know you would be storing up stress and expense in the future.

If a healthy Goldendoodle is important to you, save up until you can afford one. Good breeders do not sell their dogs on general purpose websites or in pet shops. Many reputable Goldendoodle breeders do not have to advertise, such is the demand for their puppies. Often breeders have their own websites, you have to learn to spot the good ones from the bad ones, so do your research.

We strongly recommend visit the breeder personally at least once and follow our **Top 12 Tips for Selecting a Good Breeder** to help you make the right decision. Buying a poorly-bred puppy may save you a few hundred pounds or dollars in the short term, but could cost you thousands in extra veterinary bills in the long run; not to mention the terrible heartache of having a sickly dog. Rescue groups know only too well the dangers of buying a poorly-bred dog; years of problems can arise, usually health-related, but there can also be temperament issues, or bad behavior due to lack of socialization at the breeder's. If possible, look for a GANA member or one listed on the Health Tested Goldendoodle and Labradoodle BreederDirectory at **www.goldendoodle-labradoodle.org**.

....

GANA

The Goldendoodle Association of North America (GANA) is a great place to start your search if you live in the USA or Canada. Unfortunately, there is no similar organization in the UK or Europe, as Goldendoodles are not as popular in these countries, so European buyers should rely on looking for breeders who health test their dogs.

It states: "GANA is the first and only breed club established for the Goldendoodle. A registry database has been created to document lineage. Membership is limited to breeders that provide proof of health clearances achieved on all their breeding dogs and that have agreed to a Code of Ethics regarding their breeding practices and the care of their dogs. To ensure you are working with a breeder that meets these standards, look for the GANA logo (pictured) on their website."

Mission statement: "GANA's primary objective is to promote and guide the development of the Goldendoodle to achieve breed standards while maintaining optimum health. GANA guides breeders to the common goal of establishing reliability in coat, type, health, and temperament. It is imperative that the breed's ancestry be documented to allow pedigree and health information to be accessed as the breed's development moves forward. GANA has established a registry that will document this development. Without careful consideration and proper use of the records, the future of the Goldendoodle could be compromised.

A Code of Ethics and Accredited Breeder Rules and Requirements have been created to assure the common goal of the betterment of the breed is followed by all member breeders. Protecting the integrity of the Goldendoodle is in the best interest of all of us as we are the beneficiaries of this wonderful breed."

Code of Ethics

Members have to agree to a strict Code of Ethics which guarantees, as far as possible, the health and welfare of the breeding stock and puppies. Main points include:

- ✓ I shall at all times ensure all dogs under my control are appropriately cared for in regards to shelter, food, water, exercise, and veterinary care

- ✓ I will register/license my dogs with all state and local required organizations. If a kennel license is required, I will not operate a breeding program without obtaining one

- ✓ I shall always breed with the soundness or betterment of the Goldendoodle in mind. I will not breed any dog/bitch that has not been tested or has failed any of the requirements listed in the "Required Health Tests"

- ✓ I will not sell/trade any of my dogs or puppies to any commercial animal wholesaler or retail pet dealers/traders

- ✓ I will not sell/trade/release a puppy under the age of seven weeks or before the minimum age requirement for my state

- ✓ I will give/sell/trade all puppies with a written spay/neuter requirement or I will have the puppies desexed before leaving me unless puppies are sold with breeding rights

- ✓ I will have all puppies examined by my vet prior to placement as pets or breeders and will provide proof of this exam to the new owner upon their request
- ✓ I will educate new puppy owners to the best of my ability as to the proper care and welfare of the puppy

- ✓ I will offer email and phone support to new puppy owners before and after the puppy leaves my care

- ✓ I agree to help rehome any dog that originated from my breeding stock should the need arise

- ✓ I will provide records of all vaccinations, dewormings, and veterinary care as well as a GANA Puppy Registration Certificate with each puppy that leaves my care

- ✓ I will not guarantee hypo-allergenic qualities or non-shedding coats to any customer

- ✓ I will keep written records of my breeding stocks' offspring and document any noticed or reported genetic defects. I will not pair those that show repeated defects of an inhibiting nature in their offspring

✓ I will provide a warranty for life inhibiting genetic defects until at least 2 years of age. I understand that each breeder's warranty will vary somewhat, but I will not require a puppy/dog to be returned for a warranty to be exercised. The required use of any supplements or specific brand of food is not allowed. Exercise limitations can be requested, but not required. It is at my discretion as to whether to offer monetary assistance or to replace the puppy with a like puppy. The minimum monetary assistance is 50% of the purchase price of the puppy not including shipping fees. A copy of your warranty and/or Bill of Sale must be posted on your website at all times. (Pictured is a litter bred by Amy Lane.)

✓ I will not breed any dog/bitch to a related dog/bitch within three generations

✓ I will select breeding pairs with the specific goal of producing the best health, conformation, temperament, and coats

✓ I will make certain that any buyer given breeding rights with a puppy understands and follows ethical breeding practices

✓ I will not surrender a pet or breeding dog to any rescue, animal control, or shelter. I will find an appropriate pet home

✓ I will keep my dogs up to date on necessary vaccines for my area. I will vaccinate all puppies between six to eight weeks of age. I will deworm all puppies a minimum of two times prior to eight weeks of age

✓ I agree that I either own the breeding rights or have contracted the use of the breeding rights for all dogs used in my breeding program.

All accredited breeders MUST test at least for the following:

➤ HIPS – hip score of FAIR, GOOD or EXCELLENT for dogs aged seven months or older
➤ HEART – OFA permanent heart clearance
➤ EYES - Bi-annual CERF exam, certificate from OFA or CERF
➤ VWD (von Willebrand Disease, a canine bleeding disorder) - At least one clear in the breeding pair. Poodles and Goldendoodles can be cleared by parentage or by DNA testing, Golden Retrievers are not required to be tested as they are not at risk for vWd

To move up from Red Ribbon to Blue Ribbon level, breeders must also carry out tests for:

➤ ELBOWS – Preliminary or permanent clear rating after the age of seven months
➤ PATELLAS (hind leg knees) - Permanent clear rating (Mini/Toy Poodles and Mini/Medium Goldendoodles only)

In addition, there is recommended testing at all levels for Degenerative Myelopathy (a disease of the spinal cord), Ichthyosis (a skin disease in Golden Retrievers) and annual eye exams. Health testing does not come cheap and with such rigorous exams, you can see now why healthy Goldendoodle puppies are so expensive.

Amy Lane, founder of GANA, told The Goldendoodle Handbook: "Pricing for a Goldendoodle varies due to a number of reasons. If both parent dogs of a litter have been fully health tested and proven to be free and clear of the genetic issues that are prevalent in the Poodle and Golden Retriever breeds, a higher price is set to cover the costs of all this testing, as well as the removal of dogs from the breeding program that ended up not passing a health test certification along the way.

"Cheaper prices can be found for puppies produced by backyard breeders and puppy mills (breeders that do not concern themselves about the health of the puppies they produce nor the conditions in which the adults kept.) Many breeders charge a higher price for smaller Goldendoodles as it takes more generations of selective breeding to downsize, since one of the beginning generation parents is always a Golden Retriever, which is a large breed.

"From health tested parents, the typical price ranges from $2,000 to $3,500 for a puppy from a respected breeder. Most Goldendoodle puppies sold for less than $2,000 are typically from puppy mills, back yard breeders, or perhaps breeders new to the breeding world that have not established their reputation." Here's the link to the list of GANA members: http://goldendoodleassociation.com/dogtrack/guest/memberbreeders.aspx.

As yet, there is no similar organization in the UK or Europe, as Goldendoodles are not as popular in these countries. European buyers should rely on looking for breeders who conform to many of the points listed in the GANA Code of Ethics. (This handsome Medium multigen pup was bred by Debbie Dixon, of Zippity Doodles Goldendoodles, Colorado.)

Of course, there are no cast iron guarantees that your puppy will be healthy and have a good temperament, but choosing a breeder who conforms to a code of ethics is a very good place to start. If you live in Europe or, for whatever reason, you're not able to buy a puppy from a breeder with a proved track record, how do you avoid buying one from a 'backstreet breeder' or puppy mill? These are people who just breed puppies for profit and sell them to the first person who turns up with the cash. Unhappily, this can end in heartbreak for a family months or years later when their puppy develops health or temperament problems due to poor breeding.

Price is a good guide, and with Goldendoodles you often do get what you pay for. A cheap puppy usually means that corners have been cut somewhere along the line – and it's often health. If a pup is advertised at a few hundred dollars or pounds, then you can bet your last dollar that the dam and sire are not superb examples of their breed, that they haven't been fully health tested, and that often the puppies are not being fed premium quality food or even kept in the house with the family where the breeder should start to socialize and housetrain them. Here's some advice on what to avoid:

Where NOT to buy a Goldendoodle Puppy

Due to the high cost of Goldendoodle puppies – as well as waiting lists for litters - unscrupulous breeders have sprung up to cash in on this hugely popular crossbreed. While new owners might think they have bagged 'a bargain,' this more often than not turns out to be false economy and an emotionally disastrous decision when the puppy develops health problems due to poor breeding, or behavioral problems due to lack of socialization during the critical early phase of his or her life.

In September 2013 The UK's Kennel Club issued a warning of a puppy welfare crisis, with some truly sickening statistics. As many as one in four puppies bought in the UK may come from puppy farms - and the situation is no better in North America. The Press release stated: "As the popularity of online pups continues to soar:

- **Almost one in five pups bought (unseen) on websites or social media die within six months**
- One in three buy online, in pet stores and via newspaper adverts - outlets often used by puppy farmers – this is an increase from one in five in the previous year
- The problem is likely to grow as the younger generation favor mail order pups, and breeders of fashionable crossbreeds flout responsible steps."

The Kennel Club said: "We are sleepwalking into a dog welfare and consumer crisis as new research shows that more and more people are buying their pups online or through pet shops, outlets often used by cruel puppy farmers, and are paying the price with their pups requiring long-term veterinary treatment or dying before six months old. The increasing popularity of online pups is a particular concern. Of those who source their puppies online, half are going on to buy 'mail order pups' directly over the internet." The KC research found that:

- One third of people who bought their puppy online, over social media or in pet shops failed to experience 'overall good health'
- Almost one in five puppies bought via social media or the internet die before six months old
- Some 12% of puppies bought online or on social media end up with serious health problems that require expensive on-going veterinary treatment from a young age

Caroline Kisko, Kennel Club Secretary, said: "More and more people are buying puppies from sources such as the internet, which are often used by puppy farmers. Whilst there is nothing wrong with initially finding a puppy online, it is essential to then see the breeder and ensure that they are doing all of the right things. This research clearly shows that too many people are failing to do this, and the consequences can be seen in the shocking number of puppies that are becoming sick or dying. We have an extremely serious consumer protection and puppy welfare crisis on our hands."

The research revealed that the problem was likely to get worse as mail order pups bought over the internet are the second most common way for the younger generation of 18 to 24-year-olds to buy a puppy (31%.) Marc Abraham, TV vet and founder of Pup Aid, said: "Sadly, if the 'buy it now' culture persists, then this horrific situation will only get worse. There is nothing wrong with sourcing a puppy online, but people need to be aware of what they should then expect from the breeder.

"For example, you should not buy a car without getting its service history and seeing it at its registered address, so you certainly shouldn't buy a puppy without the correct paperwork and health certificates and without seeing where it was bred. However, too many people are opting to buy directly from third parties such as the internet, pet shops, or from puppy dealers, where you cannot possibly know how or where the puppy was raised.

"Not only are people buying sickly puppies, but many people are being scammed into paying money for puppies that don't exist, as the research showed that 7% of those who buy online were scammed in this way." The Kennel Club has launched an online video and has a Find A Puppy app to show the dos and don'ts of buying a puppy. View the video at www.thekennelclub.org.uk/paw

Caveat Emptor – Buyer Beware

Here are some signs that a puppy may have arrived via a puppy mill, a puppy broker (somebody who makes money from buying and selling puppies) or even an importer. Our strong advice is that if you suspect that this is the case, walk away - unless you want to risk a lot of trouble and heartache in the future.

You can't buy a Rolls Royce or a Lamborghini for a couple of thousand pounds or dollars - you'd immediately suspect that the 'bargain' on offer wasn't the real thing. No matter how lovely it looked, you'd be right - and the same applies to Goldendoodles. Here are some signs to look out for:

- ❧ Websites – buying a puppy from a website does not necessarily mean that the puppy will turn out to have problems. But avoid websites where there are no pictures of the home, environment and owners. If they are only showing close-up photos of cute puppies, click the **X** button

- ❧ Don't buy a website puppy with a shopping cart symbol next to his picture

- ❧ Don't commit to a puppy unless you have seen it face-to-face. However, some experienced Goldendoodle breeders in the US may not allow general access to litters, due to the possible spread of infection to unweaned puppies – especially if potential owners are visiting various different premises. If this is the case, the breeder may have Open Days when you can visit his or her home to see non-nursing puppies and how they are cared for and raised. If so, attend one beforehand and make sure you are happy with welfare conditions and health testing before signing on the dotted line

- ❧ If you are buying in the UK, always ask to see the parents; as a minimum, see the mother and how she looks and behaves. The situation in North America may be different. Some recognized breeders use permanent guardian homes for their breeding dogs, so the parents of your puppy may not be available when you visit. If so, ask about the parents, who keeps them and whether the dogs live in the house with the guardian

🐾 If the breeder says that the dam and sire are Kennel Club or AKC registered, insist on seeing the parents' registration papers – this only applies to first generation (F1) Goldendoodles

🐾 Ignore photographs of so-called 'champion' ancestors (unless you are buying from an approved breeder), in all likelihood these are fiction

🐾 The puppies look small for their stated age. A committed Goldendoodle breeder will not let her puppies leave before they are seven or eight weeks old

🐾 The person you are buying the puppy from did not breed the dog themselves. Don't buy from an intermediary, always buy direct from the breeder

🐾 The place you meet the puppy seller is a car park or place other than the puppies' home

🐾 The seller tells you that the puppy comes from top, caring breeders from your or another country. Not true. There are reputable, caring breeders all over the world, but not one of them sells their puppies through brokers

🐾 Ask to see photos of the puppy from birth to present day. If the seller has none, there is a reason – walk away

🐾 Price – if you are offered a cheap Goldendoodle, he or she almost certainly comes from dubious stock. Careful breeding, taking good care of mother and puppies and genetic health screening all add up to one big bill for breeders. Anyone selling their puppies at a knock-down price has certainly cut corners

🐾 If you get a rescue Goldendoodle, make sure it is from a recognized rescue group - such as IDOG International in the USA or The Doodle Trust in the UK - and not a 'puppy flipper' who may be posing as a do-gooder, but is in fact getting dogs – including stolen ones - from unscrupulous sources

In fact the whole brokering business is just another version of the puppy mill and should be avoided at all costs. Bear in mind that for every cute Goldendoodle puppy you see from a puppy mill or broker, other puppies have died. Good Goldendoodle breeders will only breed from dogs which have been carefully selected for health, temperament, physical shape and lineage. There are plenty out there, it's just a question of finding one. And the good news is that there are signs to help the savvy buyer spot a good breeder.

Top 12 Tips for Choosing a Good Breeder

1. Choose a Goldendoodle breeder whose dogs are health tested with certificates to prove it.

2. Choose a Goldendoodle breeder whose dogs are health tested with certificates to prove it.

3. Choose a Goldendoodle breeder whose dogs are health tested with certificates to prove it. No, this repetition is not a typo! It is just that we cannot stress enough how important this is with Goldendoodles. You may have chosen this hybrid because you do not want a purebred dog; the health problems of overbreeding and interbreeding are well documented. Well, both the Goldendoodle's parent breeds - Poodles and Golden Retrievers - have a number of

health issues and if you buy from untested stock (even if you are buying a multigen puppy), you risk your puppy inheriting one or all of these genetic diseases.

4. If you are in North America, visit the GANA website for a list of accredited breeders. If your chosen breeder is not registered, read the small print on the breeder's website – what health tests are carried out? This also applies to Europe where there is no breed association.
5. Good breeders keep the dogs in the home as part of the family - not outside in kennel runs, garages or outbuildings. Check that the area where the puppies are kept is clean and that the puppies themselves look clean.

6. Their Goldendoodles appear happy and healthy. Check that the pup has clean eyes, ears, nose and bum (butt) with no discharge. The pups are alert, excited to meet new people and don't shy away from visitors. (Photo courtesy of Steve and Neelie Smith

7. They are very familiar with Goldendoodles, although some may also breed other breeds and crossbreeds. If these are related types – e.g. Labradoodles or other Poodle crosses – all the better.

8. All responsible breeders should provide you with a written contract and health guarantee. They will also show you records of the puppy's visits to the vet, vaccinations, worming medication, etc. and explain what other vaccinations your puppy will need. They will agree to take a puppy back within a certain time frame if it does not work out for you, or if there is a health problem.

9. They feed their adults and puppies high quality dog food and give you some to take home and guidance on feeding and caring for your puppy. They will also be available for advice after you take your puppy home.

10. They don't always have pups available, but keep a list of interested people for the next available litter. They don't over-breed, but do limit the number of litters from their dams. Over-breeding or breeding from older females can be detrimental to the female's health.

11. If you have selected a breeder and checked if/when she has puppies available, go online to the Goldendoodle forums before you visit and ask if anyone out there already has a dog from this breeder. If you are buying from a good breeder, the chances are someone will know her dogs or at least her reputation. If the feedback is negative, cancel your visit and start looking elsewhere. A good breeder will, if asked, provide references from other people who have bought their puppies; call at least one before you commit. They will also agree to take a puppy back within a certain time frame if it does not work out for you, or if there is a health problem.

12. And finally ... good Goldendoodle breeders want to know their beloved pups are going to good homes and will ask YOU a lot of questions about your suitability as owners. DON'T buy a puppy from a website or advert where a PayPal or credit card deposit secures you a puppy without any questions.

Goldendoodle puppies should not be regarded as must-have accessories. They are not objects, they are warm-blooded, living, breathing creatures. (Photo of this lively litter courtesy of Janece Schommer, of Goldendoodle Acres, Wisconsin.)

Healthy, happy puppies and adult dogs are what everybody wants. Taking the time now to find a responsible and committed breeder with well-bred Goldendoodles is time well spent. It could save you a lot of time, money and heartache in the future and help to ensure that you and your chosen puppy are happy together for many years to come.

The Most Important Questions to Ask a Breeder

Some of these points have been covered in the previous section, but here's a reminder and checklist of the questions you should be asking.

Have the parents been health screened? Buy only a pup with DNA-tested parents. Ask to see original copies of health certificates. If no certificates are available, ask what guarantees the breeder or seller is offering in terms of genetic illnesses, and how long these guarantees last – 12 weeks, a year, a lifetime? It will vary from breeder to breeder, but good ones will definitely give you some form of guarantee – it should be stated in the puppy contract. They will also want to be informed of any hereditary health problems with your puppy, as they may choose not to breed from the dam or sire (mother or father) again. Some breeders keep a chart documenting the full family health history of the pup – ask if one exists and if you can see it.

Can you put me in touch with someone who already has one of your puppies?

Are you a member of GANA? (if in North America.) Not all good Goldendoodle breeders are members, but this is a good place to start.

How long have you been breeding Goldendoodles? You are looking for someone who has a track record with the breed.

How many litters has the mother had? Females should not have litters until they are over one year old, and then only have a few litters in their lifetime. Check the age of the mother; too young or too old is not good for her health. GANA stipulates there should be no breeding of females before one or after seven years of age.

What happens to the female(s) once she/they have finished breeding? Are they kept as part of the family, rehomed in loving homes or sent to animal shelters?

Do you breed any other types of dog? Buy from a Goldendoodle specialist, preferably one who does not breed lots of other breeds of dog - unless you know they have a good reputation.

What is so special about this litter? You are looking for a breeder who has used good breeding stock and his or her knowledge to produce healthy, handsome dogs with good temperaments, not just cute dogs in fancy colors. All Goldendoodle puppies look cute, don't buy the first one you see – be patient and pick the right one. If you don't get a satisfactory answer, look elsewhere.

What do you feed your adults and puppies? A reputable breeder will feed a top quality dog food and advise that you do the same.

What special care do you recommend? Your Goldendoodle will probably need regular grooming, trimming and ear cleaning.

What is the average lifespan of your dogs? Generally, pups bred from healthy stock tend to live longer.

How socialized and housetrained is the puppy? Good breeders will raise their puppies as part of the household and start the socialization and potty training process before they leave.

What healthcare have the pups had so far? Ask to see records of flea treatments, wormings and vaccinations.

Has the puppy been microchipped?

Why aren't you asking me any questions? A good breeder will be committed to making a good match between the new owners and their puppies. If the breeder spends more time discussing money than the welfare of the puppy and how you will care for him, you can draw your own conclusions as to what his or her priorities are – and they probably don't include improving the breed. Walk away.

Pictured is seven-week-old Dax, an F3 Medium Goldendoodle from health-tested parents bred by Laura Chaffin, of Cimarron Frontier Doodles, Oklahoma, who has been breeding Goldendoodles since 2000.

 Take your puppy to a vet to have a thorough check-up within 48 hours of purchase. If your vet is not happy with the health of the dog, no matter how painful it may be, return the pup to the breeder. Keeping an unhealthy puppy will only cause more distress and expense in the long run.

Puppy Contracts

Unlike with some other breeds and crossbreeds, ALL good Goldendoodle breeders will provide you with an official Puppy Contract. This protects both buyer and seller by providing information on diet, worming, vaccination and veterinary visits from the birth of the puppy until he or she leaves the breeder. You should also have a health guarantee for a specified time period of two years or longer.

A Puppy Contract will answer such questions as whether the puppy:

- Is covered by breeder's insurance and can be returned if there is a health issue within a certain period of time
- Was born by Cesarean section
- Has been micro-chipped and/or vaccinated and details of worming treatments
- The puppy has been partially or wholly toilet trained
- Whether the pup has been socialized and where it was kept
- And what health issues the pup and parents have been screened for
- What the puppy is currently being fed by the breeder and if any food is being supplied
- Details of the dam and sire

It's not easy for caring breeders to part with their puppies after they have lovingly bred and raised them to seven or eight weeks of age or older, and so many supply extensive care notes for new owners, which may include details such as:

- The puppy's daily routine
- Feeding schedule
- Vet and vaccination schedule
- General puppy care
- Toilet training
- Socialization

New owners should do their research before visiting a litter as once there, the cute Goldendoodle puppies will undoubtedly be irresistible and you will buy with your heart rather than your head. If you have any doubts at all about the breeder, seller or the puppy, WALK AWAY. Spending the time now to get your Goldendoodle from a good breeder with a proven track record will help to reduce the chances of health and behavior problems later on.

In the UK, The Royal Society for the Prevention of Cruelty to Animals (RSPCA) has a downloadable puppy contract endorsed by vets and animal welfare organizations .You can see a copy here and should be looking for something similar from the breeder or seller of the puppy: http://puppycontract.rspca.org.uk/webContent/staticImages/Microsites/PuppyContract/Downloads/PuppyContractDownload.pdf

Here is a typical Goldendoodle Puppy Contract as used by GANA members in North America:

GOLDENDOODLE PURCHASING CONTRACT

This agreement is between ......(Seller) and: ....(Buyer)

It is agreed between Seller and Buyer as follows:

1. **DESCRIPTION OF DOG** - The dog sold pursuant to the terms of this agreement is as follows:

Sex:_____ Whelped:_____

Color:_____ Microchip #_____

2. **SELLER'S REPRESENTATIONS**

The following conditions apply to the sale of the aforementioned dog:

The Buyer has FIVE days from the time of purchase to have the dog examined by a veterinarian and to personally inspect the dog. Any request to return the dog to the Seller <u>must be made within this time period</u> and must be accompanied by a <u>written</u> statement from a veterinarian describing all problems found. Failure to have the puppy examined within 5 days voids the health warranty.

A warranty against genetic defects is provided for two years after the date of sale, related reimbursement limited to 50% of the purchase price. Genetic defects that qualify for reimbursement are those related to hip, heart, elbow, eye, or life threatening issues. Reimbursement for genetic defects will be made only when a second opinion from a qualified veterinarian and proof of surgery expenses are provided. An official OFA hip rating will qualify as a second opinion. In the rare case of death, the puppy will be replaced free of charge if under 2 years of age. A necropsy report completed by a qualified vet must show the cause of death was caused by a genetic issue. Shipping fees are at the Buyer's expense. Seller agrees to rehome the dog should the original purchaser so request. Warranties shall apply only to original purchaser. This warranty is void in the event of an indeterminable or inconclusive diagnosis. Transfer of dog ownership shall void all such provisions of this agreement.

Seller makes no guarantee this dog will not shed or cause an allergic reaction. Buyer understands that Seller's prediction of coat type, height, and weight at adulthood are estimates only and are based on Seller's goal to match puppies with families appropriately.

(Seller) provides a certificate for 30 days of free health insurance through Trupanion (PA NY, SC, CA, FL and WA residents) and 60 days of free health insurance through Embrace for all others. Any warranty issues within the first 30 or 60 days (depending on free coverage length) will be paid out only for the deductible incurred. It is your responsibility to enroll your puppy within the first 24 hours of possession with Trupanion to enact this free coverage. (Seller) activates the free coverage through Embrace.

This dog must be spayed or neutered before 7 months of age and failure to have this done will void the health warranty. Proof of spay/neuter must be provided to the Seller within 30 days of procedure being completed to maintain your warranty. Failure to have this dog spayed or neutered prior to 8 months of age will require purchaser to pay Seller five times the purchase price. Proof of spaying/neutering by 7 months of age must accompany any request for warranty reimbursement. This puppy is being sold as a family pet and does not convey with breeding rights. If this puppy is bred, the purchaser agrees to pay the Seller ten times the purchase price of this puppy for every litter produced. All legal fees to enforce this contract will be the responsibility of the purchaser.

Under no circumstances shall the Seller be liable to the Buyer or to any third party for a dog that has been subjected to abuse, accident, negligence or misuse. Also, under no circumstances shall the Seller be liable for any consequential incidental or special damages resulting from or in any manner related to the dog.

Upon execution of this contract all veterinary care and its associated costs are the sole and exclusive responsibility of the Buyer.

3. CONSIDERATION

This dog, identified in Section 1, is being sold for the sum of $_, payable in full at the execution of this contract. In the event that said funds are not readily collectible by the Seller, for example, a refusal by a bank to honor a check tendered by the Buyer for the dog, the parties agree that the Seller shall have the right to recover from the Buyer all reasonable attorneys' fees and court costs incurred in connection with obtaining full payment.

4. MAINTENANCE

Buyer agrees to maintain this dog in good health, provide preventative health care including, but not limited to, inoculation, internal parasites, and -where indicated- heartworm preventative medication. It is agreed that your Goldendoodle will be housed indoors and fed a quality food. It is also agreed that you will maintain the dog at a healthy weight. Buyer agrees to postpone strenuous, repetitive exercise (such as agility training or running miles a day) until a minimum of one year of age. Buyer agrees to provide basic obedience training within the first year of ownership. Buyer agrees to never place this dog in a shelter, pound, or similar facility including a research laboratory.

5. FULL AND FINAL AGREEMENT

The parties agree that this writing represents the entire Agreement between them and that no other representations, either oral or written have been made regarding the dog described above. The parties further agree that no changes in this contract shall be binding upon either of them without written modifications signed by both parties.

Buyer agrees that he/she understands this contract fully, and that this contract is under the jurisdiction of the State of ……………

SELLER'S SIGNATURE & DATE

BUYER'S SIGNATURE & DATE...

BUYER'S PHONE NUMBER...

Top 12 Tips for Choosing a Healthy Goldendoodle

Once you've selected your breeder and a litter is available, you then have to decide WHICH puppy to pick. Often the breeder may ask questions about you, your family and lifestyle in order to try and match you with a puppy likely to fit in with your schedule. Here are some signs that you should look for when selecting a puppy:

1. Your chosen puppy should have a well-fed appearance. He or she should not, however, have a distended abdomen (pot belly) as this can be a sign of worms - or other illnesses (such as Cushing's disease in adults.) The ideal puppy should not be too thin either, you should not be able to see his ribs.

2. His (or her) nose should be cool, damp and clean with no discharge. (This healthy litter, bred by Candice Farrell, Ooodles of Doodles, Canada, are enjoying all the comforts that home has to offer.)

3. The pup's eyes should be bright and clear with no discharge or tear stain. Steer clear of a puppy which blinks a lot, this could be the sign of a problem.

4. His gums should be clean and pink.

5. The pup's ears should be clean with no sign of discharge, soreness or redness and no unpleasant smell.

6. Check the puppy's rear end to make sure it is clean and there are no signs of diarrhea.

7. One of the Goldendoodle's prize attributes is his or her coat; it should look clean, feel soft, not matted - and puppies should smell good! The coat should have no signs of ticks or fleas. Red or irritated skin or bald spots could be a sign of infestation or a skin condition. Also check between the toes of the paws for signs of redness or swelling.

8. Choose a puppy that moves freely without any sign of injury or lameness. It should be a fluid movement, not jerky or stiff, which could be a sign of joint problems.

9. When the puppy is distracted, clap or make a noise behind him - not so loud as to frighten him - to make sure he is not deaf.

10. Finally, ask to see veterinary records to confirm your puppy has been wormed and had his first injections.

If you are unlucky enough to have a health problem with your pup within the first few months, a reputable breeder will allow you to return the pup. Also, if you get the Goldendoodle puppy home and things don't work out for whatever reason, good breeders should also take the puppy back. Make sure this is the case before you commit.

What the Breeders Say

Our breeders have lots of advice on what to look out for when either considering or visiting a breeder. Wendi Loustau, of Mustard Seed Ranch Goldendoodles, Georgia, has been breeding Goldendoodles since 2005 and said: "Health testing is the most important thing; read the warranty BEFORE you put a deposit down. If breeders aren't doing any testing or won't show proof, this is a red flag."

Lisa Ross, Chai Kennels, Elgin, Canada: "Look out for dogs not getting along well with each other and not wanting to be with people; and parents being tucked away in another room or not allowed with the other dogs. We board and train and see too many Doodles with sketchy temperaments. You should be looking for happy, confident puppies that want to be picked up. When picked up they should be comfortable and not wanting right back down. Again, the pups should be in with the family and not fearful."

Laura Chaffin, Cimarron Frontier Doodles, Oklahoma: "Signs of a well-bred puppy, are enthusiasm to be with humans, no eye or bottom discharge, a healthy looking coat and a sound and healthy mother. I have purchased several breeding stock dogs from other breeders and I really am shocked that so many come to me with kennel shyness. I think that they must spend all their time in an outdoor kennel with limited interaction with humans.

"It is very hard to trust what the breeders say in an email or an ad online. It is the best choice to visit the breeder you are getting a puppy from. Insist on seeing at least the mother, and the father if he is on site. If the sire is not available, ask to visit the other dogs. View the environment the other dogs are in and pay attention to their temperament and health. Check the puppy's paws for filth , and check their eyes and their bottom - there should be no discharge. And ask what the puppy has been eating. Poor food quality is a poor start on their development. I think starting out with raw food or kibble that is made fresh and without corn, wheat, or soy is best.

"If buying a puppy online, be diligent to read what others have said regarding the breeder. All this is more important than registrations or pedigrees. This is because, if you see the other dogs in the breeder's procession, and if they have older dogs, you can see whether these dogs are taken care of and if the older dogs have any health issues. Plus, you can observe whether there are any temperament issues in the breed line. I think a website with pictures of all the breeding stock and information with pictures of the puppy you are interested in, in several stages of development, including pictures and information of other dogs in the breeding line, is pretty important."

Sandra Beck, of Beck Kennels, Iowa: "Look for a breeder that has done extensive health testing on breeding dogs and demand to see the testing results. These would include OFA heart, hips, elbows and patellas, as well as an annual CERF eye exam. Genetic testing for prcd-PRA and vWd at a minimum. Ask to see the parent dogs and observe if they appear healthy and well groomed. A bonus would be a breeder that takes the time to train their dogs and really enjoys them as part of their family."

Melissa Farmer, FarmerDoodles, Ohio: "When visiting, the home or kennel the environment should be clean. Dogs should look groomed and visibly healthy. Breeders should be able to produce health testing and be able to explain it to owners. Google is a powerful tool...use it. Google names and look for complaints. Look at the organizations the breeder belongs to and contact them for feedback."

Kelsey Huffer, Alki Goldendoodles, Washington State: "Asking about the health of the parents is key. As breeders of GANA, we are attempting to avoid the costly mistakes that purebreds in the AKC now face today. A breeder who cares not only about the health of her breeding stock, but also the health of the puppies will inherently put any fears to rest about 'buying a lemon.'" Pictured is Kelsey's Alki's She's My Ginnie, aged six weeks, and as a 45lb two-year-old adult, below.

"Responsible breeders will want you to tell them immediately if there are any health concerns with your puppy, so that they can mitigate these risks either in their own breeding program or with their puppy families. I think health concerns and genetic testing makes way for other responsible practices in a natural way, so I would advise this to be a focus in selecting a responsible breeder. Breeders who breed for attractive colors and markings only, or breed a large Golden Retriever to a small Poodle and call them 'Mini Goldendoodles' really have no idea about the basics of breeding and genetics. You can buy from them, but you need to understand that you are getting an unpredictable dog and financing irresponsible breeding.

"If the breeder has no interest in taking the puppy back if he/she does not work out (regardless of a refund or not) RUN, and RUN QUICKLY, because these are the types of breeders who keep local animal shelters well stocked with dogs that 'just didn't work out' or 'had to be given up because we moved.'"

Neelie Smith, River Falls Goldendoodles, South Carolina: "When visiting a breeder, the place must be clean and smell clean. Are there a lot of other dogs on the property? A good breeder should encourage you to spend time with the puppies and not rush you. Pups should be clean, no fleas and never seem frightened; pups should want to play. When searching for a pup it's helpful to look for the blue ribbon GANA status. A good breeder should have done the proper health testing on both parents and offer a two-year health guarantee. Are the puppies active, friendly, outgoing? If the puppies seem lethargic, there may be something wrong. Again look for the GANA status."

Lynne Whitmire, Fountain Falls Goldendoodles: "When someone calls me and I do not have puppies available, I give them this advice: Ask if the parents are health tested. If the breeder says yes, ask if the health documents are available to see. Don't accept a puppy whose parents have not had at least these health tests: a CERF (eye test), OFA heart and hips. We do many more tests than these. Ask if you can visit where the puppies are raised before puppy pick-up day. Pay close attention to the environment, and cleanliness of the dogs. Only buy from a breeder that will talk to you and answer all of your questions.

"Puppies should be raised in a clean, healthy environment. They should have clean, age-appropriate toys and plenty of room to run play and develop. Mom should be clean, clear eyed and healthy looking. Puppies should have shiny coats and be somewhat chubby. When you approach the puppies they should be jumping on the fence, eager to be picked up. You don't want to choose a shy, fearful puppy. One of the things that I advise against is letting the puppy choose you. Anyone who sits down with a litter of puppies will be noticed by those puppies. The first one to reach you may be the dominant female that has had her fill at the food bowl and beats everyone else to this new person. An experienced breeder is your best tool for finding the right fit for your family. Don't let the spot on a puppy's head be the reason for choosing that particular puppy."

Renee Sigman, Yesteryear Acres, Ohio: "I would say the time the breeder spends with the puppies is key; puppies need socialization. You can't really undo damage caused by lack of social contact during the four- to eight-week period in a puppy's life. Puppies need good social interactions and lots of human cuddling and playtime. Also, cleanliness is important; puppies who learn to lie in their own waste are almost impossible to housebreak. We take our puppies outside every two hours to make sure they get the hang of housebreaking from an early age."

Janece Schommer, "Warning signs are: 1. Breeders that don't do genetic testing, 2. Breeders who can't talk about genetics of their dogs, 3. Breeders who can't produce pedigrees, 4. Breeders who are willing or requesting to meet you at a 'meeting point', 5. Breeders who don't have a two-year guarantee contract, 6. Breeders who don't have a spay/neuter clause in their contract, 7. Breeders who don't have their pups examined by a licensed vet in their state before going home. Checking the internet for formal complaints and reviews may also help prospective buyers."

Dyvonia Bussey, Grace Goldens, Alabama: "Prospective buyers should be looking for healthy parents with documentation. Review how well the breeder and puppies interact. If the breeder cannot explain the personality of the puppy, they haven't spent much time with them. Look at how the puppy responds to people and breeder. Is the puppy familiar with the voice of the breeder family? Can the breeder readily supply references of past buyers? Can the breeder supply pictures of the puppies at any stage of life, sleeping, eating, playing, etc?"

Donna Shaw, Donakell Goldendoodles, Aberdeenshire, Scotland: "Ask lots of questions, see how the other dogs, look. Are the puppies kept inside, do they look healthy, how are they raised? Do you feel comfortable with everything you are told? I am more than willing to speak all day about my dogs to any people visiting me - and usually do! Beware if a breeder can't answer your questions

and go with your gut instinct! Sometimes it just doesn't feel right and if you get a funny feeling about anything, WALK away, no matter how cute the puppy is. Sometimes I've had a gut feeling about people not being suitable and let it go, and it has always proved me right. Now if I don't feel comfortable with people, then I say no - so don't be afraid to do it the other way round.

"If you're visiting a litter, make sure the puppies look happy and healthy and want to come and see you; you don't want a shy nervous puppy who isn't used to people. Again, ask questions about feeding, worming etc. and ask to see parents' health test certificates and listen to the reasons if none are available. (I'm saying this as two of my older dogs aren't hip and elbow scored, but this is due to them not testing cross breeds nine years ago. My older two and all their younger offspring are tested. Sometimes there is a reason they haven't been done but a breeder should be honest with people." Photo courtesy of Donna.

Picking the Right Temperament

You've picked a Goldendoodle, presumably, because you love this crossbreed's friendly get-along-with-everybody, including the kids, nature and the way they look. Presumably you're planning to spend a lot of time with your new puppy, as Goldendoodles love being with humans. Remember that while different Goldendoodles may share many characteristics and temperament traits, each puppy also has his own individual character, just like humans.

The pleasant temperament and friendly nature of the Goldendoodle suits most people. Visit the breeder to see how your chosen pup interacts and get an idea of his character in comparison to his littermates. Some puppies will run up to greet you, pull at your shoelaces and playfully bite your fingers. Others will be more content to stay in the basket sleeping. Watch their behavior and energy levels. Are you an active person who enjoys masses of daily exercise or would a less hyper puppy be more suitable? Choose the puppy which will best fit in with your family and lifestyle. (Photos courtesy of Lisa Ross, Chai Kennels, top, and Melissa Farmer, FarmerDoodles, bottom.)

A submissive dog will by nature be more passive, less energetic and also possibly easier to train. A dominant dog will usually be more energetic and lively. He or she may also be more stubborn and need a firmer hand when training or socializing with other dogs. If you already have a dominant dog at home, you have to be careful about introducing a new dog into the household; two dominant dogs may not live together comfortably.

There is no good or bad, it's a question of which type of character will best suit you and your lifestyle. Here are a couple of quick tests to try and gauge your puppy's temperament; they should be carried out by the breeder in familiar surroundings so the puppy is relaxed. It should be pointed out that there is some controversy over temperament testing as a dog's personality is formed by a combination of factors, which include inherited temperament, socialization, training and environment (or how you treat your dog):

- ❧ The breeder puts the pup on his or her back on her lap and gently rests her hand on the pup's chest, or

- ❧ She puts her hands under the pup's tummy and gently lifts the pup off the floor for a few seconds, keeping the pup horizontal A puppy that struggles to get free is less patient than one which makes little effort to get away. A placid, patient dog is likely to fare better in a home with young children than an impatient one. Here are some other useful signs to look out for –

- ❧ Watch how he interacts with other puppies in the litter. Does he try and dominate them, does he walk away from them or is he happy to play with his littermates? This may give you an idea of how easy it will be to socialize him with other dogs

- ❧ After contact, does the pup want to follow you or walk away from you? Not following may mean he has a more independent nature

- ❧ If you throw something for the puppy is he happy to retrieve it for you or does he ignore it? This may measure their willingness to work with humans

- ❧ If you drop a bunch of keys behind the Goldendoodle puppy, does he act normally or does he flinch and jump away? The latter may be an indication of a timid or nervous disposition. Not reacting could also be a sign of deafness

Decide which temperament would fit in with you and your family and the rest is up to you. Whatever hereditary temperament your Goldendoodle has, it is true to say that dogs that have constant positive interactions with people and other animals during the first four months of life will generally be happier and more stable. In contrast, a puppy plucked from its family too early and/or isolated at home alone for long periods will be less happy, less socialized, needier and may well display behavior problems later on.

Puppies are like children. Being properly raised contributes to their confidence, sociability, stability and intellectual development. The bottom line is that a pup raised in a warm, loving environment with people is likely to be more tolerant and accepting, and less likely to develop behavior problems.

For those of you who prefer a scientific approach to choosing the right puppy, we are including the full Volhard Puppy Aptitude Test (PAT.) This test has been developed by the highly respected Wendy and Jack Volhard who have built up an international reputation over the last 30 years for their invaluable contribution to dog training, health and nutrition. Their philosophy is: "We believe that one of life's great joys is living in harmony with your dog."

They have written several books and the Volhard PAT is regarded as an excellent method for evaluating the nature of young puppies. Jack and Wendy have also written the Dog Training for Dummies book. Visit their website at www.volhard.com for details of their upcoming dog training camps, as well as their training and nutrition groups.

....

The Volhard Puppy Aptitude Test

Here are the ground rules for performing the test: The testing is done in a location unfamiliar to the puppies. This does not mean they have to be taken away from home. A 10-foot square area is perfectly adequate, such as a room in the house where the puppies have not been.

- ✓ The puppies are tested one at a time. There are no other dogs or people, except the scorer and the tester, in the testing area.
- ✓ The puppies do not know the tester.
- ✓ The scorer is a disinterested third party and not the person interested in selling you a puppy.
- ✓ The scorer is unobtrusive and positions himself so he can observe the puppies' responses without having to move.

The puppies are tested before they are fed. The puppies are tested when they are at their liveliest. Do not try to test a puppy that is not feeling well.

Puppies should not be tested the day of or the day after being vaccinated. Only the first response counts! Tip: During the test, watch the puppy's tail. It will make a difference in the scoring whether the tail is up or down. The tests are simple to perform and anyone with some common sense can do them. You can, however, elicit the help of someone who has tested puppies before and knows what they are doing.

Social attraction - the owner or caretaker of the puppies places it in the test area about four feet from the tester and then leaves the test area. The tester kneels down and coaxes the puppy to come to him or her by encouragingly and gently clapping hands and calling. The tester must coax the puppy in the opposite direction from where it entered the test area. Hint: Lean backward, sitting on your heels instead of leaning forward toward the puppy. Keep your hands close to your body encouraging the puppy to come to you instead of trying to reach for the puppy.

Following - the tester stands up and slowly walks away encouraging the puppy to follow. Hint: Make sure the puppy sees you walk away and get the puppy to focus on you by lightly clapping your hands and using verbal encouragement to get the puppy to follow you. Do not lean over the puppy.

Restraint - the tester crouches down and gently rolls the puppy on its back for 30 seconds. Hint: Hold the puppy down without applying too much pressure. The object is not to keep it on its back but to test its response to being placed in that position.

Social Dominance - let the puppy stand up or sit and gently stroke it from the head to the back while you crouch beside it. See if it will lick your face, an indication of a forgiving nature. Continue stroking until you see a behavior you can score. Hint: When you crouch next to the puppy avoid leaning or hovering over it. Have the puppy at your side, both of you facing in the same direction.

During testing maintain a positive, upbeat and friendly attitude toward the puppies. Try to get each puppy to interact with you to bring out the best in him or her. Make the test a pleasant experience for the puppy.

Elevation Dominance - the tester cradles the puppy with both hands, supporting the puppy under its chest and gently lifts it two feet off the ground and holds it there for 30 seconds.

Retrieving - the tester crouches beside the puppy and attracts its attention with a crumpled up piece of paper. When the puppy shows some interest, the tester throws the paper no more than four feet in front of the puppy encouraging it to retrieve the paper.

Touch Sensitivity - the tester locates the webbing of one the puppy's front paws and presses it lightly between his index finger and thumb. The tester gradually increases pressure while counting to ten and stops when the puppy pulls away or shows signs of discomfort.

Sound Sensitivity - the puppy is placed in the center of the testing area and an assistant stationed at the perimeter makes a sharp noise, such as banging a metal spoon on the bottom of a metal pan.

Sight Sensitivity - the puppy is placed in the center of the testing area. The tester ties a string around a bath towel and jerks it across the floor, two feet away from the puppy.

Stability - an umbrella is opened about five feet from the puppy and gently placed on the ground. During the testing, make a note of the heart rate of the pup, this is an indication of how it deals with stress, as well as its energy level. Puppies come with high, medium or low energy levels. You have to decide for yourself, which suits your life style. Dogs with high energy levels need a great deal of exercise, and will get into mischief if this energy is not channeled into the right direction.

Finally, look at the overall structure of the puppy. You see what you get at 49 days age (seven weeks.) If the pup has strong and straight front and back legs, with all four feet pointing in the same direction, it will grow up that way, provided you give it the proper diet and environment. If you notice something out of the ordinary at this age, it will stay with puppy for the rest of its life. He will not grow out of it.

Scoring the Results

Following are the responses you will see and the score assigned to each particular response. You will see some variations and will have to make a judgment on what score to give them –

TEST	RESPONSE	SCORE
SOCIAL ATTRACTION	Came readily, tail up, jumped, bit at hands	1
	Came readily, tail up, pawed, licked at hands	2
	Came readily, tail up	3
	Came readily, tail down	4
	Came hesitantly, tail down	5
	Didn't come at all	6
FOLLOWING	Followed readily, tail up, got underfoot, bit at feet	1
	Followed readily, tail up, got underfoot	2
	Followed readily, tail up	3
	Followed readily, tail down	4
	Followed hesitantly, tail down	5
	Did not follow or went away	6
RESTRAINT	Struggled fiercely, flailed, bit	1
	Struggled fiercely, flailed	2
	Settled, struggled, settled with some eye contact	3
	Struggled, then settled	4
	No struggle	5
	No struggle, strained to avoid eye contact	6
SOCIAL DOMINANCE	Jumped, pawed, bit, growled	1
	Jumped, pawed	2
	Cuddled up to tester and tried to lick face	3
	Squirmed, licked at hands	4
	Rolled over, licked at hands	5

	Went away and stayed away	6
ELEVATION DOMINANCE	Struggled fiercely, tried to bite	1
	Struggled fiercely	2
	Struggled, settled, struggled, settled	3
	No struggle, relaxed	4
	No struggle, body stiff	5
	No struggle, froze	6
RETRIEVING	Chased object, picked it up and ran away	1
	Chased object, stood over it and did not return	2
	Chased object, picked it up and returned with it to tester	3
	Chased object and returned without it to tester	4
	Started to chase object, lost interest	5
	Does not chase object	6
TOUCH SENSITIVITY	8-10 count before response	1
	6-8 count before response	2
	5-6 count before response	3
	3-5 count before response	4
	2-3 count before response	5
	1-2 count before response	6
SOUND SENSITIVITY	Listened, located sound and ran toward it barking	1
	Listened, located sound and walked slowly toward it	2
	Listened, located sound and showed curiosity	3
	Listened and located sound	4
	Cringed, backed off and hid behind tester 5	5
	Ignored sound and showed no curiosity	6
SIGHT SENSITIVITY	Looked, attacked and bit object	1
	Looked and put feet on object and put mouth on it	2
	Looked with curiosity and attempted to investigate, tail up	3
	Looked with curiosity, tail down	4
	Ran away or hid behind tester	5
	Hid behind tester	6
STABILITY	Looked and ran to the umbrella, mouthing or biting it	1
	Looked and walked to the umbrella, smelling it cautiously	2
	Looked and went to investigate	3
	Sat and looked, but did not move toward the umbrella	4
	Showed little or no interest	5
	Ran away from the umbrella	6

The scores are interpreted as follows:

Mostly 1s - Strong desire to be pack leader and is not shy about bucking for a promotion.
Has a predisposition to be aggressive to people and other dogs and will bite.
Should only be placed into a very experienced home where the dog will be trained and worked on a regular basis.

Tip: Stay away from the puppy with a lot of 1's or 2's. It has lots of leadership aspirations and may be difficult to manage. This puppy needs an experienced home. Not good with children.

Mostly 2s - Also has leadership aspirations. May be hard to manage and has the capacity to bite. Has lots of self-confidence. Should not be placed into an inexperienced home. Too unruly to be good with children and elderly people, or other animals. Needs strict schedule, loads of exercise and lots of training. Has the potential to be a great show dog with someone who understands dog behavior.

Mostly 3s - Can be a high-energy dog and may need lots of exercise. Good with people and other animals. Can be a bit of a handful to live with. Needs training, does very well at it and learns quickly. Great dog for second-time owner.

Mostly 4s - The kind of dog that makes the perfect pet. Best choice for the first time owner. Rarely will buck for a promotion in the family. Easy to train, and rather quiet.
Good with elderly people, children, although may need protection from the children.
Choose this pup, take it to obedience classes, and you'll be the star, without having to do too much work!

Tip: The puppy with mostly 3's and 4's can be quite a handful, but should be good with children and does well with training. Energy needs to be dispersed with plenty of exercise.

Mostly 5s - Fearful, shy and needs special handling. Will run away at the slightest stress in its life. Strange people, strange places, different floor or surfaces may upset it. Often afraid of loud noises and terrified of thunderstorms. When you greet it upon your return, may submissively urinate. Needs a very special home where the environment doesn't change too much and where there are no children. Best for a quiet, elderly couple. If cornered and cannot get away, has a tendency to bite.

Mostly 6s – So independent that he doesn't need you or other people. Doesn't care if he is trained or not - he is his own person. Unlikely to bond to you, since he doesn't need you. A great guard dog for gas stations! Do not take this puppy and think you can change him into a lovable bundle - you can't, so leave well enough alone.

Tip: Avoid the puppy with several 6's. It is so independent it doesn't need you or anyone. He is his own person and unlikely to bond to you.

The Scores

Few puppies will test with all 2's or all 3's, there'll be a mixture of scores. For that first time, wonderfully easy to train, potential star, look for a puppy that scores with mostly 4's and 3's. Don't worry about the score on Touch Sensitivity - you can compensate for that with the right training equipment.

It's hard not to become emotional when picking a puppy - they are all so cute, soft and cuddly. Remind yourself that this dog is going to be with you for eight to 16 years. Don't hesitate to step back a little to contemplate your decision. Sleep on it and review it in the light of day.

Avoid the puppy with a score of 1 on the Restraint and Elevation tests. This puppy will be too much for the first-time owner. It's a lot more fun to have a good dog, one that is easy to train, one you can live with and one you can be proud of, than one that is a constant struggle.

Getting a Dog From a Shelter - Don't overlook an animal shelter as a source for a good dog. Not all dogs wind up in a shelter because they are bad. After that cute puppy stage, when the dog grows up, it may become too much for its owner. Or, there has been a change in the owner's circumstances forcing him or her into having to give up the dog.

Most of the time these dogs are housetrained and already have some training. If the dog has been properly socialized to people, it will be able to adapt to a new environment. Bonding may take a little longer, but once accomplished, results in a devoted companion.

....

So you see, it's not all about the color or the cutest face! When getting a puppy, your thought process should run something like this:

1. Decide to get a Goldendoodle
2. Decide which size of Goldendoodle would best suit you
3. Decide what generation of Goldendoodle to get
4. Find a good breeder whose dogs are DNA health tested
5. Find one with a litter available when you are ready for a puppy – or wait
6. Check on the shedding properties of your chosen breeder's pups – and remember there are no 100% guarantees for allergy sufferers
7. Decide on a male or female
8. Pick one with a suitable temperament to fit in with your family
9. Once you have decided on all the above factors, choose the color!

Some people pick a puppy based purely on how the dog looks. If coat color, for example, is very important to you, make sure the other boxes are ticked as well.

3. Bringing Your Puppy Home

Before you bring home your precious little bundle of joy, it's a smart idea to prepare your home before he or she arrives while you still have the chance. All puppies are demanding and once they land, they will swallow up most of your time. Here's a list of things you ought to think about getting beforehand:

Puppy Checklist

- ✓ A dog bed or basket
- ✓ Bedding – old towels or a blanket which can easily be washed
- ✓ If possible, a towel or piece of cloth which has been rubbed on the puppy's mother to put in the bed
- ✓ A collar, or harness, and lead
- ✓ An identification tag for the collar or harness
- ✓ Food and water bowls, preferably stainless steel
- ✓ Lots of newspapers for housetraining
- ✓ Poo(p) bags
- ✓ Puppy food – find out what the breeder is feeding and stick with it initially
- ✓ Puppy treats (preferably healthy ones, not rawhide)
- ✓ Toys and chews suitable for puppies
- ✓ A puppy coat if you live in a cool climate
- ✓ A crate if you decide to use one
- ✓ Old towels for cleaning your puppy and covering the crate

AND PLENTY OF TIME!

Later on you'll also need a longer, stronger lead, a grooming brush and comb, dog shampoo, flea and worming products (which you can buy from your vet) and maybe a travel crate. Photo of this playful nine-week-old F2 female is courtesy of UK breeder Donna Shaw, of Donakell Goldendoodles, Aberdeenshire, Scotland.

Puppy Proofing Your Home

Before your puppy arrives at his or her new home, you may have to make a few adjustments to make your home safe and suitable. Young puppies are small bundles of instinct and energy (when they are awake), with little common sense and even less self-control! All young Goldendoodles are curious, they love to play and have a great sense of fun. They often have bursts of energy before they run out of steam and spend much of the rest of the day sleeping.

They are like babies and it's up to you to look after them and set the boundaries – both physically and in terms of behavior – but one step at a time.

Create an area where the puppy is allowed to go and then keep the rest of the house off-limits until housetraining (potty training) is complete. You can use a baby gate or make your own barrier. This one at the home of breeder Christy Stevens, of Winding Creek Ranch Goldendoodles, Indiana, was designed for infants but works well with puppies too. (If your puppy is very small you may need to temporarily block the bottom part of the gate or get one with smaller gaps!)

With a bit of effort, housetraining shouldn't take long; Goldendoodles are one of the easiest canines to housetrain, according to the breeders involved in this book. One of the biggest factors influencing the success and speed of housetraining is your commitment - another reason for taking a week or two off work when your puppy arrives home.

Like babies, most puppies are mini chewing machines and so remove anything breakable and/or chewable within the puppy's reach – including wooden furniture. Obviously you cannot remove your kitchen cupboards, doors, sofas and fixtures and fittings, so don't leave your new arrival unattended for any length of time where he can chew something which is hard to replace.

Using a gate or barrier is also an effective and relatively inexpensive method of preventing a puppy from going upstairs and leaving an unwanted gift on your precious bedroom carpets. A puppy's bones are soft and recent studies have shown that if very young pups are allowed to climb or descend stairs regularly, they can develop joint problems later in life. This is worth bearing in mind, especially as some Goldendoodles can be prone to joint problems such as hip dysplasia.

You can also use a baby gate, wire or plastic panels - available online or from pet shops - to keep the puppy enclosed in a pen or a single room – preferably one with a floor which is easy to wipe clean and not too far away from a door to the garden or yard for housetraining. Many of the breeders we contacted use a puppy pen to contain a pup or pups, while giving them plenty of room to stretch their legs. Photo by Amy Lane, of Fox Creek Farm, West Virginia.

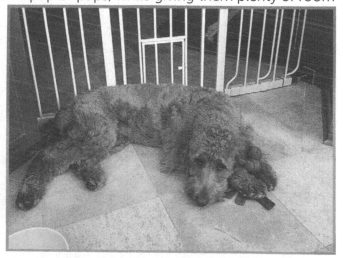

In any case, you may also want to remove your expensive oriental rugs to other rooms until your little darling is fully housetrained and has stopped chewing everything. Make sure you have some soft toys to chew which are suitable for sharp little teeth and too big to swallow.

Don't give old socks, shoes or slippers or your pup will regard your footwear as fair game. Avoid rawhide chews as they can get stuck in the dog's throat.

The puppy's designated area or room should be not too hot, cold or damp and it must be free from drafts. Puppies are sensitive to temperature fluctuations and don't do well in very hot or very cold conditions. If you live in a hot climate, your new puppy may need air conditioning in the summertime. Photo: Amy Lane.

If you have young children, you must restrict the time they spend with the puppy to a few short sessions a day. Plenty of sleep is **essential** for the normal development of a young dog. You wouldn't wake a baby every hour or so to play and shouldn't do that with a puppy. Don't invite friends round to see your new puppy for at least a day or two, preferably longer. However excited you are, your new pup needs a few days to get over the stress of leaving his mother and siblings and to start bonding with you.

Just as you need a home, your puppy needs a den. This den is a haven where your puppy feels safe, particularly for the first few weeks after the traumatic experience of leaving his or her mother and littermates. Young puppies sleep for over 18 hours a day at the beginning; some may sleep for up to 22 hours a day. This is normal. You have a couple of options with the den; you can get a dog bed or basket, or you can use a crate. Crates have long been popular in North America and are becoming increasingly used in the UK, particularly as it can be quicker to housetrain a puppy using a crate.

It may surprise some American readers to learn that the normal practice in the UK has often been – and still is - to initially contain the puppy in the kitchen or utility room, and later to let the dog roam around the house. Some owners do not allow their dogs upstairs, but many do. The idea of keeping a dog in a cage like a rabbit or hamster is abhorrent to many animal-loving Brits.

However, a crate can be a useful aid if used properly. Using one as a prison to contain a dog for hours on end certainly is cruel, but the crate has its place as a sanctuary for your dog. It is their own space and they know no harm will come to them in there. See **Chapter 5. Housetraining and Crate Training** for getting your Goldendoodle used to - and even to enjoy - being in his crate.

Most puppies' natural instinct is not to soil the area where they sleep. Put plenty of newspapers down in the area next to the den and your pup should choose to go to the toilet here if you are not quick enough to take him or her outside. Of course, they may also decide to trash their designated area by chewing their blankets and shredding the newspaper – patience is the key in this situation!

Pictured in his crate is Dobby, owned and bred by Sandra Beck, of Beck Kennel, Iowa.

If you have a garden or yard that you intend letting your puppy roam in, make sure that every little gap has been plugged. You'd be amazed at the tiny holes puppies can escape through. Also, don't leave your Goldendoodle unattended as they can come to harm, and dogs are increasingly being targeted by thieves, who are even stealing from gardens. Make sure there are no poisonous plants which your pup might chew and check there are no low plants with sharp leaves or thorns which could cause eye or other injuries.

In order for puppies to grow into well-adjusted dogs, they have to feel comfortable and relaxed in their new surroundings and they need a great deal of sleep. They are leaving the warmth and protection of their mother and littermates and so for the first few days at least, your puppy will feel very sad. It is important to make the transition from the birth home to your home as easy as possible. Your pup's life is in your hands. How you react and interact with him in the first few days and weeks will shape your relationship and his character for the years ahead.

The First Few Days

Before you collect your puppy, let the breeder know what time you will arrive and ask her not to feed the pup for three or four hours beforehand (unless you have a very long journey, in which case the puppy will need to eat something.) He will be less likely to be car sick and should be hungry when he lands in his new home.

The same applies to an adult dog moving to a new home. When you arrive, ask the breeder for an old towel or toy which has been with the pup's mother – you can leave one on an earlier visit to collect with the pup. Or take one with you and rub the mother with it to collect her scent and put this with the puppy for the first few days. It may help him to settle in. In the USA some Goldendoodles may be shipped to your home. You can still ask for a toy or towel

Make sure you get copies of any health certificates relating to the parents. A good breeder will have a Contract of Sale or Puppy Contract – **see Chapter 2. Choosing Your Goldendoodle Puppy** – which outlines your and their rights and responsibilities. It should also state that you can return the puppy if there are health issues within a certain time frame – although if you have picked your breeder carefully, it should hopefully not come to this. The breeder should also give you details of worming and any vaccinations. Most good breeders supply an information sheet and puppy pack for new owners.

You should also find out exactly what the breeder is feeding and how much. You cannot suddenly switch a dog's diet; their digestive systems cannot cope with a sudden change. In the beginning stick to whatever the puppy is used to initially. Again, good breeders will send some of the food home with the puppy.

The Journey Home

Bringing a new puppy home in a car can be a traumatic experience. Your puppy will be devastated at leaving his or her mother, brothers and sisters and a familiar environment. Everything will be strange and frightening and he will probably whimper and whine - or even howl or bark - on the way to his or her new home. If you can, take somebody with you to take care of him on that first journey. Under no circumstances have the puppy on your lap while driving. It is simply too dangerous - a Goldendoodle puppy is cute, lively and far too distracting.

The best and safest way to transport the pup is in a crate – either a purpose-made travel crate or a wire crate which he will use at home. Put a comfortable blanket in the bottom - preferably rubbed with the scent of the mother. Ask your travel companion to sit next to the crate and talk softly to the frightened little bundle of nerves. He or she will probably cry or whimper. If you don't have a crate, your passenger may wish to hold the puppy. If so, have an old towel between the person and the pup as he may quite possibly urinate (the puppy, not the passenger!)

If you have a journey of more than a couple of hours, make sure that you take water and offer the puppy a drink en route. He may need to eliminate or have diarrhea (hopefully, only due to nerves), but don't let him outside on to the ground in a strange place as he is not yet fully inoculated. If you have a long journey, cover the bottom of the crate with a waterproof material and put newspapers in half of it, so the pup can eliminate without staining the car seats.

Arriving Home

As soon as you arrive home, let your puppy into the garden or yard and when he 'performs,' praise him for his efforts.

These first few days are critical in getting your puppy to feel safe and confident in his new surroundings. Spend time with your new arrival, talk to him often in a reassuring manner. Introduce him to his den and toys, slowly allow him to explore and show him around the house –once you have puppy proofed it. Goldendoodle puppies are extremely curious - and amusing, you might be surprised at his reactions to everyday objects. Remember that puppies and babies explore by sniffing and using their mouths, so don't scold for chewing. Instead, remove objects you don't want chewed out of reach and replace them with toys he can chew.

If you have other animals, introduce them slowly and in supervised sessions - preferably once the pup has got used to his new surroundings, not as soon as you walk through the door. Gentleness and patience are the keys to these first few days, so don't over-face your puppy. Have a special, gentle puppy voice with which to talk to him and use his name often in a pleasant, encouraging manner. Never use his name to scold or he will associate it with bad things. The sound of his name should **always** make him want to pay attention to you as something good is going to happen - praise, food, play time and so on.

Resist the urge to pick the puppy up all the time – not matter how cute he is! (Photo courtesy of Renee Sigman.) Let him explore on his own legs, encouraging a little independence. One of the most important things at this stage is to ensure that your puppy has enough sleep – which is nearly all of the time - no matter how much you want to play with him or watch his antics when awake.

If you haven't decided what to call your little Goldendoodle yet, 'Shadow' might be a good suggestion, as he or she will follow you everywhere! Many puppies from different breeds do this, but Goldendoodles like to stick close to their owners – both as puppies and adults.

Our website receives many emails from worried new owners. Here are some of the most common concerns:

- 🐾 My puppy sleeps all the time, is this normal?
- 🐾 My puppy won't stop crying or whining
- 🐾 My puppy is shivering
- 🐾 My puppy won't eat
- 🐾 My puppy is very timid
- 🐾 My puppy follows me everywhere, she won't let me out of her sight

Most of the above are quite common. They are just a young pup's reaction to leaving his mother and littermates and entering into a strange new world. It is normal for puppies to sleep most of the time, just like babies. It is also normal for some puppies to whine a lot during the first couple of days. Make your new pup as comfortable as possible, ensuring he has a warm (but not too hot), quiet den away from drafts, where he is not pestered by children or other pets. Handle him gently, while giving him plenty of time to sleep. During the first few nights your puppy will whine; try your best to ignore the pitiful cries.

Unless they are especially dominant, most puppies will be nervous and timid for the first few days. They will think of you as their new mother and follow you around the house. This is also quite natural, but after a few days start to leave your puppy for a few minutes at a time, gradually building up the time. Goldendoodles, like other breeds and hybrids selectively bred primarily for companionship, can be prone to separation anxiety - particularly if they are used to being with you virtually 24/7. See **Chapter 8. Behavior** for more information.

If your routine means you are normally out of the house for a few hours during the day, get your puppy on a Friday or Saturday so he has at least a couple of days to adjust to his new surroundings. A far better idea is to book at least a week or two off work to help your puppy settle in. If you don't work, leave your diary free for the first couple of weeks. Helping a new pup to settle in is virtually a full-time job.

This is a frightening time for your puppy. Is your puppy shivering with cold or is it nerves? Avoid placing your puppy under stress by making too many demands on him. Don't allow the kids to pester the pup and, until they have learned how to handle a dog, don't allow them to pick him up unsupervised, as they could inadvertently damage his delicate little body.

If your puppy won't eat, spend time gently coaxing him. If he leaves his food, take it away and try it later. Don't leave it down all of the time or he may get used to turning his nose up at it. The next time you put something down for him, he is more likely to be hungry.

If your puppy is crying, it is probably for one of the following reasons:

- 🐾 He is lonely
- 🐾 He is hungry
- 🐾 He wants attention from you
- 🐾 He needs to go to the toilet

If it is none of these, then physically check him over to make sure he hasn't picked up an injury. Try not to fuss over him. If he whimpers, just reassure him with a quiet word. If he cries loudly and tries to get out of his allotted area, he probably needs to go to the toilet. Even if it is the middle of the night, get up (yes, sorry, this is best) and take him outside. Praise him if he goes to the toilet.

The strongest bonding period for a puppy is between eight and 12 weeks of age. The most important factors in bonding with your puppy are TIME spent with him and PATIENCE, even when he or she makes a mess in the house or chews something he shouldn't.

Remember, your Goldendoodle pup is just a baby (dog) and it takes time to learn not to do these things. Spend time with your pup and you will have a loyal friend for life. Goldendoodles are very focused on their humans and that emotional attachment between you and him may grow to become one of the most important aspects of your life — and certainly his.

Where Should the Puppy Sleep?

Where do you want your new puppy to sleep? You cannot simply allow him or her to wander freely around the house. Ideally your puppy will be in a contained area, such as a playpen or a crate, at night. While it is not acceptable to shut a dog in a cage all day, you can keep your puppy in a crate at night until he or she is housetrained. You also have to consider whether you want the pup to sleep in your bedroom or elsewhere. If your puppy is in the bedroom, try to prevent him from jumping on and off beds and/or couches or racing up and down stairs until he has stopped growing, as this can damage his joints.

If he is to sleep outside your bedroom, put him in a comfortable bed of his own, or a crate — and then block your ears for the first couple of nights He will almost certainly whine and whimper, but this won't last long and he will soon get used to sleeping on his own, without his littermates or you. Alternatively, you can follow Debbie Dixon and Janece Schommer's advice later in this chapter and let the puppy sleep near you for the first couple of nights. (Photo: Renee Sigman.)

We don't recommend letting your new pup sleep on the bed. He will not be housetrained and also a puppy needs to learn his place in the household and have his own den. It's up to you whether you decide to let him on the bed when he's older. Another point to bear in mind is that if your dog is regularly exercised, his paws and coat may pick up mud, grass, insects and other things you may not want on your bed.

While it is not good to leave a dog alone all day, it is also not healthy to spend 24 hours a day with him. He becomes too reliant on you and this increases the chance of him developing separation anxiety when you do have to leave him. A Goldendoodle puppy used to being on his own every night is less likely to develop attachment issues, so consider this when deciding where he should sleep

Many owners prefer to bite the bullet right from the start by leaving the pup in a safe place downstairs or in a different room to the bedroom, so he gets used to being on his own right from the beginning. If you do this, you might find a set of earplugs very useful for helping (you) to survive the first few nights! In a moment of weakness you might consider letting the puppy sleep in the bedroom, but think carefully about this. Dogs snuffle, snore, fart and, if not in a crate, pad around the bedroom in the middle of the night and come up to the bed to check you are still there! None of this is conducive to a good night's sleep. Our dog sleeps in his own bed in our bedroom and has separation anxiety. Any future dogs we have will sleep in a separate room from us – no matter how hard that is in the beginning when the puppy whimpers during the night.

If you decide you definitely do want your Goldendoodle to sleep in the bedroom from Day One, initially put him in a crate or similar with a soft blanket covering part of the crate. Put newspapers inside as he will not be able to last the night without urinating. Once your dog has been housetrained and can access other areas of the house, you may reconsider where he sleeps.

What the Breeders Say

We asked a number of breeders what essential advice they would give to new owners of Goldendoodle puppies. They had lots of warnings and advice for puppy proofing the yard or garden, as well as some tips for the first night or two.

Sandra Beck: "Puppy proof your home and yard; a safe fenced in yard area for puppy play is best. Remove any toxic plants and have plenty of toys available for your puppy to chew on. Goldendoodles love chewing and retrieving sticks. They also love anything left on the floor with your scent on it and, according to my vet, have even been known to swallow small pieces of clothing, requiring surgery to remove it!"

Renee Sigman: "I would be sure to not have any toxic plants out in the yard, read up on potentially toxic foods and stay away from giving puppies people food. I advise leash training when the puppy is young so that there is no chance for the pup to get into any danger."

Neelie Smith, River Falls Goldendoodles, South Carolina: "We encourage a fenced-in yard or an area where the Doodle can have plenty of room to run and play. Keep an eye on your pet if you have lots of plants and flowers, as many can be poisonous to a puppy." Photo: Neelie and Steve Smith.

Melissa Farmer, FarmerDoodles, Ohio: "Puppy proof your home and yard just like you would when bringing home a new human baby. Many plants can be toxic to dogs, and families should research what these potential dangers are for their area. New puppies should be **supervised, supervised, supervised** at all times, as they explore with their mouths and can easily ingest small, foreign objects."

Wendi Loustau Mustard Seed Ranch Goldendoodles, Georgia: "Goldendoodle puppies chew everything. The yard is the hardest place to get ready, as they usually want to chew all the vegetation. In the beginning, sleeping through the night and potty training are the first hurdles, followed by biting and jumping."

Lynne Whitmire: "Think of a puppy as a toddler; don't expose him to anything that you would not expose your toddler to. I include a list of toxic plants, indoor and out in my puppy take-home packet. Puppies chew things and many things in the yard and garden may be toxic to them, so do your homework first. My front yard is lined with hydrangea bushes, so I have to watch any young puppy that is in that area. Mushrooms can grow quickly in mulch; make sure you do not use any kind of mulch that would be toxic. If you have a yard service, call your local university or research the chemicals that are used. I recommend that puppies only be allowed in a small part of the yard that has not been treated with chemicals or fertilizer, and the same goes for pest management in your home."

Christy Stevens: "Make sure the garage is off limits. Cars can leak antifreeze, etc. and there are many dangerous items in a garage or barn. Anything on the floor is a toy, so keep everything picked up. Never leave a new puppy unsupervised. They like to chew on electrical cords, furniture, carpet, etc. They aren't being bad; this is how they explore their world and they just don't know what is acceptable yet. There needs to be some form of containment for the puppy outdoors and indoors in order to keep your puppy safe." Photo by Christy.

Janece Schommer: "When pups first arrive in your home, it will smell very different from the home they just came from. Remember, dogs are ALL about smell. To throw a pup into a kennel in a laundry room far away from everyone else can be very frightening for a puppy. Most tire easily and will fall asleep initially after a bit of protest. However, when the pup wakes a bit in the night because he realizes (smells) that he is somewhere unfamiliar AND he's all alone, instinctually, he knows that can mean bad things for him! That's when you get the whining and crying in the middle of the night.

"What I suggest to sort of break up the scariness and easy the transition from my house to yours is to bring the pup either directly into bed with you for the first couple of night or so, or put a small kennel on a chair so it is level with your bed so the pup can be reassured you are there. That way,

even though the pup wakes to being in an unfamiliar place, he or she is still not alone and is comforted by that nice new human. Then, after a couple of nights, transition the pup into the crate either in your room or the main living area. The smells of your home will now be familiar and unalarming to the new puppy.

"IF your puppy whines in the middle of the night, he may have to go potty. I recommend taking him directly outside and give the potty command. After he goes, put him right back to bed, don't turn on the lights, play with him, etc. In other words, don't make a party out of it or he will want to schedule that playtime every night. Put him right back to bed and he'll quickly figure out it's not worth getting up for, unless he really has to go."

Kelsey Huffer, Alki Goldendoodles, Washington State: "There are specific plants, like hydrangeas, that are toxic to dogs. Fencing off the garden area of a yard is a good way to protect both your plants and a curious puppy! As they age, they learn what they should and shouldn't eat. If a puppy ingests a plant that you aren't sure about, call your local poison control center or your local vet for instructions on how to induce vomiting (if caught within a reasonable amount of time.)

"Suggestions for the home include roping off or blocking most areas of your house until puppy has learned where he must go when needing to potty. A smaller area, like a corner of your kitchen or rec room, will be best for puppy when not playing. Expect him to sleep often and in unusual places!"

Laura Chaffin, Cimarron Frontier Doodles, Oklahoma: "Containment is a big issue; you never want to risk your puppy escaping from your yard. Another issue you have to think about is time. Will there be anyone home most of the day? Leaving a puppy alone for possibly nine or 10 hours a day would be very hard on a young puppy.

"Crying is usually a concern for new puppy families. I think a clock ticking sometimes helps, as does keeping the crate near someone's bed helps. Listening out for whining in the night so you can take him out to potty is a good idea. I send a blanket home with the puppy that has scent from mom and siblings on it to soothe the puppy and bring some comfort.

"I also use pet approved essential oils to help calm the puppy; these are useful resources: www.essentialoils4pets.com. www.animaleo.info/order-animaleo.html. (Laura's photo shows a little pup enjoying the companionship of mom and siblings before leaving for a brave new world and a new home.)

"Puppies who are taken to their new home too early, for instance at six weeks old, will most likely develop a biting habit. This is because they were removed from their mom and siblings too early and did not receive full training in manners from their canine family. Of course, even older puppies will mouth on the humans' hands and feet, arms, etc. They need plenty of chewing toys, and if they bite, you should cry out loudly in pain and replace your fingers with a chew toy."

Debbie Dixon, Zippity Doodles, Colorado: "Supervision is the key. With any puppy you want to be in the yard whenever they are outside. Firstly, to reward them during housebreaking, and secondly, to interrupt and redirect any negative or unsafe activities so that they don't become habits. To puppy proof your yard, review a toxic plant list before bringing puppy home. Be sure you do not have cocoa mulch in the yard and be careful of flower beds that have metal edging that pups can cut paws on.

"Don't use pesticides or weed killers, as they are absorbed through the paw pads. Avoid fertilizers-talk to your garden shop about alternatives that are healthy for pup. In winter, use melting salt for ice that is dog safe. Be sure the yard is clean of construction debris, i.e. nails, screws, pieces of roofing or metal from recent projects."

Debbie also has some detailed advice for helping new owners deal with those first few stressful days: "We give our puppies a bath (with time to air dry) and try to wear them out right before they go home so they will be more relaxed during the car journey home.

"For the first night, we recommend that when you are ready to go to bed, take pup out to go potty. When you're ready to get into bed, put pup in a crate, which should be within arm's reach, and turn out the lights. Let them cry until they fall asleep. It's OK to put your hand down for them to smell/lick you, but don't get up with pup or talk with them. Once they fall asleep, let them sleep until they wake (never wake a sleeping baby.)

"Once they wake they will need to go outside. If it's not morning, take them out without talking and turn on as few lights as possible (keep it like night.) Let them potty and put them back in the crate...and do the same over again. Remember...they can't hold it well, so don't let them walk to the door...carry them or you may have a potty mistake along the way!

"A new pup may not seem very hungry the first week or more. There is not that 'pack drive' competition for food, and most Doodles don't have big appetites anyway. Don't worry unless your puppy shows other signs that concern you (suggesting s/he might not be feeling well.) Things you can do to make their food a bit more appetizing is to alternate some of these: 1. Soak food, 2. Microwave dry food (unwetted) to warm and release oils, 3. Quickly spray a little warm water (don't soak.) All three will create different textures that might appeal to your pup.

"Wash or soak any new collars and let them dry thoroughly before letting pup wear it. Often they shrink! By shrinking first you can avoid a too tight collar." (Photo is of one-year-old Guinness, Debbie's F1b English Goldendoodle with a curly coat.)

"Eating: It's best if they are fed on a regular schedule, starting out with three times per day, then dropping down to two times (at about four to six months old.) Allow them access to their food for 10-15 minutes, during which time they should eat up to one third, or half, of their daily food allowance.

"Don't overfeed...a lean puppy dog will live longer and have less health problems (that said, make sure they get enough...they go through growing spurts and may need to eat more for a week or two here and there.)

"After that time, remove the bowl and any uneaten food until the next meal. This will help with potty training (establishing a food in/food out schedule!), with making sure they don't eat too much, but get enough.

"If you have the time, use all their meals as training incentives, that is, have them earn it a few nuggets at a time all throughout the day. Remember to increase their daily rations as they grow, based on the food/weight chart on the dog food bag. Don't feed them after about 6pm or 7 pm, so they can make it all night, and don't water them after about 7pm or 8p, until their bladders grow a bit for the same reason - times depending on how early you go to bed!

"Teach them to sit while you put down their bowl; and stay, until they look at you and you say "OK!" You can increase the time they stay as they learn the concept. When taking them outside, always use the sit/stay at the door (again making sure they make eye contact for release.) They learn not to rush out the door, but to wait for you to give them the "OK". You'll be amazed at how fast they learn this."

Candice Farrell, Ooodles of Doodles, Alberta, Canada: "Puppy proofing your home and removing any dangers such as small objects and electrical cords, is important. Making sure there are no escape routes in your yard and doing some research in regards to poisonous plants.

"It is also very important to keep your puppy close to home until vaccination boosters are complete." Pictured showing great self-control with her birthday cake is Candice's one-year-old Medium F1b, Olive.

"For the first few days keep things fairly quiet and limit the visitors to give your puppy time to adjust to its new surroundings. Try and set a consistent schedule and rules for your puppy to follow. Crate training is very important and will aid with faster house training. Lots of positive reinforcement and consistency will help with adjustment."

Amy Lane also has advice for owners with other pets: "Introducing the puppy to the older family dog may need to be done off the premises. This keeps the older dog from feeling like he/she needs to protect its home. Introducing a puppy to an existing cat is a little different. Cats that are not used to dogs or who are uncomfortable with the puppy will retreat to higher ground. Allow them to work their way back down to the living level at their pace. This friendship cannot be forced and may take many months to achieve. However, the older family dog should come around much quicker and a bond should be formed in less than a week.

"Puppy proofing is similar to baby proofing a home. Anything that can be picked up and put in a mouth is a hazard to a puppy. This is more difficult in families with young children with toys - keeping the bedroom doors to kids' rooms closed may be important. All trashcans should have lids or be placed in a cabinet or pantry.

"A list of poisonous plants for dogs is available via a Google search and an inventory of plants indoors and outdoors need to be evaluated. Goldendoodles tend to be curious and they seem to find the toy or sock that was overlooked. Once swallowed, it becomes an emergency situation. Know the closest 24 hour emergency clinic before you have the need!"

Donna Shaw: "Make sure your garden is puppy-proof, that there are no areas they can escape from. Make ponds safe so they can't fall in and drown, and don't leave things lying about a puppy can eat or hurt itself on. If you have gravel in your garden, don't leave puppies unsupervised, as they are like babies and put everything in their mouths. Stones and things like daffodil bulbs are dangerous, and don't let them eat snails or slugs! Just be sensible really and use your common sense."

"I always say to owners to start as you mean to go on. Puppies are very clever and know how to get their own way, even at eight weeks. However, you do have to make some allowances for them being taken away from everything familiar to them, but don't let them off with biting hands - even at eight weeks - as it's not so funny when a six-month-old puppy is doing it.

"Keep to their routine as much as possible, and if they do cry the first couple of nights, hopefully they have blanket from their breeder with comforting smells on it. Unless they are in pain, try to ignore them as much as possible, but reassure them quietly and assertively that everything is OK. Hopefully, if you have a well-socialized pup, this only happens the first night."

Photo of this little parti pup courtesy of Donna.

The First Few Weeks of Life

Goldendoodle breeder and GANA board member Christy Stevens, of Winding Creek Ranch, Indiana, gives an insight into the lives and minds of young puppies, which may help new owners understand what is going on inside the head of that cute little bundle of fur and instinct:

"It is truly a miracle that in just eight or nine weeks, a litter of sweet, wiggly puppies is completely developed and ready to meet the world.

For the puppies to have their best chance of survival, someone who is qualified to take care of a puppy in distress needs to be present for the delivery - after all, it isn't easy being born! Once a litter has been delivered and cared for, the first thing the pups wants to do is nurse. In fact, the only things a new-born litter does are sleep and nurse, and Mom has to stimulate them to go potty by licking their bottoms.

These tiny puppies are very fragile and vulnerable. They are born unable to hear, see or even regulate their own body temperature, so it's no wonder that they stay near Mom or piled up with their siblings. If a pup gets lost from the group, he will crawl around and cry loudly. Because his eyes and ears are sealed shut for approximately the first two weeks, finding his way back to the group can be a challenge. Thankfully, he can smell Mom and that makes it easier to stay near his food source.

During the first two weeks, puppies will do an 'Army crawl,' as their legs are not strong enough to hold up their body weight, but they soon build muscle and by the time they are three weeks old, they are wobbling around on all fours. This is the age when play within the litter begins and daily interactions with humans are advantageous. Both of these jump start the all-important socialization.

At four weeks old, a puppy is normally feeling playful and energetic when awake, but even so, sleep still dominates the majority of the day. In between naps, you can hear cute, barking and growling sounds as the puppies play with each other. At five weeks, personality differences start to become apparent. Just as with people, every puppy is an individual with unique personality traits - and these will later present the new owner with a custom set of delights and challenges.

Depending on the individual breeder, a litter of puppies will be started on a softened food to initiate weaning once the pups are three to five weeks old. Puppies love to eat so this is always a welcome change. Although they still like being with Mom, she slowly decreases her milk supply to avoid discomfort and complications. During this time the pups are very playful and eager for more stimulation. They tend to romp around Mom and start to rough play with each other. Mom doesn't take too kindly to being a jungle gym and will sometimes growl or snap at the puppies. This is not so different from human behavior, and it's her way of saying: "Give me some space!"

Socialization

Socialization begins when puppies begin to play with their litter mates. While dogs require socialization throughout their lives, puppies need it as early as three weeks old and it remains vitally important until around 16 weeks for proper development. If a puppy is raised without interaction with people, he will become fearful of human interaction. It's important to understand a puppy will go through periods of fear as well and that this is quite normal.

The peak stage of fear is between eight and 11 weeks when the puppy needs to be kept safe and secure. He may feel afraid for his life as he ventures out into his new world, full of unknown people and creatures. In many cases this is the time when puppy goes to live with his new family. What is a truly fun day for a lucky family might be the scariest day of this puppy's life. Imagine his fears and thoughts: "Where is Mom and where are my brothers and sisters? Who are these people? Where am I?" The puppy might get sick from a mixture of motion and anxiety on the way home. We may not be able to explain the situation to him, but we can make him feel safe and secure as best we can. For these reasons, Christmas morning or a birthday party is not a good time to introduce a puppy to his new surroundings.

Most breeders start sending their puppies home when they are at least eight weeks old. In most US states, it is unlawful for puppies to leave the breeder prior to eight weeks, in some states it is seven. This is a good law as puppies need to spend that time with their litter mates for proper socialization. Puppies teach each other valuable lessons while they are together, such as when biting hurts and play is too rough. The puppy should certainly be completely weaned and able to eat solid food before going to its new home.

When you bring your new puppy home, allow him time to settle in before starting to teach him commands. The first week home is a great time to focus on getting the puppy into a routine with food/water, naps, play times, potty breaks, etc. For the first few days, a puppy could seem a little bit out of sorts and he may not eat well. Be patient and don't entice him with all kinds of foods as he could get sick. He will eat when he is ready. He's just a little nervous, so keep that in mind if you were thinking of having a homecoming party for the puppy. He is going to need a chance to adjust without being overstimulated.

Bear in mind that puppies like to be in a den-like atmosphere to feel safe and secure. A crate works well, especially if there is something warm and cozy inside it. The first few nights in a new home might require the puppy being close to somebody. Trying to adjust to being alone and in a crate at the same time is really scary. I believe the crate is the best place for a puppy to sleep at night, take naps during the day and spend time in when you are out running errands. While some people feel crates are cruel, allowing a puppy to run loose all the time will not produce a well-trained puppy and may be dangerous as well. If the puppy doesn't whine to get you up during the night, let a sleeping baby sleep. Remember to always make the crate a positive and desirable place for the puppy and he'll learn to enjoy being there.

An eight-week- old puppy is going to need a lot of socialization during the next few weeks. This does not mean there is an immediate need to sign him up for a training class with other puppies. If you do, make sure it is after the fear stage (eight to 11 weeks) has passed and is in a safe, well supervised environment.

 A new puppy owner can achieve an acceptable amount of socialization in many ways. Going places in the car, other than the vet and groomer, will really help the puppy not have a negative association with going for car rides. Since puppy's vaccinations are not complete until he's around 16 weeks, safe ways of socialization should be sought. After about a week and once he's settled in, the puppy will enjoy meeting friends and family, along with their pets. It's a good idea to make sure your puppy is initially only exposed to other dogs that are fully vaccinated, dog friendly, and not too large in comparison.

Training

It's also the time for him to start learning new skills. A young puppy is very impressionable, so you can start training him at home. Remember to start slowly and understand that he is going to have a very short attention span. Training sessions should be short and fun! Work on one skill at a time and be patient. It will be so rewarding when something is finally learned. Don't underestimate the social gains your puppy will achieve just by you spending time working with him on training goals. Some easy commands to work on in the first month are 'Sit' and 'Come.'

Leash training should also be started slowly, without pulling, and should also be a very positive and rewarding experience for the puppy. Teach the puppy to walk on the left side and right next to you only or you could have a weaving walker on your hands! By the time your puppy is 12 weeks old, you should be able to take him for a short walk on the leash (even if it is only around the home or yard if he is not yet clear after his vaccinations.)

At this age you should also be prepared for him to start testing boundaries – he may seem to develop bad manners –and it is really important to put the time in to stay on top of this and be consistent. Keep working with your puppy to teach him what is acceptable behavior. You never want to reward unacceptable behavior, but certainly never use physical punishment to correct him. A negative verbal sound is all the puppy needs to understand a behavior is unacceptable, but he may need to hear it over and over again before he completely stops.

If you ever feel you are in over your head and don't understand how to correct a behavior, don't wait and assume he'll grow out of it. He won't! If you are not succeeding on your own, contact a reputable animal behaviorist to learn how to correct the behavior. The puppy is worth it.

During this stage, the puppy will also begin teething and will have a strong urge to chew on things. Some puppies chew more than others; this is completely normal. Make sure the puppy has a variety of acceptable chew toys available at all times. Try to keep a healthy perspective and understand that the puppy was not born knowing what he can chew on; this is something he needs to be taught.

Every single new behavior the puppy displays, he has learned through experiences he has had. If it's a bad behavior, that doesn't mean he is a bad puppy. He just needs someone to show him what is acceptable in a language he understands.

The puppy needs continued exposure to all sorts of situations, people and animals, all the way through to 16 weeks old when the crucial window for socialization closes. From the time a puppy joins his new family up to the age of 16 weeks, so much will have been learned. Socialization does not stop at this age; it is just that this crucial window is when the pup is most receptive.

Even though all puppy owners will look back on these first few weeks as the most challenging, the times spent cuddling and receiving puppy kisses will far outweigh the challenges! These memories will last a lifetime and someday, the question will be, "How did I ever live without my Goldendoodle?" "

All photos in 'The First Few Weeks of Life' supplied by Christy.

© Copyright 2016 Christy Stevens and Canine Handbooks

Vaccinations and Worming

It is **always** a good idea to have your Goldendoodle checked out by a vet within a few days of picking him up. Keep him away from other dogs in the waiting room as he will not be fully protected against canine diseases until the vaccination schedule is complete. All puppies need these injections; very occasionally a Goldendoodle puppy has a reaction, but this is very rare and the advantages of immunization far outweigh the disadvantages.

Vaccinations

An unimmunized puppy is at risk every time he meets other dogs as he has no protection against potentially fatal diseases – another point is that is unlikely a pet insurer will cover an unimmunized dog. It should be stressed that vaccinations are generally quite safe and side effects are uncommon. If your Goldendoodle is unlucky enough to be one of the very few that suffers an adverse reaction, here are the signs to look out for; a pup may exhibit one or more of these:

MILD REACTION - Sleepiness, irritability and not wanting to be touched. Sore or a small lump at the place where he was injected. Nasal discharge or sneezing. Puffy face and ears.

SEVERE REACTION - Anaphylactic shock. A sudden and quick reaction, usually before leaving the vet's, which causes breathing difficulties. Vomiting, diarrhea, staggering and seizures.

A severe reaction is extremely rare. There is a far, far greater risk of your Goldendoodle either being ill and/or spreading disease if he does not have the injections.

The usual schedule is for the pup to have his first vaccination at six to eight weeks of age. This will protect him from a number of diseases in one shot. In the UK these are Distemper, Canine Parvovirus (Parvo), Infectious Canine Hepatitis (Adenovirus) and Kennel Cough (Bordetella.) In the US this is known as DHPP. Puppies in the US also need vaccinating separately against Rabies. There are optional vaccinations for Coronavirus and - depending on where you live and if your dog is regularly around woods or forests - Lyme Disease.

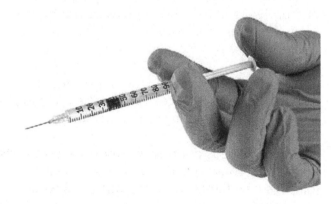

The puppy requires a second vaccination at 10 to 12 and the third and last is done at 14 to16 weeks. Seven days after that he is safe to mix with other dogs. When you take your Goldendoodle for an initial check-up within a few days of bringing him home, check with your vet exactly what shots are needed. (In the UK, the second vaccination is normally done at 10 weeks and the puppy is safe to go out a week after this. Some UK vets recommend a third vaccination at 12 weeks – check with your local vet.)

Diseases such as Parvo and Kennel Cough are highly contagious and you should not let your puppy mix with other dogs - unless they are your own and have already been vaccinated - until a week after he has completed his vaccinations, otherwise he will not be fully immunized. Parvovirus can also be transmitted by fox feces.

You shouldn't take your new puppy to places where unvaccinated dogs might have been, like the local park. This does not mean that your puppy should be isolated - far from it. This is an important time for socialization. It is OK for the puppy to mix with another dog which you 100% know has been vaccinated and is up to date with its annual boosters. Perhaps invite a friend's dog round to play in your yard/garden to begin the socialization process.

Once your puppy is fully immunized, you have a window of a few weeks when it's the best time to introduce him to as many new experiences - dogs, people, traffic, noises, other animals, etc. – This critical period before the age of four and a half or five months is when he is at his most receptive. Socialization should not stop at that age, but continue for the rest of your Goldendoodle's life; but it is particularly important to socialize young puppies.

In the UK, your dog will currently need a booster injection every year of his life. The vet should give you a record card or send you a reminder, but it's also a good idea to keep a note of the date in your diary. However, giving annual vaccines is becoming a thing of the past in the USA. Tests have shown that the Parvovirus vaccination gives most animals at least seven years of immunity, while the Distemper jab provides immunity for at least five to seven years and it is now believed that vaccinating every year can stress a dog's immune system. In the US, many vets now recommend that you take your dog for a 'titer' test once he has had his initial puppy vaccinations and one-year booster.

Titers

To 'titer or 'titering' is to take a blood sample from a dog (or cat) to determine whether he or she has enough antibodies to guarantee immunity against a particular disease, usually Parvovirus, Distemper and Adenovirus (Canine Hepatitis.) Titering is not recommended for Leptospirosis, Bordetella or Lyme Disease, as these vaccines provide only short-term protection, and many states still require proof of a Rabies vaccination.

The vet can test the blood at his or her clinic without sending off the sample, thereby keeping costs down for the owner. A titer for Parvovirus and Distemper currently costs around $100 or less. Titer levels are given as ratios and show how many times blood can be diluted before no antibodies are detected. So, if blood can be diluted 1,000 times and still show antibodies, the ratio would be 1:1000, which is a 'strong titer,' while a titer of 1:2 would be 'weak.' A strong (high) titer means that your dog has enough antibodies to fight off that specific disease and is immune from infection. A weak titer means that you and your vet should discuss revaccination - even then your dog might have some reserve forces known as 'memory cells' which will provide antibodies when needed.

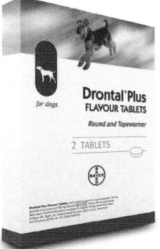

Christy Stevens adds: "Most boarding facilities now also accept titers as an alternative to vaccinations, as long as the dog has documented immunity."

Worming

All puppies need worming (or deworming.) A good breeder will give the puppies their first dose of worming medication at around two weeks old, then probably again at five and eight weeks before they leave the litter. Get the details and inform your vet exactly what treatment, if any, your pup has already had. The main types of worms affecting puppies are roundworm and tapeworm. In certain areas of the USA, the dreaded heartworm can also pose a risk. Roundworm can be transmitted from a puppy to humans – most often children - and can in severe cases cause blindness, or miscarriage in women, so it's important to keep up to date with worming.

Worms in puppies are quite common; they are often picked up through their mother's milk. If you have children, get them into the habit of washing their hands after they have been in contact with the puppy – lack of hygiene is the reason why children are most susceptible. Most vets recommend worming a puppy once a month until he is six months old, and then around every two or three months.

In the US, dogs are given a monthly heartworm pill. It should be given every month when there is no heavy frost (as frost kills mosquitos that carry the disease); giving it all year round gives the best protection. The heartworm pill is by prescription only and deworms the dog monthly for heart worm, round, hook, and whip worm.

If your Goldendoodle, like many, is often out and about running through the woods and fields with his head down, then it is important to stick to a regular worming schedule, as he is more likely to pick up worms than one which spends more time indoors.

Fleas can pass on tapeworms to dogs, but a puppy would not normally be treated unless it is known for certain he has fleas. And then only with caution. You need to know the weight of your Doodle and then speak to your vet about the safest treatment to rid your puppy of the parasites.

It is not usually worth buying a cheap worming or flea treatment from a supermarket, as they are usually far less effective than more expensive vet-recommended preparations, such as Drontal.

Many people living in the US have contacted our website claiming the parasite treatment **Trifexis** has caused severe side effects, and even death, to their dogs. Although this evidence is only anecdotal, you might want consider avoiding Trifexis to be on the safe side - even if your vet recommends it.

4. Goldendoodles for Allergy Sufferers

You are either already the proud owner of a Goldendoodle or you are thinking about becoming one. Goldendoodles make excellent family pets. They have cheerful temperaments, look cute, get on well with people and other dogs and you've heard that they are non-shedding and 'hypoallergenic'.

Some people get a 'hypoallergenic' dog thinking they are guaranteed NOT to have a reaction to the animal. The truth is... there is no such thing as 'a hypoallergenic dog.' And for people who have an allergic reaction to the protein in a dog's saliva or urine, having a 'hypoallergenic dog' with low dander isn't going to solve your problem.

Many allergy sufferers do not have a reaction to their Goldendoodle, but it is important to understand that **there is no 100% guarantee.** Every dog is different; every person's allergy is different. This is why some breeders won't let their dogs go to allergy sufferers. They simply don't want to see their beloved puppy out of a home when the sneezing starts.

Allergies are one of the main reasons why Poodle crosses have become so popular – there are now oodles of Doodles and piles of Poos in the dog world! The Poodle, with its tightly curled wool coat is regarded as a minimal shedder and 'hypoallergenic' breed.

Let's look at the hypoallergenic topic more closely. Firstly, the official definition of the word 'hypoallergenic' is "**having a decreased tendency** to provoke an allergic reaction". In other words, there is no cast iron guarantee that an allergy or asthma sufferer will not suffer a reaction to a particular individual dog or type of dog.

It is true that if you choose a 'hypoallergenic' breed or hybrid such as the Goldendoodle, you are **less likely** to have an allergic reaction. But there is no such thing as a dog breed or hybrid which will never cause an allergic reaction in someone. Allergies vary from person to person and coats vary from one dog to another. This is particularly true with the Goldendoodle, which is not a breed but a crossbreed, and there are even more variables than with a purebred. A Goldendoodle can have one of four types of coat:

- ❖ **Flat** like the Golden Retriever (also called the 'improper coat')
- ❖ **Straight,** which is fluffier than the flat coat with a longer moustache and eyebrows
- ❖ **Wavy,** which can be clipped short or left to grow like a long, wavy fleece for a 'scruffy' look
- ❖ **Curly,** which is tighter curled than the wavy, more like the Poodle's coat

Most prospective owners are looking for puppies with **wavy** or **straight** coats. Sometimes the coat will change its characteristics and even color as the puppy grows, and the type of coat may even vary within pups of the same litter. While a Poodle is regarded as a 'hypoallergenic' breed, a Golden Retriever is not and the puppies may take more after one breed or the other, although many good Goldendoodle breeders are working hard with their breeding programs to create a consistent low shedding coat. There is plenty of anecdotal evidence that many Goldendoodles, particularly multigens (or multigenerationals), shed little or no hair and do not trigger a reaction with many allergy sufferers.

Breeder Janece Schommer, of Goldendoodle Acres, Wisconsin, says: "This is due to generations of eliminating coats that shed and only keeping non-shedding and at least 1 IC-clear parent Goldendoodle for breeding. There is also a scientific way to see how much your dog will shed by DNA swabbing parents and even the offspring to see what score they receive for shedding. On a grading scale of 0 to 4, most Poodles will score a 0 and most Goldens will score a 4. Most multigenerational Goldendoodles will score a 0 or a 1 as well, as they have been produced by non-shedding parents, grandparents, great-grandparents, etc."

There has also been an exciting breakthrough in the world of dog breeding recently and that is the discovery of the IC (or improper coat) gene. A DNA test named RSP02 has been developed to see which dogs carry the recessive IC gene. This, combined with a second DNA test, results something known as "the shedding test," which shows which dogs have a high propensity towards shedding. By DNA testing, breeders can produce puppies with a more consistent no or low shed coat.

Janece is one breeder at the forefront of this technology. At the time of writing in 2016, she says: "This 'shedding test' is brand new and is only currently available from VetGen Laboratories in Ann Arbor, Michigan, as they bought the license from Cornell University, where the research work was carried out to discover the gene. I was just at the VetGen laboratory last week to learn about it.

"This will change the way people feel about what kind of coat they need. The truth is that 90% of people want a straight or wavy coat and it is hard for us breeders, knowing that we're typically only going to get 75% wavy coats in a litter, even when breeding two wavy-coated dogs." Photo: Janece Schommer.

"Testing for curl now allows us to use one dog who is -/- for curl and get a wavy litter with no curly pups.... even when bred to a Poodle. The reason this is all so important is because now we can start to create a more consistent look with the Doodle, if that's what breeders choose for their program.

"The general public may not understand, nor need to understand, coat genetics, but the DNA test does provide valuable information for families who want a wavy or straight-coated Goldendoodle. Some have previously ended up with a dog with a curly coat because they were misinformed.

"I have an unprecedented litter on the ground which is IC clear AND the puppies don't carry a curl gene; I'm quite sure this litter is the first of its kind. Given the DNA results run at VetGen, we now know that these puppies are all: 1. IC clear, 2. They tested -/- for curl, meaning all coats will be straight or wavy but still fluffy, and 3. They will be low to no shed. Seven of the 11 pups are being retained by GANA breeders.

"So, we now also have the ability to create a dog with furnishings (longer facial hair) and with a wavy or straight coat, but with little to no shedding. This is important data because at this point, all the current information says you need a CURLY coat for allergy issues, which is simply not true. What I did was simply try to recreate the DNA of other straight-haired non-shedding dogs like the Lhasa Apso, Maltese, Shih Tzu, etc."

However, it's important to bear in mind that, according to the latest advice from Kennel Clubs of both the USA and UK, **there is no such thing as a non-shedding dog!** No breeder can guarantee that a specific Goldendoodle will be suitable for a particular individual who suffers from allergies to dogs. However, when good Goldendoodle breeders select their breeding stock, coat is an important factor, and this latest genetic test will undoubtedly have an influence on the Goldendoodle. See Janece's article in **Chapter 11. Coat types and Grooming** for more detailed information.

....

Allergies - The Facts

Allergies are on the increase. Amazingly, 50 million Americans are allergy sufferers, according to the Asthma and Allergy Foundation of America. They affect as many as 30% of adults and 40% of children according to the American College of Allergy, Asthma, and Immunology. Of these, some 10 million people are pet allergy sufferers. In fact, allergic disease, including asthma, is the fifth leading chronic disease in the U.S. in people of all ages and the third most common chronic disease in children aged under 18.

In the UK, pets are the second most common cause of allergy in the home, with 40% of asthmatic children reacting to dogs. According to Allergy UK, each year the number of people affected increases by 5% and half of all sufferers are children. The UK is one of the top three countries in the world for the most allergies, with 50% of youngsters having one or more allergy within the first 18 years of life (Journal of Clinical & Experimental Allergy.)

It's a common misconception that people are allergic to animal hair, but that's not true. What they are actually allergic to are proteins - or allergens. These are secreted by the animal's oil glands and then shed with the **dander**, which is dead skin cells (like dandruff.) They are also found in dog saliva and urine - and if you are allergic to either, you are unlikely ever to be able to successfully share your home with a dog. The good news for dog lovers is that more people are allergic to cats!

This is what Allergy UK has to say: "Dog and cat allergen is found in the animals' saliva, sweat and urine. Animals frequently groom themselves, so the allergens coat the hair and skin cells (dander), which, when shed, spread throughout the home or other buildings. Once the saliva dries, it becomes airborne very easily.

"These allergens can be very persistent in the environment, with detectable levels found in homes where no pets have lived for many years, and dog allergen can be found in schools, having been brought there on the clothing and shoes of pupils and teachers. Cat allergen in particular is very 'sticky' in this way.

"In dogs, routine and proper grooming, preferably outdoors, has been shown to greatly decrease shedding of hair and may decrease skin irritation and secondary bacterial infection. Grooming, preferably by someone other than the sensitive individual, should therefore be an important part of a management strategy for dog-allergic patients."

It is possible for many pet allergy sufferers to enjoy living with a dog without spending all of their time sneezing, wheezing, itching or breaking out in rashes. Millions of people are proving the case. Any dog can cause an allergic reaction, although you stand a far higher chance of having no reaction to a dog which is a low-shedding, hypoallergenic purebred or hybrid.

Allergies and Dogs

If you are considering a Goldendoodle, then selecting an experienced breeder is essential. He or she knows her dogs and is, in all likelihood, breeding for a no or low-shedding coat. The more experience breeders have of their breeding stock, the more they know which dogs will produce low shedding puppies. Some of these may then be used in the breeding program, thereby reducing the chances of breeding pups which shed a lot. Although, as one breeder put it: "All Goldendoodles shed less than Golden Retrievers, whatever the coat type."

A word of caution needs to be made here: as an allergy sufferer you may be fine with a Goldendoodle puppy because tiny puppies often don't shed. But the coat can sometimes change in adolescence or adulthood and this could trigger a reaction later on. It would indeed cause distress if you were suddenly allergic to your adult Goldendoodle who has become a dearly-loved member of your family. If you have any doubts at all about a puppy - even a tiny reaction - don't get him.

We strongly advise against selecting a Goldendoodle solely because you believe the dog will not trigger your allergies. There are no guarantees. For those people with consistent or severe allergies, the only way to discover what triggers the allergies is to undergo a series of medical tests and immunization therapy. If you are an allergy sufferer and you decide you can't live without a dog, you do have to put in extra time to make sure that you pick the right dog and make adjustments to your home as well to increase your chances of successfully living together. Remember:

No dog is totally non-shedding No dog is totally hypoallergenic

Two further points to consider are that people's pet allergies vary greatly. Sufferers may react differently to different dogs within a breed or crossbreed, or even litter. A person may be fine with one puppy, yet have a reaction to his brother or sister. This is especially true of early generation hybrids, like F1s, where pups may have different physical characteristics and coats. Any prospective owner considering an F1 can now ask for the new shedding test on the parents or pups if coat type is an important issue for them.

In broad terms, all dogs - even so-called 'hairless' dogs - have hair, dander, saliva and urine. Therefore all dogs *can* cause allergic reactions. But not all dogs do. Some hypoallergenic dog breeds and hybrids do not affect pet allergy sufferers as much because of the amount of hair that they shed. If they are not shedding, then the dander remains trapped within the coat. Hypoallergenic dogs virtually do not molt - you might find the *occasional* dog hair or small fur ball around the house - which is why you have to have them clipped.

Choosing a puppy

If you have friends with a Goldendoodle, spend some time inside their house with their dog, stroke the dog, touch your face with the same hand - do you have a reaction? Did you have a reaction the following day? No reaction is a good start, but it doesn't automatically mean that you won't be allergic to a different Goldendoodle. (Pictured is a multigen Mini bred by Debbie Dixon, of Zippity Doodles, Colorado.)

Next step is to find a reputable breeder. Choose one with several years' experience, as he or she will have a better knowledge of how the puppies' coats will develop as the dogs grow. You should be looking for a breeder with a track record of producing low shedding pups. The revolutionary new genetic test should make this easier – does your chosen breeder test for the IC (Improper Coat) gene? If you can visit the litter, then do so, and make sure there are no cats around which could also trigger allergies. (Pictured is a multigen Mini bred by Debbie Dixon, of Zippity Doodles, Colorado.)

Although this works in the UK and other countries, this is not necessarily the case in the USA, where many top breeders restrict access to their puppies on health grounds.

Janece explains: "Good breeders in the US will rarely allow people to come and hang out with moms and pups. We simply don't want the health risk. Often people arrive at the breeder's after they have been visiting other kennels, dog shelters, etc. and most good breeders are not going to allow visitors due to the health risk to the puppies. And any breeder that doesn't allow you to visit pups before they are vaccinated is not going to let you visit mom either, as bacteria can transfer easily from mom to puppies.

"I would recommend prospective buyers first visit friends, family, neighbors, etc. who have Doodles. OR look up when and where your next local Doodle Romp will be; there will be lots of Doodles there to visit! Anyone who does have an allergic reaction should visit an allergist to determine the exact nature of their allergy.

"We ask that people make their decision on which breeder to choose based on testimonials from other owners of our puppies and that they look at the videos on our websites to show our homes, how we raise our pups and the planning and care that goes into them. In my own case, all of my pups are spoken for and selected on this basis before any buyers even meet them. I have never had anyone ever have to return one of my puppies, except in one case where the person was allergic to the dog's saliva. It is the new owner's responsibility to be tested for such."

If the breeder does allow you to visit the specific pup you are thinking of getting, handle the dog, rub your hands on your face and lick your hands after you have touched the dog in order to absorb as much potential allergen as you can on your short visit.

If possible, go back and visit the breeder before you make that life-changing commitment to buy the puppy. Take an old towel or piece of cloth and rub the puppy with it. Take this home with you and handle it to see if you get a delayed reaction - which can occur up to 48 hours later.

Check with the breeder to see if you can return the pup within a certain time period were you to have a reaction back at home. You cannot expect the breeder to take the dog back if the allergies only occur once the dog has reached adulthood.

Top 12 Tips for Reducing Pet Allergens

Here's an interesting fact: everyone with pet allergies can tolerate a certain amount of allergens (things they are allergic to.) If that person is just below his or her tolerance, any additional allergen will push him or her over the edge, thus triggering a reaction. So if you reduce the general allergen load in the home, you'll be much more successful when you bring your dog home. Here are some tips for doing just that:

1. Get a HEPA air cleaner in the bedroom and/or main living room. HEPA stands for High Efficiency Particle Air - a type of air filter that removes 99.97% of all particles.

2. Use a HEPA vacuum cleaner. Neither the HEPA air nor vacuum cleaner is cheap, but if you suffer allergies and really want to share your life and home with a dog, they are worth considering. Both will dramatically improve the quality of the air you breathe in your home. Regardless of what vacuum you use, clean and dust your home regularly.

3. Carpets trap allergens and dust, so consider having hard floor coverings in rooms.

4. Keep the dog out of your bedroom. We spend around a third of our lives here and keeping animals out can greatly reduce allergic reactions.

5. Wash your hands with an antibacterial soap after handling the dog and before eating – and make sure your children do the same. Avoid contact with other dogs and always wash your hands after you have handled any dog, including your own.

6. Get a non-allergic member of your family to brush your dog regularly - always outdoors - and regularly clean his bedding. Avoid using normal washing powder, as it may trigger a reaction in dogs with sensitive skin.

7. Do not allow your dog on the couch, bed or any other furniture. Keep him out of the car, or if this is not possible, use car seat covers or a blanket on the seat.

8. Keep your dog's skin healthy by regularly feeding a good multivitamin and a fatty acid supplement, such as Omega 3 fish oil.

9. You can try 'Allergy Control Solutions' that alter animal allergens to make them less reactive. They can be sprayed on carpets and soft furnishings, and can be added to water when washing fabrics or clothing.

10. Wipe your dog's underbelly and paws with a damp cloth - or hose him down -after walks, particularly in spring and summer when there are more allergens around.

11. Consider using an allergy-reducing spray such as Allerpet (pictured), which helps to cleanse the dog's hair of dander, saliva and sebaceous gland secretions. There are also products to reduce allergens from carpets, curtains and furniture.

12. There is always the option of consulting your doctor to discuss possible immunotherapy or medication. There are medical advanced being made in the treatment of allergies and a range of tables, sprays and even injections are currently available.

Experts aren't sure whether bathing your dog has any effect on allergy symptoms. Some studies have shown that baths reduce the amount of airborne dander, while others haven't found a difference. We wouldn't recommend bathing your dog more than once a month unless he has a skin problem, as this could cause dry skin, which would then be shed.

Of course, the only sure-fire way to GUARANTEE no allergic reaction is not to have a dog, but that's not what you want to hear! It wasn't what we wanted to hear either when we decided to get a dog more than 11 years ago, knowing that one of our family members had allergies. We followed the advice given in this chapter before we got our dog and can honestly say that none of us have ever had any reaction to Max. It pays to do your homework.

Photo courtesy of Renee Sigman, Yesteryear Acres, Ohio

5. Crate Training and Housetraining

If you are unfamiliar with them, crates may seem like a cruel punishment for a lovable Goldendoodle puppy. They are, however, becoming increasingly popular to help with housetraining (potty training) and to keep the dog safe at night or when you are not there. Breeders, trainers, behaviorists and people who show dogs all use them and, as you will read, many Goldendoodle breeders believe they are a valuable aid in helping to housebreak your dog.

Getting Your Dog Used to a Crate

If you decide to use a crate, then remember that it is not a prison to restrain the dog. It should only be used in a humane manner and time should be spent to make the puppy or adult dog feel like the crate is his own safe little haven. If the door is closed on the crate, your puppy must ALWAYS have access to water while inside. If used correctly and if time is spent getting the puppy used to the crate, it can be a godsend.

Crates may not be suitable for every Goldendoodle, which are companion creatures. They are not like hamsters or pet mice which can adapt to life in a cage; they thrive on being physically close to their humans.

Being caged all day is a miserable existence, and a crate should never be used as a means of confinement because you are out of the house all day. If you do decide to use one - perhaps to put your dog in for short periods while you leave the house, or at night - the best place for it is in the corner of a room away from cold draughts or too much heat. And remember, Goldendoodles like to be near their family - which is you and/or the other dogs.

It is only natural for any dog to whine in the beginning. He is not crying because he is in a cage. He would cry if he had the freedom of the room and he was alone - he is crying because he is separated from you. However, with patience and the right training he will get used to it and some come to regard the crate as a favorite place. Many breeders advise leaving the crate in your bedroom for the first couple of nights. And after that it is still a good idea to leave the crate where the dog can see or hear you. Some owners make the crate their dog's only bed, so he feels comfortable and safe in there.

Dogs with thick coats can overheat easily. When you buy a crate get a wire one (like the one pictured) which allows air to pass through, not a plastic one which may get very hot. If you cover the crate, don't cover it 100% or you will restrict the flow of air. The crate should be large enough to allow your dog to stretch out flat on his side without being cramped, he should be able to turn round easily and to sit up without hitting his head on the top. Here is Midwest Pet Products sizing guide for crates, based on the anticipated adult weight of your dog: www.midwestpetproducts.com/midwestdogcrates/dog-crate-sizes.

Crates aren't for every owner or every Goldendoodle, but used correctly, they can:

- 🐾 Create a canine den
- 🐾 Be a useful housetraining tool
- 🐾 Limit access to the rest of the house while your dog learns the household rules
- 🐾 Be a safe way to transport your dog in a car

If you use a crate right from Day One, cover half of it with a blanket initially to help your puppy regard it as a den. He also needs bedding and it's a good idea to put a chew in as well. A large crate may allow your dog to eliminate at one end and sleep at the other, but this may slow down his housetraining. So, if you are buying a crate which will last for a fully grown Goldendoodle, get adjustable crate dividers – or make them yourself (or put a box inside) - to block part of it off while he is small so that he feels safe and secure, which he won't do in a very big crate.

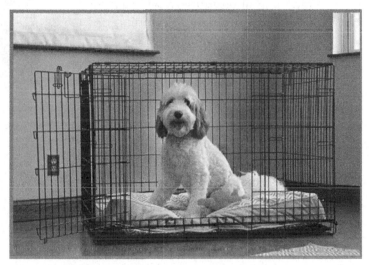

Once you've got your crate, you'll need to learn how to use it properly so that it becomes a safe, comfortable den for your dog and not a prison. Pictured is Sandra Beck's Dobby looking very much at home in his crate. Sandra, of Beck Kennel, Iowa, normally leaves the door open and Dobby takes himself in there for a nap. When he's not relaxing, Dobby likes to chew socks.

Here's a tried-and-tested method of getting your dog firstly to accept a crate, and then to actually want to spend time in there. Initially a pup might not be too happy about going inside, but he will be a lot easier to crate train than an adult dog which has got used to having the run of your house. These are the first steps:

1. Drop a few tasty puppy treats around and then inside the crate.
2. Put your puppy's favorite bedding or toy in there.
3. Keep the door open.
4. Feed your puppy's meals inside the crate. Again, keep the door open.

Place a chew or treat INSIDE the crate and close the door while your puppy is OUTSIDE the crate. He will be desperate to get in there! Open the door, let him in and praise him for going in. Fasten a long-lasting chew inside the crate and leave the door open. Let your puppy go inside to spend some time eating the chew. **IMPORTANT:** Always remove your dog's collar before leaving him unattended in a crate. A collar can get caught in the wire mesh.

After a while, close the crate door and feed him some treats through the mesh while he is in there. At first just do it for a few seconds at a time, then gradually increase the time. If you do it too fast, he will become distressed. Slowly build up the amount of time he is in the crate. For the first few days, stay in the room, then gradually leave for a short time, first one minute, then three, then 10, 30 and so on.

Next Steps

5. Put your dog in his crate at regular intervals during the day - maximum two hours.

6. Don't crate only when you are leaving the house. Place the dog in the crate while you are home as well. Use it as a 'safe' zone. Photo of Bella courtesy of Sandra Beck.

7. By using the crate both when you are home and while you are gone, your dog becomes comfortable there and not worried that you won't come back, or that you are leaving him alone. This helps to prevent separation anxiety later in life.

8. Give him a chew and remove his collar, tags and anything else which could become caught in an opening or between the bars.

9. Make it very clear to any children that the crate is NOT a playhouse for them, but a 'special room' for the dog.

10. Although the crate is your dog's haven and safe place, it must not be off-limits to humans. You should be able to reach inside at any time.

The next point is important:

11. Do not let your dog immediately out of the crate if he barks or whines, or he will think that this is the key to opening the door. Wait until the barking or whining has stopped for at least 10 seconds before letting him out.

A puppy should not be left in a crate for long periods except at night time, and even then he has to get used to it first. Whether or not you decide to use a crate, the important thing to remember is that those first few days and weeks are a critical time for your puppy. Try and make him feel as safe and comfortable as you can. Bond with him, while at the same time gently and gradually introducing him to new experiences and other animals and humans.

A crate is a good way of transporting your Goldendoodle in the car. Put the crate on the shady side of the interior and make sure it can't move around; put the seatbelt around it if necessary. If it's very sunny and the top of the crate is wire mesh, cover part of it so your dog has some shade and put the windows up and the air conditioning on. Never leave your Goldendoodle unattended in a vehicle; he can quickly overheat - or be targeted by thieves.

Allowing your dog to roam freely inside the car is not a safe option, particularly if you - like me – are a bit of a 'lead foot' on the brake and accelerator! Don't let him put his head out of the window either, he can slip and hurt himself and the wind pressure can cause an ear infection or bits of dust, insects, etc. to fly into your dog's eyes. Special travel crates are useful for the car, or for taking your dog to the vet's or a show. Try and pick one with holes or mesh in the side to allow free movement of air, rather than a solid plastic one, in which your Goldendoodle can become overheated.

Goldendoodle Breeders on Crates

Traditionally crates have been more popular in America than in the UK and the rest of Europe, but opinion is slowly changing and more owners are starting to use crates on both sides of the Atlantic. This is perhaps because people's perception of a crate is shifting from regarding it as a prison to thinking of it as a safe haven as well as a useful tool to help with housetraining and transportation, when used correctly.

Without exception, the breeders in this book believe that a crate should not be used for punishment or to imprison a dog all day while you are away from the house. This is cruel for any dog, but particularly a Doodle, who loves to be with his humans. As you will read, opinions vary as to how long a puppy should be left in a crate. The keys to successful crate training are firstly to spend time enticing the dog into the crate so that he or she starts to enjoy spending time in there. Remember, that most puppies will not initially like being in a crate and patience, along with the right techniques, are required. Secondly, never leave your Goldendoodle in there if he or she is distressed by it.

Here's what the breeders say, starting with Christy Stevens: "I highly recommend crate training - we crate train puppies all the time. In fact, we utilize crates in our Puppy Preschool Program and it's a highly successful way to teach them to eliminate outdoors. We use the rule of thumb that states a puppy should only be left in a crate for a maximum of one hour per month of age. During training, the crate should be just big enough for the puppy to turn around and stand with its head erect.

"After a puppy is completely house trained, it should have a crate that is plenty large enough to have extra room to move around. I tend to recommend one size larger than the dog, so for a small breed, I'd get a crate for a medium breed dog. It is possible to purchase a crate that is large enough for a full grown dog, but it needs a divider panel so it can grow with your puppy. We always make sure the crate is a positive place for a puppy by feeding meals or giving treats after entering the crate." Photo of a Goldendoodle behind an indoor gate courtesy of Christy.

"The crate should never be used as a time out or a place the puppy is sent to after being scolded - this will make the puppy want to avoid it altogether. If you have a puppy who seems to be having a panic attack inside the crate, you definitely need to try a slower approach to crate training. This will require allowing your puppy time to get used to the crate without being locked inside it. This can take a few weeks to a few months.

"If you force your puppy to stay inside the crate while in a state of panic, it can have irreversible negative effects on your puppy's disposition and ability to ever be able to tolerate enclosures in the future. Sometimes it is a form of separation anxiety that causes the panic. If your puppy can't get to you because of the crate, it can cause panic. Remember the reasons for the panic and try to be patient while you help your puppy through this scary and difficult adjustment."

Candice Farrell: "Goldendoodle puppies are smart and eager to please and if you are consistent from the moment your puppy comes home, the training process should be quick and easy. Using a crate when you can't watch them and blocking off areas so that the puppy is always in your sight will be very helpful. We start crate training our puppies before they go to their new homes. We crate them for short periods of time, especially when the puppies are sleeping, and then it's straight outside to potty. We give treats when the puppies go in their crates. If you have to be gone for longer than two or three hours, then a treat toy like a Kong can be a good boredom buster."

Laura Chaffin: "I am a firm believer in crate training. A young puppy can be in a crate all night if taken outside once or twice. I advise new families to end feeding by about five or six o'clock each night so that the puppy doesn't have such an urgent need to potty all night long. Also, taking up the water bowl about an hour before bed time will help. An early rise will be necessary so that the puppy does not suffer overly long from the need to potty." Photo courtesy of Laura.

Amy Lane: "Most Goldendoodle puppies are reliably housebroken by four months of age. Use of a crate is an absolute must to achieve this as no human can watch a puppy 24 hours a day. The crate provides a place where the puppy does not need supervision and as long as the crate is appropriately sized, the puppy will not soil inside the crate. However, all puppies do have a limit and the general rule is to add one to the age of the puppy (in months) and this is the maximum number of hours the puppy can be left in the crate before it will be forced to have an accident inside the crate. For example, a two-month-old puppy has a three-hour limit."

Lynne Whitmire: "I train my puppies to a crate, but seldom use it once they mature. I think crate training is important for the following reasons: it helps while potty training, and it is a safe place to contain a puppy when not supervised. Every dog will spend some time of its life in a crate; whether it is at the vet's or the groomer's a dog should be familiar with and unafraid of a crate.

"An eight-week-old puppy should have breaks from the crate every four to six hours at night. If a young puppy is forced to stay in the crate all night they will usually potty in the crate. It can also cause a urinary tract infection as a puppy will try to hold it for as long as he or she can. If a family has to be away from the puppy for more than four hours before it is 16 weeks old, I recommend they get a play fence that has a litter box. A crate should only be used for when a dog needs to sleep, is injured or needs a time out. I don't believe that dogs should ever spend extended time in a crate. A crate with an open door, a snuggly blanket and a toy can be a place of refuge for dog. Many dogs retire to their crate when they want to rest or retreat from too much noise or commotion."

Renee Sigman: "A crate is a great tool if there is no place safe to put the puppy. If you can't tether the pup or need to leave your home, a crate works great. I don't like a pup left for longer than two hours when they are young."

Janece Schommer: "I recommend using a crate for the first year while you're away, then you know your dog is safe. As far as night time goes, I think it's okay to have them crated at night until they are potty trained. After that, you may opt to have them sleep in a doggy bed or maybe your bed! The general rule of thumb for pups in crates is this: a pup can be left alone one hour for each month of age, plus one. For example, a two-month-old pup can be crated for three hours, at three months, puppy can be crated for four hours, etc. After that, they will need a potty break, lunch, play time, etc. When you come home, don't address them. Simply go to the crate, open the door and take the pup out to go potty. Don't make a big deal by greeting your puppy or you will teach them it IS a big deal when you come and go and that can create separation anxiety."

Wendi Loustau: "Crate training is by far the best way to potty train and you need to plan on using it for about two years for chewing."

Lisa Ross: "We crate train while the pups are with us and they are usually sleeping through the night when they go home. If pups are crated, it takes stress off both the pup and the family when pup is unattended. It is good to keep them crated at night and when home alone until they show a good pattern of not getting into anything or messing in the house."

Sandra Beck: "I crate all of my dogs at night and the doors are left open for them to rest at will during the day. Used properly a crate is a great tool for keeping puppies safe, as well as an aid during potty training. Puppies under six months should not be left in a crate for more than three to four hours during the day." Despite looking like a Nova Scotia Duck Tolling Retriever, Forrest, pictured, is actually an F2B flat coated Goldendoodle. Forrest sheds very little, according to his owner Sandra Beck, who took this photo.

Debbie Dixon also recommends crate training: "It makes it easier to protect the puppy from harm while unsupervised, especially at night. It makes potty training easier, and the puppies learn they have a safe place of their own. At night, we highly recommend you keep the crate in your bedroom. It's a scary, lonely time when they leave their littermates, and that is when they best bond to you. Dogs sleep together in packs....so that is one of the ways you will teach him or her to become familiar with you and a part of your pack. It also allows you to hear when your pup needs to go out at night; yes - for the first few days or weeks.

"You can also move a crate from the bedroom at night, to the kitchen or family area for when she or he needs to be in it during the day...keeping pup as near as possible to the action. I also recommend tethering the pup to a six-foot leash attached to your belt as you go about your daily routine for bonding and training. If you buy a crate the size your puppy will be as an adult, be sure to block off part of it to make the sleeping area smaller so they don't soil it."

Dyvonia Bussey: "We start crating puppies at four weeks old and we require crating in our contract. The crate is your friend while housetraining. Puppies cannot be expected to be in the crate all day and then all night. We ask our families not to crate for long periods during the day until after 15 weeks of age. After four to five months, puppies should be capable of being crated for five or six hours during the day."

Melissa Farmer: "We use the crate and highly recommend it. Use the crate to create a schedule, so that manners and housetraining are quickly achieved. As puppies, they are in and out of the crate quite frequently. As your Doodle grows into a well-trained adult, he or she typically uses the crate less."

Neelie Smith: "The first few days are hard on everyone, pup included. We recommend crate training. We crate train our pups a week before they go home in order for them to get used to it. The pup will cry the first few nights. Be PATIENT! The puppy has to get used to you and its new environment. If biting is an issue, have a toy close by. If pup nips, give him the toy to nip at." Photo courtesy of Steve and Neelie Smith.

Scottish breeder Donna Shaw says: "I do crate train my puppies before they go to new homes as nowadays a lot of people use them, so it's always best that the pups are used to them before they leave me, so it's not scary for them. I think little and often for a start is best. Feed them in the crate with the door open and put their bed in. Most of my dogs see an open crate and love going in, I never use it as a punishment and always supervise them for the first few days.

"I would not recommend leaving a Doodle in one for hours on end as we wouldn't like to be locked up for hours either, but it is good knowing they are safe and not up to mischief when you're not there. It is also good for pups when there are children about as they can have their own time out and peace to sleep, especially after meals." Donna jokes: "If all else fails, put the kids in and leave the pup out!"

....

Housetraining

How easy are Goldendoodles to housetrain?

Well, the good news is that, according to our breeders, pretty easy. But the catch is that the dog is only as good as his or her owners. In other words, the speed and success of housetraining often depends largely on one factor: the time and effort you are prepared to put in. The more vigilant you are during the early days, the quicker your dog will be housetrained. It's as simple as that. Taking the advice in this chapter and being consistent with your routines and repetitions is the quickest way to toilet train (potty train) your Goldendoodle.

You have three big factors in your favor when it comes to housetraining:

1. Goldendoodles are intelligent.
2. They are eager to please their owners and love being praised.

3. Most would sell their own mothers for a treat.

A further piece of good news is that a puppy's instinct is not to soil his own den. From about the age of three weeks, a pup will leave his sleeping area to go to the toilet. Most good breeders will already have started the housebreaking process with their puppies, so when you pick up your little bundle of joy, all you have to do is ensure that you carry on the good work.

One method of speeding up toilet training and general training is the 'tethering method' used by several breeders. Renee Sigman explains her methods: "I find you are pretty much 90% done with housetraining within the first month. Tethering the pup to you will greatly speed up the process, I like to tether for the first three weeks – all the time; it works wonders. For very headstrong puppies, it takes away their freedom and ability to do what they want. For shy puppies it gives them the confidence to learn that noises aren't scary and people come and go and they can't hide somewhere away from the action. It brings puppies to the middle and works really quickly.

"I prefer a four-foot lead, but six-foot will also work. When I am at my computer, I just loop the end of the leash around my ankle. I do that whenever I am sitting and, for all the other times, I just hook the leash to my belt loop or keep it on my wrist. Once in a while, I will get an email from a puppy buyer that says: "My puppy won't stop jumping on my two-year-old, what can I do?" To that I say, "Don't let it!"

"This is where tethering is ideal. You can stop the puppy from jumping in mid-action and keep it minding its manners all the time. You can stop a puppy from nipping, lunging, chewing etc. It has to listen to your rules and you are there to remind the pup what behavior is expected. It also prevents accidents under the dining room table, in the other room or having the pup chew up something it shouldn't. It is a pain – but three weeks of tethering can lead to a lifetime of a really well-behaved dog."

Here's what other breeders said:

Sandra Beck: "Goldendoodle puppies that are raised in a clean environment do not like to soil their living area and can be easily potty trained. Make sure you find a breeder that keeps the puppies' sleep and play area clean. Keep your puppy on a routine and you should have great success with housetraining."

Candice Farrell: "Goldendoodle puppies are smart and eager to please. If you are consistent from the moment your puppy comes home, the training process should be quick and easy. Using a crate when you can't watch them and blocking off areas so that the puppy is always in your sight will be very helpful." Pictured is Candice's Sage, a four-month-old English 'teddy bear' Goldendoodle.

Melissa Farmer: "Goldendoodles are very quickly trained. We start training our pups to use a litter box as soon as they have some decent mobility. We move into taking them outside frequently to potty as they get older. This helps the process once they go home. Our feedback is that many pups never have an accident in the house. Even with all this, I don't consider a puppy 'trained' until the bladder has matured at about four to six months. Even if everything is successful...supervise, supervise, supervise."

Kelsey Huffer: "Each dog is different. My girl, Ginnie, was potty trained within two months and my stud, Bernoulli, was still having accidents at seven months. The season in which you get your puppy will play a part in this process if you intend to take your Goldendoodle outside. Like any puppy, a Goldendoodle should not be expected to hold his or her bladder longer than general veterinary recommendations."

Wendi Loustau: "It takes from four to six months to potty train a Goldendoodle and the difference is the owner, not the dog. I find them to be very quick to train, faster than a Golden Retriever."

Laura Chaffin: "I believe Doodles are pretty easy to housetrain. Compared to hounds and the Arctic breeds, Doodles master housetraining very quickly. I start to train my puppies while they are still at my home. I like to get them used to going out - doorways, pet doors, and steps. I use pads on the floor for them to potty on, then narrow the area that they potty in, until there is just a small area with the pads to potty on. By seven weeks old, they are accustomed to going out the pet door or the house door to potty. However, they are not old enough to tell me when they need to go out, so they need to be taken out as soon as awakening, just after eating, and every hour between. Puppies can become pretty good at housetraining by 10 weeks old if they are watched and taken out regularly. A crate is always a good idea with a new puppy. And consistency in being taken out is key."

Lynne Whitmire: "I find that housetraining one of my Goldendoodle's puppies takes approximately two weeks; sometimes shorter, sometimes longer. I train my puppies to a litter box starting at four weeks old and they take to it very easily. As they mature and spend less time with mom, I take them outside every two hours. Because of this, they learn to keep their play and sleeping area fairly clean and are easier to potty train."

Dyvonia Bussey: "When a puppy leaves us, they are going eight hours without accident in the crate at night. However, we follow a strict schedule in the daytime that includes potty breaks every one to one-and-a-half hours." Photo of these two nine-week-old F1 litter mates courtesy of Dyvonia.

Janice Schommer: "Goldendoodles train much faster than average because of the intelligence of their parent breeds. When potty training, I recommend a puppy be in only one of three places: 1. Directly playing with you (not children because they get distracted and puppy sneaks off to have an accident), 2. In their kennel (crate) if you're gone, and 3. (This is what makes it fool-proof:) Put them on a leash in the house and keep them with you.

"That way, they can't sneak off to go potty. Similar to the premise behind crate training, dogs don't like to mess where they lie, so keeping them close and not able to leave works.

"If I am working in my office, I simply put the end of the leash under my chair and the pup can stay close. If I have to make dinner, I will tether them to their crate where I can see them. They have the option to go inside the crate and take a nap, have a drink of water, etc. but they don't have the opportunity to sneak off while I'm busy..."

Donna Shaw: "Housetraining seems to be an easy chore according to the feedback I get from new puppy owners, who say even after a couple of days the puppies know where to go for the toilet. I have a few in fact that have attached a small bell beside the door that the puppy rings to go out! It's pretty amazing. Goldendoodles seem to be far quicker learning toilet training than most breeds I have known over the years.

"I always tell owners to let them out as soon as they wake up, after eating and, generally speaking, every half hour during the first few days. As soon as puppies grasp the fact that they go outside, put them on one spot and have a word for it. With mine we say: "Go be clever!" and they know what's expected, or "Go pee pee!" or whatever you want to call it. If they don't do it right away, keep taking them back to the same spot again and use the word and then once they have done their business, give lots of praise and then let them run around and play."

Debbie Dixon: "Goldendoodles are fast learners. How fast usually depends on the trainer! Consistency and supervision are the key. As is crate training. Tethering is an excellent way to keep track of your puppy - and bond with them. To tether a puppy, put a six-foot leash on your puppy and tie it to your belt loop, or attach to your body in another manner. Puppy learns to follow you wherever you go, and is unable to sneak off. Use tethering when you are able, or when you might not notice puppy wandering off, i.e. while working at a desk, watching TV or reading a book.

"Families that never leave their pup unsupervised (where they can go around the corner and go potty inside unnoticed) tend to have pups potty trained within a matter of weeks with few accidents after that time. But more typically, four months is the general timeframe that pups begin to become mostly dependable. Each dog is different, and each family is different. We've seen pups go home and never have an accident, and on the opposite scale, families that took up to six months to train their pup." Photo of Medium multigen Zozo (Zippity's Trial Size) by Debbie.

Amy Lane: "The typical Goldendoodle learns quickly if their family does their due diligence in housebreaking. Most Goldendoodle puppies show a marked understanding of where they are supposed to do their business within two weeks. This does not mean they are housebroken, but if watched for cues, the puppy will indicate its bathroom needs.

"A puppy that is not housebroken should never be left loose in the house without someone watching them 100%. This would be the same with a toddler, so keeping that in mind will give the proper idea of what is involved. A puppy cannot be reprimanded for an accident if it is not caught in the act of having that accident. They associate any reprimand or reward for their actions in the last three seconds; beyond that, they can't associate appropriately.

"On that note, a new owner may find it necessary to tether the puppy to their belt on a six-foot leash so it cannot get out of sight when the owner becomes distracted. Avoiding the indoor accident is the only way to make progress on housebreaking. The more accidents that happen indoors - especially the ones noticed too late to reprimand - the longer the process will take. Most puppies are reliably housebroken by four months of age.

"Use of a crate is an absolute must to achieve this, as no human can watch a puppy 24 hours a day. The crate provides a place where the puppy does not need supervision and as long as the crate is appropriately sized, the puppy will not soil inside the crate. However, all puppies do have a limit."

Top 12 Housetraining Tips

If you're starting from scratch when you bring your new pup home, your new arrival thinks that the whole house or apartment is his den and doesn't realize it is not the place to eliminate. Therefore you need to gently and persistently teach him that it is unacceptable to make a mess inside the home. Goldendoodles, like all dogs, are creatures of routine - not only do they like the same things happening at the same times every day, but establishing a regular routine with your dog also helps to speed up training and housebreaking.

Dogs are also very tactile creatures, so they will pick a toilet area which feels good under their paws. Many dogs like to go on grass - but this will do nothing to improve your lawn, so you should think carefully about what area to encourage your Goldendoodle to use. You may want to consider a small patch of gravel crushed into tiny pieces in your garden, or a dog litter tray if you live in an apartment. Some breeders advise against using puppy pads for any length of time as puppies like the softness of the pads, which can encourage them to eliminate on other soft areas - such as your carpets or bed. Follow these tips to speed up housetraining:

1. **Constant supervision** is essential for the first week or two if you are to housetrain your puppy quickly. This is why it is important to book the week or so off work when you bring him home. Make sure you are there to take him outside regularly. If nobody is there, he will learn to urinate or poo(p) inside the house.

2. **Take your pup outside at the following times** (Photo: F1 six-week-old pup by Renee Sigman):

   🐾 As soon as he wakes – every time

   🐾 Shortly after each feed

   🐾 After a drink

   🐾 When he gets excited

   🐾 After exercise or play

   🐾 Last thing at night

   🐾 Initially every hour - whether or not he looks like he wants to go

You may think that the above list is an exaggeration, but it isn't. Housetraining a pup is almost a full-time job for the first few days. If you are serious about housetraining your puppy quickly, then clear your diary for a few days and keep your eyes firmly glued on your pup...learn to spot that expression or circling motion just before he makes a puddle - or worse – on your floor.

3. Take your Goldendoodle to **the same place** every time, you may need to use a leash in the beginning - or tempt him there with a treat. Some say it is better to only pick him up and dump him there in an emergency, as it is better if he learns to take himself to the chosen toilet spot. Dogs naturally develop a preference for going in the same place or on the same surface - often grass or dirt. Take him to the same patch every time so he learns this is his bathroom - preferably an area in a corner of your yard or garden. (Photo of F1 Mini Goldendoodle Annie courtesy of Christy Stevens.)

No pressure – be patient. You must allow your distracted little darling time to wander around and have a good sniff before performing his duties – but do not leave him, stay around a short distance away. Sadly, puppies are not known for their powers of concentration; it may take a while for them to select the perfect bathroom!

4. **Housetraining is reward-based.** Praise him or give him a treat immediately after he has performed his duties in the chosen spot. Goldendoodles love praise, and reward-based training is the most successful method for this sensitive crossbreed.

5. **Share the responsibility.** It doesn't have to be the same person who takes the dog outside all the time. In fact it's easier if there are a couple of you, as housetraining is a very time-consuming business. Just make sure you stick to the same principles, command and patch of ground.

6. **Stick to the same routine.** Dogs understand and like routine. Sticking to the same one for mealtimes, short exercise sessions, play time, sleeping and toilet breaks will help to not only housetrain him quicker, but help him settle into his new home.

7. **Use the same word** or command when telling your puppy to go to the toilet – or while he is in the act. He will gradually associate this phrase or word with toileting and you will even be able to get him to eliminate on command after some weeks or months.

8. **Use your voice if you catch him in the act indoors.** A short sharp negative sound is best - NO! ACK! EH! - it doesn't matter, as long as it is loud enough to make him stop. Then start running enthusiastically towards your door, calling him into the garden and the chosen place and patiently wait until he has finished what he started indoors. It is no good scolding your dog if you find a puddle or unwanted gift in the house but don't see him do it; he won't know why you are cross with him. Only use the negative sound if you actually catch him in the act.

9. **No punishment.** Accidents will happen at the beginning, do not punish your Goldendoodle for them. He is a baby with a tiny bladder and bowels, and housetraining takes time - it is perfectly natural to have accidents early on. Remain calm and clean up the mess with a good strong-smelling cleaner to remove the odor, so he won't be tempted to use that spot again. Dogs have a very strong sense of smell; use a special spray from your vet or a hot solution of washing powder to completely eliminate the odor. Smacking or rubbing his nose in it can have the opposite effect - he will become afraid to do his business in your presence and may start going behind the couch or under the bed, rather than outside.

10. **Look for the signs.** These may be whining, sniffing the floor in a determined manner, circling and looking for a place to go, or walking uncomfortably - particularly at the rear end! Take him outside straight away. Try not to pick him up. He has to learn to walk to the door himself when he needs to go outside.

11. **If you use puppy pads, only do so for a short time** (unless you live in an apartment and are indoor toilet training) or your puppy will get used to them. You can also separate a larger crate into two areas and put a pad in one area to help housetrain your pup. He will eliminate on the pad and keep his bed clean.

12. If you are having problems, **try the Tethering Method.**

One British breeder added this piece of advice: "If you are getting a puppy, invest in a good dressing gown and an umbrella!"

If you decide to keep your puppy in a crate overnight and you want him to learn not to soil the crate right from the very beginning, you need to have the crate in the bedroom so you can hear him whine when he needs to go. Initially this might be once or twice a night. The age at which a pup can go through the night (seven or eight hours) without needing the toilet varies a great deal. A breeder who puts in the time to housetrain her puppies is worth her weight in gold. While some owners find that their puppies are still not lasting the night at four months of age, others are delighted to report that their pups are sleeping through after only a couple of nights in their new home.

One such breeder is Amy Lane: "The average for my puppies to sleep through the night is 10 weeks of age. Many sleep through the night on the first or second night in a new home, which is at eight weeks old. I don't have a single customer that has reported it taking longer than 11 weeks of age."

If using a crate, remember that the door should not be closed until your Goldendoodle is happy with being inside. He needs to believe that this is a safe place and not a trap or prison. Rather than use a crate, many people prefer to section off an area inside one room or use a puppy pen to confine their pup. Inside this area is a bed and another area with pads or newspapers which the puppy can use as a toilet area.

....

Apartment Living

Most Goldendoodle owners live in houses, but a few live in apartments - usually with smaller Goldendoodles. If you live on the 11th floor of an apartment, housetraining can be a little trickier as you don't have easy access to the outdoors. One suggestion is to indoor housetrain your puppy. Dogs that spend much of their time indoors can be housetrained fairly easily - especially if you start early. Stick to the same principles already outlined - the only difference is that you will be placing your pup on training pads or newspaper instead of taking him outside.

Start by blocking off a section of the apartment for your new puppy. You can use a baby gate or puppy pen or make your own barrier - pick a chew-proof material. You will be able to keep a better eye on him than if he has free run of the whole place. It will also be easier to monitor his 'accidents.'

Select a corner away from his eating and sleeping area that will become his permanent bathroom area – carpets are to be avoided if at all possible. At first, cover a larger area than is actually needed - about three to four square feet - with newspaper (or training pads.) You can reduce the area as training progresses. Take your puppy there as indicated in our Housetraining Tips. Praise him enthusiastically when he eliminates on the allotted area. If you catch him doing his business out of the toilet area, pick him up and take him back there. Correct with a firm voice - never a hand. With positive reinforcement and a strict schedule, he will soon be walking to the area on his own.

Owners attempting indoor housetraining should be aware that it will generally take longer than outdoor training; some pups may resist. Also, once a dog learns to go indoors, it can be difficult to train him to eliminate outdoors. Any laziness on your part by not monitoring your puppy carefully enough - especially in the beginning – will make indoor housetraining a lot longer and more difficult process. The first week or two is crucial to your puppy learning what is expected of him.

GENERAL HOUSETRAINING TIP: As you have read, a trigger can be very effective to encourage your dog to perform his duties. Some people use a clicker or a bell - we used a word; well, two actually. Within a week or so I trained our puppy to urinate on the command of "Wee wee!" Think very carefully before choosing the word or phrase, as I often feel an idiot wandering around our garden last thing at night shouting "Max, WEE WEE!!" in an encouraging manner. (Although I'm not sure that the American expression "GO POTTY!!" sounds much better!

"How can you tell the dogs need to go out?"

6. Feeding a Goldendoodle

To keep your dog's biological machine in good working order, he or she needs the right fuel, just like a finely-tuned sports car. Feeding the correct diet is an essential part of keeping your Goldendoodle fit and healthy. However, the topic of feeding the right diet is something of a minefield. Owners are bombarded with endless choices as well as countless adverts from dog food companies, all claiming that theirs is best.

There is not one food that will give every single dog the brightest eyes, the shiniest coat, the most energy, the best digestion, the longest life and stop him from scratching or having skin problems. Dogs are individuals, just like people, which means that you could feed a premium food to a group of dogs and find that most of them do great on it, some do not so well, while a few might even get an upset stomach or even an allergic reaction. The question is: "Which food is best for my Goldendoodle?"

If you have been given a recommended food from a breeder, rescue center or previous owner, it is best to stick to this as long as your dog is doing well on it. A good breeder will know which food their dogs thrive on. If you do decide - for whatever reason - to change diet, then this must be done gradually. There are several things to be aware of when it comes to feeding:

1. Most Goldendoodles are not fussy eaters and love their food. Add to this their eagerness to please their owners and you have a powerful training tool. You can use feeding time to reinforce a simple command on a daily basis.

2. Some Goldendoodles do not do well on diets with a high grain content.

3. Some dogs have food sensitivities or allergies, leading to skin issues and scratching/biting - more on this topic later.

4. Controlling your dog's food intake is important, as obesity can trigger or worsen numerous health conditions and shorten lives.

5. There are many different options on the market. The most popular manufactured foods include dry complete diets, tinned food (with or without a biscuit mixer), and semi-moist. Some dog foods contain only natural ingredients. Then there is the option of feeding a home-made diet; while other owners feed their dogs vegetarian food. There are many different qualities of manufactured food. Often, you get what you pay for, so a more expensive food is usually – but not always - more likely to provide better nutrition in terms of minerals, nutrients and high quality meats. Cheap foods often contain a lot of grain.

However, this is not always the case - read the list of ingredients to find out. Dried foods (also called kibble in the USA) tend to be less expensive than other foods. They have improved a lot over the last few years and some of the best ones are now a good choice for a healthy, complete diet. Dried foods also contain the least fat and most preservatives. Foods such as Life's Abundance dry formulas do not contain any preservatives.

6. Sometimes elderly dogs may just get bored with their diet and go off their food. This does not necessarily mean that they are ill, simply that they have lost interest and a new food should be gradually introduced.

Our dog Max, who has inhalant allergies, is on a quality dried food made by James Wellbeloved who claims it is 'hypoallergenic,' i.e. good for dogs with allergies. Max seems to do well on it, but not all dogs thrive on dried food. We tried several other foods first; it is a question of each owner finding the best one for their dog. Ask your breeder or vet if you're unsure.

 Beware foods described as 'premium' or 'natural' or both, these terms are meaningless. Many manufacturers blithely use these words, but there are no official guidelines as to what they mean. However **"Complete and balanced"** IS a legal term and has to meet standards laid down by AAFCO (Association of American Feed Control Officials) in the USA.

Always check the ingredients on any food sack, packet or tin to see what is listed first; this is the main ingredient and it should be meat or poultry, not grain. If you are in the USA, look for a dog food endorsed by AAFCO. In general, tinned foods are 60-70% water and often semi-moist foods contain a lot of artificial substances and sugar. Choosing the right food for your Goldendoodle is important; it will certainly influence his health, coat and even temperament.

There are three stages of your dog's life to consider when feeding: Puppy, Adult and Senior (also called Veteran.) Some manufacturers also produce a Junior feed for adolescent dogs. Each represents a different physical stage of life and you need to choose the right food during each particular phase. Also, a pregnant female will require a special diet to cope with the extra demands on her body; this is especially important as she nears the latter stages of pregnancy.

Most owners feed their Goldendoodles twice a day; which helps to stop a hungry dog gulping food down in a mad feeding frenzy, and reduces the risk of Bloat (see **Chapter 9. Health** for more details.) Some owners of fussy eaters feed two different meals each day to provide variety. One meal could be dried kibble, while the other might be home-made, with fresh meat, poultry and vegetables, or a moist food. If you do this, speak with your vet to make sure the two separate meals provide a balanced diet and that they are not too rich in protein.

We will not recommend one brand of dog food over another, but do have some general tips to help you choose what to feed. There is also some advice for owners of dogs with food allergies and intolerances. Goldendoodles are not particularly prone to them; however, there is some anecdotal evidence from breeders that some Goldendoodles can have an intolerance to grain. Food allergies are a growing problem in the canine world generally. Sufferers may itch, lick or chew their paws and/or legs, or rub their face. They may also get frequent ear infections as well as redness and swelling on their face. Switching to a grain-free diet can help to alleviate the symptoms, as your dog's digestive system does not have to work as hard. In the wild, a dog or wolf's staple diet would be meat with some vegetable matter from the stomach and intestines of the herbivores (plant eating animals) he ate – but no grains. Dogs do not digest corn or wheat (which are often staples of cheap commercial dog food) very efficiently. Grain-free diets still provide carbohydrates through fruits and vegetables, so your dog still gets all his nutrients.

15 Top Tips for Feeding your Goldendoodle

1. If you choose a manufactured food, **don't pick one where meat or poultry content is NOT the first item listed on the bag.** Foods with lots of cheap cereals or sugar are not the best choice.

2. Some dogs suffer from sensitive skin, 'hot spots' or allergies. A cheap food, often bulked up with grain, will only make this worse. If this is the case, bite the bullet and **choose a high quality – usually more expensive – food, or consider a raw diet.** You'll probably save money in vets' bills in the long run and your dog will be happier. A food described as 'hypoallergenic' on the sack means 'less likely to cause allergies.'

3. **Feed your Goldendoodle twice a day**, rather than once. Smaller feeds are easier to digest, and reduce flatulence and the risk of Bloat. Puppies need to be fed more often; discuss exactly how often with your breeder.

4. **Establish a feeding regime and stick to it**. Dogs like routine. If you are feeding twice a day, feed once in the morning and then again at tea-time. Stick to the same times of day. Do not give the last feed too late, or your dog's body will not have chance to process or burn off the food before sleeping. He will also need a walk or letting out in the garden or yard after his second feed to allow him to empty his bowels. Feeding at the same times each day helps your dog establish a toilet regime.

5. **Take away any uneaten food between meals.** Most Goldendoodles are good eaters, but any dog can become fussy if food is available all day. Imagine if your dinner was left on the table for hours. Returning to the table two or three hours later would not be such a tempting prospect, but coming back for a fresh meal would be far more appetizing.

Also, when food is left all day, some dogs take the food for granted and lose their appetite. They start leaving food and you are at your wits' end trying to find something they will actually eat. Put the food bowl down twice a day and take it up after 20 minutes – even if there is some left. If he is healthy and hungry, he'll look forward to his next meal and soon stop leaving food. If your dog does not eat anything for a couple of days, it could well be a sign that he is not well.

6. **Do not feed too many tidbits and treats between meals.** Extra weight will place extra strain on your dog's joints and organs, have a detrimental effect on his health and even his lifespan. It also throws his balanced diet out of the window. Try to avoid feeding your dog from the table or your plate, as this encourages attention-seeking behavior and drooling.

7. **Never give your dog cooked bones,** as these can splinter and cause him to choke or suffer intestinal problems. If your dog is a gulper, it's a good idea to avoid giving rawhide, as dogs who rush their food have a tendency to quickly chew and swallow rawhide without first bothering to nibble it down into smaller pieces.

8. **If you switch to a new food, do the transition gradually.** Unlike humans, dogs' digestive systems cannot handle sudden changes in diet. Begin by gradually mixing some of the new food in with the old and increase the proportion so that after seven to eight days, all the food is the new one. The following ratios are recommended by Doctors Foster & Smith Inc: Days 1-3 add 25% of the new food, Days 4-6 add 50%, Days 7-9 add 75%, Day 10 feed 100% new food. By the way, if you stick to the identical brand, you can change flavors in one go.

9. **NEVER feed the following items to your dog**: grapes, raisins, chocolate, onions, Macadamia nuts, any fruits with seeds or stones, tomatoes, avocadoes, rhubarb, tea, coffee or alcohol. ALL of these are poisonous to dogs.

10. **Check your dog's feces** (aka stools, poo or poop!) If his diet is suitable, the food should be easily digested and produce dark brown, firm stools. If your dog produces soft or light stools, or has a lot of gas or diarrhea, then the diet may not suit him, so consult your vet or breeder for advice.

11. **Feed your dog in stainless steel or ceramic dishes.** Plastic bowls don't last as long and can also trigger an allergic reaction in some sensitive dogs. Ceramic bowls are best for keeping water cold.

12. **If you have more than one dog, consider feeding them separately.** Goldendoodles usually get on fine with other pets, especially if introduced at an early age. But feeding dogs together can sometimes lead to dog food aggression from a dog either protecting his own food or trying to eat the food designated for another pet.

13. **If you do feed leftovers, feed them INSTEAD of a balanced meal,** not as well as (unless you are feeding a raw diet.) High quality dog foods already provide all the nutrients, vitamins,

minerals and calories that your dog needs. Feeding tidbits or leftovers may be too rich for your Goldendoodle in addition to his regular diet and cause him to scratch or have other problems, as well as get fat.

 You can feed your dog vegetables as a healthy low-calorie treat. Get your dog used to eating raw carrots, pieces of apple, etc. as a treat while he is still a puppy and he will continue to enjoy them as treats as an adult. If you wait until he is fully grown before introducing them, he may well turn his nose up.

14. **Keep your dog's weight in check.** Obesity can lead to the development of serious health issues, such as diabetes, high blood pressure and heart disease. Although weight varies from dog to dog, a good rule of thumb is that your Goldendoodle's tummy should be higher than or, at worst, level with his rib cage. If his belly hangs down below it, he is overweight.

15. And finally, **always make sure that your dog has access to clean, fresh water.** Change the water and clean the bowl regularly – it gets slimy!

....

Types of Dog Food

We are what we eat. The right food is a very important part of a healthy lifestyle for dogs as well as humans. Here are the main options explained:

Dry dog food - also called kibble, this is a popular and relatively inexpensive way of providing a balanced diet. It comes in a variety of flavors and with differing ingredients to suit the different stages of a dog's life. Cheap foods are often false economy, particularly if your Goldendoodle does not tolerate grain/cereal very well, as they often contain a lot of grain. You may also have to feed larger quantities to ensure he gets sufficient nutrients.

Canned food - another popular choice – and it's often very popular with dogs too. They love the taste and it generally comes in a variety of flavors. Canned food is often mixed with dry kibble, and a small amount may be added to a dog on a dry food diet if he has lost interest in food. It tends to be more expensive than dried food and many owners don't like the mess. These days there are hundreds of options, some are very high quality and made from natural, organic ingredients and containing herbs and other beneficial ingredients. A part-opened tin can sometimes smell when you open the fridge door. As with dry food, read the label closely. Generally, you get what you pay for and the origins of cheap canned dog food are often somewhat dubious.

Semi-Moist - These are commercial dog foods shaped like pork chops, salamis, bacon, burgers or other meaty foods and they are the least nutritional of all dog foods. They are full of sugars, artificial flavorings and colorings to help make them visually appealing.

Goldendoodles don't care what their food looks like, they only care how it smells and tastes; the shapes are designed to appeal to us humans. While you may give your dog one as an occasional treat, they are not a diet in themselves and do not provide the nutrition that your dog needs. Steer clear of them for regular feeding.

Freeze-Dried - This is made by frozen food manufacturers for owners who like the convenience – this type of food keeps for six months to a year - or for those going on a trip with their dog. It says 'freeze-dried' on the packet and is highly palatable, but the freeze-drying process bumps up the cost.

Home-Cooked - Some dog owners want the ability to be in complete control of their dog's diet, know exactly what their dog is eating and to be absolutely sure that his nutritional needs are being met. Feeding your dog a home-cooked diet is time consuming and expensive, and the difficult thing – as with the raw diet - is sticking to it once you have started out with the best of intentions. But many owners think the extra effort is worth the peace of mind. If you decide to go ahead, you should spend the time to become proficient and learn about canine nutrition to ensure your dog gets all his vital nutrients.

What the Breeders Feed

We asked a number of Goldendoodle breeders what they fed their dogs. We are not recommending one brand over another, but the breeders' answers give a good insight as to what issues are important when considering food and why a particular brand has been chosen.

Janece Schommer, of Goldendoodle Acres, Wisconsin, USA: "I feed my dogs Life's Abundance. I like the company because of their high quality food and their high standards regarding the products that go into their food. I also love the fact that none of the food is over four weeks old when it arrives at your door, given the fact that kibble can lose vitamins and nutrients the longer it sits. I also like the fact that they have never been involved in a pet food recall, but if they did ever have a recall, they would contact everyone who purchased that product as they keep track of that. You don't have to wait to see it on TV after your dog has been sick for weeks."

Pictured is a litter of one-week-old red Medium multigenerational (multigen) Goldendoodles bred by Janece.

Amy Lane, of Fox Creek Farm, West Virginia agrees: "My dogs are fed a high quality kibble made by Life's Abundance. Choosing a food is important and my criteria are that is has to be made in the USA and be preservative, dye and grain free. Dog food recalls in the USA are

common and many times the recall is done because the tainted food has caused death in multiple dogs. Typically the tainted food is due to imported products. I chose Life's Abundance because every ingredient is USA grown and the food is manufactured in a human-grade facility and the company has never had to issue a recall."

So does Christy Stevens, of Winding Creek Ranch Goldendoodles, Indiana: "We feed Life's Abundance because it is holistic with ingredients sourced in the USA only. The company produces food in short batches and doesn't use a middle man. This allows my dogs to eat the absolute freshest, most nutrient-rich kibble possible. The company has never had a food recall and that's something to say. I also love having it shipped to me on an auto-ship program in which UPS bring it right to my door."

Michael and Lisa Ross, of Chai Kennels, Elgin, Canada, agree on the importance of feeding a top quality food: "We feed Pro Series Puppy. It is all human grade, a three-star kibble that is both grown and harvested locally."

Renee Sigman, of Yesteryear Acres, Ohio, has a slightly different approach: "We feed our dogs and puppies a blend of 20 different foods. We find it greatly reduces the chance of food allergies further down the road. Single source proteins and grains can lead to intolerance later on as the gut simply can't process anything else. By introducing a wide variety of proteins and grains, the gut is much healthier and resistant to food allergies."

Wendi Loustau, of Mustard Seed Ranch Goldendoodles, Georgia: "I always feed and recommend grain-free non-poultry based foods. I think the majority of Doodles do best on this diet." Dyvonia Bussell, of Grace Goldens, Alabama, adds: "We feed Taste of the Wild. When we bought our Golden Retriever, she was eating it and we have been pleased with the results."

UK breeder Donna Shaw, of Donakell Goldendoodles, Aberdeenshire, Scotland, says: "I feed my dogs a varied diet and not always the same brand, as I wouldn't like beans on toast every day of my life! My dogs get a change every so often, and they do enjoy some raw food as well. Sometimes the most expensive foods are not always the best and some of your cheaper brands are just as good - but do your research.

"My pups are also raised on varied diets, not just one brand, I try all sorts with them, and that way you tend not to get fussy eaters. Also, it doesn't matter how many times you tell a new owner to stick to a particular diet and food type, I have found over the years that if they have had another dog fed on a specific brand they say "She was on this food," and they change it anyway. If the pups are only used to a certain brand of food, they get upset tummies which isn't good for either the puppy or the owner, so my pups are used to getting their food changed and don't get dodgy tummies again. Two of my dogs came from Canada and I couldn't get their brand of food over here and for two weeks Mallic hardly ate a thing."

Lynne Whitmire, of Fountain Falls Goldendoodles, South Carolina, USA: "I feed most of my dogs a variety of five star dog foods. No one really knows what all dogs need to be healthy, therefore I switch three or four high grade dogs foods and this has worked well for my dogs. I avoid any food that has corn, wheat or soy; meat has to be the first ingredient. I research any dog food I use."

The Raw Diet

There is a quiet revolution going on in the world of dog food. After years of feeding dry or tinned dog food, increasing numbers of owners are now feeding a raw diet to their beloved pets. There is anecdotal evidence that many dogs thrive on a raw diet, although scientific proof is lagging behind. There are a number of claims made by fans of the raw diet, including:

- Reduced symptoms of - or less likelihood of – allergies, and less scratching
- Better skin and coats
- Easier weight management
- Improved digestion
- Less doggie odor and flatulence
- Fresher breath and improved dental health
- Helps fussy eaters
- Drier and less smelly stools, more like pellets
- Reduced risk of Bloat
- Overall improvement in general health and less disease
- Higher energy levels
- Most dogs love a raw diet

It's fair to say that most Goldendoodles breeders and owners we contacted generally found there was no need to feed a raw diet to their dogs as they thrived on commercially-prepared food, or a mixture of manufactured and home-prepared food, although several of them thought that raw was a very good option. A raw diet can, however, be expensive and time consuming and it definitely involves more research and effort on the part of the owner.

However, food intolerances and allergies, as well as other types of allergies, are on the increase and if you find your Goldendoodle is unlucky enough to be a sufferer, you might want to consider a raw diet.

Laura Chaffin, of Cimarron Frontier Doodles, Oklahoma, USA, is one breeder who is a fan: "I usually feed raw or home-cooked; there are no additives or bags sitting in warehouses. I don't like to feed dogs, corn, wheat or soy, and weaning puppies in particular need a healthy foundation for their development. I really feel like commercial kibble is usually not healthy for dogs. There are some that make it fresh and send it off from the manufacturer to consumer freshly made - like Life's Abundance - but I think raw or home-cooked is best.

"I use Barf World, fresh meat and bones, and home-cooked as well. I have also used Honest Kitchen, Sojos, and Grandma Lucy dog food. NuVet is a good supplement as well as Springtime Supplements and Nupro, and salmon oil. My dogs have never had any health problems, so it seems to be good for them." This handsome chap, bred by Laura, is seven-week-old Medium (Moyen) Goldendoodle Oscar.

Candice Farrell, of Ooodles of Doodles, Alberta Canada, says: "Raw diet is absolutely the best if you can feed it. I would, however, caution against it with small children, as the raw food can contain bacteria that doesn't affect dogs but may affect people. Raw foods are great for dogs with allergies, they result in smaller, easier to clean poops and nutrition- wise, they are the very best choice. If you can't feed raw you can add cooked real foods to your dog's kibble. Cooked eggs, raw veggies and other cooked lean proteins are great choices."

Lynne Whitmire: "I have one mini that is on a raw diet. He was a poor eater and never seemed to gain enough weight. After two years I reluctantly switched him to a raw diet and he went from nine pounds to 11 and eats a healthy amount every day. I have found the raw diet to be very beneficial for my Mini Goldendoodle. He will not eat commercially prepared raw diets, so I make up a month's worth of meals at a time and he has gained weight, energy and seems all around healthier. Because he is a small dog the cost is not prohibitive. However, unless someone has a good supply of raw meat, it can be quite costly to feed a raw diet to a large dog. Researching how to do it properly is very important as dogs need more than just meat. He also gets fish oil, probiotics and vitamins. It is also a pain to prepare and is a problem when we travel, so I would not recommend it unless needed."

Christy Stevens: "My opinion is that a raw diet can be a great option; there are many benefits to feeding raw. However, only a veterinary dietician can put together a well-rounded diet for a dog, and I would not feel comfortable trying to guess what my dog needs. At least with the Life's Abundance, I know it is well-balanced. If an owner would like to feed a raw diet, I suggest using a commercially prepared, raw diet or hiring a dietician to create a recipe or menu for your dog."

Janece Schommer: "I do feel raw diet is best for a dog, but the willingness of most new puppy owners to feed raw is low. For that reason and an easy transition into their new homes, we feed a high quality kibble with a vitamin to round out all the vitamins and nutrients a dog needs daily at a cellular level, as well as filling their caloric needs."

Donna Shaw: "I think it's down to personal taste and I am certainly not against it. My lot enjoy a mix of both and they do well on it. Varied diets are, I find, good for them, but if you are feeding a completely raw BARF diet, you need to do your research."

Amy Lane: "I do not feed a raw diet. Some people think that feeding a raw diet is a healthy alternative to dry kibble. The main problem when feeding a raw diet is that a dog needs more nutrition than plain meat provides, so one must work with a vet skilled in nutrition to work out what other additives (vegetables, etc.) need to be included to provide a nutritionally balanced diet."

(This little beauty is Amy's Medium multigen Fox Creek's All That Jazz (Jazz) aged four months.)

Renee Sigman adds: "The poop doesn't smell as bad; that is always a plus! However, a raw diet is messy and rather inconvenient for most owners." And Lisa Ross reminds anyone considering a raw diet that owners need to be extremely careful regarding hygiene when preparing raw meat - especially in households with children.

If your dog is NOT doing well on a commercially-prepared dog food, it's certainly worth considering a raw diet, which emulates the way dogs used to eat. Commercial foods may contain artificial preservatives and excessive protein and fillers – causing a reaction in some dogs. Dry, canned and other styles of processed food were mainly created as a means of convenience, but unfortunately this convenience sometimes can affect a dog's health.

Some nutritionists believe that dogs fed raw whole foods tend to be healthier than those on other diets, claiming there are inherent beneficial enzymes, vitamins, minerals and other qualities in meats, fruits, vegetables and grains in their natural forms that are denatured or destroyed when cooked. Many also believe dogs are less likely to have allergic reactions to the ingredients on this diet. But unsurprisingly, the topic is not without controversy.

Critics say that the risks of nutritional imbalance, intestinal problems and food-borne illnesses caused by handling and feeding raw meat outweigh any benefits. It's true that owners must pay strict attention to hygiene when preparing a raw diet and it may not be suitable if there are children in the household. A dog may also be more likely to ingest bacteria or parasites such as Salmonella, E. Coli and Ecchinococcus.

Frozen food can be a valuable aid to the raw diet. The food is highly palatable, made from high quality ingredients and dogs usually wolf it down. The downsides are that not all pet food stores stock it and it is expensive. There are two main types of raw diet, one involves feeding raw, meaty bones and the other is known as the BARF diet (*Biologically Appropriate Raw Food* or *Bones And Raw Food),* created by Dr Ian Billinghurst.

Raw Meaty Bones

The main principles are:

- Raw meaty bones or carcasses, if available, should form the bulk of the diet
- Table scraps both cooked and raw - such as vegetables - can be fed
- As with any diet, fresh water should be constantly available. **NOTE: Do NOT feed cooked bones, they can splinter**

Australian veterinarian Dr Tom Lonsdale is a leading proponent of the raw meaty bones diet. He believes the following foods are suitable:

- Chicken and turkey carcasses, after the meat has been removed for human consumption
- Poultry by-products, including heads, feet, necks and wings
- Whole fish and fish heads
- Sheep, calf, goat, and deer carcasses sawn into large pieces of meat and bone
- Other by-products, e.g. pigs' trotters, pigs' heads, sheep's heads, brisket, tail and rib bones
- A certain amount of offal can be included in the diet, e.g. liver, lungs, trachea, hearts, tripe

He says that low-fat game animals, fish and poultry provide the best source of food for pet carnivores. If you feed meat from farm animals (cattle, sheep and pigs), avoid excessive fat and bones that are too large to be eaten.

Some of it will depend on what's available locally and how expensive it is. If you shop around you should be able to source a regular supply of suitable raw meaty bones at a reasonable price. Start with your local butcher or farm shop. When deciding what type of bones to feed your Goldendoodle, one point to bear in mind is that dogs are more likely to break their teeth when eating large knuckle bones and bones sawn lengthwise than when eating meat and bone together.

You'll also need to think about WHERE you are going to feed your dog. A dog takes some time to eat a raw bone and will push it around the floor, so the kitchen may not be the most suitable or hygienic place. Outside is one option, but what do you do when it's raining?

Establishing the right quantity to feed is a matter of trial and error. You will reach a decision based on your dog's activity levels, appetite and body condition. High activity and a big appetite show a need for increased food, and vice versa. A very approximate guide, based on raw meaty bones, for the average dog is 15%-20% of body weight in one week, or 2%-3% a day. Table scraps should be fed as an extra component of the diet. These figures are only a rough guide and relate to adult pets in a domestic environment. Pregnant or lactating females and growing puppies may need much more food than adult animals of similar body weight.

Dr Lonsdale says: "Wherever possible, feed the meat and bone ration in one large piece requiring much ripping, tearing and gnawing. This makes for contented pets with clean teeth. Wild carnivores feed at irregular intervals. In a domestic setting, regularity works best and accordingly I suggest that you feed adult dogs and cats once daily.

If you live in a hot climate, I recommend that you feed pets in the evening to avoid attracting flies. I suggest that on one or two days each week your dog may be fasted - just like animals in the wild. On occasions you may run out of natural food. Don't be tempted to buy artificial food, fast your dog and stock up with natural food the next day. Puppies, sick or underweight dogs should not be fasted (unless on veterinary advice.)"

Table scraps and some fruit and vegetable peelings can also be fed, but should not make up more than one-third of the diet. Liquidizing cooked and uncooked scraps in a food mixer can make them easier to digest.

Things to Avoid

- Excessive meat off the bone - not balanced
- Excessive vegetables - not balanced
- Small pieces of bone - can be swallowed whole and get stuck
- Cooked bones - get stuck
- Mineral and vitamin additives - create imbalance
- Processed food - leads to dental and other diseases
- Excessive starchy food - associated with Bloat
- Onions, garlic and chocolate, grapes, raisins, sultanas, currants - toxic to pets
- Fruit stones (pips) and corn cobs - get stuck
- Milk - associated with diarrhea. Animals drink it whether thirsty or not and can get fat

Points of Concern

- Old dogs accustomed to processed food may experience initial difficulty when changed to a natural diet. Discuss the change with your vet first and then, if he or she agrees, switch your dog's diet over a period of a week to 10 days
- Raw meaty bones are not suitable for dogs with dental or jaw problems
- This diet may not be suitable if your dog gulps his food, as the bones can become lodged inside him; larger bones may prevent gulping

- The diet should be varied, any nutrients fed to excess can be harmful

- Liver is an excellent foodstuff, but should not be fed more than once weekly

- Other offal, e.g. ox stomachs, should not make up more than half of the diet

- Whole fish are an excellent source of food, but avoid feeding one species of fish constantly. Some species, e.g. carp, contain an enzyme which destroys thiamine (vitamin B1)

- If you have more than one dog, do not allow them to fight over the food; feed them separately if necessary

- Be prepared to monitor your dog while he eats the bones, especially in the beginning, and do not feed bones with sharp points. Take the bone off your dog before it becomes small enough to swallow

- Make sure that children do not disturb the dog when he is feeding or try to take the bone away

- Hygiene: Make sure the raw meaty bones are kept separate from human food and clean thoroughly any surface the uncooked meat or bones have touched. This is especially important if you have children. Feeding bowls are unnecessary. Your dog will drag the bones across the floor, so feed them outside if you can, or on a floor which is easy to clean

- Puppies can and do eat diets of raw meaty bones, but you should consult the breeder or a vet before embarking on this diet with a young dog

You will need a regular supply of meaty bones – either locally or online - and you should buy in bulk to ensure a consistency of supply. For this you will need a large freezer. You can then parcel up the bones into daily portions. You can also feed frozen bones; some dogs will gnaw them straight away, others will wait for them to thaw. More information is available from the website www.rawmeatybones.com and I would strongly recommend discussing the matter with your breeder or vet first before switching to raw meaty bones.

The BARF Diet

A variation of the raw meaty bones diet is the BARF created by Dr Ian Billinghurst, who owns the registered trademark 'Barf Diet'. A typical BARF diet is made up of 60%-75% of raw meaty bones (bones with about 50% meat, such as chicken neck, back and wings) and 25%-40% of fruit and vegetables, offal, meat, eggs or dairy foods. Bones must not be cooked or they can splinter inside the dog. There is a great deal of information on the BARF diet on the internet.

One point to consider is that a raw diet is not suitable for every dog. You could consider a gradual shift and see how your Goldendoodle copes with the raw bones. You might also consider feeding two different daily meals to your dog - one dry kibble and one raw diet, for example. If you do, then research the subject, and consult your vet to make sure that the two combined meals provide a balanced diet.

NOTE: Only start a raw diet if you have done your research and are sure you have the time and money to keep it going. There are numerous websites and canine forums with information on switching to a raw diet and everything it involves.

....

Food Allergies

Dog food allergies affect about one in 10 dogs. They are the third most common canine allergy for dogs after atopy (inhaled or contact allergies) and flea bite allergies. While there's no scientific evidence of links between specific breeds/crossbreeds and food allergies, there is anecdotal evidence from dog owners in general that some bloodlines do suffer from food allergies or intolerances. Goldendoodles are not regarded as particularly susceptible – although some can be sensitive to grain - but any individual dog of whatever breed can suffer from them.

Food allergies affect males and females in equal measures as well as neutered and intact pets. They can start when your dog is five months or 12 years old - although the vast majority start when the dog is between two and six years old. It is not uncommon for dogs with food allergies to also have other types of allergies. If your Goldendoodle is not well, how do you know if the problem lies with his food or not? Here are some common symptoms of food allergies to look out for:

- Itchy skin (this is the most common.) Your dog may lick or chew his paws or legs and rub his face with his paws or on the furniture, carpet, etc.
- Excessive scratching
- Ear infections
- Hot patches of skin
- Hair loss
- Redness and inflammation on the chin and face
- Recurring skin infections
- Increased bowel movements (maybe twice as often as usual)
- Skin infections that clear up with antibiotics but recur when the antibiotics run out

Allergies or Intolerance?

There's a difference between dog food *allergies* and dog food *intolerance*:

Typical reactions to allergies are skin problems and/or itching

Typical reactions to intolerance are diarrhea and/or vomiting

Dog food intolerance can be compared to people who get diarrhea or an upset stomach from eating spicy food. Both can be cured by a change to a diet specifically suited to your dog, although a food allergy may be harder to get to the root cause of. As they say in the canine world: "One dog's meat is another dog's poison".

Certain ingredients are more likely to cause allergies than others. In order of the most common triggers they are: **Beef, dairy products, chicken, wheat, eggs, corn, and soy** (called soya in the UK, pictured.) Unfortunately, these most common offenders are also the most common ingredients in dog foods!

By the way, don't think if you put your dog on a rice and lamb kibble diet that it will automatically cure the problem. It might, but then again there's a fair chance it won't. The reason lamb and rice were once thought to be less likely to cause allergies is simply because they have not traditionally been included in dog food recipes - therefore less dogs had reactions to them.

It is also worth noting that a dog is allergic or sensitive to an **ingredient**, not to a particular brand of dog food, so it is very important to read the label. If your dog has a reaction to beef, for example, he will react to any food containing beef, regardless of how expensive it is or how well it has been prepared.

Symptoms of food allergies are well documented. Unfortunately, the problem is that these conditions may also be symptoms of other issues such as environmental or flea bite allergies, intestinal problems, mange and yeast or bacterial infections. If your Goldendoodle suffers from ear infections, there could be a number of different causes. It is more likely to be a bacterial or yeast infection due to the lack of air circulation under the hairy ear flap, but a reaction to a certain type of food should also be considered. You can have a blood test on your dog for food allergies, but many vets now believe that this is not accurate enough.

The only way to completely cure a food allergy or intolerance is complete avoidance. This is not as easy as it sounds. First you have to be sure that your dog does have a food allergy, and then you have to discover which food is causing the reaction. Blood tests are not thought to be reliable and, as far as I am aware, the only true way to determine exactly what your dog is allergic to is to start a **food trial**. If you don't or can't do this for the whole 12 weeks, then you could try a more amateurish approach, which is eliminating ingredients from your dog's diet one at a time by switching diets – remember to do this over a period of a week to 10 days.

A food trial is usually the option of last resort, due to the amount of time and attention that it requires. It is also called **'an exclusion diet'** and is the only truly accurate way of finding out if your dog has a food allergy and what is causing it. Before embarking on one, try switching dog food. A hypoallergenic dog food, either commercial or home-made, is a good place to start. There are a number of these on the market and they all have the word **'hypoallergenic'** in the name.

Usually more expensive, hypoallergenic dog food ingredients do not include common allergens such as wheat protein or soya, thereby minimizing the risk of an allergic reaction. Many may have less common ingredients, such as venison, duck or types of fish. Here are some things to look for in a high quality food: meat or poultry as the first ingredient, vegetables, natural herbs such as rosemary or parsley, and oils such as rapeseed (canola) or salmon.

Here's what to avoid: corn, corn meal, corn gluten meal, meat or poultry by-products (as you don't know exactly what these are or how they have been handled), artificial preservatives (including BHA, BHT, Propyl Gallate, Ethoxyquin, Sodium Nitrite/Nitrate and TBHQBHA), artificial colors, sugars and sweeteners like corn syrup, sucrose and ammoniated glycyrrhizin, powdered cellulose, propylene glycol. If you can rule out all of the above, and you have tried switching diet without much success, then a food trial may be the only option left.

Food Trials

Before you embark on one of these, you need to know that they are a real pain-in-the-you-know-what to monitor. You have to be incredibly vigilant and determined, so only start one if you 100% know you can see it through to the end, or you are wasting your time. It is important to keep a diary during a food trial to record any changes in your dog's symptoms, behavior or habits.

A food trial involves feeding one specific food for 12 weeks, something the dog has never eaten before, such as rabbit and rice or venison and potato. Surprisingly, dogs are typically NOT allergic to foods they have never eaten before. The food should contain no added coloring, preservatives or flavorings. There are a number of these commercial diets on the market, as well as specialized diets that have proteins and carbohydrates broken down into such small molecular sizes that they no longer trigger an allergic reaction. These are called '**limited antigen**' or '**hydrolyzed protein**' diets.

Home-made diets are another option as you can strictly control the ingredients. The difficult thing is that this must be the **only thing** the dog eats during the trial. Any treats or snacks make the whole thing a waste of time. During the trial, you shouldn't allow your dog to roam freely, as you cannot control what he is eating or drinking when he is out of sight outdoors. Only the recommended diet must be fed. Do NOT give:

- Treats
- Rawhide (you shouldn't feed this to a Goldendoodle, anyway)
- Pigs' ears
- Cows' hooves
- Flavored medications (including heartworm treatments) or supplements
- Flavored toothpastes
- Flavored plastic toys

If you want to give a treat, use the recommended diet. (Tinned diets can be frozen in chunks or baked and then used as treats.) If you have other dogs, either feed them all on the trial diet or feed the others in an entirely different location. If you have a cat, don't let the dog near the cat litter tray. And keep your pet out of the room when you are eating. Even small amounts of food dropped on the floor or licked off of a plate can ruin an elimination trial, meaning you'll have to start all over again.

Grain

Although beef is the food most likely to cause allergies in the general dog population, there is evidence to suggest that the ingredient most likely to cause a problem in many dogs of all types is grain. Grain is wheat or any other cultivated cereal crop.

Foods that are high in grains and sugar can cause an increase in unhealthy bacteria and yeast in the stomach. This crowds out the good bacteria in the stomach and can cause toxins to occur that affect the immune system. When the immune system is not functioning properly, the itchiness related to food allergies can cause secondary bacterial and yeast infections. These often show as ear infections, skin disorders, bladder infections and reddish or dark brown tear stains. Symptoms of a yeast infection also include:

- Itchiness
- A musty smell
- Skin lesions or redness on the underside of the neck, the belly or paws

Although drugs such as antihistamines and steroids will temporarily help, they do not address the cause. Long term use of steroids is definitely not recommended as it can lead to organ problems.

Switching to a grain-free diet may help your dog get rid of the yeast and toxins in the digestive system. Some owners also feed their dogs a daily spoonful of natural live yoghurt, as this contains healthy bacteria and helps to balance the bacteria in your dog's digestive system - by the way, it works for humans too, although you need more than a spoonful! -others have switched their dogs to a raw diet. If you decide to switch, introduce the new food over a week to 10 days and be patient, it may take two to three months for symptoms to subside – but you will definitely know whether it has worked after 12 weeks.

Wheat products are known to produce flatulence in some dogs, while corn products and feed fillers may cause skin rashes or irritations. It is also worth noting that some of the symptoms of food allergies - particularly the scratching, licking, chewing and redness - can also be a sign of inhalant or contact (environmental) allergies, which are caused by a reaction to such triggers as pollen, grass or dust. Some dogs are also allergic to flea bites. See **Chapter 10. Skin and Allergies** for more details.

If you suspect your Goldendoodle has a food allergy, the first port of call should be to the vet to discuss the best course of action. Many vets' practices promote specific brands of dog food, which may or may not be the best for your dog. Whichever food you buy, make sure you first check every ingredient on the label.

How Much Food?

This is another question I am often asked. The answer is ... there is no easy answer! The correct amount of food for your dog depends on a number of factors:

- Breed/crossbreed
- Size
- Gender
- Age
- Energy levels
- Amount of daily exercise
- Health
- Environment
- Number of dogs in house
- Quality of the food

Some breeds have a higher metabolic rate than others. Goldendoodles are generally regarded as dogs with medium activity levels – although this varies greatly depending on factors such as parent breeds, size and what they get used to. Photo courtesy of Candice Farrell, Ooodles of Doodles, Alberta, Canada.

Generally smaller dogs have faster metabolisms so require a higher amount of food per pound of body weight. Female dogs can be slightly more prone to putting on weight than male dogs. Some people say that dogs which have been spayed or neutered are more likely to put on weight, although this is disputed by others. Growing puppies and young dogs need more food than senior dogs with a slower lifestyle.

Every dog is different. You can have two Goldendoodles from the same litter with different temperaments and energy levels; the energetic dog will burn off more calories. Maintaining a healthy body weight for dogs – and humans – is all about balancing what you take in with how much you burn off. If your dog is exercised for an hour or two a day and has play sessions with other dogs or humans, he will need more calories than, for example, a Goldendoodle who spends most of his time inside the home. And certain health conditions, such as an underactive thyroid, diabetes, arthritis or heart disease, can lead to dogs putting on weight, so their food has to be adjusted accordingly.

Just like us, a dog kept in a very cold environment will need more calories to keep warm than a dog in a warm climate. They burn extra calories in keeping themselves warm.

Here's an interesting fact: a dog kept on his own is more likely to be overweight than a dog kept with other dogs. This is because he receives all of the food-based attention. Manufacturers of cheaper foods usually recommend feeding more to your dog, as much of the food is made up of cereals, which are not doing much except bulking up the weight of the food – and possibly triggering allergies in your dog. The daily recommended amount listed on food sacks or tins are generally too high – after all, the more your dog eats, they more they sell! Because there are so many factors involved, there is no simple answer. However, below we have listed a broad guideline of the average number of **calories** a Goldendoodle with medium energy and activity levels needs.

We feed our dog a dried hypoallergenic dog food made by James Wellbeloved in England. Max has seasonal allergies which make him scratch, but he seems to do pretty well on this food. Here we list James Wellbeloved's recommended feeding amounts for dogs, listed in kilograms and grams. (28.3 grams=1 ounce. 1kg=2.2 pounds.) The number on the left is the dog's **adult weight** in kilograms. The numbers on the right are the amount of daily food that an average dog with average energy levels requires, measured in grams (divide this by 28.3 to get the amount in ounces.) For example, a three-month-old Goldendoodle puppy which will grow into a 10kg (22lb) adult would require around 190 grams of food per day (6.73 ounces.) **NOTE: These are only very general guidelines; your dog may need more or less than this.** Use the chart as a guideline only and if your dog appears to lose or gain weight, adjust his or her feeds accordingly.

Canine Feeding Chart

PUPPY

Size type	Expected adult body weight (kg)	Daily serving (g)					
		2 mths	3 mths	4 mths	5 mths	6 mths	> 6 mths
Small	5	95	110	115	115	110	Change to Adult or Small Breed Adult
Small	10	155	185	195	190	185	

Size type	Expected adult body weight (kg)						
Medium	17	215	265	285	285	280	
Large	25	270	350	375	375	370	
Large	32	300	400	445	450	450	
	40	355	475	525	530	530	
	50	405	545	610	625		
	60	450	605	685			Change to Large Breed Jnr
	70	485	670				
	90	580					

JUNIOR

Size type	Expected adult body weight (kg)	Daily serving (g)						
		6 mths	7 mths	8 mths	10 mths	12 mths	14 mths	16 mths
Medium	10	195	185	175	160			
Medium	17	290	285	270	245	Change to Adult		
	25	390	380	365	330	320		
	32	445	435	415	380	365		Change to Large Breed Adult
Large	40	555	545	530	500	460	460	

ADULT

Size type	Bodyweight (kg)	Daily serving (g)		
		High activity	Normal activity	Low activity
Small	5-10	115-190	100-170	85-145
Medium	10-15	190-255	170-225	145-195
Medium	15-25	255-380	225-330	195-285
Large	25-40	380-535	330-475	285-410
	40-55	535-680	475-600	410-520
Large	55-70	680-820	600-720	520-620
	70-90	820-985	720-870	620-750

SENIOR

Size type	Bodyweight (kg)	Daily serving (g)	
		Active	Normal
Small	5-10	105-175	90-150
Medium	10-15	175-235	150-205
Large	15-25	235-345	205-300
	25-40	345-495	300-425
	40-55	495-625	425-540
Large	55-70	625-750	540-650
	70-90	750-905	650-780

Overweight Dogs

It is far easier to regulate your Goldendoodle's weight and keep it at a healthy level than to try and slim down a voraciously hungry dog when he becomes overweight. Overweight and obese dogs are susceptible to a range of illnesses. According to James Howie, Veterinary Advisor to Lintbells, some of the main ones are:

Joint disease – excessive body weight may increase joint stress which is a risk factor in joint degeneration (arthrosis), as is cruciate disease (knee ligament rupture.) Joint disease tends to lead to a reduction in exercise which then increases the likelihood of weight gain, which reduces exercise further. A vicious cycle is created. Overfeeding Goldendoodles while they are growing can lead to various problems, including the worsening of hip dysplasia. Weight management may be the only

measure required to control clinical signs in some cases. (Pictured is an obese Golden Retriever.)

Heart and lung problems – fatty deposits within the chest cavity and excessive circulating fat play important roles in the development of cardio-respiratory and cardiovascular disease.

Diabetes – resistance to insulin has been shown to occur in overweight dogs, leading to a greater risk of diabetes mellitus.

Tumors – obesity increases the risk of mammary tumors in female dogs.

Liver disease – fat degeneration may result in liver insufficiency.

Reduced Lifespan - one of the most serious proven findings in obesity studies is that obesity in both humans and dogs reduces lifespan.

Exercise intolerance – this is also a common finding with overweight dogs, which can compound an obesity problem as fewer calories are burned off and are therefore stored, leading to further weight gain.

Goldendoodles are very attached to their humans. However, beware of going too far in regarding your dog as a member of the family. **You have to resist those beautiful big, pleading eyes!** It has been shown that dogs regarded as 'family members' by the owner (i.e. anthropomorphosis) are at greater risk of becoming overweight. This is because attention given to the dog often results in food being given as well.

The important thing to remember is that many of the problems associated with being overweight are reversible. Increasing exercise increases the calories burned, which in turn reduces weight. If you do put your dog on a diet, the reduced amount of food will also mean reduced nutrients, so he may need a supplement during this time.

Feeding Puppies

Puppy foods

Feeding your Goldendoodle puppy the right diet is important to help his young body and bones grow strong and healthy. Puppyhood is a time of rapid growth and development, and puppies require different levels of nutrients to adult dogs. For the first six weeks, puppies need milk about five to seven times a day, which they take from their mother. Generally they make some sound if they want to feed. At around six weeks old, puppies are weaned, which means that they are no longer dependent on their mother's milk and are ready to move on to puppy food. Goldendoodle puppies should stay with their breeders until **at least** seven or eight weeks old.

During this time, the mother is still teaching her offspring some important rules about life. Good breeders will tell you in detail what your puppy is being fed and provide you with a sample of the food to take home. Leaving the litter is a very stressful time for puppies and a change of diet is the last thing they need. You should continue feeding the same puppy food and at the same times as the breeder at least for the first few days or weeks at home. Dogs do not adapt to changes in their diet or feeding habits as easily as humans. (Pictured is a photogenic trio of four-week-old standard F1 puppies bred by Renee Sigman.)

You can then slowly change the food based on information from the breeder and your vet. This should be done very gradually by mixing in a little more of the new food each day over a period of seven to 10 days. If at any time your puppy starts being sick, has loose stools or is constipated, slow the rate at which you are switching him over. If he continues vomiting, seek veterinary advice as he may have a problem with the food you have chosen. Puppies who are vomiting or who have diarrhea quickly dehydrate.

Because of their special nutritional needs, you should only give your puppy a food that is approved either just for puppies or for all life stages. If a feed is recommended for adult dogs only, it won't have enough protein, and the balance of calcium and other nutrients will not be right for a pup. Puppy food is very high in calories and nutritional supplements, so you want to switch to a junior or adult food once he leaves puppyhood. Feeding puppy food too long can result in obesity and orthopedic problems – check with your vet on the right time to switch.

Getting the amount and type of food right for your pup is important. Feeding too much will cause him to put on excess pounds, and overweight puppies are more likely to grow into overweight adults. As a very broad guideline, dogs normally mature into fully developed adults at around two years old, although smaller dogs develop more quickly and therefore often reach maturity sooner.

DON'T:

- 🐾 Feed table scraps from the table. Your Goldendoodle will get used to begging for food; it will also affect a puppy's carefully balanced diet
- 🐾 Feed food or uncooked meat which has gone off. Puppies have sensitive stomachs, stick to a prepared puppy food suitable for Goldendoodles, preferably one recommended by your breeder

DO:

- 🐾 Regularly check the weight of your growing puppy to make sure he is within normal limits for his age. There are charts available on numerous websites, just type "puppy weight chart" into Google – you'll need to know the exact age and current weight of your puppy
- 🐾 Take your puppy to the vet if he has diarrhea or is vomiting for two days
- 🐾 Remove his food after it has been down for 15 to 20 minutes. Food available 24/7 encourages fussiness

How Often?

Puppies have small stomachs but big appetites, so feed them small amounts on a frequent basis. Establishing a regular feeding routine with your puppy will also help with toilet training. Get him used to regular mealtimes and then let him outside to do his business as soon as he has finished. Puppies have fast metabolisms, so the results may be pretty quick!

Don't leave food out for the puppy so that he can eat it whenever he wants. You need to be there for the feeds because you want him and his body on a set schedule. Smaller meals are easier for him to digest and energy levels don't peak and fall so much with frequent feeds. There is some variation between recommendations, but as a general rule of thumb:

- 🐾 Up to the age of three or four months, feed your puppy four times a day
- 🐾 Feed him three times a day until he is six months old
- 🐾 Then twice a day for the rest of his life

It's up to you to control your dog's intake and manage his or her diet. Stick to the correct amount; you're doing your pup no favors by overfeeding. Unless your puppy is particularly thin (which is highly unlikely), don't give in - no matter how much your cute Goldendoodle pleads with his big brown eyes. You must be firm and resist the temptation to give him extra food or treats.

A very broad rule of thumb is to feed puppy food for a year, but some owners start earlier on adult food, while others delay switching until their Goldendoodle is 18 months or even two years old. If you are not sure, consult your breeder or your vet.

TIP: Goldendoodles are very loving companions, they are also very motivated by food. If your dog is not responding well to a particular family member, a useful tactic is to get that person to feed the dog every day. The way to a dog's heart is often through his or her stomach.

Feeding Seniors

Once your adolescent dog has switched to an adult diet he will be on this for several years. As a dog moves towards old age, his body has different requirements to those of a young dog. This is the time to consider switching to a senior diet. Dogs are living much longer than they did 30 years ago. There are many factors contributing to this, including better vaccines and veterinary care, but one of the most important factors is better nutrition. Generally a dog is considered to be 'older' or senior if he is in the last third of his normal life expectancy.

Some owners of large breeds - such as Great Danes with a lifespan of nine years - switch their dogs from an adult to a senior diet when they are only six or seven years old. A Goldendoodle's lifespan will vary according to factors such as size and general health - a Standard may typically live for 10 to 12 years, while Minis might live to 14 or 15. The time to change to a senior food depends on these factors as well as energy levels. Look for signs of your dog slowing down or having joint problems. That may be the time to talk to your vet about switching. You can describe any changes at your dog's annual vaccination appointment, rather than having the expense of a separate consultation.

As a dog grows older, his metabolism slows down, his joints may stiffen, his energy levels decrease and he needs less exercise, just like with humans. You may notice in middle or old age that your dog starts to put weight on. The adult diet he is on may be too rich and have too many calories, this would be the time to consider switching.

Even though he is older, keep his weight in check, as obesity in old age only puts more strain on his body - especially joints and organs - and makes any health problems even worse. Because of lower activity levels, many older dogs will gain weight and getting an older dog to slim down can be very difficult. It is much better not to let your Goldendoodle get too chunky than to put him on a diet. But if he is overweight, put in the effort to shed the extra pounds. This is one of the single most important things you can do to increase your dog's quality AND length of life.

Other changes in canines are again similar to those in older humans and as well as stiff joints or arthritis, the might move more slowly and sleep more. Hearing and vision may not be so sharp and organs don't all work as efficiently as they used to, and his teeth may have become worn down. You may also notice that your old Goldendoodle isn't quite as tolerant as he used to be – particularly with boisterous puppies – they can become grumpy old men and women too!

Specially formulated senior diets are lower in protein and calories but help to create a feeling of fullness. Older dogs are more prone to develop constipation, so senior diets are often higher in fiber - at around 3% to 5%. Wheat bran can also be added to regular dog food to increase the amount of fiber - but do not try this if your Goldendoodle has a low tolerance or intolerance to grain. If your dog has poor kidney function, then a low phosphorus diet will help to lower the workload for the kidneys.

Aging dogs have special dietary needs, some of which can be provided in the form of supplements, such as glucosamine and chondroitin, which help joints. If your dog is not eating a complete balanced diet, then a vitamin/mineral supplement is recommended to prevent any deficiencies. Some owners also feed extra antioxidants to an older dog – ask your vet's advice on your next visit. Antioxidants are also found naturally in fruit and vegetables.

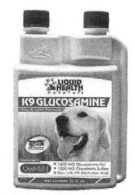

While some older dogs put on weight more easily, others have the opposite problem – they lose weight and are disinterested in food. If your old dog is losing weight and not eating well, firstly get him checked out by the vet to rule out any possible disease problems. If he gets the all-clear, your next challenge is to tempt him to eat. He may be having trouble with his teeth, so if he's on a dry food, try smaller kibble or moistening it with water.

Our dog loved his twice daily feeds until he recently got to the age of 10 when he suddenly lost interest in his daily food, a hypoallergenic kibble. We tried switching flavors within the same brand, but that didn't work. After a short while we mixed his daily feeds with a little gravy and a spoonful of tinned dog food – Bingo! He's wolfing it down again and lively as ever.

Some dogs can tolerate a small amount of milk or eggs added to their food, and home-made diets of boiled rice, potatoes, vegetables and chicken or meat with the right vitamin and mineral supplements can also work well. See **Chapter 14. Caring for Older Dogs** for more information on looking after a senior.

Reading Dog Food Labels

A NASA scientist would have a hard job understanding some dog food manufacturers' labels, so it's no easy task for us lowly dog owners. Here are some things to look out for on labels:

- ❧ The ingredients are listed by weight and the top one should always be the main content, such as chicken or lamb. Don't pick one where grain is the first ingredient, it is a poor quality feed and some Goldendoodles can develop grain intolerances or allergies - often it is specifically wheat they have a reaction to

- ❧ High up the list should be meat or poultry by-products, these are clean parts of slaughtered animals, not including meat. They include organs, blood and bone, but not hair, horns, teeth or hooves

- ❧ Guaranteed Analysis (pictured) – This guarantees that your dog's food contains the labeled percentages of crude protein, fat, fiber and moisture. Keep in mind that wet and dry dog foods use different standards. (It does not list the digestibility of protein and fat and this

Crude Protein (min)	32.25%
Lysine (min)	0.43%
Methionine (min)	0.49%
Crude Fat (min)	10.67%
Crude Fiber (max)	7.3%
Calcium (min)	0.50%
Calcium (max)	1.00%
Phosphorus (min)	0.44%
Salt (min)	0.01%
Salt (max)	0.51%

can vary widely depending on their sources.) While the guaranteed analysis is a start in understanding the food quality, be wary about relying on it too much. One pet food manufacturer made a mock product with a Guaranteed Analysis of 10% protein, 6.5% fat, 2.4% fiber,

Ingredients: Chicken, Chicken By-Product Meal, Corn Meal, Ground Whole Grain Sorghum, Brewers Rice, Ground Whole Grain Barley, Dried Beet Pulp, Chicken Fat (preserved with mixed Tocopherols, a source of Vitamin E), Chicken Flavor, Dried Egg Product, Fish Oil (preserved with mixed Tocopherols, a source of Vitamin E), Potassium Chloride, Salt, Flax Meal, Sodium Hexametaphosphate, Fructooligosaccharides, Choline Chloride, Minerals (Ferrous Sulfate, Zinc Oxide, Manganese Sulfate, Copper Sulfate, Manganous Oxide, Potassium Iodide, Cobalt Carbonate), DL-Methionine, Vitamins (Ascorbic Acid, Vitamin A Acetate, Calcium Pantothenate, Biotin, Thiamine Mononitrate (source of vitamin B1), Vitamin B12 Supplement, Niacin, Riboflavin Supplement (source of vitamin B2), Inositol, Pyridoxine Hydrochloride (source of vitamin B6), Vitamin D3 Supplement, Folic Acid), Calcium Carbonate, Vitamin E Supplement, Brewers Dried Yeast, Beta-Carotene, Rosemary Extract.

and 68% moisture (not unlike what's on many canned pet food labels) – the only problem was that the ingredients were old leather boots, used motor oil, crushed coal and water!

🐾 Chicken meal (dehydrated chicken) has more protein than fresh chicken, which is 80% water. The same goes for beef, fish and lamb. So, if any of these meals are number one on the ingredient list, the food should contain enough protein

🐾 A certain amount of flavorings can make a food more appetizing for your dog. Chose a food with a specific flavoring, like **'beef flavoring'** rather than a general **'meat flavoring'**, where the origins are not so clear

🐾 Find a food that fits your dog's age and size. Talk to your vet or visit an online Goldendoodle forum and ask other owners what they are feeding their dogs

🐾 If your Goldendoodle has a food allergy or intolerance to wheat, check whether the food is gluten free. All wheat contains gluten

🐾 The USA's FDA says: "The term **'natural'** is often used on pet food labels, although that term does not have an official definition either. AAFCO has developed a feed term definition for what types of ingredients can be considered 'natural' and "Guidelines for Natural Claims" for pet foods. For the most part, 'natural' can be construed as equivalent to a lack of artificial flavors, artificial colors, or artificial preservatives in the product." However, as artificial flavors and colors are not used in many foods, the word 'natural' on dog food does not mean a lot, neither are there legal guidelines regarding use of the word 'organic'

🐾 In the USA, dog food that meets minimum nutrition requirements has a label that confirms this. It states: *"[food name] is formulated to meet the nutritional levels established by the AAFCO Dog Food Nutrient Profiles for [life stage(s)]"*

🐾 **'Complete and balanced'** DO have a legal meaning'; these are the words to look for on a packet or tin. The FDA states: "This means the product contains the proper amount of all recognized essential nutrients needed to meet the needs of the healthy animal."

Even better, look for a food that meets the minimum nutritional requirements **'as fed'** to real pets in an AAFCO-defined feeding trial, then you know the food really delivers the nutrients it claims to. AAFCO feeding trials on real dogs are the gold standard. Brands that do costly feeding trials (including Nestle and Hill's, pictured) indicate so on the package

Vitamin E	Min.	425 IU/kg
Ascorbic Acid* (Vitamin C)	Min.	95 mg/kg
Docosahexaenoic Acid* (DHA)	Min.	0.1 %
Eicosapentaenoic Acid* (EPA)	Min.	0.15 %
Omega-3 Fatty Acids*	Min.	0.5 %

* Not recognized as an essential nutrient by the AAFCO Dog Food Nutrient Profiles.

AAFCO Statement: Animal feeding tests using AAFCO procedures substantiate that Science Diet® Puppy Healthy Development Small Bites provides complete and balanced nutrition for growing puppies and gestating or lactating adult female dogs.

Protect from moisture. Store in a cool, dry place.

NOTE: Dog food labeled *'supplemental'* isn't complete and balanced. Unless you have a specific, vet-approved need for it, it's not something you want to feed your dog for an extended period of time. Check with your vet if in doubt. If it all still looks a bit baffling, you might find the following websites very useful, I have no vested interest in either website, but have found them to be a good source of independent advice.

www.dogfoodadvisor.com provides useful information with star ratings for grain-free and hypoallergenic dogs foods for USA brands. It is run by Mike Sagman who has a medical background and analyses and rates hundreds of brands of dog food based on the listed ingredients and meat content. You might be surprised at some of his findings. In the UK there is the website www.allaboutdogfood.co.uk by David Jackson, who used to be employed in the dog food industry.

To recap: no one food is right for every dog; you must decide on the best for yours. If you have a puppy, initially stick to the same food that the breeder has been feeding the litter, and only change diet later and gradually. Once you have decided on a food, monitor your puppy or adult. The best test of a food is how well your dog is doing on it.

If your Goldendoodle is happy and healthy, interested in life, has plenty energy, is not too fat and not too thin, doesn't scratch a lot and has healthy-looking stools, then...

Congratulations, you've got it right!

7. Exercise and Training

One thing all dogs have in common — including every Goldendoodle ever born - is that they need daily exercise, and the best way to give them this is by regular walks. Here is what daily exercise does for your dog - and you:

- It strengthens respiratory and circulatory systems
- Helps get oxygen to tissue cells
- Wards off obesity
- Keeps muscles toned and joints flexible
- Aids digestion
- Releases endorphins which trigger positive feelings
- Helps to keep dogs mentally stimulated and socialized

Whether you live in a small house, an apartment or on a farm, start regular exercise patterns early so your dog gets used his daily routine and gets chance to blow off steam and excess energy. Daily exercise helps to keep your dog content, healthy and free from disease.

How Much Exercise?

The amount of exercise that each individual dog needs varies tremendously. It depends on a number of issues, including size, temperament, natural energy levels, your living conditions, whether your dog is kept with other dogs and, importantly, what he gets used to. Goldendoodles tend to be flexible and, unless you have a particularly high spirited or high energy Doodle, will settle down to a regular routine.

But all dogs need exercise. Don't make the mistake of thinking your Doodle's easy going nature means he doesn't need exercising; he does. Standard Goldendoodles are regarded as having medium to high exercise requirements and will usually take as much exercise as you are prepared to give them; smaller Doodles require less exercise. There is no one-rule-fits-all solution.

Another major factor is your Goldendoodle's ancestry. Was he bred from sporting or show Retrievers and Poodles? Many people forget that the Standard Poodle was bred to work (by retrieving water fowl), as was the Golden Retriever. Ask the breeder about your puppy's parents and grandparents.

Gundogs have high energy drives; they are not usually couch potatoes. A Goldendoodle whose parents were bred to run all day and be on the lookout for game is likely to have higher energy demands – and will probably need more mental stimulation – than one bred to have a calmer nature for the show ring. That's not so say Goldendoodles don't love snuggling up on the couch with you; they most certainly do. They just need their exercise as well. Multigen Goldendoodles produced by responsible breeders have been bred from Goldendoodles selected for their equable temperament as well as their low shedding coat, and so are not as likely to be as "full on" as dogs from a sporting heritage. It is also important to remember that Goldendoodles should be given daily mental exercise as well as physical exercise. This may take the form of games, playing with toys, challenges and events such as Agility.

Ideally, a Standard Goldendoodle should get a minimum of an hour's exercise a day – even longer is better. Smaller Goldendoodles still require a minimum of 30 minutes; again much depends on the individual dog. A fenced garden or yard where he can burn off energy is a big advantage, but should never be seen as a replacement for daily exercise away from the home. While Mini Goldendoodles require less exercise than their larger cousins, you shouldn't think about getting a Goldendoodle if you cannot commit to at least one exercise session every day. If you don't think you have the time or the energy levels for this, then look at getting a dog which requires even less physical and mental stimulation – or don't get a dog.

Your dog will enjoy going for walks on the leash (lead), but will enjoy it far more when he is allowed to run free. A Goldendoodle is never happier than when running after a ball, toy, an old stick or playing with other dogs. Goldendoodles excel at Flyball, Agility and other canine activities which involve lots of energy and mental challenges – see **Chapter 15. Goldendoodles in Action** for more information. Make sure it is safe to let your dog run free, away from traffic and other hazards. And do not let him off the leash until he has learned the recall. There is also growing concern in both North America and the UK about attacks from loose dogs in public parks and dog parks. If you are at all worried about this, avoid public areas and find woodlands, fields, a beach or open countryside where your dog can exercise safely.

Establish a Routine

Establish an exercise regime early in the dog's life. Dogs like routine. If possible, get him used to walks at the same time every day, at a time that fits in with your daily routine. For example, take your dog out after his morning feed, then perhaps for a longer walk in the afternoon or when you come home from work, and a short toilet trip last thing at night.

Daily exercise could mean a walk, a jog, playtime, playing fetch or swimming - an activity loved by most Goldendoodles. Swimming is a great way for dogs to exercise; so much so that many veterinary practices are now incorporating small water tanks, not only for remedial therapy, but also for canine recreation. Most Goldendoodles will dash in and out of the water all day if you'll let them – they are, after all originally bred from the Poodle –

or 'puddle dog' as it was called in Germany, where the breed originated.

Remember that swimming is a lot more strenuous for a dog than walking or even running. Don't constantly throw that stick or ball into the water - your Goldendoodle will fetch it back until he drops; it's great fun and he wants to please you. The same is true if he is following you on your cycle; overstretching him could place a strain on his heart. He should exercise within his limits.

Whatever routine you decide on, your Goldendoodle should be getting walked at least once or more a day and you should stick to it. If you begin by taking your dog out three times a day and then suddenly stop, he will become restless and attention-seeking because he has been used to having more exercise. Conversely, don't expect a dog used to very little exercise to suddenly go on day-long hikes; he will probably struggle. Standard and Medium Goldendoodles may make suitable hiking or jogging companions, but they need to build up to that amount of exercise gradually - and such strenuous activity is not suitable for puppies.

To those owners who say their dog is happy and getting enough exercise playing in the yard or garden, just show him his leash and see how he reacts. Do you think he is excited at the prospect of leaving the property and going for a walk? Of course he is! Nothing can compensate for interesting new scents, meeting other dogs, playing games, frolicking in the snow or going swimming.

Goldendoodles are extremely playful with a great sense of fun and love all these activities. Exercising a dog requires a big commitment from owners – you are looking at daily walks for perhaps 12 or more years when you get a Goldendoodle. Don't think that as your dog gets older, he won't need exercising. Older dogs need exercise to keep their body, joints and systems functioning properly. They need a less strenuous regime, but still enough to keep them physically and mentally active. Regular exercise can add months or even years to a dog's life. Look on the bright side, a brisk walk is a great way of keeping both you and your dog fit – even when it's raining or snowing. (Photo of a multigen puppy at nine weeks courtesy of Melissa Farmer.)

Most Goldendoodles love snow, but it can present problems if they have long, wavy or curly hair. Snow sticks, leading to clumps of snow and ice building up on their paws, legs and tummy. It can build up quickly and heavily. An added problem can be salt or de-icing products on roads and pathways, as some contain ingredients which are poisonous to dogs. As your dog licks or chews at its fur to remove some of the ice balls, it can ingest a dangerous quantity of these chemicals and become ill. This does not mean that you should not go out in the snow; with a bit of thought both you and your dog can enjoy the Winter Wonderland. Use a dog sweater or coat, you can also use coconut oil, which is natural, non-sticky and good for the dog's skin. It acts as an ice repellent and stops it sticking to your dog's fur. Spray it on paws, legs and tummy to cut down on ice balls and when you get home, bathe your dog's paws in warm (NOT HOT) water to defrost the ice. There are also special dog boots (pictured), which are highly effective in preventing ice balls from forming on your dog's paws – provided you can get the boots to stay on.

Mental Stimulation

Goldendoodles are very intelligent. They inherit their brains from both their Poodle and Golden Retriever ancestors. This is good news when it comes to training, as they can learn very quickly. But the downside is that this intelligence needs to be fed. Without sufficient mental challenges, a Goldendoodle can become bored, unresponsive, destructive attention-seeking and/or needy. You should factor in play time with your Goldendoodle – even old ones.

If your Goldendoodle's behavior deteriorates or he suddenly starts chewing things he's not supposed to or barking a lot, the first question you should ask yourself is: "Is he getting enough exercise?" Boredom through lack of exercise or mental stimulation (such being alone and staring at four walls a lot) leads to bad behavior and it's why some Goldendoodles end up in rescue centers, through no fault of their own. On the other hand, a Goldendoodle at the heart of the family getting plenty of daily exercise and play time is a happy dog and a companion second to none.

Exercising Puppies

There are strict guidelines to stick to with puppies, as it is important not to over-exercise young pups. Their bones and joints are developing and cannot tolerate a great deal of stress, so playing fetch for hours on end with your adolescent or baby Goldendoodle is not a good option. You'll end up with an injured dog and a pile of vet's bills.

We are often asked how much to exercise a pup. It does, of course, vary depending on whether you have a Mini, Medium or Standard Goldendoodle as well as the dog's natural energy level. Puppies, like babies, have different temperaments and some will be livelier and need more exercise than others.

The worst danger is a combination of over exercise and overweight when the puppy is growing. Do not take him out of the yard or garden until he has completed his vaccinations and it is safe to do so – unless you carry him around to start the socialization process. Then start with short walks on the leash every day. A good guideline is:

Five minutes of on-leash exercise per month of age

until the puppy is fully grown. That means a total of 15 minutes when he is three months (13 weeks old), 20 minutes when four months (17 weeks) old, and so on.

Slowly increase the time as he gets used to being exercised on the leash and this will gradually build up his muscles and stamina. Too much walking on pavements early on places stress on young joints. It's OK, however, for your young pup have free run of your garden or yard (once you have plugged any gaps in the fence), provided it has a soft surface such as grass, not concrete. He will take things at his own pace and stop to sniff or rest. Once he is fully grown, your dog can go out for much longer walks on the leash. And when your little pup has grown into an adorable adult with a skeleton capable of carrying him through a long and healthy life, it will have been worth all the effort.

A long, healthy life is best started slowly

Puppies have enquiring minds. Get your pup used to being outside the home environment and experiencing new situations as soon as he is clear after vaccinations. Start to train him to come back to you so that you are soon confident enough to let him roam off the leash. Under no circumstances leave a puppy imprisoned in a crate for hours on end. Goldendoodles are extremely sociable; they love being physically close to their humans and do not like being left alone for long periods.

If you are considering getting two puppies, it you might consider waiting until the first pup is older so he can teach the new arrival some good habits. Some say that if you keep two puppies from the same litter, their first loyalty may be to each other, rather than to you as their owner. (Others say this is simply untrue!) Photo: Amy Lane.

As already outlined, your Goldendoodle will get used to an exercise routine. If you over-stimulate and constantly exercise him as a puppy, he will think this is the norm. This is fine with your playful little pup, but may not be such an attractive prospect when your fully-grown Goldendoodle constantly needs and demands your attention and exercise a year or two later, or your work patterns change and you have not so much time to devote to him. The key is to start a routine that you can stick to.

Exercise Tips

❧ Goldendoodles are intelligent and playful with a sense of fun. They need to use their brains. Make time to play indoor and outdoor games, such as Fetch or Hide-The-Toy, regularly with your dog - even elderly Goldendoodles like to play

❧ Don't strenuously exercise your dog straight after or within an hour of a meal as this can cause bloat, particularly in large dogs. Canine bloat causes gases to build up quickly in the stomach, blowing it up like a balloon, which cuts off normal blood circulation to and from the heart. The dog can go into shock and then cardiac arrest within hours. If you suspect this is happening, get to a vet immediately

❧ If you want your dog to fetch a ball, don't fetch it back yourself or he will never learn to retrieve! Train him when he's young by

giving him praise or a treat when he brings the ball or toy back to your feet

🐾 Do not throw a ball or toy repeatedly; your Goldendoodle will do fetch it to please you and because it's great fun. Stop the activity after a while - no matter how much he begs you to throw it again. He may become over-tired, damage his joints, pull a muscle, strain his heart or otherwise injure himself. Keep an eye out for heavy panting and other signs of over-exertion or overheating

🐾 The same goes for swimming, which is an exhausting exercise for a dog. Repeatedly retrieving from water may cause him to overstretch himself and get into difficulties. Gentle swimming is a good low-impact activity for older Goldendoodles

🐾 Some dogs, particularly adolescent ones, may try to push the boundaries when out walking on the leash. If your Goldendoodle stares at you and tries to pull you in another direction, ignore him. Do not return his stare, just continue along the way you want to go, not him!

🐾 Follow the tips earlier in this chapter and/or invest in a set of doggie boots if your Goldendoodle spends a lot of time in snow. It can actually be quite painful for your dog when his legs and face become covered in snowballs. Bathe your dog's legs in lukewarm water - **never** hot – at home afterwards to wash off snowballs and salt

🐾 Vary your exercise route – it will be more interesting for both of you. (Photo of multigen Alki's Bernoulli courtesy of Kelsey Huffer.)

🐾 If exercising off-leash at night, buy a battery-operated flashing/illuminated collar for your dog

🐾 Exercise older dogs slowly and gently once they start to slow down - especially in cold weather when it is harder to get their bodies moving. Have a cool-down period at the end of the exercise to reduces stiffness and soreness; it helps to remove lactic acids from the dog's body

🐾 Make sure your dog has constant access to fresh water. Dogs can't sweat and many Goldendoodles don't shed much either. They need to drink water to cool down

Admittedly, when it is pouring down with rain, freezing cold (or scorching hot), the last thing you want to do is to venture outdoors with your dog. But the lows are more than compensated for by the highs. Exercise helps you to bond with your dog, keeps you both fit; you see different places and meet new companions - both canine and human. In short, it enhances both your lives.

Socialization

Your adult Goldendoodle's character will depend largely on two things. The first is his temperament, which he is born with, and presumably one of the reasons you have chosen a Goldendoodle. (The importance of picking a good breeder who selects breeding stock based on temperament, physical characteristics and health cannot be over-emphasized.) The second factor is environment – or how you bring him up and treat him. In other words, it's a combination of **nature and nurture**. These two factors will form his character. And one absolutely essential aspect of nurture is **socialization.**

Scientists have come to realize the importance that socialization plays in a dog's life. We also now know that there is a fairly small window which is the optimum time for socialization - and this is up to the age of up to around four months (16 weeks) of age. (Photo: Lisa Ross)

Most young animals, including dogs, are naturally able to get used to their everyday environment - until they reach a certain age. When they reach this age they become much more suspicious of things they haven't yet experienced. This is why it often takes longer to train an older dog.

The age-specific natural development allows a puppy to get comfortable with the normal sights, sounds, people and animals that will be a part of his life. It ensures that he doesn't spend his life jumping in fright or growling at every blowing leaf or bird in song. The suspicion that dogs develop in later puppyhood – after the critical window - also ensures that they do react with a healthy dose of caution to new things that could really be dangerous - Mother Nature is clever!

Socialization means learning to be part of society, or integration. When we talk about socializing puppies, it means helping them learn to be comfortable within a human society that includes many different types of people, environments, buildings, sights, noises, smells, animals and other dogs. Your Goldendoodle may already have a wonderful temperament, but he still needs socializing to avoid him thinking that the world is tiny and it revolves around him, which leads to unwanted adult behavior traits.

The ultimate goal of socialization is to have a happy, well-adjusted dog that you can take anywhere. Socialization will give your dog confidence and teach him not to be afraid of new experiences. Ever seen a therapy or service Goldendoodle in action and noticed how incredibly well-adjusted to life they are? This is no coincidence. These dogs have been extensively socialized and are ready and able to deal in a calm manner with whatever situation they encounter. They are relaxed and comfortable in their own skin - just like you want your own dog to be.

You have to start socializing your puppy as soon as you bring him home - waiting until he has had all his vaccinations is leaving it too late. Start by socializing him around the house and garden and, if it is safe, carry him out of the home environment (but do not put him on the floor or allow him to sniff other dogs until he's got the all-clear after his shots.) Regular socialization should continue until your dog is around 18 months of age. After that, don't just forget about it. Socialization isn't only for puppies; it should continue throughout your dog's life. As with any skill, if it is not practiced, your dog will become less proficient at interacting with other people, animals, and environments.

Developing the Well-Rounded Adult Dog

Well-socialized puppies usually develop into safer, more relaxed and enjoyable adult dogs. This is because they're more comfortable in a wider variety of situations than poorly socialized canines. Dogs which have not been properly integrated are much more likely to react with fear or aggression to unfamiliar people, dogs and experiences.

Goldendoodles which are relaxed about other dogs, honking horns, cats, cyclists, veterinary examinations, crowds and noise are easier to live with than dogs who find these situations challenging or frightening. Well socialized dogs also live more relaxed, peaceful and happy lives than dogs which are constantly stressed by their environment. Socialization isn't an "all or nothing" project. You can socialize a puppy a bit, a lot, or a whole lot. The wider the range of experiences you expose him to, the better his chances are of becoming a more relaxed adult. (Photo: Lisa Ross.)

Don't over-face your little puppy. Socialization should never be forced, but approached systematically and in a manner that builds confidence and curious interaction. If your pup finds a new experience frightening, take a step back, introduce him to the scary situation much more gradually, and make a big effort to do something he loves during the situation or right afterwards.

For example, if your puppy seems to be frightened by noise and vehicles at a busy junction, a good method would be to go to quiet road, sit with dog away from - but within sight of - the traffic. Every time he looks towards the traffic say "YES" and reward him with a treat. Keep each session he is still stressed, so you need to move further away. When your dog takes the food in a calm manner, he is becoming more relaxed and getting used to traffic sounds, so you can edge a bit nearer - but still just for short periods until he becomes totally relaxed.

Meeting Other Dogs

When you take your gorgeous and vulnerable little pup out with other dogs for the first few times, you are bound to be a little nervous. To start with, introduce your puppy to just one other dog — one which you know to be friendly, rather than taking him straight to the park where there are lots of dogs of all sizes racing around, which might frighten the life out of your timid little darling. Always make the initial introductions on neutral ground, so as not to trigger territorial behavior. You want your Goldendoodle to approach other dogs with confidence, not fear.

From the first meeting, help both dogs experience good things when they're in each other's presence. Let them sniff each other briefly, which is normal canine greeting behavior. As they do, talk to them in a happy, friendly tone of voice; never use a threatening tone.

Don't allow them to sniff each other for too long as this may escalate to an aggressive response. After a short time, get the attention of both dogs and give each a treat in return for obeying a simple command, such as "sit" or "stay." Continue with the "happy talk," food rewards, and simple commands. Here are some signs of fear to look out for when your dog interacts with other canines. (Photo: Renee Sigman.)

- Running away

- Freezing on the spot

- Tail lifted in the air

- Ears high on the head

- Frantic/nervous behavior, such as excessive sniffing, drinking or playing with a toy frenetically

- A lowered body stance or crouching

- Lying on his back with his paws in the air – this is a submissive gesture

- Lowering of the head, or turning the head away

- Lips pulled back baring teeth and/or growling

- Hair raised on his back (hackles)

Some of these responses are normal. A pup may well crouch on the ground or roll on to his back to show other dogs he is not a threat. Try not to be over-protective, your Goldendoodle has to learn how to interact with other dogs, but if the situation looks like escalating into something more aggressive, calmly distract the dogs or remove your puppy – don't shout or shriek. The dogs will pick up on your fear and this in itself could trigger an unpleasant situation.

Another sign to look out for is eyeballing. In the canine world, staring a dog in the eyes is a challenge and may trigger an aggressive response. This is more relevant to adult dogs, as a young pup will soon be put in his place by bigger or older dogs; it is how they learn. The rule of thumb with puppy socialization is to keep a close eye on your pup's reaction to whatever you expose him to so that you can tone things down if he seems at all frightened.

Always follow up a socialization experience with praise, petting, a fun game or a special treat. One positive sign from a dog is the play bow, when he goes down on to his front elbows but keeps his backside up in the air. This is a sign that he is feeling friendly towards the other dog and wants to play. Although Goldendoodles are not naturally aggressive dogs, aggression is often grounded in fear, and a dog which mixes easily is less likely to be aggressive. Similarly, without frequent and new experiences, some dogs can become timid and nervous when introduced to new experiences.

Take your new dog everywhere you can. You want him to feel relaxed and calm in any situation, even noisy and crowded ones. Take treats with you and praise him when he reacts calmly to new situations. Once he has settled into your home, introduce him to your friends and teach him not to jump up. If you have young children, it is not only the dog who needs socializing! Youngsters also need training on how to act around dogs, so both parties learn to respect the other.

Once excellent way of getting your new puppy to meet other dogs in a safe environment is by joining a puppy or kindergarten class. Ask around locally if any classes are being run. Some vets and dog trainers run puppy classes for very junior pups who have had all their vaccinations. These help pups get used to other dogs of similar age.

Breeders on Exercise and Socialization

We asked a number of Goldendoodle breeders about the suitability of Goldendoodles as family pets and the amount of exercise they need. Bear in mind that many breeders have several dogs and large plots of land and so, to some extent, the dogs exercise themselves for much of the time. Most Goldendoodle owners have just one dog and therefore need to take the dog out for exercise and interaction with other canines.

Lynne Whitmire, Fountain Falls Goldendoodles, South Carolina: "I find that Goldendoodles do well with other family pets, especially when introduced at an early age. I do training with my dogs which involves having them sit and stay while I feed chickens around them. If they get agitated I have them lie down. Doodles need to be introduced to children at an early age. I had an owner call me and say that their Doodle, who had never been around children till recently seemed very shy and even fearful when they went to the local park in their new home. I recommended training sessions with known children that involved them giving the dog treats as a reward for approaching them. It wasn't long before the Doodle loved going to the park and would wag his tail when he saw a child.

"Early socialization is very important and is an important part of Fountain Falls' puppy raising protocol. We have a 12, 12 and 12 puppy protocol. At least 12 people (we try to have men, woman, black, white, young, old and babies, if possible, meet and interact with the puppies) 12 animals other than their mom, 12 sounds, 12 textures - cement, carpet, hardwood, sand, mud, grass, gravel, water, leaves, woods walks, rubber, decks. (Photo courtesy of Lynne.)

"Although I usually take a four-mile walk most days, they also have five acres of underground fence in which to run and play. Doodles love playmates. I find that having another Doodle or dog to play with encourages them to get more exercise. All I have to say is: "There is a bunny in the yard!" and they are out the door, running, sniffing and enjoying the outdoors. My nine-pound Doodle and 70-pound Doodle adore each other and love to be outdoors."

Amy Lane, Fox Creek Farm, West Virginia: "Young puppies are accepting of new situations and people, so it is critical they be exposed to children of all ages as well as other puppies and dogs in the first few months of ownership. Missing this window for exposure can prove to make a dog skittish around things that are new to them later in life. A properly socialized Goldendoodle loves children and learns how to act differently with each child, i.e. more gentle with the toddler and more rambunctious with the teenager. A Goldendoodle that grows up in a home without young children or another dog and is isolated for the first many months or even years may be fearful of children and lack the social skills necessary to appropriately interact with other dogs.

"I find that the larger the Goldendoodle is, the more exercise they seem to need. This may be because a smaller dog playing inside the house is not as disruptive as a large dog running around inside. Each dog varies somewhat, but every dog should have at least moderate exercise daily to stay in good shape. Taking a dog on leashed walks is great, but allowing them to run and play off leash is recommended as well on a daily basis. The need to take the dog on a mile walk is a good incentive for the humans to exercise daily as well! Puppies should not go jogging with their humans until they are at least one year of age and are done with growing."

Janece Schommer, Goldendoodle Acres, Wisconsin:" They are a medium exercise dog. They don't need to be constantly exercised, but truly enjoy a morning and evening walk with you."

Candice Farrell, Ooodles of Doodles, Alberta, Canada: "If your puppy comes from a breeder that makes it her priority to make sure the puppies are well socialized and exposed to a variety of experiences, they will be curious, playful and ready for new experiences, such as meeting new people and pets. It is important to keep your puppy well socialized and exposed to new things." Photo courtesy of Candice.

Christy Stevens, Winding Creek Ranch, Indiana: "In almost all cases, Goldendoodles are amazing around children as young as babies. Of course, no puppy should ever be left with a baby or toddler unattended; they can hurt each other without meaning to. I've known of a few cases where puppies will resource guard around children, but that's usually because a child frequently takes something away that the dog has placed value on.

"Since a dog can typically recognize a child as a lower member of the pack, he or she can act with a show of dominance toward the child. This isn't a breed-specific behavior. It is very important a new puppy owner have an animal behaviorist, as a resource, for situations like this. If caught early, a family and their Goldendoodle can easily be trained to correct any issues that arise. Most of the time, it's simply the dog/human communication gap that is the problem. Goldendoodle puppies generally get along great with other pets they are raised with, even cats.

"Some Goldendoodles are more active than others. It is important to try and get a puppy with the right level of activity to fit your family dynamics; if you aren't very active, you may not do well with a dog that requires a lot of play time. If you want a pup that will grow up to enjoy being a running partner, you will not be well matched with a puppy who is a couch potato. Every Goldendoodle will have different requirements based on their personality. Size will only factor in as to whether or not the exercise can take place in the house or will require more room and therefore be better outdoors.

"Our Doodles get a variety of exercise: leash walks, off-leash walks, swimming and playing ball. It's important to have off-leash exercise, even as simple a game as Fetch in the back yard will help burn off any excess energy and make for a happier, more obedient puppy."

Kelsey Huffer, Alki Goldendoodles, Washington State:" My unspayed female is naturally territorial, but other spayed females and neutered males are generally very docile. Some may have a prey drive, depending on their parentage (another good questions to ask the breeder, if you have other small pets or farm animals like chickens.) With children, every single Goldendoodle I've met has had this empathic ability to understand that these miniature people are more delicate. It's a wonderful thing to see my girl interacting with children, and I'm proud of her composure every time!"

Wendi Loustau, Mustard Seed Ranch Goldendoodles, Georgia: "We exercise them for at least an hour a day, but it depends on the individual dog (walking is not exercise.) Goldendoodles generally react very well around children and other pets; they love people and dogs. Of course, it depends on the individual children and other dogs, though."

Laura Chaffin, Cimarron Frontier Doodles, Oklahoma: "I guess I think of exercise as running, not walking, a dog. I like to have them run hard at least once every day. This is good for small and large dogs. Taking a walk is good, but they really need to run.

"I have found every one of my Goldendoodles to be very safe around children. The Standards are very dependable around children. Breeders need to be cautious when breeding Miniature Goldendoodles, because some Miniature or Toy Poodles can feel threatened by children or strangers, and become reactive. Poodles with this temperament type should never be used for breeding Miniature Goldendoodles. Always select mild mannered, submissive Poodles for breeding. These, usually male, Poodles produce very lovely and child-safe Miniature Goldendoodles."

Sandra Beck, Beck Kennel, Iowa: "It is important to socialize and expose your pup to many new situations at an early age, this will go a long way in boosting their confidence as they mature. Goldendoodles love to learn new things and obedience training opens up a whole new level of relationship between you and your furry family member. Remember to keep training sessions short and enjoyable for both of you. Each Goldendoodle has its own personality traits, just like us. If socializing has begun at a young age they are very loving towards children and other friendly dogs. However, I believe a shy or timid puppy in a litter will do best in a home with no children or other pets to compete with."

Donna Shaw, of Donakell Goldendoodles, Aberdeenshire, Scotland, has been breeding Goldendoodles since 2002 and says: "Well to be honest, my lot don't go out every day on huge long walks as we have a one-acre garden they run around in. Having a few of them means they do tend to exercise themselves, but we do still enjoy our forest walks and they love the beach. Photo of Donna's daughter Kelly Milne competing at Agility with a sprightly 10-year-old Teddy (Teddy the One and Only.)

"We also have our own Agility Club and our Doodles get a lot of exercise there too. One thing I have found is that they adapt really well to any type of lifestyle, whether an older couple taking them out even just one walk a day, to people who enjoy hillwalking or jogging with them."

"The main thing I find is they aren't like your average dog. If one day you can't manage a long walk, they aren't the type to be bouncing off the walls, which is good - especially if sometimes you aren't able to take them out for one reason or another. I do prefer to sell my pups to people with a garden at the very least."

When asked: "How do you find Goldendoodles react around children and other family pets?" Donna replied: "That is their main appeal for me; they are fantastic around children of all ages. Lots of my Goldendoodles have done to autistic children or children with learning difficulties and the difference they make to them is unbelievable. I just think the Goldendoodles sense this and are so gentle and forgiving with them. I have 10 Doodles, five cats, chickens and ducks, and the dogs are fantastic with each and every one of them and accept anything! They seem to be drawn towards children, and I have never seen another breed quite like this."

Lisa Ross, Chai Kennel, Elgin, Canada: "Ours get out in a large fenced area many times a day. If we go walking lots they come along, if we sit around the house they do that as well. They do well with exercise, but they don't demand it or tear apart the house because they didn't get it. I am sure this does vary."

Dyvonia Bussey, of Grace Goldens, Alabama: "We chose the F1 Goldendoodle because they are so kid-friendly; we are a family with three kids. Children come and go at our house daily and we have never had a problem with any of our Doodles or Retrievers. All dogs should be exercised daily. It keeps them out of trouble."

....

Obedience Training

Training a young dog is like bringing up a child. Put in the effort early on to teach them the guidelines and you will be rewarded with a well-adjusted, sociable, individual who will be a joy to live with. Goldendoodles are intelligent, incredibly eager to please and love being with their humans. All of this adds up to one of the easiest breeds of all to train - but only if you are prepared to put in the time too.

Goldendoodles make wonderful companions for us humans, but let yours behave exactly however he wants, and you may well finish up with a willful, attention-seeking adult. Goldendoodles make such natural companion for humans - after all, that is what they are bred for – that it becomes all too easy to treat them like a human and spoil them. The secret of training Goldendoodles can be summed up quite simply:

Praise, Patience, Consistency and Plenty of Rewards.

Praise and treats are the two prime motivators; training should ALWAYS be reward-based, never punishment-based. Goldendoodles are sensitive critters. Many owners would say they have empathy (the ability to understand the feelings of others) and they do not respond well to heavy-handed training methods. They are also highly intelligent, making it easy for them to pick up comands - provided you make it clear exactly what you want them to do; don't give conflicting signals.

Psychologist and canine expert Dr Stanley Coren has written a book called *"The Intelligence of Dogs"* in which he ranks 140 breeds. He used "understanding of new commands" and "obey first command" as his standards of intelligence, surveying dog trainers to compile the list. He says there are three types of dog intelligence:

- Adaptive Intelligence (learning and problem-solving ability.) This is specific to the individual animal and is measured by canine IQ tests
- Instinctive Intelligence. This is specific to the individual animal and is measured by canine IQ tests
- Working/Obedience Intelligence. This is breed-dependent

The brainboxes of the canine world are the 10 breeds ranked in the 'Brightest Dogs' section of his list. All dogs in this class:

- Understand New Commands with Fewer than Five Repetitions
- Obey a First Command 95% of the Time or Better

It will come as no surprise to anyone who has even been into the countryside and seen sheep being worked by a farmer and his right-hand man (his dog) to learn that the Border Collie is the most intelligent of all dogs. The second smartest dog is the Poodle and fourth on the list is the Golden Retriever —so the Goldendoodle has brains on **both** sides of the family.

By the author's own admission, the drawback of this rating scale is that it is heavily weighted towards obedience-related behavioral traits, which are often found in working dogs, rather than understanding or creativity (found in hunting dogs.) As a result, some breeds, such as the Bully breeds (Bulldogs, Mastiffs, Bull Terriers, Pug, Rottweiler, etc.), are ranked quite low on the list, due to their stubborn or independent nature. But as far as Goldendoodles are concerned, given their ancestry, it's true to say that you are starting out with a puppy that not only has the intelligence to pick up new commands very quickly, but he also really wants to learn and please you. Three golden rules when training a Goldendoodle are:

1. Training must be reward-based, not punishment based
2. Keep sessions short or your dog will get bored
3. Keep sessions fun, give your Goldendoodle a challenge and a chance to shine

You might also consider enlisting the help of a professional trainer — although that option may not be within the budget of many new owners. If it is, then choose a trainer registered with the Association of Professional Dog Trainers (APDT); you can find a list for all countries here: https://apdt.com. Make sure the one you choose uses positive reward-based training methods, as the old alpha-dominance theories have been discredited.

When you train your dog, it should never be a battle of wills between you and him; it should be a positive learning experience for you both. Bawling at the top of your voice or smacking should play no part in training. (Photo: Renee Sigman.)

If you have a high spirited, high energy Goldendoodle, you have to use your brain to think of ways which will make training challenging for your dog and to persuade him that what you want him to do is actually what **he** wants to do. He will come to realize that when he does something you ask of him, something good is going to happen – verbal praise, pats, treats, play time, etc.

Establishing the natural order of things is not something forced on a dog through shouting or violence; it is brought about by mutual consent and good training. Like most dogs, Goldendoodles are happiest and behave best when they know and are comfortable with their place in the household. They may push the boundaries, especially as adolescents, but stick to your rules and everything will run much smoother. All of this is done with positive techniques.

Sometimes your dog's concentration will lapse, particularly with a pup or adolescent dog. Keep training short and fun. If you have adopted an older dog, you can still train him, but it will take a little longer to get rid of bad habits and instill good manners. Patience and persistence are the keys here.

Common Training Questions

1. **At what age can I start training my puppy?** As soon as he arrives home. Begin with a few minutes a day.

2. **How important is socialization for Goldendoodles?** Extremely, this can't be emphasized enough. Your puppy's breeder should have already begun this process with the litter and then it's up to you to keep it going when the pup arrives home. Up to 16 weeks' old puppies can absorb a great deal of information, but they are also vulnerable to bad experiences. Pups who are not properly exposed to different people and other animals can find them very frightening when they do finally encounter them when older.

   They may react by cowering, barking, growling, or biting. Food possession can also become an issue with some dogs. But if they have positive experiences with people and animals before they turn 16 weeks of age, they are less likely to be afraid or try to establish dominance later. Don't just leave your dog at home in the early days, take him out and about with you, get him used to new people, places and noises. Goldendoodles that miss out on being socialized can develop behavioral issues as adults.

3. **What challenges does training involve?** Chewing is an issue with most puppies; mouthing and nipping are natural behaviors for puppies. This is particularly true of puppies from working ancestors and, given that both the Poodle and Golden Retriever were both bred to retrieve game with their mouths, it is no wonder that Goldendoodles are "mouthy" when young.

So train your puppy only to chew the things you give him – don't give him your footwear, an old piece of carpet or anything that resembles anything you don't want him to chew. Buy purpose-made long-lasting chew toys.

Jumping up is a common issue with lively Goldendoodles. They love everybody and are so enthusiastic about life, so it's often a natural reaction when they see somebody. You don't, however, want your fully grown dog to jump up on grandma when he has just come back from a romp through the muddy woods. Teach him not to jump up while he is still small.

12 Tips for Training Your Goldendoodle

1. **Start training and socializing early.** Like babies, puppies learn quickly and it's this learned behavior which stays with them through adult life. Old dogs can be taught new tricks, but it's a lot harder to unlearn bad habits. It's best to start training with a clean slate. Puppy training should start with a few minutes a day from Day One when you bring him home.

2. **Your voice is a very important training tool.** Your dog has to learn to understand your language and you have to understand him. Commands should be issued in a calm, authoritative voice - not shouted. Praise should be given in a happy, encouraging voice, accompanied by stroking or patting. If your dog has done something wrong, use a stern voice, not a harsh shriek. This applies even if your dog is unresponsive at the beginning.

3. **Avoid giving your dog commands you know you can't enforce.** Every time you give a command that you don't enforce, he learns that commands are optional. **And one command equals one response.** Give your dog only one command - twice maximum - then gently enforce it. Repeating commands or nagging will make your Goldendoodle tune out. They also teach him that the first few commands are a bluff. Telling your dog to **"SIT, SIT, SIT, SIT!!!"** is neither efficient nor effective. Give your dog a single "SIT" command, gently

place him in the sitting position and then praise him.

4. **Train your dog gently and humanely.** Goldendoodles do not respond well to being shouted at or hit. Keep training sessions short and upbeat so the whole experience is enjoyable for you and him. If obedience training is a bit of a bore, pep things up a bit by 'play training'. Use constructive, non-adversarial games such as Go Find, Hide and Seek or Fetch.

5. **Begin your training around the house and garden or yard.** How well your dog responds to you at home affects his behavior away from the home as well. If he doesn't respond well at home, he certainly won't respond any better when he's out and about where there are 101 distractions, such as food scraps, other dogs, people, cats, interesting scents, etc.

6. **Mealtimes are a great time to start training your dog.** Teach him to sit and stay at dinnertime and breakfast, rather than simply putting the dish down and allowing him to dash over immediately. He might not know what you mean in the beginning, so gently place him into the sitting position while you say "Sit." Then place a hand on his chest during the "Stay" command - gradually letting go – and then give him the command to eat his dinner, followed by encouraging praise - he'll soon get the idea.

7. **Use your dog's name often and in a positive manner.** When you bring your pup or new dog home, start using his name often so he gets used to the sound of it. He won't know what it means in the beginning, but it won't take him long to realize you're talking to him. DON'T use his name when reprimanding, warning or punishing. He should trust that when he hears his name, good things happen. His name should always be a word he responds to with enthusiasm, never hesitancy or fear. Use the words "No" or "Bad Boy/Girl" in a stern - not shouted - voice instead. Some parents prefer not to use the word "No" with their dog, as they use it often around the human youngsters and it is likely to confuse the young canine! You can make a sound like **"ACK!"** instead. Say it sharply and the dog should stop whatever it is he is doing wrong.

8. **Don't give your dog lots of attention (even negative attention) when he misbehaves.** Goldendoodles love their owners' attention. If he gets lots of attention when he jumps up on you, his bad behavior is being reinforced. If he jumps up, push him away, use the command "No" or "Down" and then ignore him.

9. **Have a "No" sound.** When a puppy is corrected by his mother – for example if he bites her with his sharp baby teeth – she growls at him to warn him not to do it again. When your puppy makes a mistake, make a short sharp sound like **"Ack!"** to tell the puppy not to do that again. This works surprisingly well.

10. **Timing is critical to successful training.** When your puppy does something right, praise him immediately. If you wait more than a few seconds he will have no idea what he has done right. Similarly, when he does something wrong, correct him straight away. For example, if he eliminates in the house, don't shout and certainly don't rub his nose in it; this will only make things worse. If you catch him in the act, use your "No" or "Ack" sound and immediately carry him out of the house. Then use the toilet command (whichever word you have chosen) and praise your pup or give him a treat when he performs. If your pup is constantly eliminating indoors, you are not keeping a close enough eye on him.

11. **Give your dog attention when YOU want to** – not when he wants it. When you are training, give your puppy lots of positive attention when he is good. But if he starts jumping up, nudging you constantly or barking to demand your attention, ignore him. Don't give in to his demands. Wait a while and pat him when you want and after he has stopped demanding your attention.

12. **Start as you mean to go on.** In other words, in terms of rules and training, treat your cute little Goldendoodle as though he were fully grown; introduce the rules you want him to live by as an adult. If you don't want your dog to take over your couch or bed or jump up at people when he is an adult, don't allow him to do it when he is small. You can't have one set of rules for a pup and one set for a fully grown dog, he won't understand. Also, make sure that everybody in the household sticks to the same set of rules. Your dog will never learn if one person lets him jump on the couch and another person doesn't.

Remember this simple phrase: **TREATS, NOT THREATS.**

....

Teaching Basic Commands

Sit

Teaching the Sit command to your Goldendoodle is relatively easy. Teaching a young pup to sit still is a bit more difficult! In the beginning you may want to put your protégé on a leash to hold his attention.

1. Stand facing each other and hold a treat between your thumb and fingers just an inch or so above his head. Don't let your fingers and the treat get any further away or you might have trouble getting him to move his body into a sitting position. In fact, if your dog jumps up when you try to guide him into the Sit, you're probably holding your hand too far away from his nose. If your dog backs up, you can practice with a wall behind him.

   NOTE: It's rather pointless paying for a high quality, possibly hypoallergenic dog food and then filling him with trashy treats. Buy premium treats with natural ingredients which won't cause allergies, or use natural meat, fish or poultry tidbits.

2. As he reaches up to sniff it, move the treat upwards and back over the dog towards his tail at the same time as saying "Sit". Most dogs will track the treat with their eyes and follow it with their noses, causing their snouts to point straight up.

3. As his head moves up toward the treat, his rear end should automatically go down towards the floor. TaDa! (drum roll!)

4. As soon as he sits, say "Yes!" give him the treat and tell your dog (s)he's a good boy or girl. Stroke and praise him for as long as he stays in the sitting position. If he jumps up on his back legs and paws you while you are moving the treat, be patient and start all over again. Another method is to put one hand on his chest and with your other hand, gently push down on his rear end until he is sitting, while saying "Sit". Give him a treat and praise, even though you have made him do it, he will eventually associate the position with the word 'sit'.

5. Once your dog catches on, leave the treat in your pocket (or have it in your other hand.) Repeat the sequence, but this time your dog will just follow your empty hand. Say "Sit" and bring your empty hand in front of your dog's nose, holding your fingers as if you had a treat. Move your hand exactly as you did when you held the treat.

6. When your dog sits, say "Yes!" and then give him a treat from your other hand or your pocket.

7. Gradually lessen the amount of movement with your hand. First, say "Sit" then hold your hand eight to 10 inches above your dog's face and wait a moment. Most likely, he will sit. If he doesn't, help him by moving your hand back over his head, like you did before, but make a smaller movement this time. Then try again. Your goal is to eventually just say "Sit" without having to move or extend your hand at all.

Once your dog reliably sits on cue, you can ask him to sit whenever you meet and talk to people (admittedly, it may not work, but it might calm him down a bit.) The key is anticipation. Give your Goldendoodle the cue before he gets too excited to hear you and before he starts jumping up on the person just arrived. Generously reward your dog the instant he sits. Say "Yes" and give him treats every few seconds while he holds the Sit.

Whenever possible, ask the person you're greeting to help you out by walking away if your dog gets up from the sit and lunges or jumps towards him or her. With many consistent repetitions of this exercise, your dog will learn that lunging or jumping makes people go away, and polite sitting makes them stay and give him attention.

'Sit' is a useful command and can be used in a number of different situations. For example, when you are putting his leash on, while you are preparing his meal, when he returned the ball you have just thrown, when he is jumping up, demanding attention or getting over-excited.

Come

This is another basic command which you can teach right from the beginning. Teaching your dog to come to you when you call (also known as the recall) is an important lesson. A dog who responds quickly and consistently can enjoy freedoms that other dogs cannot. Although you might spend more time teaching this command to your Goldendoodle than any other, the benefits make it well worth the investment. By the way, "Come" or a similar word is better than "Here" if you intend using the "Heel" command, as these words sound too similar.

No matter how much effort you put into training, no dog is ever going to be 100% reliable at coming when called and especially not a strong-willed Goldendoodle or one with a high prey drive. Dogs are not machines.

They're like people in that they have their good days and their bad days. Sometimes they don't hear you call, sometimes they're paying attention to something else, sometimes they misunderstand what you want, and sometimes a Goldendoodle simply decides that he would rather do something else.

Whether you're teaching a young puppy or an older dog, the first step is always to establish that coming to you is the best thing he can do. Any time your dog comes to you whether you've called him or not, acknowledge that you appreciate it. You can do this with smiles, praise, affection, play or treats. This consistent reinforcement ensures that your dog will continue to "check in" with you frequently.

1. Say your dog's name followed by the command **"Come!"** in an enthusiastic voice. You'll usually be more successful if you walk or run away from him while you call. Dogs find it hard to resist chasing after a running person, especially their owner. He should run towards you. NOTE: Dogs tend to tune us out if we talk to them all the time. Whether you're training or out for an off-leash walk, refrain from constantly chattering to your dog - no matter how much of a brilliant conversationalist you are! If you're quiet much of the time, he is more likely to pay attention when you call him. When he does, praise him and give him a treat.

2. Often, especially outdoors, a dog will start off running towards you but then get distracted and head off in another direction. Pre-empt this situation by praising your dog and cheering him on when he starts to come to you and before he has a chance to get distracted. Your praise will keep him focused so that he'll be more likely to come all the way to you.

   If he stops or turns away, you can give him feedback by saying "Uh-uh!" or "Hey!" in a different tone of voice (displeased or unpleasantly surprised.) When he looks at you again, smile, call him and praise him as he approaches you.

Progress your dog's training in baby steps. If he's learned to come when called in your kitchen, you can't expect him to be able to do it straight away at the park or on the beach or in the woods when he's surrounded by distractions. When you first try this outdoors, make sure there's no one around to distract your dog. It's a good idea to consider using a long training leash - or to do the training within a safe, fenced area. Only when your dog has mastered the recall in a number of locations and in the face of various distractions can you expect him to come to you regularly.

Down

There are a number of different ways to teach this command. It is one which does not come naturally to a young pup, so it may take a little while for him to master. Don't make it a battle of wills and, although you may gently push him down, don't physically force him down against his will. This will be seen as you asserting dominance in an aggressive manner and your Goldendoodle will not respond well.

1. Give the **Sit** command.

2. When your dog sits, don't give him the treat immediately, keep it in your closed hand. Slowly move your hand straight down toward the floor, between his front legs. As your dog's nose follows the treat, just like a magnet, his head will bend all the way down to the floor. When the treat is on the floor between your dog's paws, start to move it away from him, like you're drawing a line along the floor. (The entire luring motion forms an L-shape.)

3. At the same time say "Down" in a firm manner.

4. To continue to follow the treat, your dog will probably ease himself into the Down position. The instant his elbows touch the floor, say "Yes!" and immediately let him eat the treat. If your dog doesn't automatically stand up after eating the treat, just move a step or two away to encourage him to move out of the Down position. Then repeat the sequence above several times. Aim for two short sessions of five minutes or so per day.

If it doesn't work, try using a different treat. And if your dog's back end pops up when you try to lure him into a Down, quickly snatch the treat away. Then immediately ask your dog to sit and try again. It may help to let your dog nibble on the treat as you move it toward the floor. If you've tried to lure your dog into a Down but he still seems confused or reluctant, try this trick:

🐾 Sit down on the floor with your legs straight out in front of you. Your dog should be at your side. Keeping your legs together and your feet on the floor, bend your knees to make a "tent" shape

🐾 Hold a treat right in front of your dog's nose. As he licks and sniffs the treat, slowly move it down to the floor and then underneath your legs. Continue to lure him until he has to crouch down to keep following the treat

🐾 The instant his belly touches the floor, say "Yes!" and let him eat the treat. If your dog seems nervous about following the treat under your legs, make a trail of treats for him to eat along the way

Some dogs find it easier to follow a treat into the Down from a standing position.

* Hold the treat right in front of your dog's nose, and then slowly move it straight down to the floor, right between his front paws. His nose will follow the treat

* If you let him lick the treat as you continue to hold it still on the floor, your dog will probably plop into the Down position

* The moment he does, say "Yes!" and let him eat the treat

Many dogs are reluctant to lie on a cold floor. It may be easier to teach yours to lie down on a carpet or warm surface. The next step is to introduce a hand signal. You'll still reward him with treats, though, so keep them nearby or hidden behind your back.

* Start with your dog in a Sit

* Say "Down"

* Without a treat in your fingers, use the same hand motion you did before

* As soon as your dog's elbows touch the floor, say "Yes!" and immediately get a treat to give him. Important: Even though you're not using a treat to lure your dog into position, you must still give him a reward when he lies down. You want your dog to learn that he doesn't have to see a treat to get one. Clap your hands or take a few steps away to encourage him to stand up. Then repeat the sequence from the beginning several times for a week or two.

When your dog readily lies down as soon as you say the cue and then use your new hand signal, you're ready for the next step. You probably don't want to keep bending all the way down to the floor to make your Goldendoodle lie down. To make things more convenient, you can gradually shrink the signal so that it becomes a smaller movement. To make sure your dog continues to understand what you want him to do, you'll need to progress slowly.

Repeat the hand signal, but instead of guiding your dog into the Down by moving your hand all the way to the floor, move it almost all the way down. Stop moving your hand when it's an inch or two above the floor. Practice the Down exercise for a day or two, using this slightly smaller hand signal. Then you can make your movement an inch or two smaller, stopping your hand three or four inches above the floor.

After practicing for another couple of days, you can shrink the signal again. As you continue to gradually stop your hand signal farther and farther from the floor, you'll bend over less and less. Eventually, you won't have to bend over at all. You'll be able to stand up straight, say "Down," and then just point to the floor.

Your next job is a bit harder - it's to practice your dog's new skill in many different situations and locations so that he can lie down whenever and wherever you ask him to. Slowly increase the level of distraction, for example, first practice in calm places, like different rooms in your house or in your garden, when there's no one else around. Then increase the distractions, practice at home when family members are moving around, on walks and then at friends' houses, too.

Stay

This is a very useful command, but it's not so easy to teach a lively and distracted young Goldendoodle pup to stay still for any length of time. Here is a simple method to get your dog to stay; if you are training a young dog, don't ask him to stay for more than a few seconds at the beginning.

1. This requires some concentration from your dog, so pick a time when he's relaxed and well exercised or just after a game or mealtimes, especially if training a youngster. Start with your dog in the position you want him to hold, either the Sit or Down position.

2. Command your dog to sit or lie down, but instead of giving a treat as soon as he hits the floor, hold off for one second. Then say "Yes!" in an enthusiastic voice and give him a treat. If your dog tends to bounce up again instantly, have two treats ready. Feed one right away, before he has time to move; then say "Yes!" and feed the second treat.

3. You need a release word or phrase. It might be "Free!" or "Here!" or a word which you only use to release your dog from this command. Once you've given the treat, immediately give your release cue and encourage your dog to get up. Then repeat the exercise, perhaps up to a dozen times in one training session, gradually wait a tiny bit longer before releasing the treat. (You can delay the first treat for a moment if your dog bounces up.)

4. A common mistake is to hold the treat high and then give the reward slowly. As your dog doesn't know the command yet, he sees the treat coming and gets up to meet the food.

Instead, bring the treat toward your dog quickly - the best place to deliver it is right between his front paws. If you're working on a Sit-Stay, give the treat at chest height.

5. When your dog can stay for several seconds, start to add a little distance. At first, you'll walk backwards, because your Goldendoodle is more likely to get up to follow you if you turn away from him. Take one single step away, then step back towards your dog and say "Yes!" and give the treat. Give him the signal to get up immediately, even if five seconds haven't passed. The stay gets harder for your dog depending on how long it is, how far away you are, and what else is going on around him.

Trainer shorthand is **"distance, duration, distraction."** For best success in teaching a stay, work on one factor at a time. Whenever you make one factor more difficult, such as distance, ease up on the others at first, then build them back up. That's why, when you take that first step back from your dog, adding **distance,** you should cut the **duration** of the stay.

6. Now your dog has mastered the Stay with you alone, move the training on so that he learns to do the same with distractions. Have someone walk into the room, or squeak a toy or bounce a ball once. A rock-solid stay is mostly a matter of working slowly and patiently to

start with. Don't go too fast, the ideal scenario is that your Goldendoodle never breaks out of the Stay position until you release him.

If he does get up, take a breather and then give him a short refresher, starting at a point easier than whatever you were working on when he cracked.

Don't use the "Stay" command in situations where it is unpleasant for your Goldendoodle. For instance, avoid telling him to stay as you close the door behind you on your way to work. Finally, don't use Stay to keep a dog in a scary situation.
If you think he's tired or had enough, leave it for the day and come back later – just finish off on a positive note by giving one very easy command you know he will obey, followed by a reward.

 Training requires lots of treats. From the beginning feed your puppy healthy treats, such as carrot pieces or apple slices, and he will continue to regard these as rewards when older. Just as with humans, it is difficult to convince an adult dog that fruit and veg are something special if they have not eaten them much as a child! Melissa Farmer has another tip: "Make sure the treats are just small enough for puppy to get a little taste. If puppy spends too much time eating the treat, you lose his interest. Plus, too many treats can cause stomach upset. I use Bil-Jac training treats - the small size - cut up into even smaller pieces."

Puppy Biting

All puppies spend a great deal of time chewing, playing, and investigating objects. All of these normal activities involve them using their mouths and their needle-sharp teeth. Like babies, this is how they investigate the world. When puppies play with people, they often bite, chew and mouth on people's hands, limbs and clothing.

Play biting is normal for puppies, they do it all the time with their littermates. They bite moving targets with their sharp teeth; it's a great game. But when they arrive in your home, they have to be taught that human skin is sensitive and body parts are not suitable material for biting. Biting is never acceptable, not even from a small dog or puppy.

As a puppy grows and feels more confident in his surroundings, he may become bolder and his bites may hurt someone – especially if you have children or elderly people at home. Make sure every time you have a play session, you have a soft toy nearby and when he starts to chew your hand or feet, clench your fingers (or toes!) to make it more difficult and distract him with a soft toy in your other hand.

Keep the game interesting by moving the toy or rolling it around in front of him. (He may be too young to fetch it back if you throw it.) He may continue to chew you, but will eventually realize that the toy is far more interesting and lively than your boring hand.

If he becomes over-excited and too aggressive with the toy, if he growls a lot, stop playing with him and **walk away**. Although it might be quite cute and funny now, you don't want your Goldendoodle doing this as an adult. Remember, if not checked, any unwanted behavior traits will continue into adulthood, when you certainly don't want him to bite a child's hand – even accidentally.

When you walk away, don't say anything or make eye or physical contact with your puppy. Simply ignore him; this is extremely effective and often works within a few days. If your pup is more persistent and tries to bite your legs as you walk away, thinking this is another fantastic game, stand still and ignore him.

If he still persists, tell him "No!" in a very stern voice, then praise him when he lets go. If you have to physically remove him from your trouser leg or shoe, leave him alone in the room for a while and ignore his demands for attention if he starts barking.

Many Goldendoodles are very sensitive and another method which can be very successful is to make a sharp cry of "Ouch!" when your pup bites your hand – even when it doesn't hurt. This worked very well for us. Your pup may well jump back in amazement, surprised that he has hurt you.

Divert your attention from your puppy to your hand. He will probably try to get your attention or lick you as a way of saying sorry. Praise him for stopping biting and continue with the game. If he bites you again, repeat the process. A sensitive Goldendoodle will soon stop biting you. You may also think about keeping the toys you use to play with your puppy separate from other toys. That way he will associate certain toys with having fun with you and will work harder to please you.

Goldendoodles love playing and you can use this to your advantage by teaching your dog how to play nicely with you and the toy and then by using play time as a reward for good behavior.

 If your puppy is either in a hyperactive mood or over-tired, he is not likely to be very receptive to training. Choose your moments; he will respond better when relaxed.

Clicker Training

Clicker training is a method of training that uses a sound - a click - to tell an animal when he does something right. The clicker is a tiny plastic box held in the palm of your hand, with a metal tongue that you push quickly to make the sound.

The clicker creates an efficient language between a human trainer and a trainee. First, the owner or trainer teaches a dog that every time he hears the clicking sound, he gets a treat. Once the dog understands that clicks are always followed by treats, the click becomes a powerful reward.

When this happens, the trainer can use the click to mark the instant the animal performs the right behavior. For example, if a trainer wants to teach a dog to sit, she'll click the instant his rump hits the floor and then deliver a tasty treat. With repetition, the dog learns that sitting earns rewards.

So the 'click' takes on huge meaning. To the animal it means: "What I was doing the moment my trainer clicked, *that's* what she wants me to do." The clicker in animal training is like the winning buzzer on a game show that tells a contestant he's just won the money! Through the clicker, the trainer communicates precisely with the dog, and that speeds up training.

Although the clicker is ideal because it makes a unique, consistent sound, you do need a spare hand to hold it. For that reason, some trainers prefer to keep both hands free and instead use a one-syllable word like "Yes!" or "Good!" to mark the desired behavior.

In the following steps, you can substitute the word in place of the click to teach your Doodle what the sound means. It's easy to introduce the clicker, spend half an hour or so teaching your dog that the sound of the click means "Treat!" Here's how:

1. Sit and watch TV or read a book with your dog in the room. Have a container of treats within reach.

2. Place one treat in your hand and the clicker in the other. (If your dog smells the treat and tries to get it by pawing, sniffing, mouthing or barking at you, just close your hand around the treat and wait until he gives up and leaves you alone.)

3. Click once and immediately open your hand to give your dog the treat. Put another treat in your closed hand and resume watching TV or reading. Ignore your dog.

4. Several minutes later, click again and offer another treat.

5. Continue to repeat the click-and-treat combination at varying intervals, sometimes after one minute, sometimes after five minutes. Make sure you vary the time so that your dog doesn't know exactly when the next click is coming. Eventually, he'll start to turn toward you and look expectantly when he hears the click - which means he understands that the sound of the clicker means a treat is coming his way.

If your dog runs away when he hears the click, you can make the sound softer by putting it in your pocket or wrapping a towel around your hand that's holding the clicker. You can also try using a different sound, like the click of a retractable pen or the word "Yes."

Clicker Training Basics

Once your dog seems to understand the connection between the click and the treat, you're ready to get started.

1. Click just once, right when your pet does what you want him to do. Think of it like pressing the shutter of a camera to take a picture of the behavior.

2. Remember to follow every click with a treat. After you click, deliver the treat to your pet's mouth **as quickly as possible.**

3. It's fine to switch between practicing two or three behaviors within a session, but work on one command at a time. For example, say you're teaching your Goldendoodle to sit, lie down and raise his paw. You can do 10 repetitions of sit and take a quick play break. Then do 10 repetitions of down, and take another quick break. Then do 10 repetitions of stay, and so on. Keep training sessions short and stop before you or your dog gets tired of the game.

4. End training sessions on a good note, when your dog has succeeded with what you're working on. If necessary, ask him to do something you know he can do well at the end of a session.

Collar and Leash Training

You have to train your Goldendoodle to get used to a collar or harness and leash, and then he has to learn to walk nicely with them. Teaching these manners can be challenging because many young Goldendoodles are very lively and don't necessarily want to walk at the same pace as you.

All dogs will pull on a leash initially. This isn't because they want to show you who is boss, it's simply that they are excited to be outdoors and are forging ahead. If you are worried about pulling on your dog's neck, you might prefer to use a body harness instead. A harness takes the pressure away from a dog's sensitive neck area and distributes it more evenly around the body. Those with a chest ring for the leash can be effective for training. When your dog pulls, the harness turns him around.

Another option is to start your dog on a padded collar and then change to a harness once he has learned some leash etiquette —although padded collars can be quite heavy. Some Doodles don't mind collars; some will try to fight them, while others will slump to the floor like you have hung a two-ton weight around their necks! You need to be patient and calm and proceed at a pace comfortable to him; don't fight your dog and don't force the collar on.

1. The secret to getting a collar is to buy one that fits your puppy now - not one he is going to grow into - so choose a small lightweight one that he will hardly notice. A big collar may be too heavy and frightening. You can buy one with clips to start with, just put it on and clip it together, rather than fiddling with buckles, which can be scary when he's wearing a collar for the first time. Stick to the principle of positive reward-based training and give him a treat once the collar is on, not after you have taken it off. Then gradually increase the length of time you leave the collar on.

IMPORTANT: If you leave your dog unattended in a crate, or leave him alone in the house, take off the collar. He is not used to it and it may get caught on something, causing panic or injury to your dog. So put the collar on when there are other things that will occupy him, like when he is going outside to be with you, or in the home when you are interacting with him. Or put it on at mealtimes or when you are doing some basic training. Don't put the collar on too tight, you want him to forget it's there. If he scratches the collar, get his attention by encouraging him to follow you or play with a toy so he forgets the irritation.

2. Once your puppy is happy wearing the collar, introduce the leash. An extending or retractable one is not particularly suitable for starting off with, as they are not very strong and no good for training him to walk close. Buy a fixed-length leash. Start off in the house, don't try to go out and about straight away. Think of the leash as a safety device to stop him running off, not something to drag him around with. You want a Goldendoodle that doesn't pull, so don't start by pulling him around. You definitely don't want to get into a tug-of-war contest.

3. Attach the leash to the collar and give him a treat while you put it on. The minute it is attached, use the treats (instead of pulling on the leash) to lure him beside you, so that he gets used to walking with the collar and leash. As well as using treats you can also make good use of toys to do exactly the same thing - especially if your dog has a favorite. Walk around the house with the leash on and lure him forwards with the toy.

It might feel a bit odd but it's a good way for your pup to develop a positive relationship with the collar and leash with the minimum of fuss. Act as though it's the most natural thing in the world for you to walk around the house or apartment with your dog on a leash – and just hope that the neighbors aren't watching! Some dogs react the moment you attach the leash and they feel some tension on it – a bit like when a horse is being broken in for the first time. Drop the leash and allow him to run round the house or yard, dragging it after him, but be careful he doesn't get tangled and hurt himself. Try to make him forget about it by playing or starting a short fun training routine with treats. Treats are a huge distraction for most Goldendoodles. While he is concentrating on the new task, occasionally pick up the leash and call him to you. Do it gently and in an encouraging tone.

4. The most important thing is not to yank on the leash. If it is gets tight, just lure him back beside you with a treat or a toy while walking. All you're doing is getting him to move around beside you. Remember to keep your hand down (the one holding the treat or toy) so your dog doesn't get the habit of jumping up at you. If you feel he is getting stressed when walking outside on a leash, try putting treats along the route you'll be taking to turn this into a rewarding game: good times are ahead... That way he learns to focus on what's ahead of him with curiosity and not fear.

Take collar and leash training slowly, give your Goldendoodle time to process all this new information about what the leash is and does. Let him gain confidence in you, and then in the leash and himself. Some dogs can sit and decide not to move. If this happens, walk a few steps away, go down on one knee and encourage him to come to you using a treat, then walk off again.

For some pups, the collar and leash can be restricting and they will react with resistance. Some dogs are perfectly happy to walk alongside you off-leash, but behave differently when they have one on. Proceed in tiny steps if that is what your puppy is happy with, don't over face him, but stick at it if you are met with resistance. With training, your puppy **will** learn to walk nicely on a leash; it is just a question of when, not if.

Walking on a Leash

There are different methods, but we have found the following one to be successful for quick results. Initially, the leash should be kept fairly loose. Have a treat in your hand as you walk, it will encourage your dog to sniff the treat as he walks alongside. He will not pull ahead, as he will want to remain near the treat.

Give him the command **Walk** or **Heel** and then proceed with the treat in your hand, keep giving him a treat every few steps initially, then gradually extend the time between treats. Eventually, you should be able to walk with your hand comfortably at your side, periodically (every minute or so) reaching into your pocket to grab a treat to reward your dog.

If your dog starts pulling ahead, first give him a warning, by saying "**No**" or "**Easy,**" or a similar command. If he slows down, give him a treat. But if he continues to pull ahead so that your arm becomes fully extended, stop walking and ignore your dog. Wait for him to stop pulling and to look up at you. At this point reward him for good behavior before carrying on your walk. Be sure to quickly reward him with treats and praise any time he doesn't pull and walks with you with the leash slack. If you have a lively young pup who is dashing all over the place on the leash, try starting training when he is already a little tired - after a play or exercise session – (but not exhausted.)

Another method is what dog trainer Victoria Stillwell describes as the Reverse Direction Technique. When your dog pulls, say "**Let's Go!**" in an encouraging manner, then turn away from him and walk off in the other direction, without jerking on the leash. When he is following you and the leash is slack, turn back and continue on your original way. It may take a few repetitions, but your words and body language will make it clear that pulling will not get your dog anywhere, whereas walking calmly by your side - or even slightly in front of you - on a loose leash will get him where he wants to go.

There is an excellent video (in front of a beautiful house!) which shows Victoria demonstrating this technique and highlights just how easy it is with a dog that's easy to please. It only lasts three minutes and is well worth watching: https://positively.com/dog-behavior/basic-cues/loose-leash-walking.

CREDIT: With thanks to the American Society for the Prevention of Cruelty to Animals for assistance with parts of this chapter. The ASPCA has a great deal of good advice and training tips on its website at: http://www.aspca.org/pet-care/virtual-pet- behaviorist/dog- behavior/training-your-dog

....

Breeders' Training Tips

Lynne Whitmire: "I advise all of my new owners to go to obedience classes. Even people that have experience with dog training will benefit from the newest positive techniques. It is also valuable socializing experienced for the young dog. I hear from many of my families that our puppies are the 'stars' of the classes.

"I find Doodles to be smart and eager to please. I tell my families that Doodles want to please their people most of the time. It is up to us to learn how to communicate. Of course, there are those times when a Goldendoodle wants to play and "doodle zoom." If I hear from people that they are having behavior problems it mostly comes down to a few reasons. The biggest problem is that the Goldendoodle is not getting enough exercise; although they can sometimes be couch potatoes, they still need plenty of exercise.

"A Doodle that is not getting enough exercise can become destructive and difficult to control. Imagine keeping a teenage boy in his room for eight hours while you are at work and expecting him to behave quietly when you come home. Doodles have a sharp mind and if they are left alone too much they become bored. A bored Doodle will find something to do - and it may not be to your liking: digging, chewing, or tearing up toys or furniture is often a sign that they are not getting enough stimulation. Doggy day care, long walks, and playing in the yard are ways to alleviate the situation. Doodles love to go on car rides.

The third reason is inconsistent commands, and expectations. I urge older children and all adults to attend the obedience classes. Everyone needs to be using the same commands and follow the same rules of behavior. If one person feeds the puppy from the table, then the puppy will naturally expect it from everyone."

Christy Stevens: "Goldendoodles are extremely intelligent and a great choice for owners at novice level and up. However, there are certain things a person needs to understand about how to communicate with their pup if they want to be successful. Always try to think about the message you are sending your dog.

"Did you innocently reward your dog for unwanted behavior? Did you confuse your dog by correcting after too much time has passed? Taking time to understand the language of a dog will help a great deal when raising a puppy. The most important thing is making sure you have time for a new puppy. In fact, the greatest requirement is time. If you want to have a well-trained, adjusted and socialized dog, you need to give him your time - and it will be very rewarding in the end."

Melissa Farmer, FarmerDoodles, Ohio: "Goldendoodles love to please and want to learn. Don't try to do everything at once. Don't move into teaching tricks/obedience until your manners are in place. My recommendation to new families is to only work on the following things: housetraining, crate training, bonding and basic manners...such as no jumping or nipping. Set up a consistent schedule/routine. Taking these steps, you will often see things like automatic sit starting to happen. Once these steps have been successfully completed, move into more formal training of commands."

Candice Farrell: "Smart, eager to please puppies make the best students and that is exactly what you are getting with a Goldendoodle. Keep training time positive and fun and your puppy will excel!"

Amy Lane: "Goldendoodles are extremely intelligent and have a great desire to please. Teaching them what pleases you is in the best interest of the human and the dog. If you teach a Goldendoodle tricks, they love to perform, as it pleases you and provides them with a reward.

"To train a dog, one has to understand how a dog thinks and processes information. If you are new to raising a puppy, it is beneficial to hire a trainer to assist you. Most new dog owners need to be taught how to communicate with their dog; once they have mastered this, they can continue to teach more tricks or behaviors on their own. It is much easier to teach a desired behavior than it is to change an undesirable behavior. Therefore, it is critical that appropriate training begins at eight weeks of age, otherwise, you are always trying to correct unwanted behavior, instead of moving forward with new desirable behavior.

"A big problem is with humans that treat their puppy like a human and try to establish human behaviors which are impossible for dogs. Puppies need to learn there are boundaries and need to have consequences when those boundaries are crossed. They need immediate rewards to enforce the good behavior, unlike a child that can be promised a reward at a later date, such as going for out for an ice cream cone.

Janece Schommer: "Goldendoodles are very easy to train. My best piece of advice for new puppy owners is to have a trained professional come to your home to teach you how to raise your new puppy. There is no shame in not knowing how to raise a pup if you've never done it before and having a professional there, in the flesh, makes it easy to spot mistakes owners are making and offer quick solutions. These are very smart pups!

"Don't get me wrong, Goldendoodles are great dogs, but a good professional can teach you how to make your dog phenomenal!! You're going to be spending the next 12-15 years with this dog. Isn't it worth putting in your time the first six months?" Photo courtesy of Janece.

Kelsey Huffer: "Goldendoodles are very sensitive to requests, very food motivated, and very eager to please. Sometimes you might get a strong willed pup (in my experience, a male) who is too excited about the world to care about a command. It sounds silly, but making sure their eyes are clear of any facial hair is also important for the dog to see your handle signals!"

Laura Chaffin: "I find Goldendoodles very easy to train. To train to come when called, I always whistle and call when it is feeding time. This way, the pup learns that my whistle or call equates to something very good, and if the puppy is running off, a loud whistle and call will bring him back. Also, when the pups are engaged in eating, I make different noises, loud, sharp, vacuum, saw, etc. so that the sound will associate with something comforting. This lessens the pups startling with loud, strange noises. I think the most important things to teach the pup are: to come when called, house manners, crate training, submission to owners, leash, not jumping up, and no biting."

Wendi Loustau: "They are very easy. Most anyone can train most Goldendoodles without any professional help - though I tell everyone to budget for training in case they happen upon any bad habits or behaviors that need to be corrected."

Donna Shaw: "I think training Goldendoodles is extremely easy as they are so intelligent and fast learners, but you have to be consistent with it right from the first day you get them. There is no point in leaving it till they are six months old then wondering why your dog is not behaving.

"Yes, they may be puppies, but training is important and you can still make training fun. I have got a training sheet I give out with my puppy packs and go through it with people and explain why you need to do all the points in the sheet. It's really good as what we as breeders see as second nature can be totally new to people who have never had a dog before."

8. Canine Behavior

Just as with humans, a Goldendoodle's personality is made up of a combination of temperament and character.

Temperament is the nature – or inherited traits - a dog is born with, a predisposition to act or react in a certain way. Not only will a responsible breeder produce puppies from physically healthy dams and sires, but she will also look at the temperament of her dogs and breed from those with good traits.

Character is what develops through the dog's life and is formed by a combination of temperament and environment. How you treat your Goldendoodle will have a huge effect on his or her personality and behavior. Starting off on the right foot with good routines for your puppy is very important; so treat your dog well, spend time with him, socialize, exercise and play with him. All dogs need different environments, scents and experiences to keep them stimulated and well-balanced. Praise good behavior, use positive methods and keep training short and fun. At the same time, be consistent so your dog learns the guidelines quickly. All of these measures will help your Goldendoodle grow into a happy, well-adjusted and well-behaved adult dog who is a delight to be with.

If you adopt a Goldendoodle from a rescue center, you may need a little extra patience. These eager-to-please people-loving dogs may also arrive with some baggage. They have been abandoned by their previous owners for a variety of reasons - or perhaps forced to produce puppies in a puppy mill - and may very well still carry the scars of that trauma. They may feel nervous and insecure or they may not know how to properly interact with a loving owner. Your time and patience is needed to teach these poor animals to trust again and to become happy in their new forever homes.

Understanding Canine Emotions

As pet lovers, we are all too keen to ascribe human traits to our dogs; this is called *anthropomorphism* – "the attribution of human characteristics to anything other than a human being." Most of us dog lovers are guilty of that, as we come to regard our pets as members of the family - and Goldendoodles certainly regard themselves as members of the family....in fact some are convinced that they are the center of it and we belong to them!

An example of anthropomorphism might be that the owner of a male dog might not want to have him neutered because he will "miss sex," as a human might if he or she were no longer able to have sex. This is simply not true. A male dog's impulse to mate is entirely governed by his hormones, not emotions. If he gets the scent of a bitch on heat, his hormones (which are just chemicals) tell him he has to mate with her. He does not stop to consider how attractive she is or whether she is '**the**

one' to produce his puppies. No, his reaction is entirely physical, he just wants to dive in there and get on with it!

It's the same with females. When they are on heat, a chemical impulse is triggered in their brain making them want to mate – with any male, they aren't at all fussy. So don't expect your little princess to be all coy when she is on heat, she is not waiting for Prince Charming to come along - the tramp down the road or any other scruffy pooch will do! It is entirely physical, not emotional. Food is another issue. A dog will not stop to count the calories of that lovely treat (you have to do that.) No, he or she is driven by food and just thinks about getting the treat.

Goldendoodles are very loving and extremely eager to please you, and if yours doesn't make you laugh from time to time, you must have had a humor by-pass. (Photo of Michael and Lisa Ross's Doodle by Sammy G Photography.)

They also want to spend most of their time with their owners. All of these characteristics add up to one thing: an extremely endearing and loving family member that it's all too easy to reward - or spoil. Treating a Goldendoodle like a child – or a puppy like a baby - is a habit to be avoided.

It's fine to treat your dog like a member of the family - as long as you keep in mind that he is canine and not human. Understand his mind, patiently train him to learn his place in the household and that there are some rules he needs to follow – like not jumping up at people or onto the couch when he's covered in mud - and you will be rewarded with a companion who is second to none and fits in beautifully with your family and lifestyle.

Dr Stanley Coren is a psychologist well known for his work on canine psychology and behavior. He and other researchers believe that in many ways a dog's emotional development is equivalent to that of a young child. Dr Coren says: "Researchers have now come to believe that the mind of a dog is roughly equivalent to that of a human who is two to two-and-a-half years old. This conclusion holds for most mental abilities as well as emotions. Thus, we can look to the human research to see what we might expect of our dogs.

"Just like a two-year-old child, our dogs clearly have emotions, but many fewer kinds of emotions than found in adult humans. At birth, a human infant only has an emotion that we might call excitement. This indicates how excited he is, ranging from very calm up to a state of frenzy. Within the first weeks of life the excitement state comes to take on a varying positive or a negative flavor, so we can now detect the general emotions of contentment and distress. In the next couple of months, disgust, fear, and anger become detectable in the infant. Joy often does not appear until the infant is nearly six months of age and it is followed by the emergence of shyness or suspicion. True affection, the sort that it makes sense to use the label "love" for, does not fully emerge until nine or ten months of age."

So, Goldendoodles can truly love us – but we knew that already! According to Dr Coren, dogs can't feel shame, so if you are housetraining your puppy, don't expect him to be ashamed if he makes a mess in the house, he can't; he simply isn't capable of feeling shame. But he will not like it when you ignore him when he's behaving badly, and he will love it when you praise him for eliminating outdoors. He is simply responding to your reaction with his simplified range of emotions.

Dr Coren also believes that dogs cannot experience guilt, contempt or pride. I'm no expert but I'm not sure I totally agree. Take your Doodle to a local dog training class or agility event and just watch him perform - surely your dog's delight is something akin to pride? And they can certainly experience joy. Goldendoodles love your attention, and when they are showing off and lapping up your attention, their reaction can only be described as a mixture of pure joy and pride. What about when they run through the muddy woods and come back with a wonderful present for you in the form of a small, deceased furry mammal - isn't there a hint of pride then?

Many owners and breeders believe that Goldendoodles are intuitive and that they can show empathy - "the ability to understand and share the feelings of another" - and this is one reason why they make such excellent therapy and service dogs. Like many companion breeds, after a while they get into tune with the rhythms of the household and pick up on the mood and emotions of the owner. Your dog's ancestor, the Poodle, is known for being intuitive and having the ability to sense his or her owners' moods, and the Golden Retriever has a temperament second to none.

One emotion which all dogs can experience is jealousy – with Goldendoodles this may be displayed when you give your precious attention to animals other than themselves. Or they may guard their food. An interesting article was published in the PLOS (Public Library of Science) Journal in summer 2014, following an experiment into whether dogs get jealous. Building on research that shows that six-month old infants display jealousy, scientists studied 36 dogs in their homes and video recorded their actions when their owners displayed affection to a realistic-looking stuffed canine.

Over three-quarters of the dogs were likely to push or touch the owner when they interacted with the decoy (pictured.) The envious mutts were more than three times as likely to do this for interactions with the stuffed dog, compared to when the owners gave their attention to other objects, including a book. Around a third tried to get between the owner and the plush toy, while a quarter of the put-upon pooches snapped at the dummy dog!

"Our study suggests not only that dogs do engage in what appear to be jealous behaviors, but also that they were seeking to break up the connection between the owner and a seeming rival," said Professor Christine Harris from University of California in San Diego. The researchers believe that the dogs understood that the stuffed dog was real. The authors cite the fact that 86% of the dogs sniffed the toy's rear end during and after the experiment!

"We can't really speak of the dogs' subjective experiences, of course, but it looks as though they were motivated to protect an important social relationship. Many people have assumed that jealousy is a social construction of human beings - or that it's an emotion specifically tied to sexual and romantic relationships," said Professor Harris: "Our results challenge these ideas, showing that animals besides ourselves display strong distress whenever a rival usurps a loved one's affection."

Typical Goldendoodle Traits

1. Goldendoodles are bred as companion dogs. They are social and sociable dogs and should have a naturally sweet and happy temperament. The definition of "social" is "needing companionship and therefore best suited to living in communities (or families.)"

2. When properly socialized, they make wonderful companions and family dogs and are known for being good with children. Some breeders say that their Doodles are drawn to children and even have an affinity with them.

3. They do not like being left alone for long. If you are away from the home a lot, consider another breed of dog not so dependent on humans for happiness – or wait until you have more time for a dog.

4. One thing which surprises some new owners is the amount of exercise some need, particularly larger dogs, such as Standards. Your Goldendoodle's ancestors were sporting breeds.

5. They love running off the leash, they are generally good swimmers and most love snow (Photo: Christy Stevens.) They also love chilling out and snuggling up with their owners, provided they have had enough exercise.

6. Goldendoodles have been described as "Velcro dogs;" they want to be with you 24/7 and will often follow you from room to room. Spend some time apart to avoid separation anxiety - which they are prone to - and which is stressful for both dog and owner.

7. Goldendoodles are highly intelligent and eager to please you, and are among the easiest of all breeds to train - provided you put the time in. They can be trained to a very high level and also excel in canine competitions where physical and mental agility is required. They need mental as well as physical stimulation, and love both indoor and outdoor games as well as challenging activities which make them think.

8. The same goes for housetraining (potty training); a Goldendoodle can pick it up very quickly, as long as you are extremely vigilant in the beginning.

9. An under-exercised, under-stimulated Goldendoodle will display poor behavior, as any dog would.

10. They are not aggressive dogs and generally get on well with other dogs, provided they have been properly socialized.

Cause and Effect

Treated well, socialized and trained, Goldendoodles make incomparable canine companions. They are affectionate and sociable, they love being around people, form close bonds and entertain their humans - which is why once you've had one, no other dog seems quite the same.

But sometimes Goldendoodles, just like other breeds and crossbreeds, can develop behavior problems.

There are numerous reasons for this; every dog is an individual with his or her own temperament and environment, both of which influence the way he or she interacts with you and the world. Poor behavior may result from a number of factors, including:

- Poor breeding
- Lack of socialization
- Boredom, due to lack of exercise or mental challenges
- Being left alone too long
- A change in living conditions
- Anxiety or insecurity
- Fear
- Being spoiled
- Being badly treated

Bad behavior may show itself in a number of different ways, such as:

- Constantly demanding attention
- Chewing or destructive behavior
- Jumping up
- Excessive barking
- Nipping or biting
- Soiling or urinating inside the house
- Growling
- Aggression towards other dogs or people

This chapter looks at some familiar behavior problems. Although every dog is different, some common causes of unwanted behavior are covered, along with tips to help improve the situation.

The best way to avoid poor behavior is to put in the time early on to socialize and train your dog, and nip any potential problems in the bud. If you are rehoming a dog, you may need extra time and patience to help your new arrival unlearn some bad habits he has picked up along the way.

Ten Ways to Avoid Bad Behavior

Different dogs have different reasons for exhibiting bad behavior; there is no simple cure for everything. Your best chance of ensuring your dog does not become badly behaved is to start out on the right foot by following these simple guidelines:

1. **Buy from a good breeder**. They use their expertise to match suitable breeding couples, taking into account temperament (as well as health, size, coat and color.)

2. **Start training early** - you can't start too soon. Like babies, Goldendoodle puppies have incredibly enquiring minds which can quickly absorb a lot of new information. You can start teaching your puppy to learn his own name as well as some simple commands as soon as you bring him home.

3. **Basic training should start with good manners**: e.g. housetraining, chew prevention, puppy biting and not jumping up, followed by simple obedience commands such as 'Sit', 'Come', 'Stay' and familiarization with a collar and leash or harness. Adopt a gentle approach and keep training sessions short. Goldendoodles are sensitive to you and your mood and do not respond well to harsh words or treatment. Start with five or 10 minutes a day and build up. Often the way a dog responds to his or her environment is a result of owner training and management – or lack of it. Puppy classes or adult canine obedience classes are a great way to start, but make sure you do your homework afterwards. Spend a few minutes each day reinforcing what you have both learned in class - owners need training as well as Goldendoodles!

4. **Start socialization right away** - We now realize the vital role that early socialization plays in developing a well-rounded adult dog. It is essential to expose your dog to other people, places, animals and experiences as soon as possible. Give him a few days to settle in and then start – even if this means carrying him places until his vaccination schedule is complete. Lack of socialization is one of the major causes of unwanted behavior traits. Exposing your Goldendoodle to as many different things as possible goes a long way to help a dog to become a more stable, happy and trustworthy companion.

   IMPORTANT: Socialization does not end at puppyhood. Dogs are social creatures that thrive on seeing, smelling and even licking. While the foundation for good behavior is laid down during the first few months, good owners will reinforce social skills and training throughout a dog's life. Goldendoodles love to be the center of attention and it is important that they learn when young that they are not the center of the universe! Socialization helps them to learn their place in that universe and to become comfortable with it.

5. **Reward your dog for good behavior.** All training should be based on positive reinforcement; so praise and reward your dog when he does something good. Generally Goldendoodles are very keen to please their owners, and this trait speeds up the training process. The main aim of training is to build a good understanding between you and your dog.

6. **Ignore bad behavior**, no matter how hard this may be. If, for example, your dog is chewing his way through your shoes, couch or toilet rolls, remove him from the situation and then ignore him. For some dogs, even negative attention is some attention. Or if he is constantly demanding your attention, ignore him. Remove yourself from the room so he learns that you give attention when you want to give it, not when he demands it. The more time you

spend praising and rewarding good behavior while ignoring bad behavior, the more likely he is to respond to you. If your pup is a chewer - and most are - make sure he has plenty of durable toys to keep him occupied. Goldendoodles can chew their way through flimsy toys in no time.

7. **Take the time to learn what sort of temperament your dog has.** Is she by nature a nervous or confident girl? What was she like as a puppy, did she rush forward or hang back? Did she fight to get upright when on her back or was she happy to lie there? Is she a couch potato or a ball of fire? Your puppy's temperament will affect her behavior and how she responds to the world around her. A timid Goldendoodle will certainly not respond well to a loud approach on your part, whereas an energetic, strong-willed one will require more patience and exercise.

8. **Exercise and stimulation.** A lack of either is another major reason for dogs behaving badly. Regular daily exercise, indoor or outdoor games and toys are all ways of stopping your dog from becoming bored or frustrated.

9. **Learn to leave your dog.** Just as leaving your dog alone for too long can lead to problems, so can being with him 100% of the time. The dog becomes over-reliant on you and then gets stressed when you leave him. This is called *separation anxiety* and something which Goldendoodles are susceptible to, like many breeds which thrive on human contact. When your dog is a puppy, or when he arrives at your house as an adult, start by leaving him for a few minutes every day and gradually build it up so that after a few weeks or months you can leave him for up to four hours.

10. **Love your Goldendoodle – but don't spoil him,** however difficult that might be. You don't do your dog any favors by giving him too many treats, constantly responding to his demands for attention or allowing him to behave as he wants inside the house.

Separation Anxiety

It's not just Goldendoodles that experience separation anxiety - people do too. About 7% of adults and 4% of children suffer from this disorder. Typical symptoms for humans are:

- ❧ Distress at being separated from a loved one
- ❧ Fear of being left alone

Our canine companions aren't much different to us. When a dog leaves the litter, his owners become his new family or pack.

Separation anxiety is on the increase and recognized by behaviorists as the most common form of canine stress.

Millions of dogs suffer from it - as much as 10% to 15% of the canine population. Both male and female Goldendoodles are susceptible because they are companion dogs and thrive on being with people. It is an exaggerated fear response caused by separation from their owner.

It can be equally distressing for the owner - I know because our dog, Max, suffers from this. He howls whenever we leave home without him. Fortunately his problem is only a mild one. If we return after only a short while, he's usually quiet. Although if we silently sneak back home and look, he's never asleep. Instead he's waiting by the patio door looking and listening for our return.

It can be embarrassing. Whenever I go to the Post Office, I tie him up outside and even though he can see me through the glass door, he still barks his head off - so loud that the people inside can't make themselves heard. Luckily the lady behind the counter is a dog lover and, despite the large **'GUIDE DOGS ONLY'** sign outside, she lets Max in. He promptly dashes through the door and sits down beside me, quiet as a mouse!

Tell-Tale Signs

Does your Goldendoodle do any of the following?

- 🐾 Follow you from room to room whenever you're home?

- 🐾 Get anxious or stressed when you're getting ready to leave the house?

- 🐾 Howl, whine or bark when you leave?

- 🐾 Tear up paper or chew cushions, couches or other things?

- 🐾 Dig, chew, or scratch at doors and windows trying to join you?

- 🐾 Foul or urinate inside the house, even though he is housetrained? (This **only** occurs when left alone)

- 🐾 Exhibit restlessness - such as licking his coat excessively, pacing or circling?

- 🐾 Greet you ecstatically every time you come home – even if you've only been out to empty the trash?

- 🐾 Wait by the window or door until you return?

- 🐾 Dislike spending time alone in the garden or yard?

- 🐾 Howl or whine when one family member leaves - even though others are still in the room or car?

If so, he or she may suffer from separation anxiety. Fortunately, in many cases this can be cured, or at least reduced. Dogs are pack animals and being alone is not a natural state for them. Puppies should be patiently taught to get used to isolation slowly and in a structured way if they are to be comfortable with it. A puppy will emotionally latch on to his new owner, who has taken the place of his mother and siblings.

He will want to follow you everywhere initially and, although you want to shower him with love and attention, it's important to leave your new puppy alone for short periods in the beginning to avoid him becoming totally dependent on you. In our case, I was working from home when we got Max. With hindsight, we should have regularly left him alone for short periods more often in the first few months.

Adopted dogs may be particularly susceptible to separation anxiety. They may have been abandoned once already and fear it happening again. And separation anxiety is not uncommon in elderly dogs. Pets age and, like humans, their senses - such as hearing and sight - deteriorate. They become more dependent on their owners and can then get more anxious when they are separated from them - or even out of view.

It may be very flattering and cute that your dog wants to be with you all the time, but insecurity and separation anxiety are forms of panic, which is distressing for your dog. If he shows any signs, help him to become more self-reliant and confident; he will be a happier dog. So what can you do if your dog is showing signs of canine separation anxiety? Every dog is different, but here are tried and tested techniques which have proved effective for some dogs.

Ten Tips to Reduce Separation Anxiety

1. Practice leaving your dog for short periods, starting with a minute or two and gradually lengthening the time you are out of sight.

2. Tire your Goldendoodle before you leave him alone. Take him for a walk or play a game before leaving.

3. Keep arrivals and departures low key and don't make a big fuss. For example, when I come home, Max is hysterically happy and runs round whimpering with a toy in his mouth. I make him sit and stay and then let him out into the garden without patting or acknowledging him. I pat him several minutes later. (He is improving.)

4. Leave your dog a 'security blanket,' such as an old piece of clothing you have recently worn which still has your scent on it, or leave a radio on - not too loud - in the room with the dog. Avoid a heavy rock station! If it will be dark when you return, leave a lamp on a timer.

5. Associate your departure with something good. As you leave, give your dog a rubber toy, like a Kong, filled with a tasty treat. This may take his mind off of your departure. (We've tried this with Max, but he refuses to touch the treat until we return home - and then wolfs it down.)

6. If your dog is used to a crate, then crate him when you go out. Many dogs feel safe there, and being in a crate can also help to reduce destructiveness. Always take the collar off first. Pretend to leave the house, but listen for a few minutes. Never leave a dog in a crate all day.

Warning: if your dog starts to show major signs of distress, remove him from the crate immediately as he may injure himself. You can also leave your dog in a pen, which gives him more freedom. (Photo: Amy Lane.)

7. Structure and routine can help to reduce anxiety. Carry out regular activities, such as feeding and exercising, at the same time every day.

8. Dogs read body language very well, many Goldendoodles are intuitive. They may start to fret when they think you are going to leave them. One technique is to mimic your departure routine when you have no intention of leaving. So put your coat on, grab your car keys, go out of the door and return a few seconds later. Do this randomly and regularly and it may help to reduce your dog's stress levels when you do it for real.

9. Some dogs show anxiety in new places, get him used to different environments and people.

10. Getting another dog to keep the first one company can help, but first ask yourself whether you have the time and money for two or more dogs. Can you afford double the vet's and food bills?

Sit-Stay-Down

Another technique for helping to reduce separation anxiety is to practice the common "sit-stay" or "down-stay" exercises using positive reinforcement. The goal is to be able to move briefly out of your dog's sight while he is in the "stay" position. Through this your dog learns that he can remain calmly and happily in one place while you go about your normal daily life. You have to progress slowly with this. Get your dog to sit and stay and then walk away from him for five seconds, then 10, 15 and so on, gradually increase the distance you move away from your dog. Reward your dog with a treat every time he stays calm.

Then move out of sight or out of the room for a few seconds, return and give him the treat if he is calm, gradually lengthen the time you are out of sight. If you're watching TV with your Goldendoodle snuggled up at your side and you get up for a snack, say 'stay' and leave the room. When you come back, give him a treat or praise him quietly. It is a good idea to practice these techniques after exercise or when your dog is a little sleepy (but not exhausted), as he is likely to be more relaxed.

Canine Separation Anxiety is NOT the result of disobedience or lack of training. It's a psychological condition; your dog feels anxious and insecure. NEVER punish your Goldendoodle for showing signs of separation anxiety – even if he has chewed your best shoes. This will only make him worse.

NEVER leave your dog unattended in a crate for long periods or if he is frantic to get out, it can cause physical or mental harm. If you're thinking of leaving an animal all day in a crate while you are out of the house, get a rabbit or a hamster - not a dog.

Excessive Barking

Goldendoodles, especially youngsters and adolescents, will behave in ways you might not want them to, until they learn that this type of unwanted behavior doesn't earn any rewards. Doodles are not normally excessive barkers, but any dog can bark a lot, until he learns not to.

Some puppies start off by being noisy from the outset, while others hardly bark at all until they reach adolescence or adulthood. Our website gets emails from dog owners worried that their young dogs are not barking enough. However, we get many more from owners whose dogs are barking too much!

Some Goldendoodles will bark if someone comes to the door – and then welcome them like old friends - while others remain quiet. However, they do not make good guard dogs, as they want to be friends with everyone.

There can be a number of reasons why your dog barks too much. He may be lonely, bored or demanding your attention. He may be possessive and over-protective and so barks (or howls) his head off when others are near you. Excessive, habitual barking is a problem that should be corrected early on before it gets out of hand and drives you and your neighbors nuts.

The problem often develops during adolescence or early adulthood as your dog becomes more confident. If your barking dog is an adolescent, he is probably still teething, so get him a good selection of hardy chew toys, such as a Nylabone, or stuff a Kong Toy with a treat or peanut butter to keep him occupied and gnawing. But give him these when he is quiet, not when he is barking, so he doesn't think they are rewards for barking.

Your behavior can inadvertently encourage excessive barking. If your dog barks non-stop for several minutes and then you give him a treat to quieten him, he associates his barking with getting a nice treat. A better way to deal with it is to say in a firm voice: **"Quiet"** after he has made a few barks. When he stops, praise him and he will get the idea that what you want him to do is stop. The trick is to nip the bad behavior in the bud before it becomes ingrained.

If he's barking to get your attention, ignore him. If that doesn't work, leave the room and don't allow him to follow you, so you deprive him of your attention. Do this as well if his barking and attention-

seeking turns to nipping. Tell him to **"Stop"** in a firm voice - not shouting - remove your hand or leg and, if necessary, leave the room. (Photo: Sandra Beck.)

As humans, we can use our voice in many different ways: to express happiness or anger, to scold, to shout a warning, and so on. Dogs are the same; different barks and noises give out different messages. **Listen** to your dog and try and get an understanding of 'Goldendoodle language!' Learn to recognize the difference between an alert bark, an excited bark, a demanding bark, a nervous, high pitched bark, an aggressive bark or a plain "I'm barking 'coz I can bark" bark!

If your Goldendoodle is barking at other dogs, arm yourselves with lots of treats and spend time calming your dog down. When he or she starts to bark wildly at another dog - usually this happens when your dog is on a leash – distract him by letting him sniff a treat in your hand. Make your dog sit down and give a treat. Talk in a gentle manner and keep showing and giving your dog a treat for remaining calm and not barking. There are several videos on YouTube which show how to deal with this problem in the manner described here.

Speak and Shush!

Goldendoodles are not good guard dogs, they couldn't care less if somebody breaks in and walks off with the family silver – they are more likely to approach the burglar for a pat or a treat. But if you do have a problem with excessive barking when somebody visits your home, the 'Speak and Shush' technique is one way of getting a dog to quieten down. If your Goldendoodle doesn't bark and you want him to, a slight variation of this method can also be used effectively to get him to bark as a way of alerting you that someone is at the door.

When your dog barks at an arrival at your house, gently praise him after the first few barks. If he persists, gently tell him that that is enough. Like humans, some dogs can get carried away with the sound of their own voice, so try and discourage too much barking from the outset. The Speak and Shush technique teaches your dog or puppy to bark and be quiet on command. Get a friend to stand outside your front door and say "Speak" - or "Woof" or "Alert." This is the cue for your accomplice to knock or ring the bell – don't worry if you both feel like idiots; it will be worth the embarrassment!

When your Goldendoodle barks, praise him profusely. You can even bark yourself in encouragement...After a few good barks, say "Shush" and then dangle a tasty treat in front of his nose. He will stop barking as soon as he sniffs the treat, because it is physically impossible for a dog to sniff and woof at the same time.

Praise him again as he sniffs quietly and then give him the treat. Repeat this routine a few times a day and your dog will quickly learn to bark whenever the doorbell rings and you ask him to speak. Eventually your dog will bark after your request but BEFORE the doorbell rings, meaning he has learned to bark on command. Even better, he will learn to anticipate the likelihood of getting a treat following your "Shush" request and will also be quiet on command.

With Speak and Shush training, progressively increase the length of required shush time before offering a treat - at first just a couple of seconds, then three, five, 10, 20, and so on. By alternating instructions to speak and shush, the dog is praised and rewarded for barking on request and also for stopping barking on request.

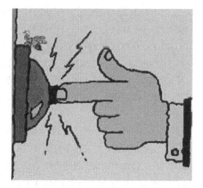

To get your Goldendoodle to bark on command, you need to have some treats at the ready, waiting for that rare bark. Wait until he barks - for whatever reason - then say "Speak" or whatever word you want to use, praise him and give him a treat. At this stage, he won't know why he is receiving the treat. Keep praising him every time he barks and give him a treat. After you've done this for several days, hold a treat in your hand in front of his face and say "Speak." Your Goldendoodle will probably still not know what to do, but will eventually get so frustrated at not getting the treat that he will bark. At which point, praise him and give him the treat. We trained our dog to do this quite quickly and now he barks his head off when anybody comes to the door or whenever we give him the command: "Speak" (he's not quite so good on the Shush!)

Always use your encouraging 'teacher voice' when training; speak softly when instructing your dog, and reinforce the Shush with whisper-praise. The more softly you speak, the more your dog will be likely to pay attention. Goldendoodles respond very well to training when it is kept fun and short.

Aggression

Some breeds are more prone to aggression than others. Fortunately, this is a problem not often seen in Goldendoodles. However, given a certain set of circumstances, any dog can growl, bark or even bite. As well as snarling, lunging, barking or biting, other physical signs of aggression include raised hackles, top lip curled back to bare teeth, ears set high and tail raised.

All puppies bite; they explore the world with their noses and mouths. But it is important to train your cute little pup not to bite, as he may cause a serious injury if he continues as an adult. **And remember, any dog can bite** when under stress – even a Goldendoodle. Here are some different types of aggressive behavior:

- Growling at you or other people
- Snarling or lunging at other dogs while on the leash
- Growling or biting if you or another animal goes near his food
- Growling if you pet or show attention to another animal
- Being possessive with toys
- Marking territory by urinating inside the house
- Growling and chasing other small animals/cars/joggers and/or strangers
- Standing in your way, blocking your path
- Pulling and growling on the leash

Goldendoodles love your attention, but they can also become possessive of you, their food or toys, which in itself can lead to bullying behavior. Aggression may be caused by a lack of socialization, an adolescent dog trying to see how far he can push the boundaries, nervousness, being spoiled by the owner, jealousy or even fear. This fear often comes from a bad experience the dog has suffered or from lack of proper socialization. Another form of fear-aggression is when a dog becomes over-protective/possessive of his owner, which can lead to barking and lunging at other dogs or humans.

An owner's treatment of a dog can be a further reason. If the owner has been too harsh with the dog, such as shouting, using physical violence or reprimanding the dog too often, this in turn causes poor behavior. Aggression breeds aggression. Dogs can also become aggressive if they are consistently left alone, cooped up, under-fed or under-exercised. A bad experience with another dog or dogs can be a further cause. If your dog has been the victim of an attack by other dog or dogs, you may find that he starts to snarl at other dogs, particularly while on the leash. This is fuelled by fear and he needs to slowly regain his confidence and learn that not all dogs want to attack him, so don't overface him with too many dogs at once.

In fact, many dogs are more combative on the leash. This is because once on it, they cannot run away and escape - **fight or flight** - they know they can't run away, so they make themselves as frightening as possible. They therefore bark or growl to warn off the other dog or person. Socializing your Goldendoodle when young is vital. If your Goldendoodle suddenly shows a change of behavior and becomes aggressive, have him checked out by a vet to rule out any underlying medical reason for the crankiness, such as toothache or earache. Raging hormones can be another reason for aggressive actions. Consider having your Goldendoodle spayed or neutered if he or she has not already been done. A leveling-off of hormones can lead to a more laid-back dog.

Another reason for dogs to display aggression is because they have been spoiled by their owners and have come to believe that the world revolves around them. Not spoiling your Goldendoodle and teaching him or her what is acceptable behavior in the first place is the best preventative measure. Early training, especially during puppyhood and before he or she develops unwanted habits, can save a lot of trouble in the future.

Professional dog trainers employ a variety of techniques with a dog which has become aggressive. Firstly they will look at the causes and then they almost always use reward-based methods to try and cure aggressive or fearful dogs. **Counter conditioning** is a positive training technique used by many to help change a dog's aggressive behavior towards other dogs. A typical example would be a dog which snarls, barks and lunges at other dogs while on the leash. It is the presence of other dogs which is triggering the dog to act in a fearful or anxious manner.

Every time the dog sees another dog, he or she is given a tasty treat to counter the aggression. With enough steady repetition, the dog starts to associate the presence of other dogs with a tasty treat. Properly and patiently done, the final result is a dog which calmly looks to the owner for the treat whenever he or she sees another dog while on the leash.

 Whenever you encounter a potentially aggressive situation, divert your Goldendoodle's attention by turning his head away from the other dog and towards you, so that he cannot make eye contact with the other dog.

Aggression Towards People

Desensitization is the most common method of treating aggression. It starts by breaking down the triggers for the behavior one small step at a time. The aim is to get the dog to associate pleasant things with the trigger, i.e. people or a specific person whom he previously feared or regarded as a threat. This is done through using positive reinforcement, such as praise or treats. Successful desensitization takes time, patience and knowledge. If your dog is starting to growl at people, there are a couple of techniques you can try to break him of this bad habit before it develops into full-blown biting.

One method is to arrange for some friends to come round, one at a time. When they arrive at your house, get them to scatter kibble on the floor in front of them so that your dog associates the arrival of people with tasty treats:

As they move into the house, and your dog eats the kibble, praise your dog for being a good boy or girl. Manage your dog's environment. Don't over-face him.

Most Goldendoodles love children, but if yours is at all anxious around them, separate them or carefully supervise their time together in the beginning. Children typically react enthusiastically to dogs and some dogs may regard this as frightening or an invasion of their space.

Some dogs, particularly spoiled companion dogs, may show aggression towards the partner of the owner. Several people have written to our website on this topic and it usually involves a partner or husband. Often the dog is jealous of the attention the owner is giving to the other person, or it could be that the dog feels threatened by him. This is not uncommon with Toy breeds. If this does arise, the key is for the partner to gradually gain the trust of the dog. He or she should show that they are not a threat by speaking gently to the dog and giving treats for good behavior. Avoid eye contact, as the dog may see this as a challenge. If the subject of the aggression lives in the house, then try letting this person give the dog his daily feeds. The way to a Goldendoodle's heart is often through his stomach!

A crate is also a useful tool for removing an aggressive dog from the situation for short periods of time, allowing him out gradually and praising good behavior. As with any form of aggression, the key is to take steps to deal with it **immediately.**

Coprophagia (Eating Feces)

It is hard for us to understand why a dog would want to eat his or any other animal's feces (stools, poop or poo, call it what you will), but it does happen. There is plenty of anecdotal evidence that some dogs love the stuff. Nobody fully understands why dogs do this, it may simply be an unpleasant behavior trait or there could be an underlying reason. It is also thought that the inhumane and useless housetraining technique of "sticking the dog's nose in it" when he has eliminated inside the house can also encourage coprophagia.

If your dog eats feces from the cat litter tray - a problem several owners have contacted us about - the first thing to do is to place the litter tray somewhere where your dog can't get to it – but the cat can. Perhaps on a shelf or put a guard around it, small enough for the cat to get through but not your Goldendoodle. Our dog sometimes eats cow or horse manure when out in the countryside. He usually stops when we tell him to and he hasn't suffered any after effects – so far. But again, this is a very unpleasant habit as the offending material sticks to the fur around his mouth and has to be cleaned off.

Sometimes he rolls in the stuff and then has to be washed down. You may find that your Goldendoodle will roll in fox poop to cover the fox's scent. It's a good idea to avoid areas you know are frequented by foxes if you can, as their feces can transmit several diseases, including Canine Parvovirus or lungworm – although neither of these should pose a serious health risk if your dog is up to date with vaccinations/titers and worming medication.

Vets have found that canine diets with low levels of fiber and high levels of starch increase the likelihood of coprophagia. If your dog is eating poop, first check his diet is nutritionally complete – is the first ingredient on the packet or tin corn (bad) or meat (good)? Does he look underweight? Check you are feeding the right amount. If there is no underlying medical reason, you'll have to try and modify your dog's behavior. Remove cat litter trays, clean up after your dog and don't allow him to eat his own feces. If it's not there, he can't eat it. Don't reprimand for this behavior. A better technique is to distract your dog while he is in the act and then remove the offending material.

Coprophagia is sometimes seen in pups aged between six months to a year and often disappears after this age.

....

In extreme cases, when a dog exhibits persistent bad behavior that the owner is unable to correct, a canine professional may be the answer. However, this is not an inexpensive option. Far better to spend time training and socializing your dog as soon as you get him or her.

Important: This chapter provides a general overview of canine behavior. If your Goldendoodle exhibits persistent behavioral problems - particularly if he or she is aggressive towards people or other dogs - consider seeking help from a reputable canine behaviorist, such as those listed the Association of Professional Dog Trainers at https://apdt.com.

9. Goldendoodle Health

There is not a single breed or crossbreed (hybrid) without the potential for some genetic weaknesses. All dogs - whether pedigrees, crossbreeds or Heinz 57s - can develop genetic health problems, just as people can inherit diseases from their parents and grandparents. It's all to do with genes passed down through the generations.

Specific genetic diseases within purebred dogs are not uncommon. For example, German Shepherds are more prone to hip problems than some other breeds, and 30% of Dalmatians have problems with their hearing. If you get a German Shepherd or a Dalmatian, your dog is not bound to suffer from these issues, but he or she will statistically be more likely to have them than a breed with no history of the complaint.

The way that these problems are being reduced within the breeds is by selective breeding from health-tested stock, i.e. NOT breeding from dogs which carry the gene or genes for specific health issues. And with Goldendoodles, the DNA testing of dams and sires (puppy parents) is the key to identifying which dogs may pass on a disease. By not breeding from these dogs, responsible breeders are playing a major role in reducing genetic illnesses.

Many people believe that a crossbreed will naturally be healthier than a pedigree or purebred dog. This can be true, but is not automatically the case. Mating a Poodle with a Golden Retriever does not **guarantee** healthier hybrid puppies – two unhealthy parents will in all likelihood produce unhealthy pups. For a more information on this topic, read the section on **Hybrid Vigor, Chapter 1.**

There's also the belief that a bigger gene pool caused by mixing these two breeds may lower the chances of a dog developing certain inherited diseases. But if a breeder interbreeds her dogs (i.e. mates closely related dogs, as has often happened with purebred lines in the past), then the gene pool becomes reduced again, leading to a greater chance of health problems.

The Goldendoodle is a crossbreed, yet can be susceptible to certain eye or joint problems, and Cavapoos, for example, are at medium risk of suffering from cataracts and other eye issues. You can't see inside your puppy, but your chances of getting a puppy with no hereditary problems is **greatly increased** if you buy from a good breeder who DNA health tests her breeding stock. It's also a good idea to ask to physically see the parents (or at least the mother, if possible) and all of their and the puppy's health certificates.

Amy Lane, Fox Creek Farm, West Virginia, and founder of GANA (Goldendoodle Association of North America), says: "There are many health issues that are prevalent in the Goldendoodle's parent breeds (Golden Retriever and Poodle) and any health issue shared by both breeds can affect the Goldendoodle. Currently, GANA requires or recommends testing and certification for: heart problems (sub aortic stenosis), eyes (multiple disorders, with cataracts being the most common), hip and elbow dysplasia, patella luxation, the bleeding disorder von Willebrands Disease, two mutations of Progressive Retinal Atrophy (one a Poodle mutation and the other a Golden Retriever

mutation and both cause incurable blindness), and Degenerative Myelopathy, which causes paralysis of the rear end. Another health issue that has no known test is cancer.

"One of the biggest threats to the Goldendoodle is caused by breeders who do no health testing on their parent dogs, or who breed dogs with known health issues. Breeders that inbreed their dogs cause recessive genes in their lines to become dominant expressed genes. The American Kennel Club (AKC) does not require any health testing to be done on breeding purebred dogs. It is my goal to ensure the Goldendoodle never becomes an AKC-recognized breed, as GANA would not be able to enforce good breeding practices, such as breeding only fully health-tested dogs to only unrelated dogs."

Janece Schommer, of Goldendoodle Acres, Wisconsin, has this advice for prospective owners: "All large breed dogs share hip dysplasia as a potential health issue. The best way to prevent it occurring is by genetic testing. Make sure you get a pup whose parents, grandparents, etc. have had their hips approved by either OFA or PennHip (BVA in the UK.)

"The biggest threat to the future of the Goldendoodle, in my opinion, would be not to learn the lessons from purebred breeds. As certain traits or looks were being developed, other things were happening genetically that were unknown at the time. Once all dogs in a breed are affected or carry a genetic issue, there is no way to eliminate it from their gene pool. GANA is dedicated to developing the healthiest dogs possible. We're careful in our genetic testing to ensure that we are creating healthy dogs on the inside as well as beautiful dogs on the outside. GANA is the only Goldendoodle registry in America and requires any breeders who would like to be members to do genetic testing of their potential breeding stock before they can be labeled 'a GANA dog'."

Goldendoodle Insurance

Another point to consider is insurance for your new puppy or adult dog. The best time to get pet insurance is BEFORE you bring your dog home and before any health issues develop. Don't wait until you need to seek veterinary help – bite the bullet and take out annual insurance. If you can afford it, take out life cover. This may be more expensive, but will cover your dog throughout his or her lifetime - including for recurring or chronic ailments, such as eye or joint problems. Some breeders give free four-week insurance in their puppy packs, which gives new owners sufficient time to sort out long term cover.

Insuring a healthy puppy or adult dog is the only sure fire way to ensure vets' bills are covered before anything unforeseen happens - and you'd be a rare owner if you didn't use your policy at least once during your dog's lifetime. Fortunately, Goldendoodles are not one of the most expensive dogs to insure - even so, it's not cheap. Insurance may cost up to £50 a month in the UK, depending on the level of cover ($25 to $75 in the US) - and if you make a claim, the monthly premium will increase. On the plus side, you'll have peace of mind and you'll know how much you have to shell out every month.

The other side of the coin is that with advances in veterinary science, there is so much more vets can do to help an ailing dog - but at a cost. Surgical procedures often rack up bills of thousands of pounds or dollars. In the US, Embrace Pet Insurance estimates the cost of diagnosing and treating hip dysplasia at anything from $1,500 to $6,000 dollars, and up to $5,000 for cataracts. The company says on its website: "Pet insurance for Goldendoodles costs more than for mixed breed dogs. This is because Goldendoodles are more likely than mixed breed dogs to make claims for hereditary conditions that are expensive to treat."

In the UK, Bought By Many has teamed up with insurers More Than to launch a policy specifically for Goldendoodles which offers a 20% discount on their normal rates. Visit http://bit.ly/1QiFzoi for details. Cover for a 10-week-old puppy ranges from around £12 to £26 a month.

Another point to consider is that desirable purebreds and crossbreeds like the Goldendoodle are at increasing risk of theft by criminals, including organized gangs. With the purchase price of puppies rising, dognapping more than quadrupled in the UK between 2010 and 2015; with some 50 dogs a day being stolen. Some 49% of dogs are snatched from owners' gardens and 13% from peoples' homes. If you take out a policy, check that theft is included. Although nothing can ever replace Man's Best Friend, a good insurance policy will ensure that you are not out of pocket.

In the US, Consumers' Advocate have named the top 10 pet insurance companies, taking into account reimbursement policies, coverage and customers' reviews. Here is their league table: 1. Healthy Paws, 2. PetPlan, 3. Trupanion, 4. Embrace, 5. Pets Best, 6. PetFirst, 7. VPI Pet Insurance, 8. Pet Partners, 9. ASPCA Pet Health Insurance, 10. Pet Premium.

The information in this chapter is not written to frighten new owners, but to help you to recognize symptoms of the main conditions affecting Goldendoodles and enable you to take prompt action should the need arise. There are also a number of measures you can take to prevent or reduce the chances of certain physical and behavioral problems developing, including keeping your dog's weight in check and giving him regular daily exercise.

....

Three Golden Tips

There are three golden tips for anybody thinking about owning a Goldendoodle which will in all likelihood save you a lot of money and heartache.

Tip Number 1: Buy a well-bred puppy

Scientists have come to realize the important role that genetics play in determining a person's long-term health – and the same is true of dogs. This means ensuring your puppy comes from a reputable breeder who selects the parents based on a number of factors; mainly health and temperament. Pictured is a litter bred by Janece Schommer. A good Goldendoodle breeder selects their stock based on:

* General health and DNA testing of the parents
* Temperament
* Conformation (physical structure)
* Coat type

Although well-bred Goldendoodle puppies are expensive, many responsible breeders do not make a lot of money from their sale, often incurring high bills for health checks, veterinary fees, specialized food, etc. The main concern of a good breeder is to produce healthy puppies with good temperaments.

It's better to spend time beforehand choosing a puppy which has been properly bred than to spend a great deal of time and money later as your wonderful pet bought from an online advert or pet shop develops health problems due to poor breeding, not to mention the heartache that causes. So spend some time to find a reputable breeder and read **Chapter 2. Choosing a Puppy** for information on finding one and knowing the right questions to ask.

* Don't buy a puppy from a pet shop. No reputable breeder allows their pups to end up in pet shops

* Don't buy a puppy from a small ad on a general website

* Don't buy a pup or adult Goldendoodle unseen with a credit card – visit the breeder at least once. This does not always happen in the USA due to distances involved. We would always recommend visiting the breeder's house, but if you don't, then make 100% sure you have done your research and you've chosen a puppy from fully DNA-tested parents.

Tip Number 2: Get pet insurance as soon as you get your dog

Don't wait until he or she has a health issue and needs to see a vet. Most insurers will exclude all pre-existing conditions on their policies. When choosing insurance check the small print to make sure that any condition which might occur is covered, and that if the problem is a chronic (long term) or recurring one, then it will continue to be covered year after year. When you are working out costs for getting a puppy, factor in the annual or monthly cost of good pet insurance and trips to a vet for check-ups, vaccinations, etc.

Tip Number 3: Find a good vet

Ask around your pet-owning friends, rather than just going to the first one you find. A vet that knows your dog from his or her vaccinations as a puppy and then right through his or her life is more likely to understand your dog and diagnose quickly and correctly when something is wrong. If you visit a big veterinary practice, ask for the vet by name when you make an appointment. We all want our dogs to be healthy -so how can you tell if yours is? Well, here are some positive things to look for in a healthy Goldendoodle.

The Signs of a Healthy Goldendoodle

1. **Ears** – If you are choosing a puppy, gently clap your hands behind the pup (not so loud as to frighten him) to see if he reacts. If not, this may be a sign of deafness. Ears can be a problem with some Goldendoodles. The folded ear flaps can hide dirt and dust and should be inspected regularly for infection or ear mites as part of your normal grooming process. An unpleasant smell, redness or inflammation are all signs of infection. Some wax inside the ear – usually brown or yellowy - is normal; lots of wax or crusty wax is not. Tell-tale signs of an ear infection are scratching the ears or shaking the head a lot, usually accompanied by an unpleasant odor around the ears.

2. **Coat and skin** – these are easy-to-monitor indicators of a healthy dog. A Goldendoodle's coat, regardless of length and curliness, should be soft to the touch. Dandruff, bald spots, a dull lifeless coat, a discolored or oily coat, or one which loses excessive hair, can all be signs that something is amiss. Skin should be smooth without redness. If your dog is scratching, licking or

biting himself a lot, he may have a condition which needs addressing before he makes it worse. Open sores, scales, scabs, red patches or growths can be a sign of a problem. Signs of fleas, ticks and other external parasites should be treated immediately. Check there are no small black specks, which may be fleas, on the coat or bedding.

3. **Mouth** – Gums should be a healthy pink or with black pigmentation. A change in color can be an indicator of a health issue. Paleness or whiteness can be a sign of anemia or lack of oxygen due to heart or breathing problems. Blue gums or tongue area sign that your Goldendoodle is not breathing properly. Red, inflamed gums can be a sign of gingivitis or other tooth disease. Again, your dog's breath should smell OK. Young dogs will have sparkling white teeth, whereas older dogs will have darker teeth, but they should not have any hard white, yellow, green or brown bits.

4. **Nose** – a dog's nose is an indicator of health symptoms. It should normally be moist and cold to the touch as well as free from clear, watery secretions. Any yellow, green or foul smelling discharge is not normal - in younger dogs this can be a sign of canine distemper. A Goldendoodle's nose can be black, pink or a similar color to the coat.

5. **Weight** –Dogs may have weight problems due to factors such as diet, overfeeding, lack of exercise, allergies, diabetes, thyroid or other problems. A general rule of thumb is that your dog's stomach should be above his rib cage when standing, and you should be able to feel his ribs beneath his coat without too much effort. If his stomach hangs below, he is overweight or may have a pot belly, which can also be a symptom of other conditions.

6. **Eyes** - a healthy Goldendoodle's eyes are dark and shiny with no yellowish tint. The area around the eyeball (the conjunctiva) should be a healthy pink, paleness could be a sign of underlying problems. A red swelling in the corner of one or both eyes could by a sign of cherry eye. Sometimes the dog's third eyelid (the nictating membrane) is visible at the eye's inside corner - this is normal. There should be no thick, green or yellow discharge from the eyes. A cloudy eye could be a sign of cataracts.

7. **Attitude** – a generally positive attitude and personality is the sign of good health. Goldendoodles are engaged, people-loving dogs, so symptoms of illness may include one or all of the following: not eating food, a general lack of interest in his or her surroundings, lethargy and sleeping a lot (more than normal.) The important thing is to look out for any behavior which is out of the ordinary for your individual dog.

8. **Energy** – Your dog should have good energy levels with fluid and pain-free movements. Lethargy or lack of energy – if it is not the dog's normal character – could be a sign of an underlying problem.

9. **Smell** –Goldendoodles are not known for having an unpleasant 'doggie odor'. Your dog should smell good! If there is a musty, 'off' or generally unpleasant smell coming from his body, it could be a sign of yeast infection. There can be a number of reasons for this, often his ears not being cleaned and groomed properly, or occasionally an allergy to a certain type of food. You need to get to the root of the problem. If he's healthy, then he's probably overdue a bath!

10. **Temperature** – The normal temperature of a dog is 101°F to 102.5°F. (A human's is 98.6°F.) Excited or exercising dogs may run a slightly higher temperature. Anything above 103°F or below 100°F should be checked out. The exceptions are female dogs about to give birth that will often have a temperature of 99°F. If you take your dog's temperature, make sure he or she is relaxed and *always* use a purpose-made canine thermometer, like the one pictured here for rectal use.

11. **Stools** –poo, poop, business, feces– call it what you will - it's the stuff that comes out of the less appealing end of your Goldendoodle on a daily basis! It should be firm and brown, not runny, with no signs of worms or parasites. Watery stools or a dog not eliminating regularly are both signs of an upset stomach or other ailments. If it continues for a day or two, consult your vet. If puppies have diarrhea they need checking out much quicker as they soon dehydrate.

So now you know some of the signs of a healthy dog – what are the signs of an unhealthy one? There are many different symptoms that can indicate that your beloved canine companion isn't feeling great. If you don't yet know your dog, his habits, temperament and behavior patterns, then we recommend you spend some time to get acquainted with him.

What are his normal character and temperament? Lively or calm, playful or serious, a joker or an introvert, bold or nervous, happy to be left alone or loves to be with people, a keen appetite or a fussy eater? How often does he empty his bowels, does he ever vomit? (Dogs often eat grass to make themselves sick, this is perfectly normal and a natural way of cleansing the digestive system.) You may think your Goldendoodle can't talk, **but he can!** If you really know your dog, his character and habits, then he CAN tell you when he's not well. He does this by changing his patterns. Some symptoms are physical, some emotional and others are behavioral.

It's important for you to be able to recognize these changes as soon as possible. Early treatment can be the key to keeping a simple problem from snowballing into a serious illness. If you think your dog is unwell, it is useful to keep an accurate and detailed account of his symptoms to give to the vet, perhaps even take a video of him on your mobile phone. This will help the vet to correctly diagnose and effectively treat your dog.

....

Four Vital Signs of Illness

1. **Temperature** - A new-born puppy will have a temperature of 94-97°F. This will reach the normal adult body temperature of 101°F at about four weeks old. Anything between 100°F and 103°F is regarded as normal. A dog's temperature is normally taken via the rectum. If you do this, be very careful. It's easier if you get someone to hold your dog while you do this. Digital thermometers are a good choice, but **only use one specifically made for rectal use,** as normal glass thermometers can easily break off in the rectum.

   Ear thermometers are now available (pictured), making the task much easier, although they can be expensive and don't suit all dogs' ears. (Walmart has started stocking them.) Remember that exercise or excitement can cause the temperature to rise by 2°F to 3°F when your dog is actually in good health, so better to wait until he is relaxed and calm before taking his temperature. If it is above or below the norms, give your vet a call.

2. **Respiratory Rate -** Another symptom of canine illness is a change in breathing patterns. This varies a lot depending on the size and weight of the dog. An adult dog will have a respiratory rate of 15-25 breaths per minute when resting. You can easily check this by counting your dog's breaths for a minute with a stopwatch handy. Don't do this if he is panting; it doesn't count.

3. **Heart Rate -** You can feel your Goldendoodle's heartbeat by placing your hand on his lower ribcage – just behind the elbow. Don't be alarmed if the heartbeat seems irregular compared to a human. It IS irregular in some dogs. Your Goldendoodle will probably love the attention, so it should be quite easy to check his heartbeat. Just lay him on his side and bend his left front leg at the elbow, bring the elbow in to his chest and place your fingers or a stethoscope on this area and count the beats.

   - Small dogs like Petites have a normal rate of 90 to 140 beats per minute

   - Medium-sized dogs have a normal rate of 80 to 120 beats

   - Big dogs like Standard Goldendoodles have a normal rate of 70 to 120 beats

   - A young puppy has a heartbeat of around 220 beats

   - An older dog has a slower heartbeat

4. **Behavior Changes -** Classic symptoms of illness are any inexplicable behavior changes. If there has NOT been a change in the household atmosphere, such as another new pet, a new baby, moving home, the absence of a family member or the loss of another dog, then the following symptoms may well be a sign that all is not well:

   - Depression

   - Anxiety and/or trembling

   - Falling or stumbling

   - Loss of appetite

   - Walking in circles

   - Being more vocal - grunting, whining and/or whimpering

   - Aggression – Goldendoodles are normally friendly, so this can be a sign of ill health

   - Tiredness - sleeping more than normal and/or not wanting to exercise

   - Abnormal posture

Your Goldendoodle may normally show some of these signs, but if any of them appear for the first time or worse than usual, you need to keep him under close watch for a few hours or even days. Quite often he will return to normal of his own accord. Like humans, dogs have off-days too. If he is showing any of these symptoms, then don't over-exercise him, and avoid stressful situations and hot or cold places. Make sure he has access to clean water. There are many other signals of ill health, but these are four of the most important. Keep a record for your vet, if your dog does need professional medical attention, most vets will want to know:

WHEN the symptoms first appeared in your dog

WHETHER they are getting better or worse, and

HOW FREQUENT the symptoms are. Are they intermittent, continuous or increasing?

We have highlighted some of the indicators of good and poor health to help you monitor your dog's wellbeing. Getting to know his or her character, habits and temperament will go a long way towards spotting the early signs of ill health. The next section looks in detail at some of the most common ailments affecting Goldendoodles, with complicated medical terminology explained in simple terms. We also cover the symptoms and treatments of various conditions.

Hip Dysplasia

Canine Hip Dysplasia (CHD) is the most common cause of hind leg lameness in dogs; dysplasia means 'abnormal development'. It is also the most common heritable orthopedic problem seen in dogs, affecting virtually all breeds, but is more common in large breeds. The condition develops into degenerative osteoarthritis of the hip joints.

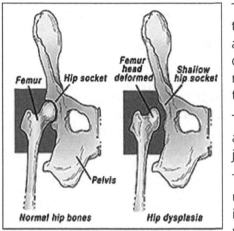

The hip is a ball and socket joint. Hip dysplasia is caused when the head of the femur (thigh bone) fits loosely into a shallow and poorly-developed socket in the pelvis. Most dogs with dysplasia are born with normal hips, but due to their genetic make-up (and possibly other factors such as diet), the soft tissues that surround the joint develop abnormally.

The right hand side of our picture shows a shallow hip socket and a deformed femur head, causing hip dysplasia. The healthy joint is on the left.

The joint carrying the weight of the dog and becomes loose and unstable, muscle growth lags behind normal development and is often followed by degenerative joint disease or osteoarthritis, which is the body's attempt to stabilize the loose hip joint. Early diagnosis gives your vet the best chance to tackle the problem as soon as possible, minimizing the chance of arthritis developing. Symptoms range from mild discomfort to extreme pain. A puppy with canine hip dysplasia usually starts to show signs between five and 13 months old.

Symptoms

- 🐾 Lameness in hind legs, particularly after exercise
- 🐾 Difficulty or stiffness when getting up or climbing uphill
- 🐾 A 'bunny hop' gait
- 🐾 Dragging the rear end when getting up
- 🐾 Waddling rear leg gait
- 🐾 A painful reaction to stretching the hind legs, resulting in a short stride
- 🐾 A side-to-side sway of the croup (area above the tail) with a tendency to tilt the hips down if you push down on the croup
- 🐾 A reluctance to jump, exercise or climb stairs

Causes and Triggers

Canine hip dysplasia is usually inherited, but there are also factors which can trigger or worsen the condition, including:

1. Overfeeding, especially on a diet high in protein and calories

2. Excess calcium, also usually due to overfeeding
3. Extended periods without exercise   or too much vigorous exercise - especially when your dog's bones are growing
4. Obesity
5. Injury can cause an otherwise normal hip joint to develop arthritis

Advances in nutritional research have shown that diet plays an important role in the development of hip dysplasia. Feeding a high-calorie diet to growing dogs can trigger a predisposition to hip dysplasia, as the rapid weight gain places increased stress on the hips. During their first year of life, Goldendoodle puppies should be fed a diet which contains the correct amount of calories, minerals and protein, thereby reducing the risk of hip dysplasia. Ask your breeder or vet for advice on the best diet.

Exercise may be another risk factor. Dogs that have a predisposition to the disease may have an increased chance of getting it if they are over-exercised at a young age. On the other hand, dogs with large leg muscle mass are **less** likely to get dysplasia than dogs with small muscle mass. The key here is **moderate, low impact exercise for fast-growing young dogs**. Activities which strengthen the gluteus muscles, such as running and swimming, are probably a good idea. Whereas high impact activities that apply a lot of force to the joint, such and jumping and catching Frisbees, are not recommended with young Goldendoodles.

Treatment

As with most conditions, early detection leads to a better outcome. Your vet will take X-rays to make a diagnosis. Treatment is geared towards preventing the hip joint getting worse and decreasing pain. Various medical and surgical treatments are now available to ease the dog's discomfort and restore some mobility. Treatment depends upon several factors, such as the dog's age, how bad the problem is and, sadly, how much money you can afford to spend on treatment – another reason for taking out pet insurance.

Management of the condition usually consists of restricting exercise, keeping body weight down and then managing pain with analgesics and anti-inflammatory drugs. As with humans, cortisone injections may sometimes be used to reduce inflammation and swelling. Cortisone can be injected directly into the affected hip to provide almost immediate relief for a tender, swollen joint. In severe cases, surgery may be an option, especially with older dogs.

Hip Testing

Both the dam and sire of your puppy should have been 'hip scored' - or tested - for hip dysplasia and the results available for you to see. Thirty years ago the British Veterinary Association (BVA) and Kennel Club set up a hip screening program for dogs in the UK, which tests them using radiology and gives them a rating or 'hip score'. In the USA the OFA (Orthopedic Foundation for Animals) administers the tests.

The hip score is the total number of points given for nine points examined by X-ray, the lower score the better. The best score for each hip is 0 and the worst is 53 and, as a dog has two hips, the total score will be between 0 and 106. Although there are no official statistics for the Goldendoodle, the OFA has carried out tests on many breeds in the USA and found that more than one in five of the 145,000 Golden Retrievers tested were affected, ranking them 41st highest out of 177 breeds for hip dysplasia problems. A lower percentage of Poodles were affected at 12.1%, ranking them 92nd. Worst affected breed was the Bulldog, with 73.4% of dogs having signs of hip dysplasia.

You can see now why responsible breeders should only breed from stock which has a proven low hip score. Continual breeding from affected dogs spreads the disease like wildfire, and if you don't know if your puppy's parents have been tested, then you are taking a big risk. For Goldendoodles, the parents should have a hip score of one to 10, with no single hip having a higher score than six.

In these X rays, Figure A (left) is the healthy hip, Figure B shows lateral tilting, C shows outward rotation

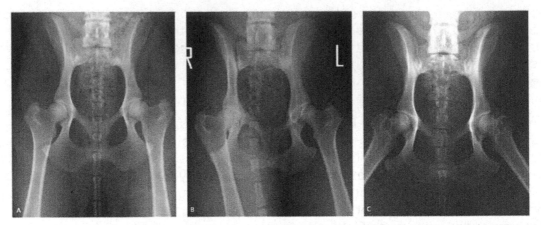

The Kennel Club is responsible for publishing BVA/KC hip dysplasia results for all pedigree dogs in the UK. However, as the Goldendoodle is a crossbreed, there are no official statistics. The KC gives a 'breed median score,' which is the score of the 'average' dog in that breed (i.e. an equal number of dogs in have better and worse scores.) For the Golden Retriever this is 11, it's 10 for the Miniature and Standard Poodle and 13 for the Toy Poodle.

In the UK, the current cost of a hip score is only £57, and the cost of a joint hip and elbow test is £90. The tests are much cheaper in the US: hip testing costs $35 for an individual pup or $90 for the whole litter, and $40 for a joint hip and elbow test. Given the price of Goldendoodle puppies, all breeders can afford to have their potential breeding stock tested. Ethically, they should have all stock tested, as non-breeding from dogs carrying the hip dysplasia genes is the way to reduce this painful disease.

When buying a Goldendoodle pup, ask to see the original hip score certificate, which is green in the UK. If the breeder does not own the stud dog, a photocopy of his results should also be available. The same applies with elbow tests outlined on the next page, when results are on a gold-colored form. Veterinary MRI and radiology specialist Ruth Dennis, of the Animal Health Trust, states: "For dogs intended for breeding, it is essential that the hips are assessed before mating to ensure that they are free of dysplastic changes or only minimally affected."

Elbow Dysplasia

Elbow Dysplasia (ED) simply means 'abnormal development of the elbow.' It affects many breeds and is thought to be on the increase in the canine population. It more commonly seen in large breed fast-growing puppies, such as Golden Retrievers. It starts in puppyhood and affects the dog for the rest of his life. There are a number of causes, but the biggest one is thought to be genetic, with the disease being passed on from dam or sire to puppy. And it is a combination of genes, rather than a single gene, which causes ED. Dogs who show no symptoms can still be carriers of the disease.

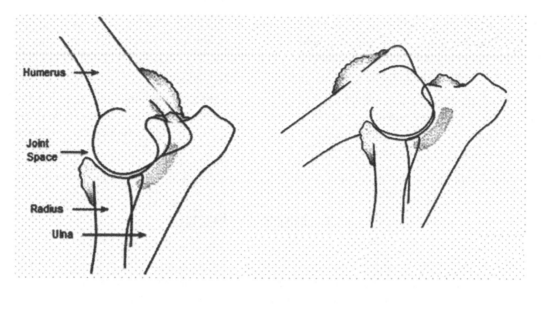

| 4a | 4b |

Osteoarthritic changes to the shape and structure of the elbow joint. The shaded areas on figure 4a (left, extended elbow) and 4b (right, flexed elbow) represent the changes to bone and cartilage as a result of UAP and other forms of elbow dysplasia. Images courtesy of the British Veterinary Association.

Other factors such as rate of growth, diet and level of exercise may influence the severity of the disease in an individual dog, but they cannot prevent it or reduce the potential of the dog to pass it on to offspring.

Many bones in a new-born puppy are not a single piece of bone, but several different pieces with cartilage in between. This is especially true of long limb bones. As the puppy grows, the cartilage changes into bone and several pieces of bone fuse together forming one entire bone. For instance, the ulna, a bone in the forearm, starts out as four pieces that eventually fuse into one bone.

Elbow dysplasia occurs when certain parts of the joint develop abnormally as a dog grows. Some parts of the joint may have abnormal development, resulting in an uneven joint surface, inflammation, lameness and arthritis. It eventually results in elbow arthritis which may be associated with joint stiffness (reduced range of motion) and lameness. The most notable symptom is a limp. Your Goldendoodle may hold his leg out away from his body while walking, or even lift a front leg completely, putting no weight on it.

Signs may be noted as early as four months old and many dogs will go through a period between six months and a year old when symptoms will be at their worst. After this, most will occasionally show less severe symptoms.

Treatment

As yet there is no DNA test for Elbow Dysplasia. Vets diagnose the condition by taking X-rays of the affected joint or joints and treatment varies depending on the exact cause of the condition.

A young dog is usually placed on a regular, low-impact exercise program - swimming can be a good exercise. Owners must carefully manage their dog's diet and weight. Oral or injected medication such as non-steroid anti-inflammatory drugs (NSAIDS) may be prescribed to reduce pain and inflammation and to make your dog more comfortable,

After the age of 12 to 18 months, the dog's lameness becomes less severe and some individuals function very well. Elbow dysplasia is a lifelong problem, although some can be very effectively helped with surgery. In most cases, degenerative joint disease (arthritis) will occur as the dog gets older, regardless of the type of treatment.

Luxating Patella

Luxating patella, also called 'floating kneecap' or 'slipped stifle' is a painful condition similar to a dislocated knee cap. It is often congenital (present from birth) and typically affects small and miniature breeds. Goldendoodles bred from Miniature or Toy Poodles may be susceptible to luxating patella. In the USA, GANA requires patella certifications on breeding dogs.

Symptoms

A typical sign would be if your dog is running across the park when he suddenly pulls up short and yelps with pain. He might limp on three legs and then after a period of about 10 minutes, drop the affected leg and start to walk normally again. If the condition is severe, he may hold up the affected leg for a few days. Dogs that have a luxating patella on both hind legs may change their gait completely, dropping their hindquarters and holding the rear legs further out from the body as they walk. In the most extreme cases they might not even use their rear legs, but walk like a circus act by balancing on their front legs so their hindquarters don't touch the ground.

Genetics, injury and malformation during development can all cause this problem. Because the most common cause is genetics, a dog with luxating patella should never be used for breeding. If you are buying a puppy, ask if there is any history in either parent. Often sufferers are middle-aged dogs with a history of intermittent lameness in the affected rear leg or legs - although puppies as young as four to six months old can also be affected.

A groove in the end of the femur (thigh bone) allows the knee cap to glide up and down when the

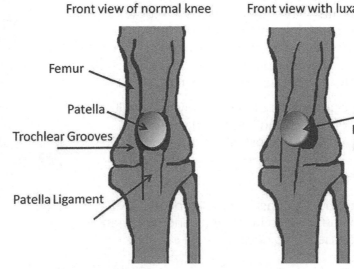

Front view of normal knee   Front view with luxating patella

Femur

Patella

Trochlear Grooves

Patella Ligament

Luxating Patella
Kneecap is dislocated outside of its normal trochlear groove.

knee joint is bent, while keeping it in place at the same time. If this groove is too shallow, the knee cap may luxate – or dislocate. It can only return to its natural position when the quadricep muscle relaxes and increases in length, which is why a dog may have to hold his leg up for some time after the dislocation. Sometimes the problem can be caused by obesity, the excess weight putting too much strain on the joint – another good reason to keep your dog's weight in check.

Treatment

There are four grades of patellar luxation, ranging from Grade I, which causes a temporary lameness in the joint, to Grade IV, in which the patella cannot be realigned manually. This gives the dog a bow-legged appearance. If left untreated, the groove will become even shallower and the dog will become progressively lamer, with arthritis prematurely affecting the joint.

This will cause a permanently swollen knee and reduce your dog's mobility. It is therefore important to get your Goldendoodle in for a veterinary check-up ASAP if you suspect he may have a luxating patella.

In severe cases, surgery is an option, although this should not be undertaken lightly. The groove at the base of the femur may be surgically deepened to better hold the knee cap in place. This operation is known as a **trochlear modification**. The good news is that dogs generally respond well, whatever the type of surgery, and are usually completely recovered within one to two months.

....

PRA (Progressive Retinal Atrophy)

PRA is the name for a collection of progressive diseases which lead to blindness. First recognized at the beginning of the 20th century in Gordon Setters, this inherited condition has been documented in over 100 breeds and some mixed breeds.

Golden Retrievers and Miniature and Toy Poodles are recognized as being among the breeds which can be affected by the disease - although the type of PRA affecting the Golden Retriever is different from that affecting the Poodle.

The type which can affect Golden Retrievers (and Goldendoodles) is prcd-PRA, or progressive rod cone degeneration PRA, also called GPRA - General Progressive Retinal Atrophy. There is a DNA test for the specific GR-PRA1 genetic mutation.

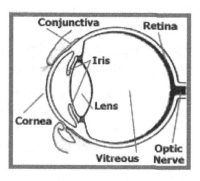

This disease causes cells in the retina at the back of the eye to degenerate and die, even though the cells seem to develop normally early in life. The rod cells operate in low light levels and are the first to lose normal function, and so the first sign is night blindness. Puppies are born with normal eyesight and this generally begins to deteriorate from around the age of three to five years.

Then the cone cells gradually lose their normal function in full light situations. Most affected dogs will eventually go blind. (Conditions that might look like prcd-PRA could be another disease and might not be inherited. Not all retinal disease is PRA and not all PRA is the prcd form of PRA.) Annual eye exams by a veterinary ophthalmologist will build a history of eye health that will help to diagnose disease. Prcd-PRA is inherited as a recessive trait.

This means that the faulty gene must be inherited **from both parents** in order to cause disease in an offspring. So for a puppy to get the disease, both his father and mother were either a carrier or sufferer. A dog that inherits only one copy of the abnormal gene (from his mother OR father) will have no signs of the disease, but will be a carrier. Poodles do not carry this gene, so if one parent is a Poodle, the puppy will not suffer, although they will be a carrier of the disease. Testing for GR-PRA1 is mandatory for all North American breeders registered with GANA.

Poodles also suffer from PRA - but a different type to the Golden Retriever. The OFA says: "The prcd gene is the cause of most, but not all, cases of PRA in Poodles. There appears to be at least two different genetic forms of PRA in Poodles, even though the clinical signs of PRA in all diseased dogs are very similar. One form cannot be distinguished from another form based on a clinical exam. This is significant – a dog that is Normal/Clear for prcd-PRA could still be at risk for having or carrying another form of PRA.

"While annual eye exams by veterinary ophthalmologists are recommended for all breeds, this is especially important for Toy and Miniature Poodles since there is more than one form of PRA known to affect the breed. Research on Poodles is continuing in order to identify the remaining gene(s) that cause other types of PRA."

Sadly, there is no cure, but prcd-PRA can be avoided in future generations by DNA testing of breeding dogs. If your Goldendoodle is affected, it may be helpful to read other owners' experiences of living with blind dogs at www.eyevet.org and www.blinddogs.com.

Eye Testing

There are various ways of testing for hereditary eye conditions. In North America there is the OptiGen prcd-*PRA* Test and the biannual OFA eye exams. Breeders using the Optigen test get one of three results:

CLEAR: these dogs have two normal copies of DNA. Clear dogs will not develop PRA as a result of the mutation

CARRIER: these dogs have one copy of the mutation and one normal copy of DNA. These dogs will not develop PRA themselves as a result of the mutation, but they can pass the mutation on to half of their offspring. Carriers can safely be bred to Clear dogs with no risk of creating affected offspring.

GENETICALLY AFFECTED: these dogs have two copies of the mutation and will almost certainly develop PRA during their lifetime.

In the UK there is the British Veterinary Association (BVA) Eye Test, which is carried out each year due to the fact some diseases have a late onset. If you are buying a puppy, it is highly advisable to check if the parents have been tested and given the all-clear. Always ensure the breeder lets you see the original certificate (which is white in the UK) and not a photocopy.

The UK tests also give one of three results: CLEAR, CARRIER and AFFECTED. In the US, the OFA statistics show that 9.4% of all Poodles tested were carriers for PRA. A carrier can safely be bred to a Clear dog and, according to GANA, it is not recommended that a PRA Carrier be removed from a breeding program if he or she has other excellent traits to pass on.

It is, however, essential that a Carrier be bred only to a Clear, as this will produce healthy puppies. If a breeder decides to breed from one of these puppies, he or she should first confirm via a DNA test that the puppy is Clear.

Identifying dogs with genes which are affected by the disease and NOT breeding from them is the key to eradicating the problem.

Hereditary Cataracts

These can be found in Golden Retrievers, Standard Poodles and certain other breeds. Inheritance of hereditary cataracts varies between breeds with some showing recessive inheritance and others dominant. It is therefore important that both parents of **any** Goldendoodle puppy have a clear current annual eye certificate.

The most common type in Golden Retrievers are bilateral (in both eyes), juvenile-onset cataracts, Despite the name, juvenile cataracts may not appear until your dog is five or six years old. The severity of the cataracts in Retrievers varies considerably; often they are quite small and have little effect on the dog. However, if they are more serious, corrective surgery is possible. In Standard Poodles hereditary cataracts usually only appear in young dogs, but are equal in both eyes and cause blindness.

Hereditary cataracts are usually first diagnosed when the owner sees their dog bumping into furniture, or when his pupils have changed color. The vet will refer the dog to a specialist who will carry out the same eye exam that is done for breeding stock. The process is painless and simple, drops are put into the eyes and after a few minutes the dog is taken into a dark room for examination and diagnosis.

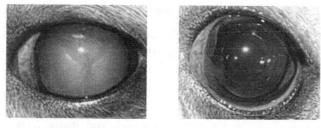

Left: eye with cataracts. Right: same eye with artificial lens

Treatment

If you think your Goldendoodle may have cataracts, it is important to get him to a vet as soon as possible. Early removal of cataracts can restore vision and provide a dramatic improvement in the quality of your dog's life. Surgery is the only treatment in serious cases (unless the cataracts are caused by another condition like canine diabetes.) Despite what you may have heard, laser surgery does not exist for canine cataracts.

The good news is that surgery is almost always (85-90%) successful. The dog has to have a general anesthetic, but the operation is often performed on an outpatient basis. The procedure is similar to small incision cataract surgery in people. An artificial lens is often implanted in the dog's eye to replace the cataract lens. Dogs can see without an artificial lens, but the image will be blurry. Discuss with the vet or ophthalmologist whether your dog would benefit from an artificial lens. Even better news is that once the cataract is removed, it does not recur. However before your dog can undergo this procedure, he has to be fit and healthy. Afterwards he will probably have to stay overnight at the surgery so the professionals can keep an eye on him. Once back home, he will wear a protective Elizabethan collar, or E collar, for one to two weeks while his eye is healing.

You have to keep him quiet and calm (not always easy –especially with an E collar on.) You'll also have to give him eye drops, perhaps four times a day for the first week and then less frequently after that. The success of cataract surgery depends very much on the owner doing all the right things, but all the effort will be worth it when your Goldendoodle regains his sight.

Glaucoma

Glaucoma is a condition which puts pressure on the eye, and if the condition becomes chronic or continues without treatment, it will eventually cause permanent damage to the optic nerve, resulting in blindness.

A normal eye contains a fluid called aqueous humor to maintain its shape, and the body is constantly adding and removing fluid from inside of the eye to maintain the pressure inside the eye at the proper level. Glaucoma occurs when the pressure inside the eyeball becomes higher than normal. Just as high blood pressure can damage the heart, excessive pressure inside the eye can damage the eye's internal structures. Unless glaucoma is treated quickly, temporary loss of vision or even total blindness can result.

The cornea and lens inside the eye are living tissues, but they have no blood vessels to supply the oxygen and nutrition they need; these are delivered through the aqueous humor. In glaucoma, the increased pressure is most frequently caused by this fluid not being able to properly drain away from the eye. Fluid is constantly being produced and if an equal amount does not leave the globe, then the pressure starts to rise, similar to a water balloon. As more water is added the balloon stretches more and more. The balloon will eventually burst, but the eye is stronger so this does not happen. Instead the eye's internal structures are damaged irreparably.

Secondary glaucoma means that it is caused by another problem, such as a wound to the eye. Primary glaucoma is normally inherited and this is the type of glaucoma which Poodles can suffer from.

Symptoms

Even though a puppy may carry the gene for this disorder, the disease itself does not usually develop until a dog is at least two or three years old; usually a little while after reaching maturity. The dog has to first reach maturity, with primary glaucoma, both eyes are rarely affected equally or at the same time, it usually starts in one eye several months or even years before it affects the second one. Glaucoma is a serious disease and it's important for an owner to be able to immediately recognize early signs. If treatment is not started within a few days - or even hours in some cases - of the pressure increasing, the dog will probably lose sight in that eye. Here are the early signs:

- Pain
- A dilated pupil or one pupil looks bigger than the other
- Rapid blinking
- Cloudiness in the cornea at the front of the eye
- The whites of an eye look bloodshot
- One eye looks larger or sticks out further than the other one
- Loss of appetite, which may be due to headaches
- Change in attitude, less willing to play, etc.

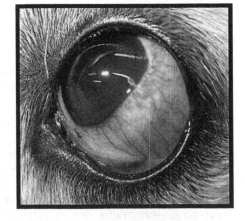

Most dogs will not display all of these signs at first, perhaps just one or two. A dog rubbing his eye with his paw, against the furniture or carpet or your leg is a common - and often unnoticed- early sign. Some dogs will also seem to flutter the eyelids or squint with one eye.

The pupil of the affected eye will usually dilate (get bigger) in the early stages of glaucoma. It may still react to all bright light, but it will do so very slowly. Remember that glaucoma, even primary glaucoma, is usually going to initially affect just one of the eyes. If the pupil in one eye is larger than in the other, something is definitely wrong and it could be glaucoma.

If you suspect your dog has glaucoma, get him to the vet as soon as possible, i.e. **immediately,** not the day after, this is a medical emergency. The vet will carry out a manual examination and test your dog's eye pressure using a tonometer on the surface of the eye. There is still a fair chance that the dog may lose sight in this eye, but a much better chance of saving the second eye with the knowledge and preventative measures learned from early intervention.

Treatment revolves around reducing the pressure within the affected eye, draining the aqueous humor and providing pain relief, as this can be a painful condition for your dog. There are also surgical options for the long-term control of glaucoma. As yet it cannot cured.

Other Eye Issues

Retinal Dysplasia

This is one of the several eye diseases which Goldendoodles can inherit. Retinal dysplasia is a disorder in which the cells and layer of retinal tissue at the back of the eye do not develop properly. One or both eyes may be affected. It can be detected by a vet using an ophthalmoscope when the puppy is six weeks old or even younger. The retina looks like layers of folded tissue rather than one flat layer.

There are three different types of the condition. Focal or Multifocal Retinal Dysplasia, which causes streaks and dots in the central retina and may cause blind spots, which sometimes lessen as the dog ages. Geographic Retinal Dysplasia occurs when horseshoe or irregular lesions appear, leading to possible visual impairment and sometimes blindness. The most serious type is Complete Retinal Dysplasia, which causes blindness and may be accompanied by a range of secondary eye problems, such as cataract or glaucoma. There is no treatment for Retinal Dysplasia.

Entropion and Ectropion

Entropion is a condition in which the edge of the lower eyelid rolls inward, causing the dog's fur to rub the surface of the eyeball, or cornea. In rare cases the upper lid can also be affected, and one or both eyes may be involved. This painful condition is thought to be hereditary.

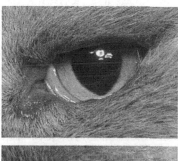

The affected dog will scratch at his painful eye with his paws and this can lead to further injury. If your Goldendoodle is to suffer from entropion, he will usually show signs at or before his first birthday. You will notice that his eyes are red and inflamed and they will produce tears. He will probably squint.

The tears typically start off clear and can progress to a thick yellow or green mucus. If the entropion causes corneal ulcers, you might also notice a milky-white color develop. This is caused by increased fluid which affects the clarity of the cornea. For your poor dog, the irritation is constant. Imagine how painful and uncomfortable it would be if you had permanent hairs touching your eyes. It makes my eyes water just thinking about it.

It's important to get your dog to the vet as soon as you suspect entropion, before he scratches his cornea and worsens the problem. The condition can cause scarring around the eyes or other issues which can jeopardize vision if left untreated. A vet will make the diagnosis after a painless and relatively simple inspection of your dog's eyes. But before diagnosing entropion, he or she will have to rule out other issues, such as allergies, which might also be making your dog's eyes red and itchy. Some vets may delay surgery for young dogs and treat the condition with medication until the dog's face is fully formed to avoid having to repeat the procedure later.

In mild cases, the vet may successfully prescribe eye drops, ointment or other medication. However, the most common treatment for severe cases is a fairly straightforward surgical procedure to pin back the lower eyelid. Discuss the severity of the condition and all possible options with your vet before proceeding to surgery.

Ectropion is a condition where the lower lids turn outwards. This causes the eyelids to appear droopy, and one or both eyes may be involved. It can occur in any breed, but certain breeds have a higher incidence of the condition. 'Acquired ectropion' can occur in any dog at any age and it means that a reason other than genetics has caused the eyelid to sag. These include:

- Facial nerve paralysis
- Hypothyroidism
- Scarring secondary to injury
- Chronic inflammation and infection of the tissues surrounding the eyes
- Surgical overcorrection of entropion
- Neuromuscular disease

Ectropion causes the lower lid to droop, thereby exposing the conjunctiva and forming a pouch or pocket where pollens, grasses and dust can collect and rub against the sensitive conjunctiva. This is a consistent source of irritation to the dog, and leads to increased redness of the conjunctiva and the production of tears which flow over the lower lid and face, often causing a brownish staining of the fur below the eyes. A thick mucus discharge may appear along the eyelid margin and the dog may rub or scratch his eyes if it becomes uncomfortable.

Diagnosis is usually made following a physical examination. If the dog is older, blood and urine tests may be performed to search for an underlying cause. Your vet may also perform corneal staining to see if any ulcers are present.

Many dogs live normal lives with ectropion and some require no treatment. However, others develop repeated eye infections due to dirt and dust collecting within the eye. Therefore, the risks are minor except in severe cases, where secondary eye infections may develop. If eye irritations do develop, you should see your vet.

Mild cases can be treated with lubricating eye drops and ointments to prevent the cornea and conjunctiva from drying out. Special eye (ophthalmic) antibiotics will be used to combat any corneal ulcers. These medications will alleviate irritations and/or infections when they occur.

In severe cases, surgery is undertaken to remove excess tissue to tighten the lids and remove the abnormal pocket which is trapping the dirt, etc. and this is usually successful. In some cases, your vet may recommend performing two separate operations in order to avoid over-correction, which could cause entropion to develop.

Distichiasis and Trichiasis

Distichiasis is the medical term for eyelashes irritating a dog's eyes. (Trichiasis is backwards-growing eyelashes.) With this condition small eyelashes abnormally grow on the inner surface or the very edge of the eyelid, and both upper and lower eyelids may be affected. Some breeds are affected more than others, suggesting that it is an inherited trait. Golden Retrievers, Cocker Spaniels, Boxers and Pekingese are among those most commonly affected.

The affected eye becomes red, inflamed, and may develop a discharge. The dog will typically squint or blink a lot, just like a human with a hair or other foreign matter in the eye. The dog will often rub his eye against furniture, other objects or the carpet. In severe cases, the cornea can become ulcerated and it looks a blue color. If left, the condition usually worsens and severe ulcerations and infections develop which can lead to blindness. The dog can make the condition worse by scratching or rubbing his eyes.

Treatment usually involves surgery or electro- or cryo-epilation, where a needle is inserted into the hair follicle and an ultra-fast electric current is emitted. This current produces heat which destroys the stem cells responsible for hair growth. This procedure may need to be repeated after several months because all of the abnormal hairs may not have developed at the time of the first treatment -although this is not common with dogs older than three years.

If surgery is performed, the lid is actually split and the areas where the abnormal hairs grow are removed. Both treatments require anesthesia and usually result in a full recovery. After surgery, the eyelids are swollen for four to five days and the eyelid margins turn pink. Usually they return to their normal color within four months. Antibiotic eye drops are often used following surgery to prevent infections.

Breeder options for these eye problems can be found at: www.offa.org/eye_breederoption.html

---

von Willebrand's Disease

Von Willebrand's Disease is a common inherited bleeding disorder similar to hemophilia in humans. In Von Willebrand's Disease (vWD), the dog lacks a substance which helps to form blood clots.

Technically speaking this substance (called 'von Willebrand's factor') forms clots and stabilizes something called Factor VIII in the normal clotting process. Dogs with von Willebrand's Disease bleed excessively as their blood does not clot properly. Some breeds have a higher incidence of vWD than others - including Poodles - which can be passed on to Goldendoodles. However, if Goldendoodles are affected by the condition, it will be Type 1 von Willebrand's, which is the least severe form of the disease.

Humans can also suffer from vWD. This disease is named after Erik Adolf von Willebrand, a Finnish doctor who documented and studied a rare bleeding disorder in an isolated group of people in 1924. He showed that the disease was inherited, rather than caught by infection.

Symptoms

The main symptom is excessive bleeding:

- Nosebleeds
- Blood in the feces (black or bright red blood)
- Bloody urine
- Bleeding from the gums
- Females bleeding excessively from the vagina

- Bruising of skin

- Prolonged bleeding after surgery or trauma

- Blood loss anemia if there is prolonged bleeding

If bleeding occurs in the stomach or intestine, you may notice something unusual in your dog's feces; his stools may have blood in them or be black and tarry or bright red. Some dogs will have blood in their urine, while others may have bleeding in their joints. In this last case, the symptoms are similar to those of arthritis.

The diagnosis is made through a test to check the levels of von Willebrand's factor in the blood. If you are buying a puppy, you can check that the parents have been DNA tested for vWD and ask to see the certificate giving them the all-clear.

Sadly, as yet there is no cure for von Willebrand's Disease. The only way to stop the spread of the disease is to have dogs tested and to prevent breeding from affected animals. Since this is a recessive gene, **both** parents have to carry the gene for the puppies to be affected. Therefore, a Carrier can successfully be bred to a Clear dog to produce healthy offspring that will not be affected.

Without treatment, an Affected dog can bleed to death after surgery or what otherwise might normally be considered a less than life-threatening injury. The only proven way to treat vWD is with transfusions of blood collected from healthy dogs. Some dogs with von Willebrand's Disease are also **hypothyroid**, meaning they have lower than normal levels of thyroid hormone. These dogs benefit from thyroid hormone replacement therapy. A drug called DDAVP may help dogs with bleeding episodes. It can be administered into the nose to increase clotting, but opinion is still divided as to whether this treatment is effective.

Hypothyroidism

Hypothyroidism is a common hormonal disorder in dogs and is due to an under-active thyroid gland. The gland (located on either side of the windpipe in the dog's throat) does not produce enough of the hormone thyroid, which controls the speed of the metabolism. Dogs with very low thyroid levels have a slow metabolic rate. It occurs mainly in dogs over the age of five. Some Goldendoodles have been known to have been affected by this condition.

Generally, hypothyroidism occurs most frequently in larger, middle-aged dogs of either gender. The symptoms are often non-specific and quite gradual in onset, and they may vary depending on breed and age. Most forms of hypothyroidism are diagnosed with a blood test and the OFA provides a registry for thyroid screening in the USA.

Symptoms are listed here in order, with the most common ones being at the top of the list:

- High blood cholesterol

- Lethargy

- Hair loss

- 🐾 Weight gain or obesity
- 🐾 Dry coat or excessive shedding
- 🐾 Hyper pigmentation or darkening of the skin, seen in 25% of cases
- 🐾 Intolerance to cold, seen in 15% of dogs with the condition

Treatment

Although hypothyroidism is a type of auto-immune disease and cannot be prevented, symptoms can usually be easily diagnosed and treated. Most affected dogs can be well-managed on thyroid hormone replacement therapy tablets. The dog is placed on a daily dose of a synthetic thyroid hormone called thyroxine (levothyroxine.) The dog is usually given a standard dose for his weight and then blood samples are taken periodically to monitor him and the dose is adjusted accordingly.

Depending upon your dog's preferences and needs, the medication can be given in different forms, such as a solid tablet, in liquid form, or a gel that can be rubbed into your dog's ears. Once treatment has started, he will be on it for the rest of his life.

In some less common situations, surgery may be required to remove part or all of the thyroid gland.

Another treatment is radioiodine, where radioactive iodine is used to kill the overactive cells of the thyroid. While this is considered one of the most effective treatments, not all dogs are suitable for the procedure and lengthy hospitalization is often required. Happily, once the diagnosis has been made and treatment has started, whichever treatment your dog undergoes, the majority of symptoms disappear.

NOTE: **Hyper**thyroidism (as opposed to **hypo**thyroidism) is caused by the thyroid gland producing **too much** thyroid hormone. It is quite rare in dogs, more often seen in cats. A common symptom is the dog being ravenously hungry, but losing weight.

Heart Problems

Subaortic Stenosis (SAS)

This is one of the most commonly inherited heart diseases in dogs and the Golden Retriever is one of the affected breeds - along with other large dogs such as Rottweilers, Great Danes and German Shepherd Dogs. Quite often the disease is discovered when the vet hears a heart murmur as he examines a puppy in for his initial vaccinations. Not all puppies with SAS have heart murmurs and sometimes the murmurs come and go.

An affected puppy is born with an abnormally narrow passage leading from the heart to the aorta, due to muscular and fibrous tissues growing more than they should. When the puppy is born, the heart is only slightly abnormal. These tissues can remain like this or they can continue to grow until they prevent blood from flowing through the bottleneck. As the blood becomes more restricted, the heart has to work harder and harder and the murmur becomes louder and more serious.

Dogs may seem perfectly healthy and active, even in severe cases. However, they may also display one or more of the following symptoms:

- 🐾 Weakness
- 🐾 Breathing difficulty (dyspnea)

- Fainting (syncope)
- In extreme cases, sudden death

The vet will diagnose SAS by a physical exam using a stethoscope and using a chest X-ray or an electrocardiogram (ECG) check for any irregularities in the heart's rhythm (arrhythmias.) However, the test of choice is usually an echocardiogram (cardiac ultrasound) which shows a monitor image of the inside of the heart in real time.

Very mild cases of SAS require no treatment at all, whereas severe cases can be life threatening. Puppies often outgrow heart murmurs, but if a pup still has a murmur at the age of six months, then the likely cause is SAS or another heart condition. If the disease is mild, treatment is not required. However, it can get worse as a growing dog reaches its adult age and body size. Recently a new surgical procedure has become available using a special 'cutting' balloon to reduce the obstruction and initial results are positive.

Dogs with moderate or severe SAS may need medication, most commonly beta blockers in tablet form which help to prevent the heart from beating too fast and control arrhythmias. Dogs with moderate or severe SAS should avoid bursts of sudden activity or intense exertion, and they should never be used for breeding.

Congestive Heart Failure (CHF)

This is relatively common among the canine population in general and occurs when the heart is not able to pump enough blood around the dog's body.

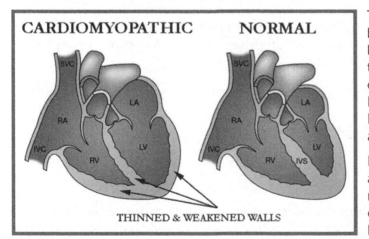

The heart is a mechanical pump. It receives blood in one half and forces it through the lungs, then the other half pumps the blood through the entire body. The two most common forms of heart failure in dogs are Degenerative Valvular Disease (DVD) and Dilated Cardiomyopathy (DCM), also known as an enlarged heart.

In people, heart disease usually involves the arteries that supply blood to the heart muscle becoming hardened over time, causing the heart muscles to receive less blood than they need. Starved of oxygen, the result is often a heart attack.

In dogs, hardening of the arteries (arteriosclerosis) and heart attacks are very rare. However, heart disease is very common.

In dogs, heart disease is often seen as heart failure, which means that the muscles 'give out.' This is usually caused by one chamber or side of the heart being required to do more than it is physically able to do. It may be that excessive force is required to pump the blood through an area and over time the muscles fail.

Unlike a heart attack in humans, heart failure in the dog is a slow insidious process that occurs over months or years. In these cases, once symptoms are noted, they will usually worsen over time until the animal is placed on treatment.

Heart failure in older dogs is usually due to problems with the mitral valve of the heart, and occurs most commonly in smaller breeds, including small Poodles, Yorkshire Terriers, Lhasa Apsos and Pomeranians, although Golden Retrievers are also susceptible. Symptoms are:

- 🐾 Tiredness
- 🐾 Decreased activity levels
- 🐾 **Restlessness,** pacing around instead of settling down to sleep
- 🐾 **Intermittent coughing** - especially during exertion or excitement. This tends to occur at night, sometimes about two hours after the dog goes to bed or when he wakes up in the morning. This coughing is an attempt to clear fluid in the lungs and is often the first sign of a mitral valve disorder. As the condition worsens, other symptoms may appear:
- 🐾 Lack of appetite
- 🐾 Rapid breathing
- 🐾 Abdominal swelling (due to fluid)
- 🐾 Noticeable loss of weight
- 🐾 Fainting
- 🐾 Paleness

If your dog is exhibiting a range of the above symptoms, the vet may suspect Congestive Heart Failure and will carry out tests to make sure. As with SAS, these may include listening to the heart, chest X-rays, an electrocardiogram, echocardiogram and/or blood tests,

If the heart problem is due to an enlarged heart (DCM) or valve disease, the condition cannot be reversed. Instead, treatment focuses on manages the symptoms with various medications, which may change over time as the condition worsens. The vet may also prescribe a special low salt diet for your dog, as sodium (found in salt) determines the amount of water in the blood. Your dog's exercise will have to be controlled. There is some evidence that vitamin and other supplements may be beneficial, so discuss this with your vet.

The prognosis (outlook) for dogs with Congestive Heart Failure depends on the cause and severity, as well as their response to treatment. CHF is progressive, so your dog can never recover from the condition. But once diagnosed, he can live a longer, more comfortable life with the right medication and regular check-ups.

Heart Murmurs

These are not uncommon in dogs. Our dog was diagnosed with a Grade 2 murmur several years ago and, of course, your heart sinks when the vet gives you the terrible news. But once the shock is over, it's important to realize that there are several different severities of the condition and, at its mildest, it is no great cause for concern.

Our dog is 11 now and, as the saying goes: "fit as a butcher's dog," with seemingly no signs of the heart murmur (except through the vet's stethoscope.) However, we are always on alert for a dry, racking cough, which is a sign of fluid in the lungs. So far it hasn't happened, touch wood.

Literally, a heart murmur is a specific sound heard through a stethoscope, resulting from the blood flowing faster than normal within the heart itself or in one of the two major arteries. Instead of the normal 'lubb dupp' noise, an additional sound can be heard that can vary from a mild 'pshhh' to a loud 'whoosh'. The different grades are:

> **Grade 1** - barely audible
> **Grade 2** - soft, but easily heard with a stethoscope
> **Grade 3** - intermediate loudness; most murmurs which are related to the mechanics of blood circulation are at least grade III
> **Grade 4** - loud murmur that radiates widely, often including opposite side of chest
> **Grades 5 and Grade 6** - very loud, audible with stethoscope barely touching the chest; the vibration is also strong enough to be felt through the animal's chest wall

Murmurs are caused by a number of factors; there may be a problem with the heart's valves or it could be other conditions, such as hyperthyroidism, anemia or heartworm.

In puppies, there are two major types of heart murmurs, and they will probably be detected by your vet at the first or second vaccinations. The most common type is called an innocent 'flow murmur.' This type of murmur is soft - typically Grade 2 or less - and is not caused by underlying heart disease. An innocent flow murmur typically disappears by four to five months of age. However if a puppy has a loud murmur - Grade 3 or louder - or if the heart murmur is still easily heard with a stethoscope after five or six months of age, the likelihood of the puppy having an underlying congenital (from birth) heart problem such as SAS becomes much higher. The thought of a puppy having congenital heart disease is extremely worrying, but it is important to remember that the disease will not affect all puppies' life expectancy or quality of life.

A heart murmur can also develop suddenly in an adult dog with no prior history of the problem. This is typically due to heart disease that develops with age. In toy and small breeds, a heart murmur may develop in middle-aged to older dogs due to an age-related thickening and degeneration of one of the valves in the heart, the mitral valve. (This is the type our dog has.)

This thickening of the valve prevents it from closing properly and as a result it starts to leak, this is known as mitral valve disease. The more common type of heart disease affecting larger dog breeds in middle age is Dilated Cardiomyopathy (DCM.)

Addison's Disease

Addison's Disease in dogs is also known as 'hypoadrenocorticism'. There are two bean-shaped organs near the kidneys called adrenal glands. Although they are quite small, they produce two critical hormones: cortisol - a hormone which deals with stress - and aldosterone, which regulates the amount of salt in the body. Both are essential for normal bodily functions.

Cortisol has an effect on sugar, fat and protein metabolism and is partially responsible for a dog's

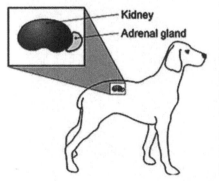

Kidney
Adrenal gland

'fight or flight' response during stressful periods. Aldosterone helps to regulate the electrolytes sodium and potassium in the body, particularly in stressful situations. When the adrenal glands do not function properly, a metabolism and electrolyte imbalance occurs. (Incidentally, Cushing's Disease (hyperadrenocorticism) is the exact opposite and occurs when the adrenal gland produces too much of these hormones.)

Goldendoodles are not particularly susceptible to Cushing's Disease, however, Standard Poodles are regarded as a high-incidence breed for Addison's Disease, along with German

Shepherds, Great Danes, Newfoundlands, West Highland Terriers, Bearded Collies and some other breeds. The causes are not yet known, although they are generally thought to be genetic, often related to autoimmune disorders. It has symptoms in common with many other ailments, which makes diagnosis difficult and sometimes only arrived at by a process of elimination. But once correctly diagnosed, it can be successfully treated and the dog can live a normal active life.

Symptoms

The symptoms can be vague and may initially simply appear as if the dog is off-color. Sometimes the dog also has hypoglycemia (low blood sugar), and the condition can be initially confused with other problems, such as seizures, pancreatic tumor, food poisoning, twisted stomach, parvovirus, back or joint problems. This has earned Addison's Disease the nicknames 'the Great Mimic' and 'the Great Imitator'.

Symptoms may wax and wane over months or years making diagnosis difficult. If the adrenals continue to deteriorate, ultimately the dog will have an acute episode called an 'Addisonian crisis'. At this point many dogs are diagnosed with renal failure, as the kidneys are unable to function properly.

Typically they are given IV solutions, which may produce an almost miraculous recovery. This, too, is a great indication that failure of the adrenal glands, rather than of the kidneys, is creating the symptoms. Addison's more often affects young to middle-aged female dogs; however, a dog of any age can develop the disease and with Standard Poodles, both males and females are susceptible. The average age at diagnosis is four years, although it has been found in puppies as well as dogs up to 12 years old. Across the general canine population, about 70% of affected dogs are female. Here are some general signs to look out for:

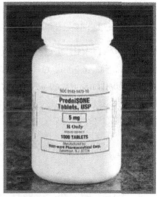

- ❧ Lethargy
- ❧ Lack of appetite
- ❧ Diarrhea
- ❧ Vomiting
- ❧ Weight loss
- ❧ Tremors or shaking
- ❧ Muscle weakness
- ❧ Pain in hindquarters

General muscle weakness might mean that your dog that can't jump onto the bed or sofa as he has done in the past. He may also shiver or have muscle tremors. The most important thing to remember is that you know your dog better than anyone, so if something seems not right, get it checked out by a vet, who will make the diagnosis by a blood test called the ACTH stimulation test. However, because the disease is not very common and has a wide variety of symptoms, this is usually done after several other tests have been carried out to eliminate more common diseases.

Before you reach this stage, one of the first things your vet may test for is electrolyte levels, particularly sodium and potassium. The results may point towards Addison's, but this is not a definitive diagnosis. Other factors, such as whipworms (found in the USA) can also cause irregular electrolyte levels.

Treatment

There are several medications used to treat chronic Addison's Disease. Your vet will prescribe daily glucocorticoids, such as Prednisolone (pictured), and/or mineralocorticoids, such as

Fludrocortisone. There is also a newer, sometimes more effective, option of an injection every 25 days of Percorten-V (DOCP.) The dog will need medication and monitoring for the rest of his life, but the good news is that most dogs properly treated for Addison's return to a full and happy life.

Canine Bloat (Gastric Torsion)

Canine bloat is a serious medical condition which requires urgent medical attention. Without it, the affected dog can die.

Bloat is known by several different names: twisted stomach, gastric torsion or, to give the ailment its medical term, Gastric Dilatation-Volvulus (GDV.) It occurs when the dog's body becomes overstretched with too much gas. The reasons for it are not fully understood, but there are some well-known risk factors. Bloat occurs mainly in larger breeds, particularly those with deep chests like Great Danes, Doberman Pinschers and Setters, but these are not the only breeds affected and it can happen to smaller dogs.

It also happens more - but not exclusively- to dogs over seven years of age and it is more common in males than in females. The risks increase if the stomach is very full, either with food or with water. A dog which is fed once daily and eats very quickly, or gets access to the food store and gorges itself, could be at higher risk. Exercising after eating or after a big drink increases the risk, and stress can also act as a trigger. Bloat occurs when gas is taken in as the dog eats or drinks. It can occur with or without the stomach twisting (volvulus.) As the stomach swells with gas, it can rotate 90° to 360°. The twisting stomach traps air, food and water inside, and the bloated organ stops blood flowing properly to veins in the abdomen. This leads to low blood pressure, shock and even damage to internal organs.

Bloat can kill a dog in less than one hour. If you suspect your Goldendoodle has bloat, get him into the car and off to the vet immediately. Even with treatment, mortality rates range from 10% to 60%. With surgery, this drops to 15% to 33%.The causes are not completely clear, despite research being carried out into the condition. However, the following conditions are generally thought to be contributory factors:

 Air is gulped down as the dog eats or drinks. This is thought more likely to cause a problem when the dog's bowls are on the floor. Some owners buy or construct a frame for the bowls so they are at chest height. However, some experts believe that this may actually increase the risk of bloat. Discuss the situation with your vet. Another option is to moisten your dog's food to slow him down. You can also buy a plastic bowl with molded lumps in the base (pictured) which slow down your dog when eating

 A large meal eaten once a day. For this reason, many owners of large dogs feed their dog two smaller feeds every day

 Diet may be a factor: avoid dog food with high fats or which use citric acid as a preservative; also avoid food with tiny pieces of kibble. Don't overfeed your dog; try and prevent him from eating too fast and avoid feeding scraps, as these may upset his stomach and lead to bloat

 Drinking too much water just before, during or after eating. Remove the water bowl just before mealtimes, but be sure to return it soon after

- Vigorous exercise before or after eating. Allow one hour either side of mealtimes before allowing your dog strenuous exercise

- Age, temperament and breeds: older dogs are more susceptible than younger ones and more males suffer than females. Deep-chested dogs are most at risk

- Stress can possibly be a trigger, with nervous and aggressive dogs being more prone to the illness. Try and maintain a peaceful environment for your dog

Symptoms

Bloat is extremely painful and the dog will show signs of distress, although it may be difficult to distinguish them from other types of stress. He may stand uncomfortably or seem to be anxious for no apparent reason. Another symptom is dry retching: the dog will often attempt to vomit every five to 30 minutes, but nothing is fetched up, except perhaps foam.

Other signs include swelling of the abdomen – this will usually feel firm like a drum – general weakness, difficulty breathing or rapid panting, drooling or excessive drinking. His behavior will change and he may do some of the following: whine, pace up and down, look for a hiding place or lick the air. **Bloat is an emergency condition. Get your dog to a veterinary surgery immediately.**

Epilepsy

Thanks to www.canineepilepsy.co.uk for assistance with this article. If your Goldendoodle has epilepsy, we recommend reading this excellent website to gain a greater understanding of the illness.

Poodles and Golden Retrievers both have a slightly higher incidence of epilepsy than average, which means that Goldendoodles may also have a slightly higher risk of having epilepsy. The characteristics of genetic epilepsy tend to show up between 10 months and three years of age, but dogs as young as six months or as old as five years can show signs.

Anyone who has witnessed their dog having a seizure (convulsion) knows how frightening it can be. Seizures are not uncommon in dogs, but many dogs only ever have one. If your dog has had more than one seizure, it may be that he or she is epileptic. Just as with people, there are medications to control seizures in dogs, allowing them to live more normal lives.

'Epilepsy' means repeated seizures due to abnormal activity in the brain and is caused by an abnormality in the brain itself. It can affect any breed of dog and in fact affects around four or five dogs in every 100. In some breeds it can be hereditary. If seizures happen because of a problem somewhere else in the body, such as heart disease (which stops oxygen reaching the brain), this is not epilepsy. Your vet may do tests to try to find the reason for the epilepsy, but in many cases no cause can be identified.

Symptoms

Some dogs seem to know when they are about to have a seizure and may behave in a certain way. You will come to recognize these signs as meaning that a seizure is likely. Often dogs just seek out their owner's company and come to sit beside them when a seizure is about to start. Once the seizure starts, the dog is unconscious – he cannot hear or respond to you. Most dogs become stiff, fall onto their side and make running movements with their legs. Sometimes they will cry out and may lose control of their bowels or bladder.

Most seizures last between one and three minutes - **it is worth making a note of the time the seizure starts and ends** because it often seems that a seizure goes on for a lot longer than it actually does.

After a seizure, dogs behave in different ways. Some dogs just get up and carry on with what they were doing, while others appear dazed and confused for up to 24 hours afterwards. Most commonly, dogs will be disoriented for only 10 to 15 minutes before returning to their old self. They often have a set pattern of behavior that they follow - for example going for a drink of water or asking to go outside. It is common for a pattern to develop and, should your dog suffer from epilepsy, you will gradually recognize this as specific to your dog.

Most seizures occur while the dog is relaxed and resting quietly. It is very rare for one to occur while exercising, and they often happen in the evening or at night. In a few dogs, seizures seem to be triggered by particular events or stress.

The most important thing is to **stay calm**. Remember that your dog is unconscious during the seizure and is not in pain or distressed. It is likely to be more distressing for you than for him. Make sure that he is not in a position to injure himself, for example by falling down the stairs, but otherwise do not try to interfere with him. **Never** try to put your hand inside his mouth during a seizure or you are very likely to get bitten.

Seizures can cause damage to the brain and if your dog has repeated occurrences, it is likely that further seizures will occur in the future. The damage caused is cumulative and after a lot of incidents there may be enough brain damage to cause early senility (with loss of learned behavior and housetraining or behavioral changes.)

It is very rare for dogs to injure themselves during a seizure. Occasionally they may bite their tongue and there may appear to be a lot of blood, but is unlikely to be serious; your dog will not swallow his tongue. If a seizure goes on for a very long time (more than 10 minutes), his body temperature will rise and this can cause damage to other organs, such as the liver and kidneys as well as the brain. In very extreme cases, some dogs may be left in a coma after severe seizures. If you can, record your dog's seizure on a mobile phone, as it will really help the vet.

When Should I Contact the Vet?

Generally, if your dog has a seizure lasting more than five minutes, or is having more than two or three a day, you should contact your vet. When your dog starts fitting, make a note of the time. If he comes out of it within five minutes, allow him time to recover quietly before contacting the vet. It is far better for him to recover quietly at home rather than be bundled into the car and carted off to the vet right away.

However, if your dog does not come out of the seizure within five minutes, or has repeated seizures close together, contact your vet immediately, as he or she will want to see your dog as soon as possible. If this is his first seizure, the vet may ask you to bring him in for a check and some routine blood tests. Always call the practice before setting off to be sure that there is someone there who can help your dog.

There are many things other than epilepsy which cause seizures in dogs. When your vet first examines your dog, he or she will not know whether your dog has epilepsy or another illness. It's unlikely that the vet will see your dog during a seizure, so it is **vital** that you're able to describe in some detail just what happens. You might want to make notes or record it on your mobile phone. The vet may need to run a range of tests to ensure that there is no other cause; these may include blood tests, possibly X-rays, and maybe even a scan (MRI) of your dog's brain. If no other cause can be found, then a diagnosis of epilepsy may be made. If your Goldendoodle already has epilepsy, remember these key points:

- Don't change or stop any medication without consulting your vet
- See your vet at least once a year for follow-up visits
- Be skeptical of 'magic cure' treatments

It is not usually possible to remove the cause of the seizures, so your vet will use medication to control them. Treatment will not cure the disease, but it will manage the signs – even a well-controlled epileptic will have occasional seizures. Sadly, as yet there is no cure for epilepsy, so don't be tempted with 'instant cures' from the internet.

There are many drugs used in the control of epilepsy in people, but very few of these are suitable for long-term use in a dog. Two of the most common are Phenobarbital and Potassium Bromide (some dogs can have negative results with Phenobarbital.) There are also a number of holistic remedies advertised, but we have no experience of them or any idea if any are effective. Do your research and ask on the forums for other owners' experiences.

Many epileptic dogs require a combination of one or more types of drug to achieve the most effective control of their seizures. Treatment is decided on an individual basis and it may take some time to find the best combination and dose of drugs for your pet. You need patience when managing an epileptic pet. It is important that medication is given at the same time each day.

Once your dog has been on a treatment for a while, he will become dependent on the levels of drug in his blood at all times to control seizures. If you miss a dose of treatment, blood levels can drop and this may be enough to trigger a seizure. Each epileptic dog is an individual and a treatment plan will be designed specifically for him based on the severity and frequency of the seizures and how he respond to different medications.

Keep a record of events in your dog's life, note down dates and times of episodes and record when you have given the medication. Each time you visit your vet, take this diary along with you so he or she can see how your dog has been since his last check-up. If seizures are becoming more frequent, it may be necessary to change the medication. The success or otherwise of treatment may depend on YOU keeping a close eye on your Goldendoodle to see if there are any physical or behavioral changes.

It is rare for epileptic dogs to stop having seizures altogether. However, provided your dog is checked regularly by your vet to make sure that the drugs are not causing any side effects, there is a good chance that he will live a full and happy life. Remember, live **with** epilepsy not **for** epilepsy With the proper medical treatment, most epileptic dogs have far more good days than bad ones. Enjoy all those good days. Visit www.canineepilepsy.co.uk for more information.

Canine Diabetes

This is not an issue which particularly affects Goldendoodles any more than any other type of dog, but can affect dogs of all breeds, sizes and both genders. It does, however, affect obese dogs more than ones of a normal weight.

There are two types: *diabetes mellitus* and *diabetes insipidus*. Diabetes mellitus (sugar diabetes) is the most common form and affects one in 500 dogs. Thanks to modern veterinary medicine, the condition is now treatable and need not shorten your Goldendoodle's lifespan or interfere with his quality of life. Diabetic dogs undergoing treatment now have the same life expectancy as non-diabetic dogs of the same age and gender.

However, if left untreated, the disease can lead to cataracts, increasing weakness in the legs (neuropathy), other ailments and even death. In dogs, diabetes is typically seen anywhere between the ages of four to 14, with a peak at seven to nine years. Both males and females can develop it; unspayed females have a slightly higher risk. The typical canine diabetes sufferer is middle-aged, female and overweight, but there are also juvenile cases.

Diabetes insipidus is caused by a lack of vasopressin, a hormone which controls the kidneys' absorption of water.

Diabetes mellitus occurs when the dog's body does not produce enough insulin and cannot successfully process sugars.

Dogs, like us, get their energy by converting the food they eat into sugars, mainly glucose. This glucose travels in the dog's bloodstream and individual cells then remove some of that glucose from the blood to use for energy. The substance that allows the cells to take glucose from the blood is a protein called *insulin,* which is created by beta cells in the pancreas, next to the stomach. Almost all diabetic dogs have Type 1 diabetes; their pancreas does not produce any insulin. Without it, the cells have no way to use the glucose that is in the bloodstream, so the cells 'starve' while the glucose level in the blood rises.

Your vet will use blood samples and urine samples to check glucose concentrations in order to diagnose diabetes. Early treatment helps to prevent further complications developing. Common symptoms of Diabetes mellitus are:

- Extreme thirst
- Excessive urination
- Weight loss
- Increased appetite
- Coat in poor condition
- Lethargy
- Vision problems due to cataracts

Cataracts and Diabetes - Some diabetic dogs do go blind. Cataracts may develop due to high blood glucose levels causing water to build up in the eyes' lenses. This leads to swelling, rupture of the lens fibers and the development of cataracts.

In many cases, the cataracts can be surgically removed to bring sight back to the dog. Vision is restored in 75% to 80% of diabetic dogs that undergo cataract removal. However, some dogs may stay blind even after the cataracts are gone, and some cataracts simply cannot be removed. Blind dogs are often able to get around surprisingly well, particularly in a familiar home.

Treatment

This starts with the right diet. Your vet will prescribe meals low in fat and sugars and recommend medication. Many cases of canine diabetes can be successfully treated with diet and medication. More severe cases may require insulin injections. In the newly-diagnosed dog, insulin therapy begins at home.

Normally, after a week of treatment, you return to the vet who will do a series of blood sugar tests over a 12-14 hour period to see when the blood glucose peaks and when it hits its lows. Adjustments are then made to the dosage and timing of the injections.

"I DON'T SEE TABLE SCRAPS."

Your vet will explain how to prepare and inject the insulin. You may be asked to collect urine samples using a test strip (a small piece of paper that indicates the glucose levels in urine.)

If your dog is already having insulin injections, beware of a 'miracle cure' offered on some internet sites. It does not exist.

There is no diet or vitamin supplement which can reduce your dog's dependence on insulin injections because vitamins and minerals cannot do what insulin does in the dog's body. If you think that your dog needs a supplement, discuss it with your vet first to make sure that it does not interfere with any other medication.

Managing your dog's diabetes also means managing his activity level. Exercise burns up blood glucose the same way that insulin does. If your dog is on insulin, any active exercise on top of the insulin might cause him to have a severe low blood glucose episode, called **'hypoglycemia'**.

 Keep your dog on a reasonably consistent exercise routine. Your usual insulin dose will take that amount of exercise into account. If you plan to take your dog out for some extra demanding exercise, such as running round with other dogs, give him only half of his usual insulin dose.

* You can usually buy specially formulated diabetes dog food from your vet

* You should feed the same type and amount of food at the same time every day

* Most vets recommend twice-a-day feeding for diabetic pets. It is OK if your dog prefers to eat more often

* If you have other pets in the home, they should also be placed on a twice-a-day feeding schedule, so that the diabetic dog cannot eat from their bowls. Help your dog to achieve the best possible blood glucose control by not feeding him table scraps or treats between meals

* Watch for signs that your dog is starting to drink more water than usual. Call the vet if you see this happening, as it may mean that the insulin dose needs adjusting. Remember:

Food raises blood glucose - Insulin and exercise lower blood glucose - Keep them in balance.

For more information on canine diabetes visit www.caninediabetes.org

Canine Cancer

This is the biggest single killer of dogs of whatever breed and will claim the lives of one in four dogs. It is the cause of nearly half the deaths of all dogs aged 10 years and older, according to the American Veterinary Medical Association. Early detection is critical, some things to look out for are:

- Swellings anywhere on the body
- Lumps in a dog's armpit or under his jaw
- Sores that don't heal
- Bad breath
- Weight loss
- Poor appetite, difficulty swallowing or excessive drooling
- Changes in exercise or stamina level
- Labored breathing
- Change in bowel or bladder habits

If your dog has been spayed or neutered, the risk of certain cancers decreases. These cancers include uterine and mammary cancer in females, and testicular cancer in males (if the dog was neutered before he was six months old.) Along with controlling the pet population, spaying is especially important because mammary cancer in female dogs is fatal in about 50% of all cases.

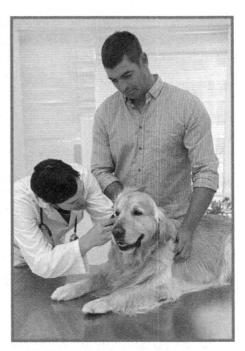

Just because your dog has a skin growth doesn't mean that it's cancerous. As with humans, tumors may be benign (harmless) or malignant (harmful.) Your vet will probably confirm the tumor using X-rays, blood tests and possibly ultrasounds. He or she will then decide whether it is benign or malignant via a biopsy in which a tissue sample is taken and examined under a microscope. If your dog is diagnosed with cancer, there is hope. Advances in veterinary medicine and technology offer various treatment options, including chemotherapy, radiation and surgery. Unlike with humans, a dog's hair will not fall out with chemotherapy.

Treatment

Canine cancer is growing at an ever-increasing rate. One of the difficulties is that your pet cannot tell you when a cancer is developing, but if cancers can be detected early enough through a physical or behavioral change, they often respond well to treatment. Over recent years, we have all become more aware of the risk factors for human cancer. Responding to these by changing our habits is having a significant impact on human health.

For example, stopping smoking, protecting ourselves from over-exposure to strong sunlight and eating a healthy, balanced diet all help to reduce cancer rates. We know to keep a close eye on ourselves, go for regular health checks and report any lumps and bumps to our doctors as soon as they appear. Increased cancer awareness is definitely improving human health.

The same is true with your dog. While it is impossible to completely prevent cancer from occurring, a healthy lifestyle with a balanced diet and regular exercise can help to reduce the risk. Also, be aware of any new lumps and bumps on your dog's body and any changes in his behavior.

The success of treatment will depend on the type of cancer, the treatment used and on how early the tumor is found. The sooner treatment begins, the greater the chances of success. One of the best things you can do for your dog is to keep a close eye on him for any tell-tale signs. This shouldn't be too difficult and can be done as part of your regular handling and grooming. If you notice any new bumps, for example, monitor them over a period of days to see if there is a change in their appearance or size. If there is, then make an appointment to see your vet as soon as possible. It might only be a cyst, but better to be safe than sorry.

Research into earlier diagnosis and improved treatments is being conducted at veterinary schools and companies all over the world. Advances in biology are producing a steady flow of new tests and treatments which are now becoming available to improve survival rates and canine cancer care. If your dog is diagnosed with cancer, do not despair, there are many options and new, improved treatments are constantly being introduced.

Our Happy Ending

We know from personal experience that canine cancer can be successfully treated if it is diagnosed early enough. Our dog Max was diagnosed with T-cell lymphoma when he was four years old.

We had noticed a black lump on his anus which grew to the size of a small grape. We took him to the vet within the first few days of seeing the lump and, after a test, he was diagnosed with the dreaded T-cell lymphoma. This is a particularly nasty and aggressive form of cancer which can spread to the lymph system and is often fatal for dogs.

As soon as the diagnosis was confirmed, our vet Graham operated and removed the lump. He also had to remove one of his anal glands, but as dogs have two this was not a serious worry. Afterwards, we were on tenterhooks, not knowing if another lump would grow or if the cancer had already spread to his lymph system.

After a few months, Max had another blood test and was finally given the all-clear. He is now happy, healthy and 11 years old. We were very lucky. I would strongly advise anyone who suspects that their dog has cancer to get him or her to your local vet as soon as possible.

Disclaimer: The author of this book is not a qualified veterinarian. This chapter is intended to give owners an indication of some of the illnesses which may affect their dogs and the symptoms to look out for. If you have any concerns regarding the health of your dog, our advice is always the same: consult a veterinarian.

10. Skin and Allergies

Allergies are a growing concern for owners of many breeds and crossbreeds. Visit any busy vet's surgery these days – especially in spring and summer – and it's likely that one or more of the dogs is there because of some type of sensitivity. When bred from healthy parents, Goldendoodles are not considered particularly susceptible as far as allergies and skin problems are concerned. However, they can inherit or develop issues, visit any Goldendoodle forum and you'll see there are plenty of itchy dogs out there.

....

Any individual dog can have issues. Skin conditions, allergies and intolerances are on the increase in the canine world as well as the human world. How many children did you hear of having asthma or a peanut allergy when you were at school? Not many, I'll bet, yet allergies and adverse reactions are now relatively common – and it's the same with dogs. As yet the reasons are not clear; it could be to do with breeding, but there is no clear scientific evidence to back this up.

This is a complicated topic and a whole book could be written on this subject alone. While many dogs have no problems at all, some suffer from sensitive skin, allergies, yeast infections and/or skin disorders, causing them to scratch, bite or lick themselves excessively on the paws and other areas. Symptoms may vary from mild itchiness to a chronic reaction.

The Goldendoodle breeders and owners we asked about this topic were mainly of the opinion that their dog(s) have had no problems. If you haven't already bought your puppy, it would be one question to ask the breeder. One quite common condition with Goldendoodles is ear infections due to their furry, floppy ears – more about these later.

As with humans, the skin is the dog's largest organ. It acts as the protective barrier between your dog's internal organs and the outside world; it also regulates temperature and provides the sense of touch. Surprisingly, a dog's skin is actually thinner than ours, and it is made up of three layers:

1. **Epidermis** or outer layer, the one that bears the brunt of your dog's contact with the outside world

2. **Dermis** is the extremely tough layer mostly made up of collagen, a strong and fibrous protein. This where blood vessels deliver nutrients and oxygen to the skin, and it also acts as your dog's thermostat by allowing his body to release or keep in heat, depending on the outside temperature and your dog's activity level

3. **Subcutis** is a dense layer of fatty tissue that allows your dog's skin to move independently from the muscle layers below it, as well as providing insulation and support for the skin

Human allergies often trigger a reaction within the respiratory system, causing us to wheeze or sneeze, whereas allergies or hypersensitivities in a dog often cause a reaction in his or her **skin.**

Skin can be affected from the **inside** by things that your dog eats or drinks.

Skin can be affected from the **outside** by fleas, parasites, inhaled or contact allergies triggered by grass, pollen, man-made chemicals, dust, mold etc. These environmental allergies are especially common in some Terriers as well as the Miniature Schnauzer, Bulldog and certain other breeds.

Like all dogs, a Goldendoodle can suffer from food allergies or intolerances as well as environmental allergies. Canine skin disorders are a complex subject. Some dogs can run through fields, digging holes and rolling around in the grass with no after-effects at all. Others may spend a lot of time indoors and have an excellent diet, but still experience severe itching.

Skin problems may be the result of one or more of a wide range of causes - and the list of potential remedies and treatments is even longer. It's by no means possible to cover all of them in this chapter. The aim here is to give a broad outline of some of the ailments most likely to affect Goldendoodles and how to deal with them. We have also included remedies tried with some success by ourselves (we have a dog with skin issues) and other owners of affected dogs, as well as advice from a holistic specialist.

This information is not intended to take the place of professional help. We are not animal health experts and you should always contact your vet as soon as your dog appears physically unwell or uncomfortable. This is particularly true with skin conditions:

If a vet can find the source of the problem early on, there is more chance of successfully treating it before it has chance to develop into a more serious condition with secondary issues.

There is anecdotal evidence from some owners that switching to a raw diet or raw meaty bones diet can significantly help some canines with skin issues. See **Chapter 6. Feeding a Goldendoodle** for more information.

One of the difficulties with this type of ailment is that the exact cause is often difficult to diagnose, as the symptoms may also be common to other issues. If environmental allergies are involved, some specific tests are available costing hundreds of pounds or dollars. You will have to take your vet's advice on this, as the tests are not always conclusive and if the answer is dust or pollen, it can be difficult to keep your lively dog away from the triggers while still having a normal life - unless you and your Goldendoodle spend all your time in a spotlessly clean city apartment (which is, frankly, unlikely!) It is often a question of managing a skin condition, rather than curing it.

Skin issues and allergies often develop in adolescence or early adulthood, which in a Goldendoodle may be anything from a few months to two or three years old. Our dog Max was perfectly normal until he reached two when he began scratching, triggered by environmental allergies - most likely pollen. He's now 11 and over the years he's been on various different remedies which have all worked for a time. As his allergies are seasonal, he normally does not have any medication between October and March. But come spring and as sure as daffodils are daffodils, he starts scratching again. Luckily, they are manageable and Max lives a happy, normal life.

 Another issue reported by some dog owners is food allergy or intolerance (there is a difference) – often to grain. Allergies and their treatment can cause a lot of stress for dogs and owners alike. The number one piece of advice is that if you suspect your Goldendoodle has an allergy or skin problem, try to **deal with it right away** - either via your vet or natural remedies – before the all-too-familiar scenario kicks in and it develops into a chronic (long term) condition.

Whatever the cause, before a vet can diagnose the problem you have to be prepared to tell him or her all about your dog's diet, exercise regime, habits, medical history and local environment. The vet will then carry out a thorough physical examination, possibly followed by further (expensive) tests, before a course of treatment can be prescribed. You'll have to decide whether these tests are worth it and whether they are likely to discover the exact root of the problem.

Sebaceous Adenitis

SA is a rare inflammatory skin disease that affects the skin glands of young and middle age dogs. It most commonly affects Poodles, Akitas and Samoyeds, although other breeds (and some cats and horses) can also be infected. Because it affects some Poodles, it can also be passed on to Goldendoodles.

Sebaceous glands are microscopic glands found below the skin which secrete an oily substance (sebum) to lubricate the dog's skin and hair. SA is a type of autoimmune disease where the dog's sebaceous glands become inflamed and are eventually destroyed. The exact cause is as yet unknown and is the subject of current research. There are two types of the condition - one for long or double coated breeds, such as the Poodle, and one for short coated breeds - each has different symptoms. (The diagram shows a normal sebaceous gland.)

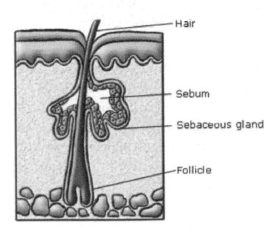

For Poodles and Goldendoodles, the symptoms are:

- Alopecia (hair loss), often in a circular pattern
- Silvery scales or dandruff which sticks to the fur
- A rancid or musty odor
- Matted hair

- 🐾 Dull, brittle or coarse hair
- 🐾 Intense itching and scratching
- 🐾 Bacterial infections along the hair follicle
- 🐾 Skin lesions on the head or back

One of the problems with diagnosis is that there are a number of other conditions with similar symptoms. These include **Seborrhea,** where the dog's body produces keratin, which results in flaking and itching of the skin; **Demodicosis,** an overgrowth of skin mites that can cause itching, hair loss and swelling; **Dermatophytosis,** a fungal infection which also causes itching and flaking, and **Endocrine Skin Disease.**

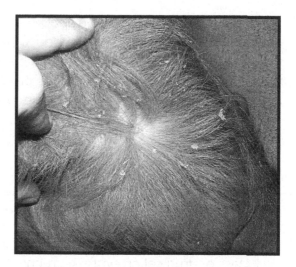

To test for SA, a vet may take skin scrapings and endocrine function tests and usually a skin biopsy. There is no cure for the condition and treatment is generally lifelong. It usually involves regular bathing with antiseborrheic shampoos (such as Malaseb or Veterinary formula Clinical Care), soaking the dog in mineral oils, giving fatty acid supplements and, in more in more severe cases, the prescription of steroids. To prevent this disease from being passed on to Goldendoodles, The Health Tested Goldendoodle and Labradoodle Breeder and Kennel Directory, which can be found online at www.goldendoodle-labradoodle.org, recommends a minimum of two tests within a three-year period for all breeding Standard Poodles.

Ichthyosis

This is a condition which affects several breeds, including Golden Retrievers – both European and American - Westies, some other Terriers, Dobermans and Jack Russells. According to Genetic Veterinary Science Inc: "The Mutation of the PNPLA1 gene associated with Ichthyosis (Golden Retriever type) has been identified in the Goldendoodle. Though the exact frequency in the overall Goldendoodle population is unknown, approximately 44% out of 1,600 Golden Retrievers tested from Australia, France, Switzerland, and the United States were carriers of the mutation and approximately 29% were affected."

Ichthyosis (named after the Greek word for 'fish,' due to the scales seen on affected dogs) causes a pronounced thickening of the outer layer of the dog's skin and footpads and rough skin which gets covered with thick greasy flakes or scales. The condition is normally present from birth, with white scales soon developing on a puppy's skin. It worsens with age, with progressive blackening of the skin, which becomes dry and rough, but typically does not cause itching.

The rough skin is covered with thick greasy scales, some of which stick to the skin and hair, and some of which flake off. The dog's general health does not appear to be affected, but the skin changes are chronic (long term) and severe, and because of the marked thickening of the footpads, the whole paw may be enlarged and painful.

Ichthyosis is relatively easy to diagnose in a young puppy, due to the condition of the skin. If these skin changes are seen in an older dog, other causes of Seborrhea ('excessive discharge of sebum from the sebaceous glands') must also be considered. In either case, the diagnosis is confirmed through a skin biopsy. This is a simple procedure done with local anesthetic, in which your vet removes a small sample of your dog's skin for testing by a veterinary pathologist.

It is possible to manage the condition in affected dogs, but it requires a lot of effort on the part of the owner in partnership with the vet. Treatment includes frequent baths using a mild anti-seborrheic shampoo and moisturizing rinses, along with plenty of brushing and a diet rich in fatty acids. If you Google "Ichthyosis Golden Retriever" you will be able to read of other owners' experiences and tips for dealing with the disease.

One glimmer of hope on the treatment front is that there has been some reported success with a new class of drug called synthetic retinoids. If your dog suffers from Ichthyosis, ask your vet about these. Although the condition is often severe and long term, the dog is usually not in pain and if you are prepared to put the time in, he or she can have a good quality of life. The only way to eradicate this disease is by not breeding from affected dogs, or those which are carriers. There is now a DNA test for the condition carried out by the Antagene research lab in France.

....

Types of Allergies

'*Canine dermatitis*' means inflammation of a dog's skin and it can be triggered by numerous things, but the most common by far is allergies. Vets estimate that one in four dogs at their clinics is there because of some kind of allergy. Symptoms are:

- Chewing on paws
- Rubbing the face on the carpet
- Scratching the body
- Scratching or biting the anus
- Itchy ears, head shaking
- Hair loss
- Mutilated skin with sore or discolored patches or hot spots

A Goldendoodle who is allergic to something will show it through skin problems and itching; your vet may call this '*pruritus*'. It may seem logical that if a dog is allergic to something he inhales, like certain pollen grains, his nose will run; if he's allergic to something he eats, he may vomit, or if allergic to an insect bite, he may develop a swelling. But in practice this is seldom the case. The skin is the largest canine organ in the body and with dogs it is this which is often affected by allergies, causing a mild to severe itching sensation over the body and maybe a chronic ear infection.

Dogs with allergies often chew their feet until they are sore and red. You may see yours rubbing his face on the carpet or couch or scratching his belly and flanks. Because the ear glands produce too much wax in response to the allergy, ear infections can occur, with bacteria and yeast - which is a fungus - often thriving in the excessive wax and debris. But your Goldendoodle doesn't have to suffer from allergies to get ear infections, the lack of air flow under the floppy hairy ears make them prone to the condition. By the way, if your dog does develop a yeast infection and you switch to a grain-free diet, avoid those which are potato-based, as these contain high levels of starch.

Holistic vet Dr Jodie Gruenstern says: "Grains and other starches have a negative impact on gut health, creating insulin resistance and inflammation. It's estimated that up to 80% of the immune system resides within the gastrointestinal system; building a healthy gut supports a more appropriate immune response. The importance of choosing fresh proteins and healthy fats over processed, starchy diets (such as kibble) can't be overemphasized."

An allergic dog may cause skin lesions or 'hot spots' by constant chewing and scratching. Sometimes he will lose hair, which can be patchy, leaving a mottled appearance. The skin itself may be dry and crusty, reddened, swollen or oily, depending on the dog. It is very common to get secondary bacterial skin infections due to these self-inflicted wounds. An allergic dog's body is reacting to certain molecules called 'allergens.' These may come from:

- Trees
- Grass
- Pollens
- Foods and food additives, such as specific meats, grains or colorings
- Milk products
- Fabrics, such as wool or nylon
- Rubber and plastics
- House dust and dust mites
- Mold
- Flea bites
- Chemical products used around the house

These allergens may be **inhaled** as the dog breathes, **ingested** as the dog eats or caused by **contact** with the dog's body when he walks or rolls. However they arrive, they all cause the immune system to produce a protein (IgE), which causes various irritating chemicals, such as histamine, to be released. In dogs these chemical reactions and cell types occur in sizeable amounts only within the skin, hence the scratching.

Inhalant Allergies (Atopy)

The most common allergies in dogs are inhalant and seasonal (at least at first; some allergies may develop and worsen.) Substances which can cause an allergic reaction in dogs are similar to those causing problems for humans. Goldendoodles are not particularly susceptible to inhalant allergies, but any individual dog can suffer from them.

A clue to diagnosing these allergies is to look at the timing of the reaction. Does it happen all year round? If so, this may be mold, dust or some other trigger which is permanently in the environment. If the reaction is seasonal, then pollens may well be the culprit. A diagnosis can be made by allergy testing - either a blood or skin test where a small amount of antigen is injected into the dog's skin to test for a reaction. The blood test can give false positives, so the skin test is many veterinarians' preferred method.

Whether or not you take this route will be your decision; allergy testing is not cheap, it takes time and may require your dog to be sedated. And there's also no point doing it if you are not going to go along with the recommended method of treatment afterwards, which is immunotherapy, or **'hyposensitization',** and this can also be an expensive and lengthy process.

It consists of a series of injections made specifically for your dog and administered over weeks or months to make him more tolerant of specific allergens. It may have to be done by a veterinary dermatologist if your vet is not familiar with the treatment. Vets in the US claim that success rates can be as high as 75% of cases. These tests work best when carried out during the season when the allergies are at their worst. But before you get to this stage, your vet will have had to rule out other potential causes, such as fleas or mites, fungal, yeast or bacterial infections and hypothyroidism. Due to the time and cost involved in skin testing, most mild cases of allergies are treated with a combination of avoidance, fatty acids and antihistamines.

Environmental or Contact Irritations

These are a direct reaction to something the dog physically comes into contact with. It could be as simple as grass, specific plants, dust or other animals. If the trigger is grass or other outdoor materials, the allergies are often seasonal. The dog may require treatment (often tablets, shampoo or localized cortisone spray) for spring and summer, but be perfectly fine with no medication for the other half of the year. This is the case with our dog.

 If you suspect your Goldendoodle may have outdoor contact allergies, here is one very good tip guaranteed to reduce his scratching: get him to stand in a tray or large bowl of water on your return from a walk. Washing his feet and under his belly will get rid of some of the pollen and other allergens, which in turn will reduce his scratching and biting. This can help to reduce the allergens to a tolerable level.

Other possible triggers include dry carpet shampoos, caustic irritants, new carpets, cement dust, washing powders or fabric conditioners. If you wash your dog's bedding or if he sleeps on your bed, use a fragrance-free - if possible, hypoallergenic - laundry detergent and avoid fabric conditioner.

The irritation may be restricted to the part of the dog - such as the underneath of the paws or belly - which has touched the offending object. Symptoms are skin irritation - either a general problem or specific hotspots - itching (pruritis) and sometimes hair loss. Readers sometimes report to us that their dog will incessantly lick one part of the body, often the paws, anus, belly or back.

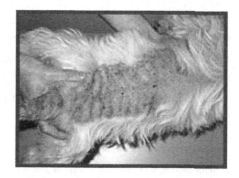

Flea Bite Allergies

These are a very common canine allergy and affect dogs of all breeds. To compound the problem, many dogs with flea allergies also have inhalant allergies. Flea bite allergy is typically seasonal, worse during summer and autumn – peak time for fleas - and is worse in warmer climates where fleas are prevalent.

This type of allergy is not to the flea itself, but to proteins in flea saliva, which are deposited under the dog's skin when the insect feeds. Just one bite to an allergic Goldendoodle will cause intense and long-lasting itching. If affected, the dog will try to bite at the base of his tail and scratch a lot. Most of the damage is done by the dog's scratching, rather than the flea bite, and can result in his fur falling out or skin abrasions.

Some Goldendoodles will develop hot spots. These can occur anywhere, but are often along the back and base of the tail. Flea bite allergies can only be totally prevented by keeping all fleas away from the dog. Various flea prevention treatments are available – see the section on **Parasites**. If you suspect your dog may be allergic to fleas, consult your vet for the proper diagnosis and medication.

Diet and Food Allergies

Food is the third most common cause of allergies in dogs. Cheap dog foods bulked up with grains and other ingredients can cause problems. Some owners have reported their dogs having problems with wheat and other grains. If you feed your dog a dry commercial dog food, make sure that it's a high quality, preferably hypoallergenic, one and that the first ingredient listed on the sack is meat or poultry, not grain. Without the correct food, a dog's whole body - not just his skin and coat - will continuously be under stress and this manifests itself in a number of ways. The symptoms of food allergies are similar to those of most allergies:

- Itchy skin affecting primarily the face, feet, ears, forelegs, armpits and anus
- Excessive scratching
- Chronic or recurring ear infections
- Hair loss
- Hot spots
- Skin infections that clear up with antibiotics, but return after the antibiotics have finished
- Possible increased bowel movements, maybe twice as many as normal

The bodily process which occurs when an animal has a reaction to a particular food agent is not very well understood, but the veterinary profession does know how to diagnose and treat food allergies. As many other problems can cause similar symptoms to food allergies (and also the fact that many sufferers also have other allergies), it is important that any other problems are identified and treated before food allergies are diagnosed. Atopy, flea bite allergies, intestinal parasite hypersensitivities, sarcoptic mange and yeast or bacterial infections can all cause similar symptoms. This can be an anxious time for owners as vets try one thing after another to get to the bottom of the allergy.

The normal method for diagnosing a food allergy is elimination. Once all other causes have been ruled out or treated, then a food trial is the next step – and that's no picnic for owners either - see **Chapter 6. Feeding a Goldendoodle** for more information. As with other allergies, dogs may have short-term relief by taking fatty acids, antihistamines, and steroids, but removing the offending items from the diet is the only permanent solution.

Acute Moist Dermatitis (Hot Spots)

Acute moist dermatitis or 'hot spots' are not uncommon. A hot spot can appear suddenly and is a raw, inflamed and often bleeding area of skin. The area becomes moist and painful and begins spreading due to continual licking and chewing. They can become large, red and irritated in a short pace of time. The cause is often a local reaction to an insect bite; fleas, ticks, biting flies and even mosquitoes have been known to cause acute moist dermatitis. Other causes of hot spots include:

- Allergies - inhalant allergies and food allergies
- Mites
- Ear infections
- Poor grooming
- Burs or plant awns
- Anal gland disease
- Hip dysplasia or other types of arthritis and degenerative joint disease

The good news is that, once diagnosed and with the right treatment, hot spots disappear as soon as they appeared. The underlying cause should be identified and treated, if possible. Check with your vet before treating your Goldendoodle for fleas and ticks at the same time as other medical treatment (such as anti-inflammatory medications and/or antibiotics), as he or she will probably advise you to wait. Treatments may come in the form of injections, tablets or creams – or your dog might need a combination of them. Your vet will probably clip and clean the affected area to help the effectiveness of any spray or ointment and your poor Goldendoodle might also have to wear an E-collar until the condition subsides, but usually this does not take long.

Interdigital Cysts

If you've ever noticed a fleshy red lump between your dog's toes that looks like an ulcerated sore or a hairless bump, then it was probably an interdigital cyst - or 'interdigital furuncle' to give the condition its correct medical term. These can be very difficult to get rid of, since they are not the primary issue, but often a sign of some other condition. Goldendoodles don't generally suffer from them any more than other breeds, but it is thought some Poodles do.

Actually these are not cysts, but the result of *furunculosis*, a condition of the skin which clogs hair follicles and creates chronic infection. They can be caused by a number of factors, including allergies, obesity, poor foot conformation, mites, yeast infections, ingrown hairs or other foreign bodies, and obesity.

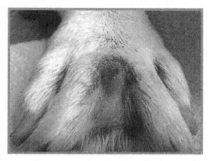

These nasty-looking bumps are painful for your dog, will probably cause him to limp and can be a nightmare to get rid of. Vets might recommend a whole range of treatments to get to the root cause of the problem. It can be extremely expensive if your dog is having a barrage of tests or biopsies and even then you are not guaranteed to find the underlying cause. The first thing he or she will probably do is put your dog in an E-collar to stop him licking the affected area, which will never recover properly as long as he's constantly licking it. This again is stressful for your dog.

Here are some remedies your vet may suggest:

- Antibiotics and/or steroids and/or mite killers
- Soaking his feet in Epsom salts twice daily to unclog the hair follicles
- Testing him for allergies or thyroid problems
- Starting a food trial if food allergies are suspected
- Shampooing his feet
- Cleaning between his toes with medicated (benzoyl peroxide) wipes
- A referral to a veterinary dermatologist
- Surgery

If you suspect your Goldendoodle has an interdigital cyst, take him to the vet for a correct diagnosis and then discuss the various options. A course of antibiotics may be suggested initially, along with switching to a hypoallergenic diet if a food allergy is suspected. If the condition persists, many owners get discouraged, especially when treatment may go on for many weeks.

 Before you resort to any drastic action, first try soaking your Goldendoodle's affected paw in Epsom salts for five or 10 minutes twice a day. After the soaking, clean the area with

medicated wipes, which are antiseptic and control inflammation. In the US these are sold under the brand name Stridex pads in the skin care section of any grocery, or from the pharmacy. If you think the cause may be an environmental allergy, wash your dog's paws and under his belly when you return from a walk, this will help to remove pollen and other allergens.

Surgery can be effective, but it is a drastic option and although it might solve the immediate problem, it will not deal with whatever is triggering the interdigital cysts in the first place. Not only is healing after this surgery a lengthy and difficult process, it also means your dog will never have the same foot as before - future orthopedic issues and a predisposition to more interdigital cysts are a couple of problems which can occur afterwards.

All that said, your vet will understand that interdigital cysts aren't so simple to deal with, but they are always treatable. Get the right diagnosis as soon as possible, limit all offending factors and give medical treatment a good solid try before embarking on more drastic cures.

....

Parasites

Demodectic Mange

Demodectic mange is also known as red mange, follicular mange or puppy mange. It is caused by the tiny mite Demodex canis – pictured - which can only be seen through a microscope. The mites actually live inside the hair follicles on the bodies of virtually every adult dog, and most humans, without causing any harm or irritation. In humans, the mites are found in the skin, eyelids and the creases of the nose ...try not to think about that!

The Demodex mite spends its entire life on the host dog. Eggs hatch and mature from larvae to nymphs to adults in 20 to 35 days and the mites are transferred directly from the mother to the puppies within the first week of life by direct physical contact. Demodectic mange is not a disease of poorly kept or dirty kennels. It is generally a disease of young dogs with inadequate or poorly developed immune systems (or older dogs suffering from a suppressed immune system.)

Vets currently believe that virtually every mother carries and transfers mites to her puppies, and most are immune to the mite's effects, but a few puppies are not and they develop full-blown mange. They may have a few (less than five) isolated lesions and this is known as localized mange – often around the head. This happens in around 90% of cases, but in the other 10% of cases, it develops into generalized mange which covers the entire body or region of the body. This is most likely to develop in puppies with parents that have suffered from mange. Most lesions in either form develop after four months of age. It can also develop around the time when females have their first season, typically around nine months old, and may be due to a slight dip in the bitch's immune system.

Symptoms – Bald patches are usually the first sign, usually accompanied by crusty, red skin which sometimes appears greasy or wet. Usually hair loss begins around the muzzle, eyes and other areas on the head. The lesions may or may not itch. In localized mange, a few circular crusty areas appear, most frequently on the head and front legs of three to six-month-old puppies. Most will self-heal as the puppies become older and develop their own immunity, but a persistent problem needs treatment.

With generalized mange there are bald patches over the entire coat, including the head, neck, body, legs, and feet. The skin on the head, side and back is crusty, often inflamed and oozes a clear fluid. The skin itself will often be oily to touch and there is usually a secondary bacterial infection. Some puppies can become quite ill and can develop a fever, lose their appetites and become lethargic. If you suspect your puppy has generalized demodectic mange, get him to a vet straight away.

There is also a condition called pododermatitis, when the mange affects a puppy's paws. It can cause bacterial infections and be very uncomfortable, even painful. The symptoms of this mange include hair loss on the paws, swelling of the paws (especially around the nail beds) and red/hot/inflamed areas which are often infected. Treatment is always recommended, and it can take several rounds to clear it up.

Diagnosis and Treatment – The vet will normally diagnose demodectic mange after he or she has taken a skin scraping. As these mites are present on every dog, they do not necessarily mean the dog has mange. Only when the mite is coupled with lesions will the vet diagnose mange. Treatment usually involves topical (on the skin) medication and sometimes tablets. In 90% of cases localized demodectic mange resolves itself as the puppy grows.

If the dog has just one or two lesions, these can usually be successfully treated using specific creams and spot treatments. With the more serious generalized demodectic mange, treatment can be lengthy and expensive. The vet might prescribe an anti-parasitic dip every two weeks. Owners should always wear rubber gloves when treating their dog, and it should be applied in an area with adequate ventilation. It should also be noted that **some dogs – especially Toy breeds - can react to these dips,** so check with your vet as to whether it will be suitable. Most dogs with a severe issue need six to 14 dips every two weeks. After the first three or four dips, your vet will probably take another skin scraping to check the mites have gone. Dips continue for one month after the mites have disappeared, but dogs shouldn't be considered cured until a year after their last treatment.

Other options include the heartworm treatment Ivermectin. This isn't approved by the FDA for treating mange, but is often used to do so. It is usually given orally every one to two days, or by injection, and can be very effective. **Again, some dogs react badly to it.** Another drug is Interceptor (Milbemycin oxime), which can be expensive as it has to be given daily. However, it is effective on up to 80% of the dogs who did not respond to dips –but should be given with caution to pups under 21 weeks of age.

Dogs that have the generalized condition may have underlying skin infections, so antibiotics are often given for the first several weeks of treatment. Because the mite flourishes on dogs with suppressed immune systems, you should try to get to the root cause of immune system disease, especially if your Goldendoodle is older when he or she develops demodectic mange.

Sarcoptic Mange (Scabies)

Also known as canine scabies, this is caused by the parasite *Sarcoptes scabiei*. This microscopic mite can cause a range of skin problems, the most common of which is hair loss and severe itching. The mites can infect other animals such as foxes, cats and even humans, but prefer to live their short lives on dogs. Fortunately, there are several good treatments for this mange and the disease can be easily controlled.

In cool, moist environments, they live for up to 22 days. At normal room temperature they live from two to six days, preferring to live on parts of the dog with less hair. These are the areas you may see

him scratching, although it can spread throughout the body in severe cases. Diagnosing canine scabies can be somewhat difficult, and it is often mistaken for inhalant allergies. Once diagnosed, there are a number of effective treatments, including selamectin (Revolution), an on-the-skin solution applied once a month which also provides heartworm prevention, flea control and some tick protection. Various Frontline products are also effective – check with your vet for the correct ones.

Because your dog does not have to come into direct contact with an infected dog to catch scabies, it is difficult to completely protect him. Foxes and their environment can also transmit the mite, so keep your dog away from areas where you know foxes are present.

Fleas

When you see your dog scratching and biting, your first thought is probably: "He's got fleas!" and you may well be right. Fleas don't fly, but they do have very strong back legs and they will take any opportunity to jump from the ground or another animal into your Goldendoodle's lovely warm coat. You can sometimes see the fleas if you part your dog's fur.

And for every flea that you see on your dog, there is the awful prospect of hundreds of eggs and larvae in your house or apartment. So if your dog is unlucky enough to catch fleas, you'll have to treat your environment as well as your dog in order to completely get rid of them.

The best form of cure is prevention. Vets recommend giving dogs a preventative flea treatment every four to eight weeks. This may vary depending on your climate, the season - fleas do not breed as quickly in the cold - and how much time your dog spends outdoors. Once-a-month topical (applied to the skin) insecticides - like Frontline and Advantix - are the most commonly used flea prevention products on the market. You part the skin and apply drops of the liquid on to a small area on your dog's back, usually near the neck. Some kill fleas and ticks, and others just kill fleas - check the details.

It is worth spending the money on a quality treatment, as cheaper brands may not rid your Goldendoodle completely of fleas, ticks and other parasites. Sprays, dips, shampoos and collars are other options, as are tablets and injections in certain cases, such as before your dog goes into boarding kennels or has surgery. Incidentally, a flea bite is different from a flea bite allergy.

NOTE: There is considerable anecdotal evidence from dog owners of various breeds that the US flea and worm tablet *Trifexis* may cause severe side effects in some dogs. You may wish to read some owners' comments at: www.max-the-schnauzer.com/trifexis-side-effects-in-schnauzers.html

Ticks

A tick is not an insect, but a member of the arachnid family, like the spider. There are over 850 types of them, divided into two types: hard shelled and soft shelled. Ticks don't have wings - they can't fly, they crawl. They have a sensor called Haller's organ which detects smell, heat and humidity to help them locate food, which in some cases is a Goldendoodle. A tick's diet consists of one thing and one thing only – blood! They climb up onto tall grass and when they sense an animal is close, crawl on him.

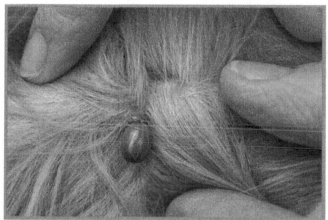

Ticks can pass on a number of diseases to animals and humans, the most well-known of which is **Lyme Disease**, a serious condition which causes lameness and other problems. Dogs which spend a lot of time outdoors in high risk areas, such as woods, can have a vaccination against Lime Disease.

If you do find a tick on your Goldendoodle's coat and are not sure how to get it out, have it removed by a vet or other expert. Inexpertly pulling it out yourself and leaving a bit of the tick behind can be detrimental to your dog's health. Prevention treatment is similar to that for fleas. If your dog has particularly sensitive skin, he might do better with a natural flea or tick remedy.

Heartworm

Heartworm is a serious and potentially fatal disease affecting pets in North America and many other parts of the world. It is caused by foot-long worms (heartworms) that live in the heart, lungs and associated blood vessels of affected pets, causing severe lung disease, heart failure and damage to other organs in the body.

The dog is a natural host for heartworms, which means that heartworms living inside the dog mature into adults, mate and produce offspring. If untreated, their numbers can increase; dogs have been known to harbor several hundred worms in their bodies. Heartworm disease causes lasting damage to the heart, lungs and arteries, and can affect the dog's health and quality of life long after the parasites are gone. For this reason, prevention is by far the best option and treatment - when needed - should be administered as early as possible.

The mosquito (pictured) plays an essential role in the heartworm life cycle. When a mosquito bites and takes a blood meal from an infected animal, it picks up baby worms which develop and mature into 'infective stage' larvae over a period of 10 to 14 days. Then, when the infected mosquito bites another dog, cat or susceptible wild animal, the infective larvae are deposited onto the surface of the animal's skin and enter the new host through the mosquito's bite wound. Once inside a new host, it takes approximately six months for the larvae to develop into adult heartworms. Once mature, heartworms can live for five to seven years in a dog. In the early stages of the disease, many

dogs show few or no symptoms. The longer the infection persists, the more likely symptoms will develop. These include:

- A mild persistent cough
- Reluctance to exercise
- Tiredness after moderate activity
- Decreased appetite
- Weight loss

As the disease progresses, dogs may develop heart failure and a swollen belly due to excess fluid in the abdomen. Dogs with large numbers of heartworms can develop sudden blockages of blood flow within the heart leading to the life-threatening caval syndrome. This is marked by a sudden onset of labored breathing, pale gums and dark, bloody or coffee-colored urine. Without prompt surgical removal of the heartworm blockage, few dogs survive.

Although more common in the south eastern US, heartworm disease has been diagnosed in all 50 states. And because infected mosquitoes can fly indoors, even dogs which spend much time inside the home are at risk. For that reason, the American Heartworm Society recommends that you get your dog tested every year and give your dog heartworm preventive treatment for 12 months of the year.

Thanks to the American Heartworm Society for assistance with the section.

Ringworm

This is not actually a worm, but a fungus and is most commonly seen in puppies and young dogs. It is highly infectious and often found on the face, ears, paws or tail. The ringworm fungus is most prevalent in hot, humid climates but, surprisingly, most cases occur in autumn and winter. Ringworm infections in dogs are not that common, in one study of dogs with active skin problems, less than 3% had ringworm.

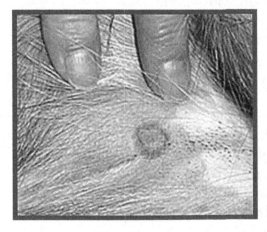

Ringworm is transmitted by spores in the soil and by contact with the infected hair of dogs and cats, which can be typically found on carpets, brushes, combs, toys and furniture. Spores from infected animals can be shed into the environment and live for over 18 months, but fortunately most healthy adult dogs have some resistance and never develop symptoms. The fungi live in dead skin, hairs and nails - and the head and legs are the most common areas affected.

Tell-tale signs are bald patches with a roughly circular shape (pictured.) Ringworm is relatively easy to treat with fungicidal shampoos or antibiotics from a vet. Humans can catch ringworm from pets, and vice versa. Children are especially susceptible, as are adults with suppressed immune systems and those undergoing chemotherapy.

Hygiene is extremely important. If your dog has ringworm, wear gloves when handling him and wash your hands well afterwards. And if a member of your family catches ringworm, make sure they use separate towels from everyone else or the fungus may spread. (As an adolescent I caught ringworm from horses at stables where I worked at weekends - much to my mother's horror - and was treated like a leper by the rest of the family until it had cleared up!)

Bacterial infection (Pyoderma)

Pyoderma literally means 'pus in the skin' (yuk!) and fortunately this condition is not contagious. Early signs of this bacterial infection are itchy red spots filled with yellow pus, similar to pimples or spots in humans. They can sometimes develop into red, ulcerated skin with dry and crusty patches.

Pyoderma is caused by several things: a broken skin surface, a skin wound due to chronic exposure to moisture, altered skin bacteria, or impaired blood flow to the skin. Dogs have a higher risk of developing an infection when they have a fungal infection or an endocrine (hormone gland) disease such as hyperthyroidism, or have allergies to fleas, food or parasites.

Pyoderma is often secondary to allergic dermatitis and develops in the sores on the skin which happen as a result of scratching. Puppies often develop 'puppy pyoderma' in thinly-haired areas such as the groin and underarms. Fleas, ticks, yeast or fungal skin infections, thyroid disease, hormonal imbalances, heredity and some medications can increase the risk. If you notice symptoms, get your dog to the vet quickly before the condition develops from *superficial pyoderma* into *severe pyoderma*, which is very unpleasant and takes a lot longer to treat.

Bacterial infection, no matter how bad it may look, usually responds well to medical treatment, which is generally done on an outpatient basis. Superficial pyoderma will usually be treated with a two to six-week course of antibiotic tablets or ointment. Severe or recurring pyoderma looks awful, causes your dog some distress and can take months of treatment to completely cure. Medicated shampoos and regular bathing, as instructed by your vet, are also part of the treatment. It's also important to ensure your dog has clean, dry, padded bedding.

Canine Acne

This is not uncommon and - just as with humans - generally affects teenagers, often between five and eight months of age with dogs. Acne occurs when oil glands become blocked causing bacterial infection and these glands are most active in teenagers. Acne is not a major health problem as most of it will clear up once the dog becomes an adult, but it can reoccur. Typical signs are pimples, blackheads or whiteheads around the muzzle, chest or groin. If the area is irritated, then there may some bleeding or pus that can be expressed from these blemishes.

Hormonal Imbalances

These occur in dogs of all breeds. They are often difficult to diagnose and occur when a dog is producing either too much (hyper) or too little (hypo) of a particular hormone. One visual sign is often hair loss on both sides of the dog's body. The condition is not usually itchy. Hormone imbalances can be serious as they are often indicators that glands which affect the dog internally are not working properly. However, some types can be diagnosed by special blood tests and treated effectively.

Ear Infections

The Goldendoodle's long, floppy ears, coupled with the fact that many are low shedders, means that the crossbreed can be susceptible to ear infections.

Infection of the external ear canal (outer ear infection) is called otitis externa and is one of the most common types seen. The fact that your dog has recurring ear infections does not necessarily mean that his ears are the source of the problem – although they might be.

One common reason for them in Goldendoodles is moisture in the ear canal, which in turn allows bacteria to flourish there. However, some dogs with chronic or recurring ear infections have inhalant or food allergies or low thyroid function (hypothyroidism.) Sometimes the ears are the first sign of allergy. The underlying problem must be treated or the dog will continue to have long term ear problems. Tell-tale signs include your dog shaking his head, scratching or rubbing his ears a lot, or an unpleasant smell coming from the ears.

If you look inside the ears, you may notice a reddy brown or yellow discharge, it may also be red and inflamed with a lot of wax. Sometimes a dog may appear depressed or irritable; ear infections are painful. In chronic cases, the inside of his ears may become crusty or thickened. Dogs can have ear problems for many different reasons, including:

- Allergies, such as environmental or food allergies
- Ear mites or other parasites
- Bacteria or yeast infections
- Injury, often due to excessive scratching
- Hormonal abnormalities, e.g. hypothyroidism
- The ear anatomy and environment, e.g. excess moisture
- Hereditary or immune conditions and tumors

In reality, many Goldendoodles have ear infections due to the structure of the ear. The long, hairy ears often prevent sufficient air flow inside the ear. This can lead to bacterial or yeast infections - particularly if there is moisture inside. These warm, damp and dark areas under the ear flaps provide an ideal breeding ground for bacteria.

Treatment depends on the cause and what – if any - other conditions your dog may have. Antibiotics are used for bacterial infections and antifungals for yeast infections. Glucocorticoids, such as dexamethasone, are often included in these medications to reduce the inflammation in the ear. Your vet may also flush out and clean the ear with special drops, something you may have to do daily at home until the infection clears.

A dog's ear canal is L-shaped, which means it can be difficult to get medication into the lower (horizontal) part of the ear. The best method is to hold the dog's ear flap with one hand and put the ointment or drops in with the other, if possible tilting the dog's head away from you so the liquid flows downwards **with gravity**. Make sure you then hold the ear flap down and massage the medication into the horizontal canal before letting go of your dog, as the first thing he will do is shake his head – and if the ointment or drops aren't massaged in, they will fly out.

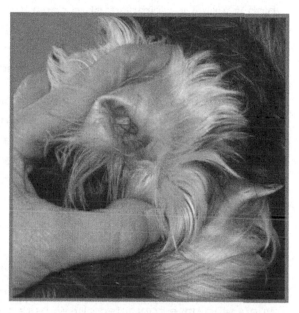

Nearly all ear infections can be successfully managed if properly diagnosed and treated. But if an underlying problem remains undiscovered, the outcome will be less favorable. Deep ear infections can damage or rupture the eardrum, causing an internal ear infection and even permanent hearing loss. Closing of the ear canal (*hyperplasia* or *stenosis)* is another sign of severe infection. Most extreme cases of hyperplasia will eventually require surgery as a last resort; the most common procedure is called a 'lateral ear resection'.

Our dog had a lateral ear resection three or four years ago following years of recurring ear infections and the growth of scar tissue. It was surgery or deafness, the vet said. We opted for surgery and our dog has been free of ear infections ever since. However, it is an **extremely** painful procedure for the dog and should only be considered as a very last resort.

To avoid or alleviate recurring ear infections, check your dog's ears and clean them regularly. Hair should be regularly plucked from inside your Goldendoodle's ears – either by you or a groomer, or both. If your Goldendoodle is one of the very many who enjoys swimming, great care should be taken to ensure the inside of the ear is thoroughly dry afterwards - and after bathing at home. There is more information in **Chapter 11. Coat Types and Grooming.**

When cleaning or plucking your dog's ears, be very careful not to put anything too far down inside. Visit YouTube to see videos of how to correctly clean without damaging them. DO NOT use cotton buds, these are too small and can damage the ear. Some owners recommend regularly cleaning the inside of ears with cotton wool and a mixture of water and white vinegar once a week or so.

If your dog appears to be in pain, has smelly ears, or if his ear canals look inflamed, contact your vet straight away. If you can nip the first infection in the bud, there is a chance it will not return. If your dog has a ruptured or weakened eardrum, ear cleansers and medications could do more harm than good. Early treatment is the best way of preventing a recurrence.

Some Allergy Treatments

Treatments and success rates vary tremendously from dog to dog and from one allergy to another, which is why it is so important to consult a vet at the outset. Earlier diagnosis is more likely to lead to a successful treatment. Some owners whose dogs have recurring skin issues find that a course of antibiotics or steroids works wonders for their dog's sore skin and itching. However, the scratching starts all over again shortly after the treatment stops.

Food allergies require patience, a change of diet and maybe even a food trial, and the specific trigger is notoriously difficult to isolate — unless you are lucky and hit on the culprit straight away. With inhalant and contact allergies, blood and skin tests are available, followed by hypersensitization treatment. However, these are expensive and often the specific trigger for many dogs remains unknown. So the reality for many owners of Goldendoodles with allergies is that they manage the ailment with various medications and practices, rather than curing it completely.

Our Personal Experience

After corresponding with numerous other dog owners and consulting our vet, Graham, it seems that our experiences with allergies are not uncommon. This is borne out by the dozens of dog owners who have contacted our website about their pet's allergy or sensitivities. According to Graham, more and more dogs appearing in his waiting room every spring with various types of allergies. Whether this is connected to how we breed our dogs remains to be seen.

Our dog was perfectly fine until he was about two years old when he began to scratch a lot. He scratched more in spring and summer, which meant that his allergies were almost certainly inhalant or contact-based and related to pollens, grasses or other outdoor triggers. One option was for Max to have a barrage of tests to discover exactly what he was allergic to. We decided not to do this, not because of the cost, but because our vet said it was highly likely that he was allergic to pollens. If we had confirmed an allergy to pollens, we were not going to stop taking him outside for walks, so the vet treated him on the basis of seasonal inhalant or contact allergies, probably related to pollen.

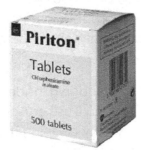

As mentioned, it's beneficial to have a shallow bath or hose outside and to rinse the dog's paws and underbelly after a walk in the countryside. This is something our vet does with his own dogs and has found that the scratching reduces as a result. Regarding medications, Max was at first put on to a tiny dose of Piriton, an antihistamine for hay fever sufferers (human and canine) and for the first few springs and summers, this worked well.

Allergies can often change and the dog can also build up a tolerance to a treatment, which is why they can be so difficult to treat. This has been the case with Max over the years. The symptoms change from season to season, although the main ones remain and they are: general scratching paw biting and ear infections. One year he bit the skin under his tail a lot (near the anus) and this was treated effectively with a single steroid injection followed by spraying the area with cortisone once a day at home for a period. This type of spray can be very effective if the itchy area is small, but no good for spraying all over a dog's body.

A couple of years ago Max started nibbling his paws for the first time - a habit he persists with - although not to the extent that they become red and raw. Over the years we have tried a number of treatments, all of which have worked for a while, before he comes off the medication In autumn for six months when plants and grasses stop growing outdoors. He manages perfectly fine the rest of the year without any treatment at all.

If we were starting again from scratch, knowing what we know now, I would investigate a raw diet, if necessary in combination with holistic remedies. Our dog is now 11, we feed him a high quality hypoallergenic dry food. His allergies are manageable, he loves his food, is full of energy and otherwise healthy, and so we are reluctant to make such a big change at this point in his life.

One season Max was put on a short course of steroids. These worked very well for five months, but steroids are not a long-term solution, as prolonged use can cause organ damage. Another spring Max was prescribed a non-steroid daily tablet called Atopica, sold in the UK only through vets. (The active ingredient is **cyclosporine**, which suppresses the immune system. Some dogs can get side effects, although Max didn't, and holistic practitioners believe that it is harmful to the dog.) This treatment was expensive, but initially extremely effective – so much so that we thought we had cured the problem completely. However, after a couple of seasons on cyclosporine he developed a tolerance to the drug and started scratching again.

A few years ago he went back on the antihistamine Piriton, a higher dose than when he was two years old, and this worked very well again. One advantage of this drug is that is it manufactured by the million for dogs and is therefore very inexpensive.

In 2013 the FDA approved **Apoquel** (oclacitinib) to control itching and inflammation in allergic dogs. In some quarters it has been hailed a wonder drug for canine allergies. In fact it has proved so popular in the UK and North America that in 2014-15 there was a shortage of supply, with the manufacturers not being able to produce it fast enough.

We have tried it with excellent results. There was some tweaking at the beginning to get the daily dose right, but it really has proved effective for us. I am writing this at the end of April. Two days ago Max suddenly started scratching like crazy - just as he does every spring. We got him into the vet pretty smartish, where he had a single steroid injection to control the itching until the Apoquel kicks in. He is now on a double dose of Apoquel for two weeks and he will continue throughout the summer on a normal, single dose, 8mg a day for his 12 Kg (26lbs) bodyweight. The tablets cost around £1 or $1.50 each; not cheap.

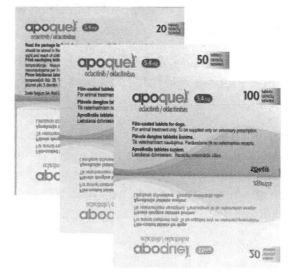

Many vets recommend adding fish oils (which contain Omega-3 fatty acids) to a daily feed to keep your dog's skin and coat healthy all year round – whether or not he has problems. We add a liquid supplement called Yumega Plus, which contains Omegas 3 and 6, to one of his two daily feeds all year round and this definitely seems to help his skin. In the past when the scratching has got particularly bad, we have bathed Max in an antiseborrheic shampoo (called Malaseb,pictured) twice a week for a limited time. This also helped, although this has not been necessary since he started on the Apoquel.

The main point is that most allergies are manageable. They may change throughout the life of the dog and you may have to alter the treatment. Max may have allergies, but he wouldn't miss his walks for anything and, all in all, he is one contented canine. We've compiled some anecdotal evidence from our website from owners of dogs with various allergies, here are some of their suggestions for alleviating the problems:

Bathing - bathing your dog using shampoos that break down the oils which plug the hair follicles. These shampoos contain antiseborrheic ingredients such as benzoyl peroxide, salicylic acid, sulfur or tar. One example is Sulfoxydex shampoo, which can be followed by a cream rinse such as Episoothe Rinse afterwards to prevent the skin from drying out.

Dabbing – Using an astringent such as witch hazel or alcohop on affected areas. We have heard of zinc oxide cream being used to some effect. In the human world, this is rubbed on to mild skin abrasions and acts as a protective coating. It can help the healing of chapped skin and nappy rash in babies. Zinc oxide works as a mild astringent and has some antiseptic properties and is safe to use on dogs, *as long as you do not allow the dog to lick it off*.

Daily supplements - Vitamin E, vitamin A, zinc and omega oils all help to make a dog's skin healthy. Feed a daily supplement which contains some of these, such as fish oil, which provides omega. Here are some specific remedies from owners. We are not endorsing them, we're just passing on the information. Check with your vet before trying any new remedies.

A medicated shampoo with natural tea tree oil has been suggested by one owner. Some have reported that switching to a fish-based diet has helped lessen scratching, while others have suggested home-cooked food is best, if you have the time to prepare the food. Another reader said: "My eight-month-old dog also had a contact dermatitis around his neck and chest. I was surprised how extensive it was. The vet recommended twice-a-week baths with an oatmeal shampoo. I also applied organic coconut oil daily for a few weeks and this completely cured the dermatitis. I also put a capsule of fish oil with his food once a day and continue to give him twice-weekly baths. His skin is great now."

Several owners have tried coconut oil with some success. Here is a link to an article on the benefits of coconut oils and fish oils, check with your vet first: www.cocotherapy.com/fishoilsvsvirginoil_coconutoil.htm

And from another reader: "I have been putting a teaspoon of canola (rapeseed) oil in my dog's food every other day and it has helped with the itching. I have shampooed the new carpet in hopes of removing any of the chemicals that could be irritating her. And I have changed laundry detergent. After several loads of laundry everything has been washed."

The Holistic Approach

As canine allergies become increasingly common, more and more owners of dogs with allergies and sensitivities are looking towards natural foods and remedies to help deal with the issues. Others are finding that their dog does well for a time with injections or medication, but then the symptoms slowly start to reappear. A holistic practitioner looks at finding the root cause of the problem and treating that, rather than just treating the symptoms.

Dr Sara Skiwski is a holistic vet working in California. She writes here about canine environmental allergies: "Here in California, with our mild weather and no hard freeze in Winter, environmental allergens can build up and cause nearly year-round issues for our beloved pets. Also seasonal allergies, when left unaddressed, can lead to year-round allergies. Unlike humans, whose allergy symptoms seem to affect mostly the respiratory tract, seasonal allergies in dogs often take the form of skin irritation/inflammation.

"Allergic reactions are produced by the immune system. The way the immune system functions is a result of both genetics and the environment: Nature versus Nurture. Let's look at a typical case. A puppy starts showing mild seasonal allergy symptoms, for instance a red tummy and mild itching in Spring. Off to the vet!

"The treatment prescribed is symptomatic to provide relief, such as a topical spray. The next year when the weather warms up, the patient is back again - same symptoms but more severe this time. This time the dog has very itchy skin. Again, the treatment is symptomatic - antibiotics, topical spray (hopefully no steroids), until the symptoms resolve with the season change. Fast forward to another Spring...on the third year, the patient is back again but this time the symptoms last longer, (not just Spring but also through most of Summer and into Fall.) By year five, all the symptoms are significantly worse and are occurring year round. This is what happens with seasonal environmental allergies. The more your pet is exposed to the allergens they are sensitive to, the more the immune system over-reacts and the more intense and long-lasting the allergic response becomes. What to do?

"In my practice, I like to address the potential root cause at the very first sign of an allergic response, which is normally seen between the ages of six to nine months old. I do this to circumvent the escalating response year after year. Since the allergen load your environmentally-sensitive dog is most susceptible to is much heavier outdoors, I recommend two essential steps in managing the condition. They are vigilance in foot care as well as fur care.

"What does this mean? A wipe down of feet and fur, especially the tummy, to remove any pollens or allergens is key. This can be done with a damp cloth, but my favorite method is to get a spray bottle filled with Witch Hazel and spray these areas. First, spray the feet then wipe them off with a cloth, and then spray and wipe down the tummy and sides. This is best done right after the pup has been outside playing or walking. This will help keep your pet from tracking the environmental allergens into the home and into their beds. If the feet end up still being itchy, I suggest adding foot soaks in Epsom salts."

Dr Sara also stresses the importance of keeping the immune system healthy by avoiding unnecessary vaccinations or drugs: "The vaccine stimulates the immune system, which is the last thing your pet with seasonal environmental allergies needs. I also will move the pet to an anti-inflammatory diet. Foods that create or worsen inflammation are high in carbohydrates. An allergic pet's diet should be very low in carbohydrates, especially grains. Research has shown that 'leaky gut,' or dysbiosis, is a root cause of immune system overreactions in both dog and cats (and some humans.) Feed a diet that is not processed, or minimally processed; one that doesn't have grain and takes a little longer to get absorbed and assimilated through the gut. Slowing the assimilation assures that there are not large spikes of nutrients and proteins that come into the body all at once and overtax the pancreas and liver, creating inflammation.

"A lot of commercial diets are too high in grains and carbohydrates. These foods create inflammation which overtaxes the body and leads not just to skin inflammation, but also to other inflammatory conditions, such as colitis, pancreatitis, arthritis, inflammatory bowel disease and ear infections. Also, these diets are too low in protein, which is needed to make blood. This causes a decreased blood reserve in the body and in some of these animals this can leads to the skin not being properly nourished, starting a cycle of chronic skin infections which produce more itching."

After looking at diet, check that your dog is free from fleas and then these are some of her suggested supplements:

✓ **Raw (Unpasteurized) Local Honey** - an alkaline-forming food containing natural vitamins, enzymes, powerful antioxidants and other important natural nutrients, which are destroyed during the heating and pasteurization processes. Raw honey has anti-viral, anti-bacterial and anti-fungal properties. It promotes body and digestive health, is a powerful antioxidant, strengthens the immune system, eliminates allergies, and is an excellent remedy for skin wounds and all types of infections. Bees collect pollen from local plants and their honey often acts as an immune booster for dogs living in the locality. Dr Sara says: "It may seem odd that straight exposure to pollen often triggers allergies, but that exposure to pollen in the honey usually has the opposite effect. But this is typically what we see. In honey, the allergens are delivered in small, manageable doses and the effect over time is very much like that from undergoing a whole series of allergy immunology injections."

✓ **Mushrooms** - make sure you choose the non-poisonous ones! Dogs don't like the taste, you so may have to mask it with another food. Medicinal mushrooms are used to treat and prevent a wide array of illnesses through their use as immune stimulants and modulators, and antioxidants. The most well-known and researched are reishi, maitake, cordyceps, blazei, split-gill, turkey tail and shiitake. The mushrooms stabilize mast cells in the body, which have the histamines attached to them. Histamine is what causes much of the inflammation, redness and irritation in allergies. By helping to control histamine production, the mushrooms can moderate the effects of inflammation and even help prevent allergies in the first place.

WARNING! Mushrooms can interact with some over-the-counter and prescription drugs, so do your research as well as checking with your vet first.

- ✓ **Stinging Nettles** - contain biologically active compounds that reduce inflammation. Nettles have the ability to reduce the amount of histamine the body produces in response to an allergen. Nettle tea or extract can help with itching. Nettles not only help directly to decrease the itch, but also work overtime to desensitize the body to allergens, helping to reprogram the immune system.

- ✓ **Quercetin** – is an over-the-counter supplement with anti-inflammatory properties. It is a strong antioxidant and reduces the body's production of histamines.

- ✓ **Omega-3 Fatty Acids** - these help decrease inflammation throughout the body. Adding them into the diet of all pets - particularly those struggling with seasonal environmental allergies – is very beneficial. If your dog has more itching along the top of their back and on their sides, add in a fish oil supplement. Fish oil helps to decrease the itch and heal skin lesions. The best sources of Omega 3s are krill oil, salmon oil, tuna oil, anchovy oil and other fish body oils, as well as raw organic egg yolks. If using an oil alone, it is important to give a vitamin B complex supplement.

- ✓ **Coconut Oil** - contains lauric acid, which helps decrease the production of yeast, a common opportunistic infection. Using a fish body oil combined with coconut oil before inflammation flares up can help moderate or even suppress your dog's inflammatory response.

Dr Sara adds: "Above are but a few of the over-the-counter remedies I like. In non-responsive cases, Chinese herbs can be used to work with the body to help to decrease the allergy threshold even more than with diet and supplements alone. Most of the animals I work with are on a program of Chinese herbs, diet change and acupuncture. So, the next time Fido is showing symptoms of seasonal allergies, consider rethinking your strategy to treat the root cause instead of the symptom."

With thanks to Dr Sara Skiwski, of the Western Dragon Integrated Veterinary Services, San Jose, California, for her kind permission to use her writings as the basis for this section.

....

This chapter has only just touched on the complex subject of skin disorders. As you can see, the causes and treatments are many and varied. One thing is true, whatever the condition, if your Goldendoodle has a skin issue, seek a professional diagnosis <u>as soon as possible</u> before attempting to treat it yourself and before the condition becomes entrenched. Early diagnosis and treatment can sometimes nip the problem in the bud.

Some skin conditions cannot be completely cured, but they can be successfully managed, allowing your dog to live a happy, pain-free life. If you haven't got your puppy yet, ask the breeder if there is a history of skin issues in her bloodlines. Once you have your pup or adult dog, remember that good quality diet and attention to cleanliness and grooming go a long way in preventing and managing canine skin problems and ear infections.

11. Coat Types and Grooming

Goldendoodles have many advantages over other breeds and crossbreeds: they get along with everybody, they are usually non-aggressive towards other dogs, they are tolerant with children, they make excellent therapy dogs, and they are easy to obedience train and housetrain. Despite these outstanding qualities, there is one other attribute which often influences a person's or family's decision to get a Goldendoodle - and that is the dog's coat.

Over the last decade there has been an explosion in the number of so-called 'designer dogs' - nearly all of them are Doodles or Poos, i.e. Poodle crosses. And the reason for the Poodle (pictured) being the dog of choice when it comes to producing hybrid (crossbreed) dogs is that, unlike many dogs, the Poodle has a single layer coat of dense, curly fur, similar to wool.

The beauty of this coat is that it sheds hardly any hair at all. This type of coat is called 'hypoallergenic', which means "**less likely** to cause an allergic reaction." Note that it does not mean that it definitely WON'T cause a reaction, see **Chapter 4** for more information on Goldendoodles for Allergy Sufferers.

Some types of 'designer dog' have received bad publicity in the Press due to uncaring breeders claiming that their Doodles of one type or another were GUARANTEED not to cause a reaction in an allergy sufferer. Let's be clear about this: no breeder can say this with 100% certainty, no matter what you may read. Most reputable Goldendoodle breeders will state in their Puppy Contract that they cannot guarantee that a puppy will be non-shedding; this is normal and truthful.

A Goldendoodle can have one of four different types of coat, although many new owners are interested in the type which sheds only minimally. Sadly, one reason why some Goldendoodles and other Doodles end up in rescue shelters is that they grow up, start shedding and are rejected by their owners. The good news is that some of the guesswork has been taken out of coat type by the recent discovery of a DNA test for what is known as the IC - or Improper Coat - gene. The test was first developed for the Portuguese Water Dog and has been modified for the Goldendoodle. An 'Improper Coat' is one where the dog has a flat coat and short hair on his head, face and legs, like the Golden Retriever, and it means that he or she is more likely to shed.

Although much more research is still to be done, this is an exciting breakthrough for Goldendoodle breeders. It means that they can DNA test their dogs for the IC gene and make sure that one dog of a breeding pair is IC clear, thereby greatly increasing the likelihood of the offspring having non- or low-shedding coats - although, technically, there is no such thing as a non-shedding coat in a dog; all dogs shed a little. Breeders do not want to remove all IC clear dogs from their breeding programs, as there are other traits attached to this gene.

Goldendoodle Coat Genetics

By Janece Schommer, of Goldendoodle Acres, Wisconsin, Vice President of GANA

Here Janece explains that the most important factor governing how your Goldendoodle will look is not what generation your puppy is – i.e. whether he is, for example F1, F1b, F2, F2b, F3 or multigen – but which coat genes go into his make-up. She writes:

Goldendoodles come in a variety of coat colors and textures. Textures can be curly, wavy, straight, or have 'improper' flat coats and smooth faces like Golden Retrievers. It's important to note that a Goldendoodle of ANY generation can present ANY of these coats. The look of your Goldendoodle is not determined by the generation, but rather due to three genes; these are: Coat Curl, Coat Length, and Furnishings:

COAT CURL (The Curl Gene – KRT71) - Goldendoodles can have straight, wavy or curly hair depending on what type of curl gene they inherit from each parent. Even if two parents have wavy coats, they can still carry a curl gene and have curly pups in a litter. It's important to ask your breeder what the coat possibilities are and if they've tested for curl.

COAT LENGTH (the Long Hair Gene - FGF5) - Since Poodles and Golden Retrievers both carry long hair genes, all Goldendoodles have longer coats, unlike a Labradoodle which can carry a short coat length given by the Labrador Retriever. Long coat length is a recessive gene, meaning you need both copies to produce a long Doodle coat - which you find in all Goldendoodles, but not in all Labradoodles.

IMPROPER COAT GENE (The Furnishings IR IC Test - RSPO2) - This gene causes the greatest variation in the look of a Goldendoodle. The term 'furnishings' refers to the longer hair on the face, i.e. moustache and eyebrows, which give the Goldendoodle that 'scruffy dog' look. Furnishings are a dominant trait, so you only need one copy from one parent to get the look. However, a breeder first needs to carry out DNA testing of the parents to ensure they don't get pups that are minus furnishings or affected with 'improper coat'. Here are two examples of Goldendoodles with furnishings:

Lucy

Malai

Below are examples of Goldendoodles who do not carry furnishing and have what are called 'improper coats.' They tend to shed more than Goldendoodles who carry furnishings.

If your family has allergies, an improper-coated Goldendoodle might not be the right fit for you. Improper coats tend to shed more than Goldendoodles with furnishings. A new DNA test has become available to test a dog's propensity for shedding and it involves the improper coat gene. Let's take a look at how it works:

The 'Shedding' Test

Collected samples of a Goldendoodle's DNA can now help to identify the amount of shedding the dog is likely to have. Found in two different genes in a dog's DNA, the 'shedability' genes are identified and calculated. Scores range from 0 to 4 with 0 being the lowest propensity towards shedding and 4 being the highest. Dogs who carry furnishings have a lower propensity for shedding than those that don't - but it's not the whole test. There is a second unrelated gene involved that also plays a very important part.

The IC Gene test is particularly important for hybrids like Goldendoodles who have both shedding and non-shedding relatives. The result of the DNA test will be more useful to prospective owners in determining the amount of shedding a pup will have than knowing the generation of the Goldendoodle they are getting.

In the past, it was thought that a curly F1b Goldendoodle (75% Poodle and 25% Golden Retriever) was needed for allergy sufferers in order to get a low to no-shed dog. This is no longer the case. Thanks to the 'shedding test', breeders can now carefully breed their parents by knowing what their shed score is, making it possible to get the same low to no-shed results in straight, wavy, or curly multigenerational Goldendoodles. The multigenerational Goldendoodle typically incorporates more Golden Retriever back into the mix, which not only increases the hybrid vigor of the offspring, but also increases the chances of the offspring having more Golden Retriever traits than an F1b.

NOTE: Even if a dog doesn't shed, a person can still be allergic to his or her dander. Allergies have to do with which proteins a person is allergic to and whether those proteins are produced by the dog or not. The proteins that cause symptoms may be found in skin cells, saliva, or urine, or any combination of the three. You need to consult an allergy specialist for accurate medical info on your potential for an allergic reaction to dogs.

Colors

Goldendoodles come in a variety of colors. Some of the common ones include cream, apricot, and red. All of these color coats are actually the same gene, it's just a matter of how much pigment gets into each coat, and follows the variation in colors with Golden Retrievers. Because of this, it is common to have a litter with lots of variations of this gene.

Goldendoodle Acres

In addition to different coat colors, Goldendoodles can also carry different coat patterns, such as parti. In order to be classified as 'a parti,' a dog must be partially white (at least 50%) and the white can accompany any other coat color. Some Goldendoodles just have patches of white on their coats and these are classified as 'abstracts.'

Textures

Goldendoodles have four main coat types: flat, straight, wavy, or curly.

The **flat coat** is also called the 'improper coat,' which was previously described, where the dog does not have furnishings.

If a Goldendoodle gets a non-curl gene from each parent, it can have a rather **straight coat**. Unlike the flat coat, this is accompanied by furnishings and a 'fluffy' texture.

When a Goldendoodle gets one curl gene from one parent and a non-curl gene from the other, he or she will have a **wavy coat**. Both of these Goldendoodles have **wavy** hair, the one on the left has had a short clip and the dog on the right has been left with a long coat.

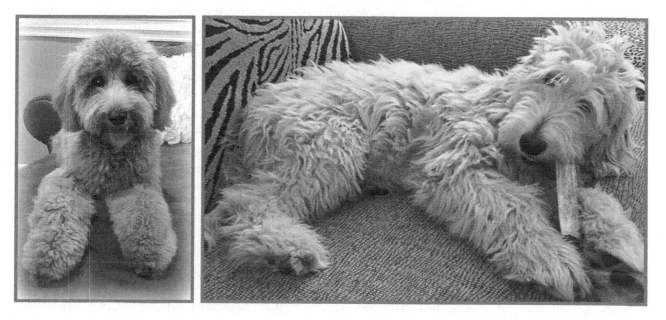

When each parent of the Goldendoodle throws a curl gene, the offspring will have a **curly coat.** All of these three dogs have curly coats. The one on the right has a short clip and the two on the left have long coats.

All photos in this section are courtesy of Janece.

Grooming your Goldendoodle

By Amy Lane, of Fox Creek Farm, West Virginia, Founder of GANA

Part of the Goldendoodle's appeal is undoubtedly the shaggy coat – but this comes at a price. Keeping a coat long enough to be 'shaggy' creates a high maintenance dog.

A Goldendoodle with a coat longer than about one inch requires a full brush out at least every other day. You'll need to use a slicker brush (a metal bristled brush, pictured) over the entire body, and follow this up with a combing out with a metal comb.

The slicker brush typically does not have bristles long enough to reach the skin, which is where mats form. The goal is to remove all tangles before they become mats - as the only remedy for a full blown mat is to cut it out. Mats tend to form first behind the ears, under the collar and in the armpits.

If you want a lower maintenance Goldendoodle, then clipping the coat to one inch or less means that you only have to give your dog a full brushing perhaps once or twice a week. Even when the coat on the body is kept fairly short, it is common to leave the hair on the head/face area perhaps twice as long. Tails are typically only trimmed two to three times a year to leave a long, flowing feathering on the tail - but these areas still need to be brushed and combed out about every other day.

Professional Grooming

Most people choose to have a professional groomer take care of the bi-monthly (roughly every eight weeks) grooming, which includes a bath, blow dry and haircut. Most groomers will also clip the nails and may even drain the anal glands if necessary. If you bathe your Goldendoodle a few times in between these visits, it will keep the coat soft and clean as well as helping your dog learn how to behave when being bathed and brushed.

Most groomers are not trainers and they don't have time to deal with unruly dogs, so it's your job to ensure yours knows how to behave during a bath and grooming session.

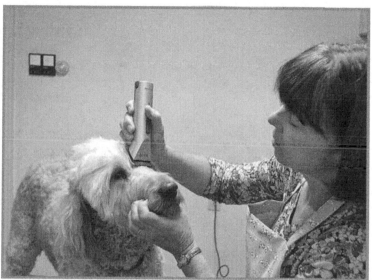

A Goldendoodle will typically need the first haircut at five to six months of age. The hair covering their eyes tends to be the first problem that many owners encounter and often clipping the hair on the bridge of the nose between the eyes is enough to ward off the first professional haircut for another month or two. CAREFULLY using a pair of clippers or a blunt-ended pair of scissors works well, allowing the puppy's eyes to become visible again." (Our photo shows Amy clipping a dog.)

Tip "Don't forget to gently massage between the toes of all four feet on a daily basis starting as soon as your pup arrives home. This desensitizes the puppy so he or she allows feet and toes to be handled. Hair grows between the toes and pads of the foot and the groomer needs to be able to clip these areas without your dog pulling his or her feet away.

New owners often have a hard time recognizing their puppies when they pick them up from the groomer's the first time. The newly-revealed adult coat may have a different texture, body or color than what they grew accustomed to when the puppy coat was present. Sometimes owners are shocked to see their puppy shaved bald as that was not what they requested. However, if the undercoat had mats, the kindest thing the groomer can do is to evenly shave off all the hair. You will then have the job of brushing more thoroughly as the coat grows back so you can avoid having a bald dog after the next haircut!

It can also be helpful if you print internet photos of Goldendoodles with haircuts you like. A picture will help describe to the groomer how you hope your puppy will look on your return. Keep in mind that you need to select pictures of dogs that have the same coat as your puppy.

If you do decide a professional groomer is worth the time and money, it is important that your dog is fully vaccinated for everything, including kennel cough, which is basically a severe cold. It is highly contagious, especially when several dogs are kept in small rooms together. Vaccines take up to a week to become effective, so make sure your dog has had his or hers well in advance of the grooming appointment.

D.I.Y.

For the do-it-yourselfer, clipping can be done in the comfort of your home. You will need either a grooming table (one with a hydraulic height adjuster is extremely helpful, especially if you have dogs of different sizes to clip) or, if not, a stable coffee table will suffice. A quality pair of clippers, scissors, clipper blades - Nos. 4, 7 and 10 (pictured) are the most common blades - and snap-on combs will be needed.

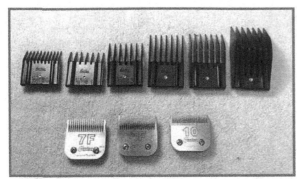

A small trim clipper with a No. 30 blade is good for areas where you want to completely remove the hair. The higher the blade number, the shorter the hair is left. The combs are used only with the No. 10 blade and allow you to leave a longer length of hair versus a complete buzz job.

Always bathe and dry your dog prior to giving a haircut as dirt on hairs quickly dulls the clipper blades, which may be used multiple times before sharpening as long as they are used only on a freshly-bathed dog. Brush the hair on the body in the **opposite direction** to the lay of the hair and clip in the **same direction** as the lay of the hair over the entire body starting on the neck leaving the head, legs and tail alone.

Then brush the hair in the opposite direction and clip again to find the hairs that were missed the first time. Brush the hair on the legs upward and use the scissors (always with the points downward) to trim the hair on the legs to the desired length. Use the trim clippers to completely remove the hair between the back legs on the belly and around the private areas under the tail as well as across the pads of the foot to remove hair that protrudes beyond the pad.

On the head, brush the hair from the back of the head forward over the eyes and trim the 'bangs' with blunt-tipped scissors at an angle on each side of the face so the eyes are visible; this gives you the length you need to match the hair on top of the head. Make sure you clip the hair very short underneath the ear under the ear flap (the ear will hide where it is clipped shorter), so air can flow into the ear canal.

Dogs with long, floppy ears are more prone to ear infections due to a lack of air circulation in the ear canal. Since Poodles have hairy ear canals (a trait uncommon in Golden Retrievers), some Goldendoodles may also have hairy ear canals. Hair in the ear canals needs to be plucked or cleaning the ears becomes impossible.

Sprinkle ear powder into the ear canal and grasp a few hairs at a time between your thumb and index finger and briskly pull the hair free. Repeat this process until the ear canal is hairless. When done, you may want to add a little more ear powder to soothe the tenderness left inside of the ear. Trim the hair short under the jaw so your Goldendoodle doesn't constantly drip water across the floor after drinking.

Last but not least, you will need to clip your dog's nails. Their nails are similar to a human's nails in that there is the nail itself and the quick. The quick is what provides blood flow to the nail and it will bleed quite a bit if you accidently cut into the quick. You'll be able to see this if your dog has white nails, but it's more difficult to see on a dog with black nails.

Always start by clipping a very small end of the tip and continue to clip a little more never going shorter than to remove the curved end of the nail. It is a good idea to have styptic powder or even corn starch handy, as it will stop the bleeding if you happen to cut into the quick. Don't forget to clip the dew claw as well if your dog has not had the dew claws removed as a puppy.

You may not be completely happy with the look of your Goldendoodle after you have clipped him for the first time! Fear not, the hair will grow back, giving you the opportunity to practice clipping again in a few months' time.

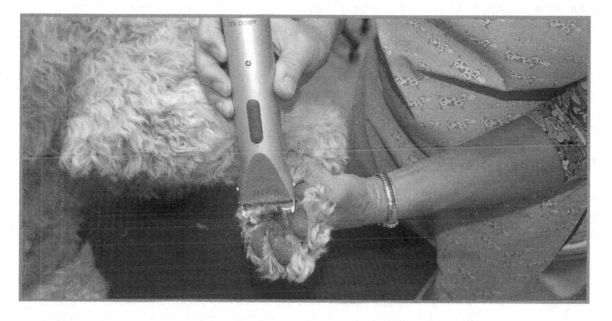

Important Little Places

In this section we look in a little more detail at how an owner can keep their Goldendoodle's ears, teeth and nails healthy through regular attention.

Ear Cleaning

It is not uncommon for some Goldendoodles to inherit very furry ears from their Poodle parents and grandparents. And, like Poodles, this makes them prone to ear infections. Ear canals surrounded by lots of hair are generally warm and moist, making them a haven for bacteria and yeast. This can lead to recurring infections and, in severe cases, the dog going deaf or needing an operation to change the shape of his ear canal.

If your dog is a low or minimal shedder, the hair inside the ear flap should be regularly plucked. You can do this at home or ask your groomer to do it during routine visits. If you do pluck the hair yourself, don't overdo it. Keep an eye out for redness or inflammation of the ear flap or inner ear. Ask your groomer for tips. Some owners also regularly bathe the inner ear with cotton wool and warm water or a veterinary ear cleaner.

If your Goldendoodle's ears have an unpleasant smell, if he scratches them a lot, rubs them on the carpet or they look red, consult your vet ASAP, as simple routine cleaning won't clear up an infection - and they are notoriously difficult to rid the dog of once he's had one.

The trick is to keep your dog's ears clean and free from too much hair right from puppyhood and hope that he never gets an ear infection.

The first method of cleaning your Goldendoodle's ears is to get a good quality ear cleaning solution from your vet's or local pet/grooming supply shop. Then squeeze the cleaner into your Goldendoodle's ear canal and rub the ear at the base next to the skull. Allow your dog to shake his or her head and use a cotton ball to gently wipe out any dirt and waxy build up inside the ear canal.

Method Two is to use a baby wipe and gently wipe away any dirt and waxy build up. In both cases it is important to only clean as far down the ear canal as you can see to avoid damaging the eardrum. The first method is preferred if you are also bathing your dog, as it will remove any unwanted water that may have got down into the ears during the bath. Clean the ears after bathing.

Teeth Cleaning

Veterinary studies show that by the age of three, 80% of dogs exhibit signs of gum disease. Symptoms include yellow and brown build-up of tartar along the gum line, red inflamed gums and persistent bad breath. You can give your dog a daily dental stick to help keep his mouth and teeth clean, but you should also brush your Goldendoodle's teeth as well.

It shouldn't be a chore, but a pleasant experience for both of you! Take things slowly in the beginning, give him lots of praise and many dogs will start looking forward to teeth brushing sessions. Use a pet toothpaste (the human variety can upset a canine's stomach); many have flavors which your dog will find tasty.

One of the real benefits comes from the actual action of the brush on the teeth. Various brushes, sponges and pads are available; the choice depends on factors such as the health of your dog's gums, the size of his mouth and how good you are at teeth cleaning!

Get your dog used to the toothpaste by letting him lick some off your finger. If he doesn't like the flavor, try a different one. Continue this until he looks forward to licking the paste – it might be instant or take days. Put a small amount on your finger and gently rub it on one of the big canine teeth at the front of his mouth.

Then get him used to the toothbrush or dental sponge you will be using, praise him when he licks it – do this for several days. The next step is to actually start brushing. Talk to your Goldendoodle in an encouraging way and praise him when you're finished.

Lift his upper lip gently and place the brush at a 45º angle to the gum line. Gently move the brush backwards and forwards. Start just with his front

teeth and then gradually do few more. You don't need to brush the inside of his teeth as his tongue keeps them relatively free of plaque.

Goldendoodles love games and, with a bit of encouragement and patience, it can become a fun task for both of you. There are various videos on YouTube which demonstrate how to clean a dog's teeth. Aim to clean your dog's teeth once a week.

Nail Trimming

Nails must be kept short for the paws to remain healthy. Long nails interfere with the dog's gait, and can make walking awkward or painful. They can also break easily. This usually happens at the base of the nail, where blood vessels and nerves are located and results in a trip to the vet's.

If you can hear the nails clicking on the floor, they're too long. Dogs which are exercised on hard surfaces such as pavements (sidewalks) naturally wear down their nails more quickly than dogs which are exercised on soft surfaces such as grass.

You can ask your groomer to trim your dog's nails. If you do it yourself, you will need a specially designed clipper. Most have safety guards to prevent you from cutting the nails too short. You want to trim only the ends, before the 'quick,' which is a blood vessel inside the nail. (It is also where we get the expression 'cut to the quick' from.) You can see where the quick ends on a white nail, but not on a dark nail. Clip only the hook-like part of the nail that turns down. It's fair to say that many dogs dislike having their nails trimmed.

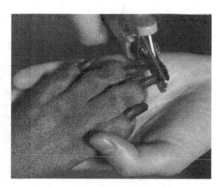

You can make it a painless procedure by getting him used to having his paws handled in puppyhood. Start trimming gently, a nail or two at a time, and your dog will learn that you're not going to hurt him. If you accidentally cut the quick, stop the bleeding with some styptic powder.

Another option is to file your dog's nails with a nail grinder tool. Some dogs may have tough nails which are hard to trim and this may be less stressful for your dog, with less chance of pain or bleeding. It may take a little while for your dog to get used to the sound of the grinder, so start with very short sessions. If you find it impossible to clip your dog's nails, or you are at all worried about doing it, take him to a vet or a groomer.

Eyes - If your dog's eye or eyes have a discharge, if they get a little sticky, or if he has dried deposits in the corner of his eyes, clean them gently with damp cotton wool. Do not use anything else unless instructed to do so by your vet. If the problem persists, consult your vet.

Anal Glands – The two anal glands, or anal sacs, are located on each side of your dog's anus (butt) between the external and internal sphincter muscles. These glands secrete a liquid that is used for marking territory and identification by other dogs, so when you see your dog sticking his nose into another dog's rear end, remember that it's his way of introducing himself!

The glands can spontaneously empty, especially during stress and if this happens, you will notice a very sudden and unpleasant change in the odor of your dog. The anal glands usually empty when your dog poops. However, they might not empty if, for example, your dog's stools are too soft and in such cases this may cause discomfort.

Expressing (emptying) the anal glands is normally done as a routine part of a trip to the groomer's. You should specify that you'd like the groomer to do this. If the groomer isn't comfortable expressing them, ask the vet to check them on your next routine visit. If you notice your dog dragging himself along on his rear end or licking or scratching his anus, he may have impacted anal glands - or he may have worms or allergies....

Either way, he needs some attention!

© Janece Schommer, Amy Lane & Canine Handbooks 2016.

12. The Birds and the Bees

Judging by the number of questions our website receives from owners who ask about the canine reproductive cycle and breeding their dogs, there is a lot of confusion about the doggie facts of life out there. Some owners want to know whether they should mate their dog, while others ask at what age they should have their dog spayed (females) *or* neutered (males.) Owners of females often ask when she will come on heat, how long this will last and how often it will occur. Sometimes they want to know how to tell if a female is pregnant or how long a pregnancy lasts. So here, in a nutshell, is a short chapter on the facts of life as far as Goldendoodles are concerned.

....

Should I Breed From My Goldendoodle?

The short and simple answer is: Unless you know exactly what you are doing or have a mentor, **NO, leave it to the experts.** You need specialist knowledge to successfully breed healthy Goldendoodles to type. The rising popularity and cost of puppies is tempting more people to consider breeding their dogs. Prices may be more than $2,000 in the USA for a puppy from a breeder with a proven track record who health tests her stock and £900 or more in the UK. But anyone who thinks it is easy money should bear in mind that responsible Goldendoodle breeding is an expensive and time consuming business when all the fees, DNA and health tests, care, nutrition and medical expenses have been taken into account.

You can't just put any two dogs together and expect perfect, healthy puppies every time; ethical and successful breeding is much more scientific than that. Pictured is a beautiful litter of puppies with their health-tested F1 mother Maggie (Fountain Falls St. Margaret), bred by Lynne Whitmire.

Responsible breeding isn't just about selling cute puppies and it's definitely not an occupation for

the uninformed. Despite what many people think, breeding is not just about the look of the dogs; health and temperament are important factors too. Many dog lovers do not realize that the single most important factor governing health and some temperament traits is genetics.

A good breeder is one whose main aim is to improve the Goldendoodle hybrid by producing healthy puppies with good temperaments and physical structures with consistently low shedding coats. This doesn't happen by accident or happy coincidence. If you want to breed first generation (F1) puppies, make sure you are very familiar with the parent breeds of Golden Retriever and Poodle (of whichever size) and the potential health issues. If you are interested in multigen (multigeneration) Goldendoodles, there are a further 101 things you need to research. Before you think of breeding from your dog, ask yourself these questions:

1. **Did you get your Goldendoodle from a good, ethical breeder?** Dogs sold in pet stores and on general sales websites are seldom good specimens and can be unhealthy.

2. **Are your dog and his or her close relatives free from a history of eye trouble?** Have you got the relevant eye certificates for your dog and seen those for his or her parents? Golden Retriever Progressive Retinal Atrophy (GR-PRA1) can be passed on to Goldendoodle puppies if one of the parents isn't completely clear of the disease. The Progressive Retinal Atrophy gene, called the prcd mutation, can also be passed on from the Poodle or from Goldendoodle to Goldendoodle.

3. **Are your dog and his or her close relatives free from other health issues?** Hip Dysplasia, Elbow and Patella Luxation, von Willebrand's Disease and heart problems are just some of the illnesses Goldendoodle puppies can inherit. Are you 100% sure your breeding dog is free from them all? Also, an unhealthy female is more likely to have trouble with pregnancy and whelping.

4. **Does your Goldendoodle have a good temperament? Does he or she socialize well with people and other animals?** If you can't tell, take your dog to training classes where the instructor can help you evaluate the dog's temperament. Dogs with poor temperaments should not be bred from, regardless of how good they look and what sort of coat they have.

5. **Has your dog got a healthy, low shedding coat and were the parents' coats similar?** If you are breeding for consistency, the coat is an important factor as many potential owners choose Goldendoodles for the hypoallergenic characteristics of the curly and wavy coat types.

6. **Do you understand canine genetics?** Do you know about the IC (Incorrect Coat) gene? There is more to breeding low shedding Goldendoodles than you might think.

7. **Do you understand COI and its implications?** COI stands for Coefficient of Inbreeding. It measures the common ancestors of a dam and sire and indicates the probability of how genetically similar they are. Breeding from too closely-related dams and sires can result in health issues for the offspring.

8. **Does your dog conform to the ideal standard/type?** Although there is no Kennel Club or AKC breed standard - as the Goldendoodle is a hybrid, not a purebred - GANA (Goldendoodle Association of North America) promotes a list of ideal attributes and has a strict Code of Ethics. Do not breed from a Goldendoodle which is not an excellent specimen, hoping that somehow the puppies will turn out better. They won't. Talk with experienced breeders and ask them for an honest assessment of your dog.

9. **Is your female at least one year old and less than seven?** Females should not be bred until they are physically mature, when they are able to carry a litter to term and are robust enough to whelp and care for a litter. They should also be less than seven years of age. Even then, not all females are suitable. Some are simply poor mothers who don't care for their puppies - which means you have to do it – others may not be able to produce enough milk.

10. **Do you know exactly what type of Goldendoodle you are going to produce?** –F1s, F1bs F2s, multigenerations? What size? (Photo by Christy Stevens of F1b English Mini Goldendoodle Freddie, aged nine weeks, and Multigen Mini Goldendoodle Zeppy, aged 11 weeks, playing together.)

11. **Are you financially able to provide good veterinary care for the mother and puppies, particularly if complications occur?** Have you considered these costs: DNA and health testing, medical care and vets' fees, supplements, whelping equipment, vaccinations and worming, extra food and stud fees? Health can be expensive, and that's in addition to routine veterinary care and the added costs of pre-natal care and immunizations for puppies. What if your female needs a Caesarean (C-section) or the puppies need emergency treatment? Can you afford the bills? If you are not prepared to make a financial commitment to a litter that could end up costing you a significant amount of money, then do not breed from your Goldendoodle.

12. **Have you got the indoor space?** The mother and puppies will need their own space in your home, which will become messy as new-born pups do not come into this world housetrained (potty trained.) It should also be warm and draught-free.

13. **Can you cope with up to a dozen or more puppies at a time?** Standard Goldendoodles may have litters of up to 14 pups.

14. **Do you have the time to provide full-time care for the mother and puppies if necessary?** Caring for the mother and newborns is a 24/7 job in the beginning, particularly the first few weeks.

15. Are you confident enough in your breeding program to offer at least a two-year health warranty on your puppies? Members of GANA offer this minimum guarantee to all new puppy parents.

16. Will you be able to find good homes for however many puppies there should be and will you be prepared to take them back if necessary? This is an important consideration for good breeders, who will not let their precious puppies go to any old home. They want to be sure that the new owners will take good care of their Goldendoodles for their lifetime. A responsible breeder will often take reservations (pre-sell) their puppies before they breed to ensure they are not creating puppies that do not have ready homes.

Mini Goldendoodle breeder Christy Stevens has some words of caution: "Young puppies are a lot of work. Most people think it's all fun and don't really understand the work that a breeder puts into raising a litter. It's the 'behind the scenes' stuff nobody sees that can be very difficult. If a person wants to consider breeding, they need to first ask themselves if they can handle it when things turn out bad. It's Mother Nature we are dealing with, so we only have so much control. Pictured are Disney, Cooper and Ellie, a trio of healthy 10-week-old F1b Mini Goldendoodles bred by Christy.

"One time, I had a female delivering her litter and she got to an umbilical cord before I could stop her. A momma dog is going to try and sever the cord and sometimes they chew way too close to the puppy. When that happens, it can create an open hole in the abdomen. I lost the puppy and it was heart-breaking. I tried really hard to save that puppy and then I blamed myself for what happened. Dog breeding isn't for the weak of heart. There are times an experience will make a breeder want to quit."

Christy adds: "The other thing is, if a person isn't willing to find good breeding stock and do all of the required health testing to make sure they are not passing down known genetic issues, they should not consider breeding. Also, a person would need to check their original puppy contract to make sure they didn't promise to spay or neuter their Goldendoodle. In such a case it may be unlawful to breed from their dog.

"And as a side note, if a breeder doesn't have a spay/neuter contract, that is a serious concern. There isn't a shortage of dogs in the world so puppies should only be produced carefully and responsibly. Part of a breeder's responsibility is making sure the offspring they produce will not be bred irresponsibly."

Amy Lane says: "Raising puppies is not for the faint of heart. Puppies need constant care and supervision. Newborns can fail quickly for a number of reasons and an experienced breeder who is attentive can pick up on the slightest changes and intervene many times in time to save lives. A small puppy in a large litter can be pushed away at feeding time by stronger, bigger puppies. A missed meal can be enough to start a puppy on a downward spiral and supervised feeding times or supplementing the puppy around the clock may become necessary for survival. Quite often, the breeder is sleep deprived for the first few weeks after the litter arrives."

"Many times families think it would be a great experience for their children to witness a birth and be a part of raising a litter of puppies just once. This isn't something that can be done properly 'just once'. Health testing and certifications need to be completed first and foremost to ensure their dog is worthy of reproducing. Finding a health-tested stud that properly complements the female is difficult because no responsible breeder will hire out their stud to a 'one-time' breeder.

"The experience of raising a litter of puppies that benefits their children may be the horrid experience another family has when their puppy grows up to be riddled with health or behavioral issues. A responsible breeder will be available for support for the life of the puppies they produce, so a one-time litter 'just for the experience' should be a 15-year commitment to the families that purchase those puppies. Having appropriate accommodation for raising a litter of puppies is also essential. A mother dog has to have a place she feels is safe for her puppies and any stress she feels is passed on to her puppies.

"Most families inexperienced with breeding do not realize that a female will typically come into heat the first time before she is a year of age. She will not be old enough by her first heat to have completed her health testing, so allowing her to become pregnant would be extremely irresponsible. Therefore, anyone wanting to provide this type of experience should do so only under the supervision of an experienced breeder or vet.

"The wonderful experience the parents wanted their children to experience can become a lesson on death instead when they find the mother dog has laid on and suffocated a puppy during the night. The stillborn puppy that cannot be revived can be an emotional picture that stays with a young child forever. Whelping and raising a litter of puppies will no doubt include experiences for the children that were not expected. "

Pictured is Amy's Fox Creek's Medium multigen All That Jazz (Jazz) at four months old on the left and eight months old on the right. Amy adds: "Puppies have different needs at different stages of their development. A warm, clean environment free of drafts (which are deadly to newborn puppies) is critical in the beginning.

As puppies grow and become more active, appropriate stimulation and interaction is necessary to continue

proper development. Changes in floor textures, toys, household noises and food all play a critical part in proper development. Knowing when to introduce softened food, allowing the puppies to play outside when the weather permits, providing climbing toys for muscle and coordination development, and exposing puppies to things such as vacuum cleaners, phones ringing, radios playing, etc. are all important, and this exposure cannot be replaced by starting at a later age."

Having said that, good Goldendoodle breeders are made, not born. Like any expert, they do their research and learn their trade over several years.

 If you are determined to breed from your dog, you must first learn a lot and the best way of doing this is to **find a mentor**; somebody who is already successfully breeding Goldendoodles. By that we mean somebody who is producing healthy puppies with good temperaments, rather someone who is making lots of money by producing lots of poor quality puppies. If you don't know anybody personally, you can contact GANA for help if you are in the USA or Canada.

GANA member Dyvonia Bussey, of Grace Goldens, Alabama, is a relative newcomer, having started breeding F1 standard Goldendoodles in 2015. She says: "Breeding dogs is the hardest thing I have ever done!

"My advice is to do your homework. I spent two years researching, interviewing, and praying before we made this decision. Every delivery is different and every female is different and I will continue learning as long as we do this. With that said, it is also very rewarding. We have met some wonderful families, and it is our goal to know them all by name and keep up with our dogs throughout their lifetimes.

"One of the things I love about GANA is the breeders that keep up with their dogs and families. I have seen many pictures of dogs that were in the breeder's first litter. It makes me smile to think that it is a relationship that will last a lifetime." Pictured is five week-old F1 Cooper, bred by Dyvonia.

Responsible breeding isn't just about selling cute puppies and it's definitely not an occupation for the uninformed. Despite what many people think, breeding is not just about the look of the dogs; health and temperament are important factors too. Many dog lovers do not realize that the single most important factor governing health and certain temperament traits is genetics.

GANA founder Amy Lane says: "All new breeders make mistakes along the way, making it quite beneficial to benefit from the knowledge of an experienced breeder. Learning how to appropriately select a puppy as a future breeding prospect, completing all the appropriate health testing certifications and selecting the right mate to compliment your dog's traits can seem like daunting tasks.

"A breeder's reputation is built on the puppies they send out into the world. GANA was created to guide the future integrity of the Goldendoodle breed and this includes mentoring new breeders to help them create healthy, quality Goldendoodle puppies. To begin the process of becoming a GANA member breeder - which includes an experienced breeder assigned to mentor you - use the **Contact Us** menu tab on our website at www.GoldendoodleAssociation.com."

GANA member Lynne Whitmire added: "A breeder should be diligent about choosing breeding dogs, and potential breeding dogs should be fully researched. Not only for details of the parents and health testing, but also the history of the dog's grandparents and great grandparents, as diseases run through certain lines of Poodles and Golden Retrievers. There are health databases that can be accessed online that have a wealth of information."

(Pictured looking very pleased with himself is Lynne's 'shadow,' Frisco, a Mini multigen.)

"It also helps to have a good relationship with other breeders and to belong to an organization such as GANA. Keeping abreast of the latest research, going to breeding seminars and speaking with other trusted breeders is key to raising healthy dogs. The availability of DNA testing is such a wonderful thing; it will avoid so many heartbreaks that have plagued dog breeders."

"The downfall is narrowing the gene pool by eliminating every dog that does not pass every test. We get into the problem of throwing out some great genes that are needed to keep the breed healthy. GANA is committed to learning from the mistakes of some of the bigger breed clubs. This is a complicated subject and it is crucial that Goldendoodle breeders stay informed about the latest findings. Education is the key."

Regardless of where you live, you can visit the GANA website or an online Goldendoodle forum, such as http://goldendoodles.com/forum_community.htm or www.doodlekisses.com/forum where other owners are willing to share their experiences. If you are considering selecting breeding stock from a particular breeder, ask others for their opinion and experiences of this breeder.

Don't go into breeding to make money or to get puppies just like your perfect Goldendoodle, and certainly not to show the kids "the miracle of birth!" If your heart is set on it, then do so for the right reason. Learn all you can beforehand, read books, visit dog shows and get-togethers and make contact with established breeders. Find yourself a mentor and make sure you have a good vet on hand who is familiar with Goldendoodles. Committed breeders use their skills and knowledge to produce healthy pups with good temperaments which conform to guidelines and ultimately improve the crossbreed.

Females and Heat

Just like all other animal and human females, a female Goldendoodle has a menstrual cycle - or to be more accurate, an estrus cycle. This is the period when she is ready (and willing!) for mating and is more commonly called *heat* or being *on heat*, *in heat* or *in season*.

A female Goldendoodle has her first cycle from about six to nine or 12 months old. She will generally come on heat every six to eight months, though it may be even longer between cycles, and the timescale becomes more erratic with old age. It can also be irregular with young dogs when cycles first begin. Heat will last on average from 12 to 21 days, although it can be anything from just a few days up to four weeks.

Within this period there will be several days which will be the optimum time for her to get pregnant. This middle phase of the cycle is called the *estrus*. The third phase, called *diestrus*, then begins. During this time, her body will produce hormones whether or not she is pregnant. Her body thinks and acts like she is pregnant. All the hormones are present; only the puppies are missing. This can sometimes lead to what is known as a 'false pregnancy'.

Breeders normally wait until a female has been in heat at least twice before breeding from her. Many believe that around two years old is the right age for a first litter as a pregnancy draws on her calcium reserves which she needs for her own growing bones. Also, some dogs are relatively slow to reach maturity. Responsible breeders also limit the number of litters from each female, as overbreeding can take too heavy a toll on her body.

While a female is on heat, she produces hormones which attract male dogs. Because dogs have a sense of smell hundreds of times stronger than ours, your girl on heat is a magnet for all the males in the neighborhood. They may congregate around your house or follow you around the park, waiting for their chance to prove their manhood – or mutthood in their case.

Don't expect your precious princess to be fussy. Her hormones are raging when she is on heat and during her most fertile days, she is ready, able and ... very willing! Keep her on a lead at all times when she is on heat. As she approaches the optimum time for mating, you may notice her tail bending slightly to one side. She will also start to urinate more frequently. This is her signal to all those virile male dogs out there that she is ready for mating.

The first visual sign you may notice is when she tries to lick her swollen rear end – or vulva, to be more precise. She will then bleed, this is sometimes called spotting. It will be a light red or brown at the beginning of the heat cycle, and some bitches (female dogs) then bleed a lot after the first week. Some can bleed quite heavily, this is normal. But if you have any concerns about the bleeding, contact your vet to be on the safe side. She may also start to 'mate' or 'hump' your leg or other dogs. These are all normal signs of heat.

Breeding requires specialized knowledge on the part of the owner, but this does not stop a female Goldendoodle on heat from being extremely interested in attention from any old mutt! To avoid an unwanted pregnancy, you must keep a close eye on her and not allow her to freely wander where she may come into contact with other dogs when she is on heat. Unlike women, female dogs do not go through the menopause and can have puppies even when they are quite old. However, a litter for an elderly Goldendoodle can also result in complications; it is generally recommended that a female not be bred after the age of seven.

If you don't want your dog to get pregnant, you should have her spayed. Many Goldendoodle puppy contracts specify that the puppy must be spayed or neutered when old enough. In North America, the UK and Europe, humane societies, animal shelters and rescue groups urge dog owners to have their pets spayed or neutered to prevent unwanted litters which contribute to too many animals in the rescue system or, even worse, euthanasia. Normally all dogs from rescue centers and shelters are spayed or neutered. Many responsible breeders also encourage early spaying and neutering – and some may even specify it in the puppy's sale contract.

Spaying

Spaying is the term used to describe the removal of the ovaries and uterus (womb) of a female dog so that she cannot become pregnant. Although this is a routine operation, it is major abdominal surgery and she has to be anaesthetized.

A popular myth is that a female should have her first heat cycle before she is spayed, but this is not the case. Even puppies can be spayed. You should consult your vet for the optimum time, should you decide to have your dog done. Note that if she is on heat or nearing her heat cycle, she cannot be spayed.

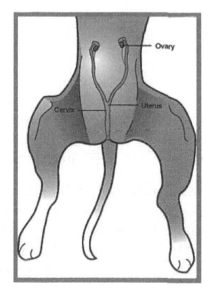

If spayed before her first heat cycle, one of the advantages is that your dog will have an almost zero risk of mammary cancer (the equivalent of breast cancer in women.) Even after the first heat, spaying reduces the risk of this cancer by 92%. Some vets claim that the risk of mammary cancer in unspayed female dogs can be as high as one in four. Some dogs may put weight on easier after spaying and will require slightly less food afterwards. As with any major procedure, there are pros and cons.

Spaying is a much more serious operation for a female than neutering is for a male. This is because it involves an **internal** abdominal operation, whereas the neutering procedure is carried out on the male's testicles, which are outside his abdomen.

For:

- Spaying prevents infections, mammary cancer and other diseases of the uterus and ovaries
- It reduces hormonal changes which can interfere with the treatment of diseases like diabetes or epilepsy
- Spaying can reduce behavior problems, such as roaming, aggression to other dogs, anxiety or fear
- It eliminates the risk of the potentially fatal disease pyometra (a secondary infection that occurs as a result of hormonal changes in the female's reproductive tract), which affects unspayed middle-aged females
- A spayed dog does not contribute to the pet overpopulation problem

Against:

- Complications can occur, including an abnormal reaction to the anesthetic, bleeding, stitches breaking and infections. This is not common
- Occasionally there can be long-term effects connected to hormonal changes. These may include weight gain, urinary incontinence or less stamina and these problems can occur years after a female has been spayed
- Older females may suffer some urinary incontinence, but it only affects a very few spayed females. Discuss it with your vet
- Cost (this is a rough estimate, vets' practices vary greatly.) This can range from $160-$480 in the USA and £100 to £300 in the UK

If you talk to your vet or a volunteer at a rescue shelter, they will say that the advantages of spaying far outweigh any disadvantages. When you take your female Goldendoodle to the vet's for her vaccinations, you can discuss at what age spaying should be considered.

....

Neutering

Neutering male dogs involves castration; the removal of the testicles. This can be a difficult decision for some owners, as it causes a drop in the pet's testosterone levels, which some humans – males in particular! - feel affects the quality of their dog's life.

Fortunately, dogs do not think like people and male dogs do not miss their testicles or the loss of sex. Our own experience is that male dogs are much happier once neutered. We decided to have our Max neutered after he went missing three times on walks – he ran off on the scent of a female on heat. Fortunately, he is microchipped and has our phone number on a tag on his collar and we were lucky that he was returned to us on all three occasions.

Unless you specifically want to breed from your dog, or he has a special job, neutering is recommended by animal rescue organizations and vets. Even then, Guide Dogs for the Blind, Hearing Dogs for Deaf People, Dogs for the Disabled, and other service and assistance dogs are routinely neutered and this does not impair their ability. There are countless unwanted puppies, especially in the US, many of which are destroyed. There is also the problem of a lack of knowledge from the owners of some breeding dogs, resulting in the production of puppies with congenital health or temperament problems.

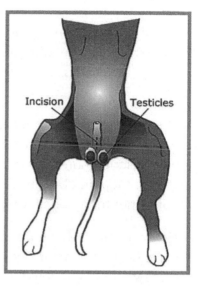

Neutering is usually performed around puberty, i.e. about six months old. It can, however, be done at any age over eight weeks, provided both testicles have descended. The operation is a relatively straightforward procedure. Dogs neutered before puberty tend to grow a little larger than dogs done later. This is because the hormone testosterone is involved in the process which stops growth, so the bones grow for longer without testosterone.

The neutering operation for a male is much less of a major operation than spaying for a female. Complications are less common and less severe than with spaying a female. Although he will feel tender afterwards, your dog should return to his normal self within a couple of days. When he comes out of surgery, his scrotum (the sacs which held the testicles) will be swollen and it may look like nothing has been done. But it is normal for these to slowly shrink in the days following surgery. Incidentally, in the USA there is on-going research into chemical alternatives to surgical neutering. Here are the main pros and cons of surgery:

For:

- 🐾 Behavior problems such as aggression and wandering off are reduced

- 🐾 Unwanted sexual behavior, such as mounting people or objects, is reduced or eliminated

- 🐾 Testicular problems such as infections, torsion (painful rotation of the testicle) are eradicated Neutering also significantly reduces the number of cases of testicular cancer

- 🐾 Prostate disease, common in older male dogs, is less likely to occur

- 🐾 A submissive entire (uncastrated) male dog may be targeted by other dogs. After he has been neutered, he will no longer produce testosterone and so will not be regarded as much of a threat by the other males, so he is less likely to be bullied

- 🐾 A neutered dog is not fathering unwanted puppies

Against:

- 🐾 As with any surgery, there can be bleeding afterwards, keep an eye out for any blood loss. Infections can also occur, generally caused by the dog licking the wound, so try and prevent him doing this. If he persists, use an E collar. In the **vast majority** of cases, these problems do not occur

- 🐾 Some dogs' coats may be affected, but supplementing their diet with fish oil can compensate for this

❖ Cost. This starts at around $130 in the USA, £80 in the UK

Here are some common myths about neutering and spaying:

Neutering or spaying will spoil the dog's character - There is no evidence that any of the positive characteristics of your dog will change. He or she will be just as loving, playful and loyal. Neutering may reduce aggression or roaming in males because they are no longer competing to mate with a female.

A female needs to have at least one litter - There is no proven physical or mental benefit to a female having a litter. Pregnancy and whelping (giving birth to puppies) can be stressful and can have complications. In a false pregnancy, a female is simply responding to the hormones in her body.

Mating is natural and necessary - Dogs are not humans, they do not think emotionally about sex or having and raising a family. Because Goldendoodles like the company of humans so much, we tend to ascribe human emotions to them. Unlike humans, their desire to mate or breed is entirely physical, triggered by the chemicals called hormones within their body. Without these hormones – i.e. after neutering or spaying – the desire disappears or is greatly reduced.

Male dogs will behave better if they can mate - This is simply not true; sex does not make a dog behave better. In fact it can have the opposite effect. Having mated once, a male may show an increased interest in females. He may also consider his status elevated, which may make him harder to control or call back.

NOTE: A recent study by The University of California suggested that it was beneficial to wait until Golden Retrievers were one year old before neutering or spaying, and some spayed female Goldens showed higher incidences of cancer. You can read the published research paper here: http://journals.plos.org/plosone/article?id=10.1371/journal.pone.0055937. Goldendoodles were not mentioned in the study; however they all carry some Golden Retriever genes. A number of Goldendoodle breeders feel that further research needs to be carried out. Our advice is to speak to your vet about the best time to spay or neuter.

Pictured here is a litter of healthy multigeneration puppies born to mother Chelsea and bred by Janece Schommer of Goldendoodle Acres, Wisconsin. The photo illustrates the different shades of color often found within the same litter.

Pregnancy

A canine pregnancy will normally last for 58 to 65 days, regardless of the size or breed of the dog. Sometimes pregnancy is referred to as the *'gestation period.'* It's a good idea to take a female for a pre-natal check-up after mating. The vet should answer any questions, such as the type of food, supplements, care and physical changes in your female.

There is a blood test available which measures levels of **relaxin**. This is a hormone produced by the ovary and the developing placenta, and pregnancy can be detected by monitoring relaxin levels as early as three weeks after mating. The levels are high throughout pregnancy and then decline rapidly after the female has given birth.

A vet can usually see the puppies using Ultrasound from around the same time. X-rays also give the breeder an idea of the number of puppies; these can help to give the vet more information, which is particularly useful if the bitch has had previous whelping problems. (Photo: Steve and Neelie Smith.) Here are some of the signs of pregnancy:

- After mating, many females become more affectionate. (However, some will become uncharacteristically irritable and maybe even a little aggressive)

- The female may produce a slight clear discharge from her vagina about one month after mating

- Three or four weeks after mating, a few females experience morning sickness – if this is the case, feed little and often. She may seem more tired than usual

- She may seem slightly depressed and/or show a drop in appetite. These signs can also mean there are other problems, so you should consult your vet

- Her teats (nipples) will become more prominent, pink and erect 25 to 30 days into the pregnancy. Later on, you may notice a fluid coming from them

- After about 35 days, or seven weeks, her body weight will noticeably increase

- Her abdomen will become noticeably larger from around day 40, although first-time mums and females carrying few puppies may not show as much

- Many pregnant females' appetite will increase in the second half of pregnancy

- Her nesting instincts will kick in as the delivery date approaches. She may seem restless or scratch her bed or the floor

- During the last week of pregnancy, females often start to look for a safe place for whelping. Some seem to become confused, wanting to be with their owners and at the same time wanting to prepare their nest. Even if the female is having a C-section, she should still be allowed to nest in a whelping box with layers of newspaper, which she will scratch and dig as the time approaches

If your female becomes pregnant – either by design or accident - your first step should be to consult a vet.

Litter Size

This varies tremendously depending on the size of the dam (mother.) An average litter size for a Golden Retriever is five to 10 puppies. A Standard Poodle may have up to 10 puppies at a time, while smaller Poodles have smaller litters. With multigenerations, a Petite Goldendoodle may typically have three to five puppies in a litter, a Mini may have four to six or seven, a Medium might have six to eight and a Standard can have eight to 10, 12 or even 14 puppies.

Amy says: "Litter sizes depend on several factors. Typically, larger dogs have more puppies than smaller dogs. A line of dogs that generally have large or small litters tend to pass this trait on to their offspring. Litters produced via artificial insemination are often smaller than those litters produced by a natural breeding due to timing of the breedings being determined by humans, instead of the natural instincts of the dogs."

False Pregnancies

As many as 50% or more of intact (unspayed) females may display signs of a false pregnancy. In the wild it was common for female dogs to have false pregnancies and to lactate (produce milk.) This female would then nourish puppies if their own mother died.

False pregnancies occur 60 to 80 days after the female was in heat - about the time she would have given birth – and are generally nothing to worry about for an owner. The exact cause is unknown. However, hormonal imbalances are thought to play an important role. Some dogs have shown symptoms within three to four days of spaying. Typical symptoms include:

- Making a nest
- Producing milk (lactating)
- Mothering or adopting toys and other objects
- Appetite fluctuations
- Barking or whining a lot
- Restlessness, depression or anxiety
- Swollen abdomen
- She might even appear to go into labor

Try not to touch your dog's nipples, as touch will stimulate further milk production. If she is licking herself repeatedly, she may need an Elizabethan collar (or E-collar, a large plastic collar from the vet) to minimize stimulation.

Under no circumstances should you restrict your Goldendoodle's water supply to try and prevent her from producing milk. This is dangerous as she can become dehydrated.

Some unspayed bitches may have a false pregnancy with each heat cycle. Spaying during a false pregnancy may actually prolong the condition, so better to wait until the false pregnancy is over and then have her spayed to prevent it happening again. False pregnancy is not a disease, but an exaggerated response to normal hormonal changes. Owners should be reassured that even if left untreated, the condition almost always resolves itself.

However, if your Goldendoodle appears physically ill or the behavioral changes are severe enough to worry you, visit your vet, who may prescribe tranquilizers to relieve anxiety, or diuretics to reduce milk production and relieve fluid retention. In rare cases, hormone treatment may be necessary.

Generally, dogs experiencing false pregnancies do not have serious long-term problems, as the behavior disappears when the hormones return to their normal levels in two to three weeks.

One exception is **Pyometra**, a disease mainly affecting unspayed middle-aged females, caused by a hormonal abnormality. Pyometra follows a heat cycle in which fertilization did not occur and the dog typically starts showing symptoms within two to four months. The signs are excessive drinking and urination, with the female trying to lick a white discharge from her vagina. She may also have a slight temperature. If the condition becomes severe, her back legs will become weak, possibly to the point where she can no longer get up without help.

Pyometra is serious if bacteria take a hold, and in extreme cases it can be fatal. It is also relatively common and needs to be dealt with promptly by a vet, who will give the dog intravenous fluids and antibiotics for several days. In most cases this is followed by spaying.

To recap: You many have the most wonderful Goldendoodle in the world, but only enter the world of canine breeding if you have with the right knowledge and motivation. Don't do it just for the money or the cute factor. Breeding poor examples only brings heartache to families in the long run when health or other issues develop.

Photo of health-tested Luna and her seven-week-old pup courtesy of Lynne Whitmire.

13. Goldendoodle Rescue

Are you thinking of adopting a Goldendoodle from a rescue organization? What could be kinder and more rewarding than giving a poor, abandoned Goldendoodle a happy and loving home for the rest of his life?

Not much really, adoption saves lives. The problem of homeless dogs is truly depressing, particularly in the USA. The sheer numbers in kill shelters there is hard to comprehend. Randy Grim states in "Don't Dump The Dog" that 1,000 dogs are being put to sleep every hour in the States. According to Jo-Anne Cousins, Executive Director at International Doodle Owners Group (IDOG) Rescue, the situations leading to a Doodle ending up in rescue can be summed up in one phrase: unrealistic expectations.

She said: "In many situations, dog ownership was something that the family went into without fully understanding the time, money and commitment to exercise and training that it takes to raise a dog. While they may have spent hours on the internet pouring over cute puppy photos, they probably didn't read any puppy training books or look into actual costs of regular vet care, training and boarding. With doodles, many are going to homes that have never had a dog before because of allergies. The marketing of doodles as "hypo-allergenic" and/or non-shedding has caused a general misconception that *all doodles* are non-shedding, or will not cause allergies to flare up."

IDOG Rescue Manager Lynda Strommer handles the charity's day-to-day operations and intakes, and says: "I'd say that shedding and anxiety are at the top of the list of reasons doodles are surrendered. So many of them shed to some degree (some quite heavy), while most people think they don't shed at all. Also, anxiety - especially separation anxiety - is common in doodles." Other reasons for rehoming are personal changes in circumstances and issues such as:

Allergies to the dog

The dog has too much energy

He nips or growls at the kids

He chews or eats things it shouldn't

The dog needs way more time and effort than the owner is able to or prepared to give

There is, however, a ray of sunshine for some of these dogs. Every year many thousands of people in North America, the UK and countries all around the world adopt a rescue dog and the story often has a happy ending.

The Dog's Point of View...

But if you are serious about adopting a Goldendoodle, you should do so with the right motives and with your eyes wide open. If you're expecting a perfect dog, you could be in for a shock. Rescue Goldendoodles can and do become wonderful companions, but much of it depends on you.

Goldendoodles are people-loving dogs. Many of them in rescue centers are traumatized. They don't understand why they have been abandoned by their beloved owners and in the beginning, may arrive with problems of their own until they adjust to being part of a loving family home again. Ask yourself a few questions before you take the plunge:

- 🐾 Are you prepared to accept and deal with any problems - such as bad behavior, shyness, aggression or making a mess in the house - which the dog may display when he initially arrives in your home?

- 🐾 How about boisterousness?

- 🐾 How much time are you willing to spend with your new pet to help him integrate back into normal family life?

- 🐾 Can you take time off work to be at home and help the dog settle in at the beginning?

- 🐾 Are you prepared to take on a new addition to your family that may live for another 10 years or so?

Here's a description of a Goldendoodle which was available for adoption through the UK's Doodle Trust. Barney would undoubtedly make a super dog for the right person or family, but only if they have the time and energy to cope with his high intelligence and huge energy drive. (The dog's name has been changed.)

Type: Goldendoodle. (Golden Retriever x Miniature Poodle)

Gender: Male   **Age:** 2 yrs

Size: 20 inches. This is deceptive though, he does weigh 20kg and is not overweight, his length is that of a much larger dog as is his strength and appetite.

Live with Children: Has lived with a teenager. Not tested with young children.

Shedding: Mats rather than sheds.

Grooming Requirements: Regular brushing and short clip to prevent matting.

House Trained: Yes   **Able to be left:** Yes. 3-4 hrs

Obedient: Yes. Responds to basic commands and would happily learn more.

Comes when called: Not when he spies someone with a flinger or there are small furries in the vicinity.

Pulls on lead: Yes on a normal collar but he has taken well to a head collar.

Exercise Requirements: High energy; two good walks per day, currently 1.5 hours morning and evening.

Mental Stimulation Requirements: Barney is a bright dog with lots to offer. He would benefit from training exercises to challenge his capability and satisfy his active and inquisitive brain.

He is reactive to the TV, both noises and visuals, the more his unwanted behaviour is ignored and desirable behaviours rewarded, the calmer he becomes.

Good with cats: Yes. After one week he accepted the comings and goings of the resident cat. He would chase a cat, and will initially growl and bark, so wouldn't be suitable for a cat that wasn't confident with dogs.

Good with dogs: Yes. Barney loves to chase, wrestle and potter along with dogs. Whilst in foster he's not met a dog he's been scared of, or been too boisterous with, he has warned off a couple of dogs, but no harm was done and they are the renowned park bullies.

Friendly with strangers: Yes. Happy to meet people out and about, and greet in the home, he will jump up, but is learning four paws on the ground is good.

Good watch dog: Barney has a wonderful bark, baying hound dog type, he will turn to look for approval/instruction.

Health Problems: None known.

Special Diet: No. Good quality kibble, and possibly raw, he has developed a penchant for duck necks. Barney is extremely lean, but has an excellent appetite, he finds it difficult to keep weight on as he runs around so much.

General Description

Barney is rocket dog, he loves life and lives it one hundred miles an hour, it is a pleasure to watch him running around, he always has a smile on his face …. but can he find an owner that can stay cool and keep up?

In a quiet home Barney will sleep the whole day through, preferably with a knee to rest his head upon, but it is important that Barney has physical and mental stimulation to satisfy his exuberance and intelligence; without he will find his own entertainment.

Barney needs an active home where there is time, and safe areas, to be off lead exploring, chasing a ball, getting wet and making friends. Barney would not be suited to a home with cream carpets and lack of human company. If Barney had a choice he would want to live with another confident dog, have stay-at-home humans and be beside the sea.

To his human companions Barney is attentive and lovable, without being overbearing, he will make a wonderful pet. Whilst in foster he has experienced limber tail, he had wagged it so much it stopped working, thankfully the wag is now back.

Barney and other Goldendoodles in rescue will make wonderful companions for the right owners. But think carefully about the implications before taking on a rescue dog - try and look at it from the dog's point of view.

What could be worse for Barney and other unlucky Goldendoodles than to be abandoned again if things don't work out between you?

Things to Consider Pre-Adoption

Adopting a rescue dog is a big commitment for all involved. It is not a cheap way of getting a Goldendoodle and shouldn't be viewed as such. It could cost you several hundred dollars - or pounds. The IDOG Adoption Fee ranges from $100 to $750, depending on the dog - generally the younger the Goldendoodle, the higher the fee. In addition, you'll have to pay vaccination and veterinary bills as well as worming and flea medication and the bill for spaying or neutering. Make sure you're aware of the full cost before committing.

Many rescue Goldendoodles have had difficult lives. You need plenty of time to help them rehabilitate. Some may have initial problems with housebreaking, others may need socialization with people as well as other dogs.

If you are serious about adopting, you may have to wait a while until a suitable dog comes up – and it's unlikely to be a puppy. One way of finding out if you, your family and home are suitable is to volunteer to become a foster home for one of the rescue centers. Fosters offer temporary homes until a forever home becomes available. It's a shorter term arrangement, but still requires commitment and patience.

And it's not just the dogs that are screened - you'll probably have to undergo a screening by the rescue organization to ensure you are suitable. You might even have to provide references, and there will almost certainly be a home visit first. Here is the list of questions on the IDOG Rescue Adoption Form:

Are you applying for a particular dog? If yes, which one?

Why are you applying for a rescue dog?

How far are you willing to travel to pick up or meet the dog?

Describe your home, yard and fence.

Do you own or rent? If you rent, do you have permission to have a dog?

Landlord's name and phone number:

Who lives in your home or visits frequently. Please include ages.

Does anyone in your home have allergies? If yes, please explain severity and type of allergy.

Does everyone in your home want to adopt a dog?

Who will be the primary caregiver for the dog?

Are there cats or small animals in the home?

Describe your lifestyle and how a dog will fit in:

How many hours a day would your dog be without human company?

Where will your dog be when you are not home?

Where will your dog sleep?

How will you exercise your dog, and how frequently?

Where will your dog be when you are on vacation?

Will this be a first dog for your family? If yes, what preparation and research have you done?

If yes, have you identified a training class to attend?

If yes, have your children been around dogs on a regular basis?

Have you had experience with a rescue dog before?

Please list your current and past pets, and their ages. If deceased, please list age and cause of death.

If you have rehomed or given up a pet, please give details:

Are your current pets spayed or neutered?

What age range would you consider?

Do you care about gender or color?

Do you care about coat type? e.g. flatter, wavy, curlier

Is any level of shedding acceptable?

What is the most important consideration for you when adopting a dog?

How would you rate your ability to train a dog?

Would you accept a dog with a manageable medical issue?

Would you accept a dog that needed to work on some behavioral issues?

Would you be willing to work with professional trainers?

Are you familiar with crate training?

Are your current animals up to date on shots and monthly heart worm medication?

Please supply one veterinarian reference and two personal non-relative references

The Doodle Trust has a list of Things to Consider BEFORE Getting a Doodle. It also warns that not ALL Doodles are guaranteed 'hypoallergenic' (less likely to cause allergies) for all allergy sufferers. Dogs vary and allergies vary from person to person. Here are some of the main points. (A couple of these points are more applicable to the UK than USA, e.g. most Goldendoodles in the UK are Standards and there are fewer multigens in Britain.) The Trust says:

Doodles have received so much positive press and many people believe they are the perfect dogs. While they make wonderful companions, they are not for everyone. These are some important considerations before you add a doodle to your family:

If you want a Golden Retriever or a Labrador that does not shed, DON'T GET A DOODLE. Most doodles shed to some degree and those that do not, do not look like either of these parent dogs.

If you are just not a Poodle person, DON'T GET A DOODLE. All doodles have Poodle in them and if the word Poodle makes you cringe, then do not get a Doodle.

If you want a low-energy dog, DON'T GET A DOODLE. Most Doodles require at least 30-60 minutes of real exercise a day. Simply letting your Doodle out in the backyard is not exercise. There are plenty of low-energy dog breeds that would be a better fit if you aren't overly active.

If you can't devote time and money into training, DON'T GET A DOODLE. Doodles are intelligent and want to please you, but they are not born with manners.

If you want an independent dog, DON'T GET A DOODLE. Doodles thrive on human companionship and most are Velcro dogs. They need your attention and will demand it.

If you want the perfect dog, DON'T GET A DOODLE. There is no such thing as a perfect dog, and just like other breeds, Doodles can have a wide variety of temperaments and health issues.

If you want a low-maintenance dog, DON'T GET A DOODLE. The look that attracts so many would-be Doodle owners requires a lot of time and money; there is major grooming involved.

If you want a dog 'for the kids to look after', DON'T GET A DOODLE. Doodles need lots of time on a daily basis, keeping their minds stimulated and reinforcing their behaviors. Kids won't keep that commitment.

If you are still interested in a Doodle, that's great! But keep in mind that some of the pre-conceived notions touted by the media that have made Doodles so popular are also reasons why so many of these dogs are abandoned by their owners. A Doodle can be a wonderful dog and will provide you with unconditional love but you must consider if this is the right type of dog for you.

Please do not break your Doodle's heart.

The Doodle Trust also has this to say about Doodles in general in the UK:

Doodles are an intelligent but challenging type of dog. They vary greatly in size and coat type and it is a common misconception that they do not shed their fur. Many of them do moult and they are not an ideal breed for allergy sufferers.

Doodles are lively, enthusiastic and sometimes boisterous dogs that require a lot of time and attention. If you are out at work for much of the time or lead a busy life, a Doodle is NOT the right breed for you. These are people dogs and they demand human companionship, they thrive as a much loved family member. If left to their own devices for long periods, they will find their own amusement and could become destructive.

Most Doodles love water and can be mud magnets, bringing in an enormous amount of dirt into your home. They are certainly not a breed for the house-proud. Some coat types require grooming on a daily basis in order to keep them mat free, whilst Doodles with a shorter coat will require less brushing.

Many Doodles also need professional grooming on a regular basis in order to keep the coat manageable and this can be expensive. You should therefore consider grooming costs on top of food, insurance, toys, vaccinations, worming, etc. It all mounts up!

Doodles are not necessarily compatible with small children and in any case it is unwise to leave any dog with small children. When considering a rescue Doodle, please also give some thought as to how this may affect any other pets you might own. Some cats for example may not take kindly to a big bouncy dog, and if you already own another dog, how will the new addition impact on them?

Most Doodles coming into rescue are large boys so there may be a considerable waiting period before we can match you with the right dog. Waiting times are further increased if you specify a certain colour and coat type and our dogs will always be matched to families by their suitability, rather than looks.

If you haven't been put you off with all of the above..... Congratulations, you may be just the family or person that poor homeless Goldendoodle is looking for!

If you can't spare the time to adopt - and adoption means forever - you might want to consider fostering. Or you could help by becoming a fundraiser to generate cash to keep these very worthy rescue groups providing such a wonderful service.

However you decide to get involved, Good Luck!

**Saving one dog will not change the world
But it will change the world for one dog**

Rescue Organizations

There are many dedicated people out there who give up their time free of charge to help find loving and permanent homes for dogs who would often otherwise be put down (euthanized). There are networks of these worthy people who have set up excellent rescue services for Goldendoodles. Here are the main ones:

USA

The International Doodle Owners Group, Inc (IDOG) Rescue was one of the first rescue groups to be set up. It is a highly-respected organization with a network of Doodle owners committed to the protection of Goldendoodles and Labradoodles. They strive to keep Doodles out of shelters by helping to find new homes for them.

It is a not-for-profit 501(c) (3) public charity group based in the USA which has affiliations with Doodle owners' groups in other countries and is endorsed by both the Australian Goldendoodle Association of America (ALAA) and the Goldendoodle Association of America (GANA).

International Doodle Owners Group
Labradoodle & Goldendoodle
Rescue, Education & Support

It is an approved rescue partner in hundreds of shelters across the USA and has an excellent reputation for helping Doodles in need, having assisted more than 1,500 since starting. Adoption fees help to cover the costs of keeping the dogs and giving them the necessary medical treatment.

IDOG Rescue has volunteers and foster homes across the USA, even internationally, operating without a shelter. As well as helping to rescue Doodles, IDOG states: "Our mission is to also provide education, resources and support to the owners and potential owners of Goldendoodles and Labradoodles to help them raise well-balanced, healthy dogs. IDOG offers counseling for behavioral issues and, when necessary, assists owners who want to rehome their dogs responsibly and safely."

Volunteers' aim is to get the dogs into homes that understand the temperament and needs of these energetic, playful and loving dogs. Any owner who finds they cannot keep their Goldendoodle for whatever reason can contact the volunteers by emailing rescue@idogrescue.com for further advice. IDOG is more than a rescue and education resource, the organization fosters a spirit of cooperation and community among Doodle owners through social networking. It highlights social activities and get-togethers, as well as specialized interests such as agility, training, therapy dog volunteer activities and other service work. It has this advice for prospective owners looking to provide a forever home:

"Seeing a dog in a photo is a great start to finding the right dog for your family, but please remember that our rescue coordinators have the very best understanding about what type of family and home environment will be most suitable for each individual dog.

"Very specific preferences will limit your chances: Sometimes people get distracted with what a dog looks like and often forget that there is a personality under all that fur. The perfect dog for you may be the opposite sex of the one you imagined. The right dog for your family might be black, or have a scruffy coat, or be a different age than you imagined.

"If you overlook some dogs because of sex, color or looks, you might just miss out on some great dogs. We urge you to consider all the dogs in our program based on their listing descriptions, and not on their photos. Please understand that our focus is on *rescuing* nice dogs and finding them good homes, not helping people find the picture-perfect dog that they can tell people they "rescued" because it is more socially acceptable.

"If your family really wants a puppy, or must have a blonde or female, or if your family has allergy issues to consider, our best recommendation is that you work with a responsible breeder to get exactly what you want. There is no shame in getting a pup from a responsible breeder.

"Please do not apply for a dog unless you are able and willing to travel to the foster's location to meet the dog. We rarely ship dogs and will do so only if we feel that it is the best option for the dog.

"Please realize that first-time dog owners comprise the majority of people who surrender dogs to shelters. For that reason, we are very hesitant to place a dog in a first time situation. Most rescue dogs need experienced owners."

IDOG Rescue does not place dogs in homes that use an electric fence or shock training collars, as they claim that this can spell disaster for rescue dogs. If you meet the criteria and are still interested, visit the website at www.idogrescue.com where you will find a detailed application form to make sure you're a suitable candidate. If fostering or adopting isn't an option for you, but you'd like to support their valuable work, you can donate online at: www.idogrescue.com/index.php/support-idog/donate-to-idog-online

The Doodle Rescue Collective Inc (DRC) was founded in 2009, It does not have a shelter, but has built up a network of over 800 registered foster volunteers across the continent.

The driving force behind the organization is joint founder member Jacqueline Yorke: "DRC is dedicated to the protection and rescue of Goldendoodles and Goldendoodles in need and to the provision of educational resources and support services to Doodle owners, aspiring owners and enthusiasts. Through its programs, it provides refuge, vet care, rehabilitation, transport and quality lifelong homes for Doodles in need."

"Through and with our programs, services, outreach and educational resources, DRC promotes, inspires and encourages humane volunteerism, responsible companion animal care, ownership and breeding practices and increases public awareness of the plight of the doodle dog associated with the "designer dog" craze and the commercial puppy mill and pet trade industry.

"Through our programs, DRC provides refuge, safe haven, vet care, rehabilitation, transport, and quality forever homes for doodle dogs in need. DRC is also dedicated to providing support services and educational resources and re-home assistance for those needing to find new forever homes for their family pets. To date, DRC has saved and placed over 1.800 doodle dogs through our successful and highly regarded Rescue/Rehome Program. DRC founders have also assisted in the rescue, transport and responsible placement of hundreds of other doodle dogs in need since 2005."

DRC is currently endorsed by the Goldendoodle Association of North America (GANA) and the Australian Goldendoodle Association of America (ALAA), and can be found online at http://doodlerescue.org and is on Facebook and on Twitter @DoodleRescue If you would like to support the cause, you can donate online at http://doodlerescue.org/page/donate.

Oodles of Doodles Inc is a Federal 501(c) (3) not-for-profit, charitable organization and was set up in January 2009 and also operates in North America. It rescues Goldendoodles, Labradoodles, "fuzzy Terriers" and Schnoodles (crosses between Schnauzers and Poodles). As with IDOG and DRC, does not have a shelter, but uses its network of foster homes.

It states: "We are committed to our Foster Partners and in-home fostering. Our dogs are socialized, vetted and loved as part of the family. Once adopted, our family and yours ensure our dogs continue to have the support of our Online Community. We will always be there for you and our dogs. We have also listed thousands of Oodles/Poodles/Doodles/Schnoodles seeking homes from all over North America. We can aid a family who needs to rehome their dog because of unforeseen circumstances or retiring breeder dogs."

"We are based in New Jersey but have dogs, fosters, rehomes and opportunities all over North America. Searchers wanted to help find listings for our site. Foster Partners wanted to help rescue more Oodles." In fact, all of the rescue organizations are looking for fosters to join their network.

Rather confusingly, the Oodles website is at www.doodlerescuecollective.com There is an ongoing dispute as to the ownership of the term 'Doodle Rescue Collective' – but whatever the ins and outs of it, the fact is that both organizations are striving to improve the outcomes for Goldendoodles who have suffered the trauma of losing their families and homes through no fault of their own. You can shop and donate at the same time on the Oodles website at: www.doodlerescuecollective.com/page/shop-to-donate

UK

The main rescue organization in the UK is the excellent **Doodle Trust** – a charity which changed its name from the Labradoodle Trust in 2014. It also rescues and rehomes Goldendoodles, Labradoodles, Cockapoos, other Poodle crosses and Poodles.

The Trust is a first class resource for information for owners and prospective owners. It provides health and welfare advice as well as giving accurate information about the nature and behavior of Poodle crossbreeds. Volunteers are keen to educate owners BEFORE they get a Doodle to help prevent so many of these wonderful people-loving dogs being abandoned by their owners. Read **Chapter 1** of the Handbook to discover what questions the Trust believes you should ask before getting a Goldendoodle – whether from a breeder or via a rescue organization.

The Doodle Trust says: "We see educating the public about Doodles as a very important part of what we do. Unscrupulous breeders are continuing to mis-sell puppies as non-shedding and allergy friendly which is very misleading. This is also one of the main reasons these dogs are coming into rescue."

This is how the Trust works when a dog needs rehoming: "If it is decided that the best thing would be to sign the dog over to us, we will deal with this as quickly as we can. We do not charge to take dogs in and all of our dogs are fostered in a loving environment in people's own homes. Our kennels are only used in emergencies or for dogs that are unsafe to put into a family environment.

The owner can keep in touch with the foster for progress reports if they so choose. However, we cannot divulge the name or address of the people who adopt from us.

"All dogs are fostered for a minimum of two weeks so that the foster can make a true assessment of the dog. If the dog has not been neutered already, we will have it done before it is rehomed. Once the dog has been assessed we look for a suitable home for it. The home must match the requirements of the dog. We do not rehome dogs to the first person that comes along.

"Once the potential new family has been found we contact them with details of the dog. If they are interested we then put them in touch with the foster so that they can learn more about the dog. During this time we will also arrange for somebody to home check the potential adopters. If the home check is passed and they like the dog they can then go ahead and meet it. If the meeting all goes well, they are given the opportunity to adopt the dog.

"Doodle Trust is committed to the welfare of any dogs that come into our care, and endeavors to make a positive contribution to their lives, no matter what the circumstances. We aim to educate people about Goldendoodles BEFORE they take the plunge, and are often called by people wondering about their suitability to own one of these lively, intelligent dogs."

The Doodle Trust can be found online at www.doodletrust.com Click on their Just Giving page to find out how to donate to keep the good work of the Trust going – and you'll be rewarded with a free mention for your efforts.

This is by no means an exhaustive list, but it does cover some of the main organizations involved. Other online resources are the Pet Finder website at www.petfinder.com and Adopt a Pet site at www.adoptapet.com. There is also the Poo Mix site at http://poomixrescue.com. Many of the dogs listed with the Goldendoodle-specific rescue organizations are also advertised on these websites. If you do visit these websites, you cannot presume that the descriptions are 100% accurate. They are given in good faith, but ideas of what constitutes a medium dog and what is a small or large one may vary. Also make sure you know what the different types of Goldendoodle look like.

Some dogs advertised may be mistakenly described as "Poodle mix and Labrador" when they may have other breeds in their genetic make-up. It does not mean they are necessarily worse dogs, but if you are attracted to the Goldendoodle for its temperament and other assets, make sure you are looking at a Goldendoodle.

NEVER buy a dog from eBay, Craig's List, Gum tree or any of the other advertising websites which sell old cars, washing machines, golf clubs etc. You might think you are getting a cheap dog, but in the long run you will pay the price. If the dog had been well bred and properly cared for, he or she would not be advertised on a website such as this. If you buy or get a free one, you may be storing up a whole load of trouble for yourselves in terms of behavioral, temperament and/or health issues due to poor breeding and/or training.

With thanks to IDOG International and The Doodle Trust for help with this chapter.

14. Caring for Seniors

If your Goldendoodle has been well looked after and has suffered no serious diseases, he or she may live 12 or 13 years; some may even live longer.

Amy Lane says: "Longevity has two main factors: good health and overall size. The larger the dog, the shorter the lifespan. Since Goldendoodles are a fairly new breed, longevity is an estimate for the most part.

"I created the first litter of Mini Goldendoodles, born on January 11th, 2002. Of the 10 puppies in the litter, one passed away at 12, two at 13, and seven of them are still alive at the age of 14.5. A standard Goldendoodle has an expected lifespan of approximately 12 years."

At some point before the end, your old dog will start to feel the effects of ageing. After having had to get up at the crack of dawn when your dog was a puppy, you may find that he likes to sleep in longer in the morning now that he is older. (Pictured is Laura Chaffin's 10-year-old F1 Bailey enjoying a well-earned rest.)

Physically, joints may become stiffer and organs, such as heart or liver, may not function as effectively. On the mental side - just as with humans - your dog's memory, ability to learn and awareness all start to dim.

Your faithful companion might become a bit grumpier, stubborn or a little less tolerant of lively dogs and children. You may also notice that he doesn't see or hear as well as he used to. On the other hand, your old friend might not be hard of hearing at all. He might have developed that affliction common to many older dogs - ours included - of 'selective hearing.' Our 11-year-old Max has bionic hearing when it comes to the word 'Dinnertime' whispered from 20 yards, yet seems strangely unable to hear the commands 'Come' or 'Down' when we are right in front of him!

You can help ease your mature dog into old age gracefully by keeping an eye on him or her, noticing the changes and taking action to help him as much as possible. This might involve a visit to the vet for supplements and/or medications, modifying your dog's environment, changing his or her diet and slowly reducing the amount of daily exercise. Much depends on the individual dog. Just as with humans, a dog of ideal weight that has been active and stimulated all of his or her life is likely to age slower than an overweight couch potato.

Keeping Goldendoodles at that optimum weight is challenging - and important - as they age. Their metabolisms slow down, making it easier to put on the pounds unless their daily calories are reduced. At the same time, extra weight places additional, unwanted stress on joints and organs, making them have to work harder than they should.

We normally talk about dogs being old when they reach the last third of their lives. This varies greatly from dog to dog and bloodline to bloodline. Some Standard Goldendoodles may start to show signs of ageing at eight years old while Minis may remain fit in mind and body long after this age. Even then it varies from dog to dog. Several Standard Goldendoodle owners have told us that their dogs are showing few signs of ageing at 10 or even 11 years old.

Physical and Mental Signs of Ageing

If your Goldendoodle is in or approaching the last third of his life, here are some signs that his body is feeling its age:

- He has generally slowed down and no longer seems as keen to go out on his walks. He tires more easily on a walk (Photo: Laura Chaffin's Standard Goldendoodle Bunny Annie Laurie, aged 11)

- He doesn't want to go outside in bad weather

- He gets up from lying down more slowly and he goes up and down stairs more slowly. He can no longer jump on to the couch or bed. These are all signs that his joints are stiffening, often due to arthritis

- He has the occasional 'accident' (incontinence) inside the house

- He is getting grey hairs, particularly around the muzzle

- He has put on a bit of weight

- He urinates more frequently

- He drinks more water

- He gets constipated

- The foot pads thicken and nails may become more brittle

- He has one or more lumps or fatty deposits on his body. Our 11-year-old dog developed two on his head recently and we took him straight to the vet, who performed an operation to remove them. They were benign (harmless), but you should always get them checked out ASAP in case they are an early form of cancer.

- He can't regulate his body temperature as he used to and so feels the cold and heat more

- He doesn't hear as well as he used to

- His eyesight may deteriorate — if his eyes appear cloudy he may be developing cataracts and you should see your vet as soon as you notice the signs

- He has bad breath (halitosis), which could be a sign of dental or gum disease. Teeth can be a particular problem with some Goldendoodles. Brush his teeth regularly and give him a daily dental stick, such as Dentastix or similar. If the bad breath persists, get him checked out by a vet

- If he's inactive he may develop callouses on the elbows, especially if he lies down on hard surfaces – this is more common with larger dogs

- It's not just your dog's body which deteriorates, his mind does too. It's all part of the normal ageing process. Here are some symptoms. Your dog may display some, all or none of these signs of mental deterioration:

- His sleep patterns change, an older dog may be more restless at night and sleepy during the day

- He barks more

- He stares at objects or wanders aimlessly around the house

- He forgets or ignores commands or habits he once knew well, such as housetraining and coming when called

- He displays increased anxiety or aggressiveness

- Some dogs may become more clingy and dependent, often resulting in separation anxiety. Others may become less interested in human contact

Understanding the changes happening to your dog and acting on them compassionately and effectively will help ease your dog's passage through his or her senior years. Your dog has given you so much pleasure over the years, now he or she needs you to give that bit of extra care for a happy, healthy old age. You can also help your Goldendoodle to stay mentally active by playing games (not too rough) and getting new toys to stimulate interest.

Helping Seniors

The first thing you can do is monitor your dog and be on the lookout for any changes in actions or behavior. Then there are lots of things you can do for him.

Food and Supplements - As dogs age they need fewer calories and less protein, so many owners switch to a food specially formulated for older dogs. These are labeled 'Senior,' 'Ageing' or 'Mature.' Check the labeling; some are specifically for dogs aged over eight, others may be for 10 or 12-year-olds.

If you are not sure if a senior diet is necessary for your Goldendoodle, talk to your vet the next time you are there. Remember, if you do change the brand, switch the food gradually over a week to 10 days. Unlike with humans, a dog's digestive system cannot cope with sudden changes of diet.

Consider feeding your Goldendoodle a supplement, such as Omega-3 fatty acids for the brain and coat, or one to help joints. There are also medications and homeopathic remedies to help relieve anxiety. Again, check with your vet before introducing anything new.

Laura Chaffin, of Cimarron Frontier Doodles, Oklahoma, is one of the first breeders of Goldendoodles, having started in 2000. She says: "I have mostly bred the Moyen or Medium Doodles, but have also bred Standards, and currently focus on the Miniatures.

"I think food is so important. I like to feed a raw or home-made diet. I also use BARF raw dog food. I haven't actually changed my older female's diet. If I had been feeding only a dry kibble all these years, I would make sure that their kidneys were healthy, and alter the protein a bit if the vet recommends. But with a raw or home-cooked diet, they are getting more moisture in the food which is very good for a senior dog. (Pictured is Bunny Annie Laurie.)

"They aren't getting the rendered protein that's in dry kibble and the extra moisture helps with elimination and constipation, I think, and keeps the dog in good shape. And giving a moist food definitely helps with constipation. If there is an elimination problem, I would go for pumpkin, dark leafy vegetables, fruits and exercise.

"I give my older dogs some turmeric via "golden paste." This is especially good for the senior dog's health to combat inflammation and cancer and is useful for detox and as an antioxidant. I also give them fish oil and digestive enzymes and different sources of probiotics - kefir (fermented milk), yogurt...I've given them sauerkraut, even kombucha (a fermented tea drink) and, of course, probiotic powders. There are good supplements available with excellent probiotics, enzymes, and super foods in them. I don't add extra fiber because I don't want the fiber to absorb all the nutrients.

"Adding bone broth to the seniors' diets also helps with digestion and overall health. I just slow cook or pressure cook bones with some meat on them with a little apple cider vinegar. I slow cook this for up to five or six days and add some to their food each day and just replace the water in the slow cooker to keep it going for the week. They love it! I also use essential oils with all my dogs. It is especially good for senior dogs as well as for transitions, anxiety and car rides. I rub it on my palms and pet them on their backs."

Amy Lane adds: "I feed Life's Abundance All Stage formula and currently have a 14.5-year-old female that is doing well on this. I also give my senior dogs glucosamine tablets daily. Glucosamine has been helpful in humans as well as horses."

Exercise - Take the lead from your dog, if he doesn't want to walk as far, then don't. But if your dog doesn't want to go out at all, you will have to coax him out. ALL senior dogs need exercise, not only to keep their joints moving, but also to keep their heart, lungs and joints exercised.

Weight - no matter how old your Goldendoodle is, he still needs a waist! Maintaining a healthy weight with a balanced diet and regular, gentler exercise are the two of the most important things you can do for your dog.

Environment - Make sure your dog has a nice soft place to rest his old bones, which may mean adding an extra blanket to his bed. This should be in a place which is not too hot or cold, as he may not be able to regulate his body temperature as well as when he was younger. If his eyesight is failing, move obstacles out of his way, reducing the chance of injuries.

Jumping on and off furniture or in or out of the car is high impact for his old joints and bones. He will need a helping hand on to and off the couch or your bed, if he's allowed up there, or even a little ramp to get in and out of the car. Make sure he has plenty of time to sleep and is not pestered and/or bullied by younger dogs, other animals or young children.

Consult a Professional - If your dog is showing any of the following signs, get him checked out by your vet:

- Increased urination or drinking - this can be a sign of something amiss, such as reduced liver or kidney function, Cushing's disease or diabetes

- Constipation or not urinating regularly could be a sign of something not functioning properly with the digestive system or organs

- Incontinence, which could be a sign of a mental or physical problem

- Cloudy eyes, which could be cataracts

- Decreased appetite – most Goldendoodles love their food and loss of appetite is often a sign of an underlying problem

- Lumps or bumps on the body - which are most often benign, but can occasionally be malignant (dangerous)

- Excessive sleeping or a lack of interest in you and his/her surroundings

- Diarrhea or vomiting

- A darkening and dryness of skin that never seems to get any better - this can be a sign of hypothyroidism

- Any other out-of-the-ordinary behavior for your dog. A change in patterns or behavior is often your dog's way of telling you that all is not well

The Last Lap

Huge advances in veterinary science have meant that there are countless procedures and medications which can prolong the life of your dog, and this is a good thing.

But there comes a time when you have to let go.

If your dog is showing all the signs of ageing, has an ongoing medical condition from which he or she cannot recover, or is showing signs of pain, mental anxiety or distress and there is no hope of improvement, then the dreaded time has come to say goodbye.

You owe it to him or her. There is no point keeping an old dog alive if all he or she has to look forward to is pain and death.

I'm even getting upset as I write this, as I think of parting from my 11-year-old not too many years into the future, as well as the wonderful dogs we have had in the past. But we have their lives in our hands and we can give them the gift of passing away peacefully and humanely at the end when the time is right.

Losing our beloved companion, our best friend, a member of the family, is truly heart-breaking for many owners. But one of the things we realize at the back of our minds when we get that lively little puppy is the pain that comes with it; knowing that we will live longer than him or her and that we will probably have to make this most painful of decisions at some point. It's the worst thing about being a dog owner.

If your Goldendoodle has had a long and happy life, then you could not have done any more. You were a great owner and your dog was lucky to have you. Remember all the good times you had together. And try not to rush out and buy another dog; wait a while to grieve for your Goldendoodle. Assess your current life and lifestyle and, if your situation is right, only then consider getting another dog and all that that entails in terms of time, commitment and expense. Goldendoodles are sensitive, often intuitive, creatures. One coming into a happy, stable household will get off to a much better start in life than a dog entering a home full of grief.

Whatever you decide to do, put the dog first.

What the Experts Say

Let's not dwell on the end stages of our dogs' lives, but focus on what life they have left - and what we can do to keep them fit and healthy as the years roll by.

Laura says: "My oldest Goldendoodle is 11 years old. She is just as active and healthy as she has been in the past, although she does sleep longer in the morning. The older ones are not usually quite as willing or patient to play with the younger ones. Although when our Doodles come in the house from being outside, they have this ritual where they all romp and play. It becomes a circus with every one jumping on the other, and the older ones jump around just as much as the younger ones.

"In terms of health issues, I suppose there could be joint issues with older Goldendoodles, or cancer and thyroid issues. I have heard of these, but not experienced them. When you brush your Goldendoodle, you should check for any skin issues or tumors. The other advice I would give is just be careful to feed them with food that is not over processed, just as we humans should not eat over-processed foods. It's also important to keep older dogs well hydrated and add supplements to help with digestion and cell health. And make sure they get to run as often as possible."

Amy Lane: "Most older Goldendoodles develop cataracts causing their vision to deteriorate. Pebbles, my 14.5-year-old, has cloudy eyes (a sign of cataracts), but still never misses a step. I find she doesn't like to walk into a completely dark room, which isn't a problem for my younger dogs. I turn on lights for her where I normally would not have done so in the past.

"It is also quite common for an older dog to have hypothyroidism, causing them to put on weight and for their coat to thin. It is important for all senior dogs to have an annual blood panel completed by their vet to keep an eye on their aging body. Many times what is found can be managed easily (such as giving Thyroxin twice daily to keep their thyroid glands working effectively.)

"In terms of behavioral changes, an older dog that experiences pain or discomfort can be less tolerable of active or rambunctious children. If long walks were a part of a dog's normal life, these walks may need to be shortened. It is up to their humans to notice this, as dogs want so badly to keep up with their humans and many times this causes lots of stiffness and discomfort after the long walk.

"I recommend annual blood work starting at the age of seven. Provide as much exercise as possible that does not cause discomfort once the exercise stops. Any dog experiencing any stiffness or whose normal athletic ability seems to be slowing should be given a glucosamine supplement to help with joint health."

All dogs are different and they age at different rates. One Goldendoodle may bounce around like a youngster at 10 years old, another might be a bit stiff with less interest in food and life. Keep an eye out for signs of ageing, help your dog approach old age gracefully by keeping him as comfortable and pain-free as possible.

Photo of 10-year-old F1 Standard Lucy enjoying a visit to the coast, courtesy of Laura Chaffin.

15. Doodles in Action

Goldendoodles as Therapy and Service Dogs

Lynne Whitmire, of Fountain Falls Goldendoodles, South Carolina, has been involved in dog breeding for decades and has focused solely on Goldendoodles since 2006. She has experience breeding and working with therapy and service Goldendoodles. Here Lynne gives an insight into what goes into the making of one of these amazing dogs who are helping to transform lives.

Therapy Dogs

A service dog needs to be intelligent, willing to work, self-confident and able to form a strong bond with its owner. He also needs to have good physical health and stamina. Goldendoodles are a natural fit for work as a service or therapy dog as they have exceptional intelligence and are easy to train, and eager to please. Low shedding and low allergy coats are a big plus for people who may need a service dog but also suffer from allergies. Goldendoodles are also sociable, non-aggressive and extremely intuitive.

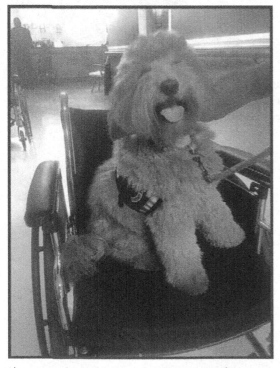

That being said, there is a lot that goes into the choosing and preparation of a service or therapy dog. Both are working dogs, but have very different functions. A therapy dog is a dog that might be trained to provide affection and comfort to people in hospitals, schools, hospices, disaster areas and to people with autism. Therapy dogs are not assistance or service dogs and, as such, are not afforded the same access to public places as service dogs.

Pictured is Lynne's Fountain Falls Chewie, a certified therapy dog with South Carolina Therapy Dogs. He earned his Canine Good Citizen at an early age and shortly afterwards passed his therapy certification. He is much loved in local care centers, the rehab center and hospice care.

A puppy that is intended for work as a therapy dog needs to be people friendly, self-assured and playful. He should not be the alpha puppy in the pack, nor the loner. A knowledgeable breeder who has had experience with therapy dogs is your best source for a puppy that will best respond to therapy dog training. A breeder who knows the personalities and temperaments of her puppies, as well as the personality traits of her lines, is what you're looking for. Temperament testing and consulting with a trainer would be an added benefit.

Once you have chosen your puppy, you should contact a certified therapy dog group that will give you guidance in raising your puppy; most therapy dog groups have trainers that they recommend.

Typical early training such as house training and basic obedience training will begin from Day One. Not rushing a puppy and using positive methods for training are a must. Once the vet gives the go-ahead after vaccinations, it is important that you enroll in puppy socialization classes to get your puppy off to the right start, and then continue with age-appropriate training.

It is also important to socialize your puppy with other dogs, types of people, animals, sounds, weather conditions and surfaces. Hopefully your pup came from a breeder that introduced these things from an early age and you need to continue this training. Your puppy also needs to be taken to places of business that allow dogs. In the US there are building supply stores, such as Lowes and Home Depot, as well as other businesses that welcome well-behaved dogs. Being around or in a shopping cart while machines, strange people and all sorts of noises are going on around them is a great way for Goldendoodle to be prepared as a therapy dog.

You want your dog to immediately be responsive to commands such as Leave It, Settle, Up, Down and Paw and going to a class that is specifically made for therapy dog training is immensely helpful. Obtaining your Canine Good Citizen badge is usually the first step toward therapy dog certification. Testing for therapy dog certification is usually not done until dogs are a year old and have been owned by the current owner at least six months.

In my local group, South Carolina Therapy Dogs, my dog and I were put through a series of tasks. We had to demonstrate basic obedience, walk by a treat on the floor and ignore it when told: "Leave It" and demonstrate a stay and recall. In the last test, I was asked to leave the room while my dog was in a Sit-Stay. Once I was out of my dog's sight, a number of people came into the room and approached him; one was in a wheelchair, another had an IV stand with them, some walked with shambling gaits.

This was to try to access the dog in an unfamiliar hospital-like setting. If a dog is accepting and does not try to run away or appear too nervous, then he or she passes that phase of the test. My dog thought it was great that he was going to get petted and approached by so many people.

I personally have found therapy work to be very rewarding. We go into health care facilities, hospices, schools, libraries, summer camps and colleges. We do everything from comforting elderly people to participating in reading programs. It's a fun way to do something worthwhile with your dog and it also enables you to meet like-minded dog lovers.

Photo: Lynne with Fountain Falls Jazzy on graduation day at Canine Assistance in Atlanta.

Service Dogs

Service dogs are a whole different category. Service dogs are defined by the US department of Justice as "A dog that is individually trained to do work or perform tasks for people with disabilities." The work of a service dog must be directly related to a person's disability. Dogs whose sole function is to provide comfort or emotional support do not qualify as service dogs; PTSD (Post Traumatic Stress Disorder) is the exception. For more information on U.S. regulations see the ADA 2010 Revised Requirements; Service Animals.

There are two ways to obtain a service dog and many organizations that provide the training. Do your research to make sure that these organizations have a good reputation. One I know personally that provides free service dogs to qualified persons with a disability is Canine Assistance. I have donated a dog to their organization and was impressed with their thoroughness.

After two years of training Jazzy, the Goldendoodle I donated, he was paired with a PTSD veteran. It was a very rewarding experience for me to see one of my Goldendoodles helping this veteran be able to live a better quality of life, which included returning to work and leading a more normal life.

The Foundation for Service Dog Support states that $15,000 is the typical price for a trained service dog. It can be much more than that depending on what route you take. Other organizations may charge more or less and some offer special pricing. It is important to do your homework when applying for service dog training. Some organizations such as Canine Assistance raise their own puppies, and they primarily use Golden Retrievers and Goldendoodles. Some organizations try to use dogs from shelters and humane societies.

For people wanting to train their own puppy it is recommended that they have a trainer to guide their efforts. As a breeder I want a certified trainer to help choose a puppy best suited for service dog work. There are some breeders that have the experience to assist in choosing and early training of a service dog. The training of a service dog takes dedication and daily attention to that end - but the results speak for themselves.

Activities for Goldendoodles

Debbie Dixon, of Zippity Doodles, Colorado, has been breeding Goldendoodles since 2004 and participating in agility and other canine events for years. Here she gives a comprehensive overview of the wide range of opportunities available to owners who want to take part in organized activities and competitions with their Goldendoodles.

Goldendoodles are a very smart, athletic, and easily trainable breed who like to be engaged with their family. If you want your Goldendoodle to get involved in a constructive activity, you'll find there are many avenues to channel their natural curiosity and intelligence, while at the same time increasing the depth of your special bond.

Goldendoodles bring an affinity for water from their founding breeds, Poodles - originally 'puddle dogs' in German - and Golden Retrievers - bred to retrieve fowl for the hunter; and many still carry the hunting instinct. This makes for a varied and rich springboard for Goldendoodles to participate in a wide variety of sports. Whether competing or for fun, getting involved in sports has many benefits. It reinforces training, builds trust, builds confidence in fearful dogs, and helps the dog/handler team to learn to work together. It's best to start by introducing your puppy to basic training classes as soon as possible, and once you have a foundation of skills, there are many options available:

Obedience - In obedience, a dog must execute tasks when directed by his handler intended to demonstrate good behavior at home and in public. It allows dog and handler to practice and demonstrate proficiency in basic manners. Canine Good Citizen (CGC) is a certification awarded by AKC for a test that demonstrates the dog knows basic commands: Heel on loose leash, Sit, Stand, Down, Stay, Come. The initial level of Obedience competition is the Companion Dog title which requires mastery of Heeling on and off leash, Stand for exam, Recall, Sit-Stay, Down-Stay. Rally (aka Rally-O) is a sport based on obedience, which follows a course of 10-20 signs instructing the owner/dog team what to do while heeling along the way. Enrolment in AKC Canine Partners (for mixed breeds) allows Goldendoodles to earn titles in Obedience as well as Agility, Rally, Tracking and Coursing ability.

Agility – This is perfect for Goldendoodles. In agility your dog works in partnership with you to complete a timed obstacle course which may include tunnels, jumps, weave poles, ramps and other obstacles. Scoring is based on speed and faults as they navigate the course.

As the dog's partner (handler), you guide the dog through a course, which is never the same, primarily using hand signals, voice, and movement/body language from a distance. The complexity of this sport is a natural for Goldendoodles, and a perfect way to engage their curiosity, intelligence, and willingness to please and perform.

Photo of Debbie's Standard F1, Olive, competing in a NADAC event courtesy of @DogAgilityPhotosForFun.

Agility is perfect for almost all owners, whether young or old, athletic or inactive. For most people, the mental process of learning the sport of agility is usually much harder for them than it is for their dog, but the reward is that it is a mind-body experience for both two and four-legged partners.

To introduce your Goldendoodle to Agility, you only need a basic obedience foundation (i.e.: Sit, Stay, Walk on Leash, Crate Training.) In fact, once your dog has completed their Canine Good Citizen (or knows the equivalent skills) and has finished growing, they are ready - although you must be careful of impacts on the bones with younger dogs.

In agility, as in some other dog sports, you learn to intimately understand your dog and how he or she thinks. This understanding grows as you learn the dynamics of teaching your dog. You start with agility training classes, learning the basics and how to compete each type of obstacle, and how to engage your dog. As your skills increase, you string together two or three obstacles in a 'course', eventually learning how to direct your Goldendoodle through an obstacle course of many elements that is fun and fulfilling for both you and your dog. While taking agility classes a dog learns to go to their crate when it's not their turn, and they learn to ignore the other dogs when they are coming on or off the course.

That's intensified in the competitions called Trials, where the sounds, sites, people and other dogs provide a great chance for socialization and further experience of focusing with distractions.

You learn to manage your dog with other unfamiliar dogs and people in a busy and stressful environment, but for the dog it's really about playing a fun game. For the handler it is a test of skills where you learn to keep your dog positive, making sure it's fun for them - because the mistakes are always the human's; not to mention only you know that a mistake was made!

Photo of Olive competing by @DogAgilityPhotosForFun.

Agility is ultimately all about the connection between dog and owner and it's beneficial whether you compete in Agility trials or just do it for fun and recreation. If and when you are ready to compete, your dog must be registered with one of the Agility clubs. There are several that organize Agility competitions (Trials), and they all have slightly different approaches and requirements. You may find that some are more suited for the beginner, or for your particular needs and style. Titles may be earned though these organizations, most of which give ribbons for participation or qualification, in addition to awards for top placement. The main ones are:

USDAA - United States Dog Agility Association www.usdaa.com

NADAC - North American Dog Agility Council www.nadac.com

AKC - American Kennel Club Agility www.akc.org/events/agility

AAC - Agility Association of Canada, FCI, IFCS, ANKC, Kennel Club UK

Flyball - This is where teams of dogs race against each other, like a relay race. Each dog jumps over a series of short hurdles to a box containing a tennis ball which the dog releases by pushing his or her paw on a spring loaded pad. Once the ball is released, the dog runs back to the start/finish line with it in his or her mouth. Flyball is a very fast - and often loud - sport! NAFA North American Flyball Association www.flyball.org

Scent detection - K9 Nosework (that's the official name!) is a fun sport that builds on a natural instinct of all dogs: to sniff. It's a search activity where dogs learn to sniff out a toy or a treat in a box. Later on a specific odor is introduced and the dogs learn to sniff it out. It's a great physical and mental activity that any dog, regardless of a size, can learn very quickly. In competition trials the dogs search several different areas for the scent box and are timed.

The fastest dog who correctly alerts the handler to the spot where the odor is coming from gets the points. Even if you don't do competition trials, a nosework class can be great way to build confidence and provide mental stimulation for the dog. Plus, you can easily play the game at home when the weather does not allow for outside exercise. www.k9nosework.com

Dock Jumping or Diving - Goldendoodles compete in this sport by jumping into a body of water as high or as far as possible. Dock Diving typically includes the categories Dock Diving, Air Retrieve and Vertical Dock Diving. It's another good way to show how sporty and capable our Goldendoodles are! Dogs need to be willing to jump into water and swim after a lure. Through North America Diving Dogs, known as NADD, www.northameriadivingdogs.com Goldendoodles can work to earn titles which can also be recognized by AKC. Other organizations: www.dockdogs.com

Disc Dog (aka Frisbee) – Here the dog works with his or her partner to either catch flying discs for distance or in a choreographed routine. There are several organizations that offer events for new and experienced handlers/dogs: AWI www.ashleywhippet.com, USDDN www.usddn.com, UFO www.ufoworldcup.org, Skyhoundz www.skyhoundz.com, Quadruped www.thequadruped.com,

Lure Coursing -This is sight hunting using mechanized lures and pulleys to simulate chasing live prey. Not all Goldendoodles will instinctively follow the lure (as the sight hound breeds do), so initial training with lure play can develop this skill. Popularity of this sport is increasing and you will often find dog training facilities offer events or opportunities to try it out, but the only competitive outlet for Goldendoodles is the AKC Coursing Ability Test. Since the stress on joints when turning can be high, it is recommended to limit Lure Coursing to dogs over one year.

Search and Rescue - This is a very intensive training and participation activity. SAR dogs use their sense of smell to search and locate victims in urban and wilderness settings. Each team (dog and handler) must pass rigorous certification and health testing. For more information visit www.DisasterDog.org, www.sardogsus.org

Hunting - In game hunting dogs can be used for searching for prey, flushing the prey out of the brush, pointing the prey, or retrieving the prey, depending on their inherent aptitude and learned skill. Many Goldendoodle owners who hunt for sport are finding that their Goldendoodles are well suited to this activity, and are often more athletic in the hunt than their Retrievers! Goldendoodles from Poodle or Golden Retriever hunting lines tend to be more suited to the task.

Barn Hunt - These competitions test the working instincts of dogs to hunt vermin. Smaller dogs who can fit through an 18-inch wide opening in a hay bale can qualify to participate. Hay bales are used to form a tunnel where the dogs can 'hunt' or locate a vermin target in the 'maze' of hay. The rat targets are humanely and safely protected in an aerated tube (usually a pet.) Older dogs, deaf dogs, and tripod dogs can also compete. Titles recognized by the AKC and UKC. www.Barnhunt.com

Skijoring - Here the dog helps to pull a person on cross country skis. Larger dogs (40+lb) are typically used in this sport, but smaller dogs can participate, even though they aren't able to actually assist in pulling, since the skier can provide the power. Dogs only need the aptitude and willingness to pull and run down a trail to participate. Both dog and owner wear a harness connected by a rope. ISDRA (International Sled Dog Racing Association) www.isdra.org

Many of these activities allow for work and play at home as well as participation with other teams in classes or competitions. The connection and fun partnership enjoyed with your dog is the real reason for getting involved in an activity with your Goldendoodle and it's the same with many of the other sports and activities suited to Goldendoodles, such as: Freestyle Dancing, Tracking, Trick Training, Paddleboarding.

Doodle Romps - A social gathering of Doodles held at local dog parks (or other dog-friendly venues), usually on a regular basis, i.e. monthly, quarterly, or yearly. The larger, regional ones are often held in the summer. Romps offer a chance to meet and socialize with other Doodle families in your area.

With a group of Doodle owners to supervise from different points in the area, play in a dog park can be a bit safer and more controlled. Doodles often have a similar play style and will seek out other Doodles, and a Romp can be the perfect outlet.

For those who are considering a Goldendoodle, a Romp can provide an avenue to meet and discuss the breed with owners who are generally more than happy to share their love for them. Sometimes Doodle romps are listed on Goldendoodle breeder websites or Facebook pages.

Local romps can often be found by searching for Doodle groups on www.meetup.com and Doodle Facebook groups.

Whichever activity you choose for you and your Goldendoodle, you'll find you both benefit from a greater understanding of each other – and have a lot of fun along the way!

Photo of Debbie and Doodles by Jaime Rowe.

List of Contributors

Breeders (in alphabetical order)

Amy Lane, Fox Creek Farm, Berkeley Springs, West Virginia, USA www.Goldendoodles.net

Candice Farrell, Ooodles of Doodles, Red Deer, Alberta, Canada ooodlesofdoodles.com

Christy Stevens, Winding Creek Ranch, Indiana, USA www.thewindingcreekranch.com

Debbie Dixon, Zippity Doodles Goldendoodles, Golden, Colorado, USA www.golden-doodle.com

Donna Shaw and Kelly Milne, Donakell Goldendoodles, Methlick, Aberdeenshire, UK www.donakellgoldendoodles.co.uk

Dyvonia Bussey, Grace Goldens, Alabama, USA www.gracegoldens.com

Janece Schommer, Goldendoodle Acres, Wisconsin, USA http://goldendoodleacres.com

Kelsey Huffer, Alki Goldendoodles, Seattle, Washington, USA www.alkigoldendoodles.com

Laura Chaffin, Cimarron Frontier Doodles, Stillwater, Oklahoma, USA www.carolinadoodles.4t.com

Lynne Whitmire, Fountain Falls Goldendoodles, South Carolina, USA http://ffgoldendoodles.com

Melissa Farmer, FarmerDoodles, Ohio, USA www.farmerdoodles.com

Michael and Lisa Ross, Chai Kennels, Elgin Canada www.chaikennels.com

Renee Sigman, Yesteryear Acres, Ohio, USA www.yesteryearacres.com

Sandra Beck, Beck Kennel, Iowa, USA www.beckkennel.com

Steve and Noelie Smith, River Falls Goldendoodles, South Carolina, USA http://riverfallsgoldendoodles.com

Wendi Loustau, Mustard Seed Ranch Goldendoodles, Georgia, USA www.mustardseeddoodles.com

Other Contributors

IDOG Rescue http://idogrescue.com

Doodle Trust http://www.doodletrust.com

Dr Sara Skiwski, The Western Dragon holistic veterinary practice, San Jose, California, USA

Cover shot: www.warrenphotographic.co.uk

Back Cover: Christy Stevens www.thewindingcreekranch.com

Useful Contacts

GANA http://goldendoodleassociation.com

Health Tested Goldendoodle and Labradoodle Breeder & Kennel Directory
http://www.goldendoodle-labradoodle.org

Continental Kennel Club https://ckcusa.com

Association of Pet Dog Trainers USA www.apdt.com

www.apdt.co.uk Association of Pet Dog Trainers UK

www.cappdt.ca Canadian Association of Professional Pet Dog Trainers

www.dogfoodadvisor.com Useful information on grain-free and hypoallergenic dog foods

www.allaboutdogfood.co.uk UK dog food advice

www.akcreunite.org Helps find lost or stolen dogs in USA, register your dog's microchip

www.idogrescue.com (USA)

www.doodlerescuecollective.com (USA)

www.doodletrust.com (UK)

There are also internet forums and Facebook groups which are a good source of information from other owners, including:

http://goldendoodles.com/forum_community.htm

www.doodlekisses.com/forum

Doodlemania on Facebook

Disclaimer

This book has been written to provide helpful information on Goldendoodles. It is not meant to be used, nor should it be used, to diagnose or treat any medical condition. For diagnosis or treatment of any animal medical problem, consult a qualified veterinarian. The author is not responsible for any specific health or allergy conditions that may require medical supervision and is not liable for any damages or negative consequences from any treatment, action, application or preparation, to any animal or to any person reading or following the information in this book. The views expressed by contributors to this book are solely personal and do not necessarily represent those of the author. References are provided for informational purposes only and do not constitute endorsement of any websites or other sources.

Author's Note: For ease of reading, the masculine pronoun 'he' is often used to represent both male and female dogs.

Made in the USA
Middletown, DE
09 May 2020